lonely planet

W9-CKP-714

# ZION & BRYCE CANYON
# NATIONAL PARKS

JEFF CAMPBELL
JOHN A VLAHIDES
DAVID LUKAS

LONELY PLANET PUBLICATIONS
Melbourne · Oakland · London

Zion & Bryce Canyon National Parks
1st edition – March 2005
ISBN 1 74059 936 5

## LONELY PLANET OFFICES

### Australia
Head Office
Locked Bag 1, Footscray, Victoria 3011
☎ 03 8379 8000, fax 03 8379 8111
talk2us@lonelyplanet.com.au

### USA
150 Linden St, Oakland, CA 94607
☎ 510 893 8555, toll free 800 275 8555
fax 510 893 8572, info@lonelyplanet.com

### UK
72–82 Rosebery Ave,
Clerkenwell, London EC1R 4RW
☎ 020 7841 9000, fax 020 7841 9001
go@lonelyplanet.co.uk

### Published by Lonely Planet Publications Pty Ltd
ABN 36 005 607 983

Cover photograph by Lonely Planet Images: Bryce Canyon National Park, Woodward Payne & Beverly Anderson (front); Delicate Arch, Utah, Arches National Park, Mark Newman (back). Many of the images in this guide are available for licensing from Lonely Planet Images: www.lonelyplanetimages.com.

Printed by SNP SPrint (S) Pte Ltd, Singapore.

# CONTENTS

Wesley Powell · Exploitation & Conservation · **Zion National Park · Bryce Canyon National Park · Southern Utah's Other Parklands** · Arches National Park · Capitol Reef National Park · Canyonlands National Park · Grand Staircase–Escalante National Monument

# THE AUTHORS

### JEFF CAMPBELL

Jeff was the coordinating author; he wrote the frontmatter, History and Zion chapters, and he collaborated with John A Vlahides on the Grand Staircase chapter.

Jeff wrote the Utah chapter for Lonely Planet's *Southwest* (3rd edition), and was the coordinating author for *USA* (3rd edition). He also contributed to *Las Vegas* (1st edition), and has been awestruck by the Southwest's deserts ever since he first visited in 1994. Having seen nearly half the USA's national parks, he's willing to wager that it doesn't get any better than this.

Jeff currently lives in San Francisco with his wife, Deanna, and his son, Jackson. All eagerly await the arrival of their newest family member.

### JOHN A VLAHIDES

John wrote the Bryce Canyon, Capitol Reef, Canyonlands, Arches and Moab chapters; he collaborated with Jeff Campbell on the Grand Staircase chapter.

John regularly writes about national parks of the western US, including Yosemite, Kings Canyon, Sequoia and Lassen Volcanic. When not hitting the trail, he works as a freelance travel writer in San Francisco, where he spends his free time touring the coast of California by motorcycle, sunning beneath the Golden Gate Bridge, skiing the Sierra Nevada and singing tenor with the San Francisco Symphony Chorus.

### DAVID LUKAS
**Geology, Ecosystem**

David has been an avid student of the natural world since the age of five. This same love took him around the world to study animals and ecosystems in Borneo, the Amazon basin and Central America. Now working as a professional naturalist, David leads natural-history tours, conducts biological surveys and writes about natural history. His articles have appeared in many national magazines, and he writes a weekly nature column for the *Los Angeles Times*. His most recent book is *Wild Birds of*

*California,* and he just finished revising the classic guidebook *Sierra Nevada Natural History.* David also contributed to Lonely Planet's *Yosemite National Park*; *Banff, Jasper & Glacier National Parks*; *Grand Canyon National Park*; and *Costa Rica* (6th edition).

## FROM THE AUTHORS

**Jeff Campbell** I am indebted to a great many people. First of all, boundless thanks to editor Kathleen Munnelly and coauthor John A Vlahides, who made a lean, mean, effortless team.

Rangers and park service employees were unfailingly gracious and helpful everywhere. At Zion, I'd particularly like to thank Ron Terry, Jeff Bradybaugh and Ray O'Neill. Museum curator Leslie Newkirk and her assistant Vicki Parkinson were a delight and never failed to make time for me. My thanks to *everyone* at the Backcountry Desk! At the Grand Staircase, Mary Dewitz offered advice and perspective.

Endless gratitude is due to Dean Wood and Travis Tomlinson for their stories, expertise and hikes. Gratitude is due in equal measure to Great Old Broads Ginger Harmon, Veronica Egan and Becky Lindberg; I'd hike with you any day. Thanks also to Heidi McIntosh of SUWA. And for freely sharing their opinions and warm friendship, many thanks to Steve and Deb Massey, Eva and Alex, Eileen and Karla and the irrepressible Joe. Rachel, sorry I missed you!

Finally, thanks to my wife for kindly not killing me, and to my son, whose enthusiasm is constant inspiration. This one's for you, Mom.

**John A Vlahides** Thank you to all my friends who put up with my disappearance while I worked on this book. Jim Aloise: I'm forever indebted to you for showing me that I'm a free man in a free universe; I surrender. Karl Soehnlein: thanks for pointing me in the right direction over and over and over again; I love you. Kate Brady, Liz Costello and David Booth: What would I do without you? Nicole Chaison: I love you, my first muse. Sondra Hall: Sorry I haven't called. Dan Fronczak and Stanley Fuller: Thanks for the faith. Bill Moore: I owe you dinner. Mom: I love you. Dad & Chris: Love you too. Barb and Tere: Ditto.

There would be no book without the wonderful work and guidance of my editor Kathleen Munnelly and my coauthor Jeff Campbell.

My life would have been miserable during the research phase of this guidebook were it not for the invaluable help of Ken Krause, Bruce Fullmer, Marian Delay, Pam Seep, Sue Fearon and the wonderful people of the National Park Service.

I dedicate this book to my dear brother Dean: I wish you were here; I'd take you to Utah.

**David Lukas** Special thanks to Mike, Ingrid, and Rex des Tombe for their generous hospitality and wonderful company while I was researching Zion National Park and for introducing me to their friend and local naturalist David Rachlis. Eileen Smith of the Zion Natural History Association graciously took time to show me around Zion, while Bryce Canyon National Park ranger Kevin Poe was a generous fountain of knowledge and stories. My traveling companion Simone Whitecloud helped me decipher this fascinating landscape and all its life, thank you.

# INTRODUCTION

The national parks of southern Utah are wild, vast and rugged almost beyond our ability to comprehend them, much less describe them. Standing at Grand View Point, the end of the Burr Trail or atop Angels Landing, what are we to make of what surrounds us? This is no gilded temple, no heavenly garden, but instead a dry, ruinous, rent and broken land that extends as far as our disbelieving eyes can see.

It remains the most remote and desolate corner of the continent, appearing much the same as when explorers Father Silvestre Escalante and John Wesley Powell first laid eyes upon it. It's shocking, and beautiful, and hard to convey. It's half the Earth's life span laid bare. It's delicate wildflowers and crumbling mesas. It's how, with enough time, rivers become like rusty knives, cleaving deep gashes in the desert's body. It's black ravens and rattlesnakes and death.

It's a wonder anyone ever comes here.

That they do, and at times in droves, is a testament to the expansive joy and amazement this desert also inspires. We become like children discovering an abandoned construction site for the first time, running everywhere and nowhere all at once in our excitement. Indeed, the erosion is so intricate and extensive, there's no single spot to aim for, no one iconic view where you can roll up to the canyon rim, snap your four consecutive pictures and call it a day. The national parks in this guide don't lack for famous vistas and formations beckoning shutterbugs like moths to the Statue of Liberty's flame, but these are never enough. The land here contains not one epiphany, but hundreds, thousands.

As you're shoulder-squeezed by a slot canyon, one hollowed bowl of rock might stop you in your tracks; as you edge up, stomach knotted, to the lip of an impossibly sheer cliff, a stalk of glowing penstemon might strike you as the greater miracle; as you pause to rest, thinking you've seen every possible hue of sandstone that 60 million years of hard work could excavate, the rising or setting sun will show you otherwise. There are cityscapes of candy-striped hoodoos and stone bridges and arches, and acres of slickrock so sinuous and sensually layered they would make Frank Gehry blush. Eventually, if you let it, the landscape gets under your skin. You see differently, until it almost feels like it has become your skin, and you're grinning through a caked mask of red dirt, loving it.

In addition to Zion and Bryce Canyon, the region's most popular national parks, this guide covers Capitol Reef, Arches and Canyonlands National Parks, as well as the Grand Staircase–Escalante National Monument. It also includes numerous other public lands and a quick detour to the North Rim of the Grand Canyon. Tourist bureaus call this the Grand Circle, and it's a compelling constellation. With a few weeks at your disposal and unlimited mileage on your rental car, you can bag six national parks, three national monuments, two wilderness areas, at least eight state parks, a national scenic byway and much more. Nowhere else in the US can you string together so much officially sanctioned scenery so easily.

The desire to see and do it all can be intense. Adventure in southern Utah means hiking two-foot ledges along thousand-foot drop-offs. It means canyoneering slot canyons so tortured the sun almost never hits bottom, and rock climbing some of the country's most famous big walls. It means river rafting, mountain biking, four-wheel driving and enough primitive backpacking to sate the most grizzled mountaineer. For adrenaline junkies, this is paradise.

It doesn't take long before you come to regard the region's Mormon pioneers and ancestral Native Americans with a new and profound respect. This land is indifferent, even hostile, to human needs, and yet people found a way to survive and even thrive here. You can thank your air-conditioned stars that they did, and that so much of this red-rock wilderness has been preserved nearly as it was. Because of this, southern Utah remains an experience and an adventure of the highest order.

## USING THIS GUIDE

The photo Highlights section presents a few tasty hors d'oeuvres from southern Utah's banquet. With so much to see, planning is essential. The Itineraries suggest what you might do in the time you have, and the Planning chapter is packed with information on seasons, costs, accommodations, transportation, good books, safety, and park and regional contact information.

Refer to the Activities chapter for things to do, then turn to the destination chapters for in-depth coverage of each national park and monument, as well as surrounding towns and sights. You'll find great trails, dirt roads, lodges and hotels, restaurants, viewpoints and Western tourist traps galore.

If you're wondering who in the world first came here and how this desert came to be, turn to the History, Geology and Ecosystem chapters.

*We know, we know, you want to see and do it all. Well, you can't –*

*and that's actually a good thing.*

# ITINERARIES

Even with a month, you'll still leave behind acres of unexplored trails, canyons, dirt roads, cliff faces and viewpoints for your next visit. If you have only a week or two, you'll need to make some hard decisions. Hopefully, we can help. The itineraries below are designed to make the most of short stays in each park and then, depending on your time and interests, offer ways you might combine visits to many of southern Utah's attractions.

## Zion National Park

### HALF A DAY

- Stop by the **visitor center** (p61) to review its interpretive exhibits and park dioramas.
- Ride the **Zion Canyon Shuttle** (p63) the length of the canyon to the **Temple of Sinawava** (p68), admiring sights along the way.
- At the Temple of Sinawava, take the **Riverside Walk** (p73), perhaps wading the North Fork Virgin River at trail's end.
- Ride the shuttle back, stopping if you have time at **Weeping Rock** (p67) or the **Court of the Patriarchs** (p66).

### ONE DAY

- Follow the half-day itinerary to Riverside Walk, then return on the shuttle to either the **Hidden Canyon Trail** (p76) or the **Emerald Pools Trail** (p74).
- Have lunch beneath the giant cottonwood at **Zion Lodge** (p67).
- Return to your car and drive **Hwy 9** (p68) through the **Zion–Mt Carmel Tunnel** to Zion's slickrock east side and **Checkerboard Mesa** (p70).
- Before returning to the canyon, hike the **Canyon Overlook Trail** (p74).
- If you have time, stop at the **Zion Human History Museum** (p69) and perhaps walk the **Pa'rus Trail** (p72).
- Have a sunset dinner at the **Bit & Spur** (p97) in Springdale.

## TWO DAYS

Follow the one-day itinerary.

- Consider a hike up the Virgin River through **The Narrows** (p77) or to the top of **Angels Landing** (p78). Either hike will take the better part of a day.
- If you missed the **Zion Human History Museum** (p69), catch it today.
- In the late afternoon, reward yourself by browsing Springdale's **fine art galleries** (p99) and recount your adventures over dinner at **Zion Pizza & Noodle** (p97) or **Oscar's Café** (p97).

## FOUR DAYS

Follow the first two-day itinerary.

### Day Three

- Take a break from hiking and visit the historic sites in **St George** (p102) or take the kids to the **Dinosaur Discovery Site** (p104) and the **Sand Hollow Aquatic Center** (p104).
- In the afternoon, drive **Kolob Terrace Rd** (p71) to Lava Point and perhaps hike the **Northgate Peaks Trail** (p81). Catch sunset on the drive back.
- Backpackers should use Days Three and Four to hike the **West Rim Trail** (p83).

### Day Four

- If you hiked **The Narrows** (p77) on Day Two, today hike to **Angels Landing** (p78), or vice versa.
- If neither hike appeals, take a three-hour **horseback ride** (p90) in Zion Canyon or an **inner-tube ride** (p90) on the Virgin River.
- Later, rent **bicycles** (p90) and bike to sights along Zion Canyon Scenic Drive, pedaling as far as your energy and the fading light allow.
- Splurge on dinner at the **Spotted Dog Café** (p98).

# Bryce Canyon National Park

## HALF A DAY

- Make the **visitor center** (p117) your first stop; watch the short introductory video.
- Head to **Sunset Point** (p121) for your first glimpse of the towering pink and orange hoodoos of Bryce Amphitheater.
- Next, head into the canyon for a one-hour hike along the **Navajo Loop Trail** (p123). If you have time, add the **Queen's Garden Trail** (p124).
- Then, either take the short drive to **Bryce Point** (p120) or head directly to **Bryce Canyon Lodge** (p138) for lunch or dinner.

- Stop first at the visitor center, then drive to **Rainbow Point** (p118).
- Hike **Bristlecone Loop Trail** (p128) for spectacular vistas and ancient trees.
- Return on the **Scenic Drive** (p118), stopping at all the major sights.
- By the time you reach **Sunrise Point** (p121), you'll be ready for lunch; head to **Bryce Canyon Lodge** (p138) or the **General Store**.
- Stroll the **Rim Trail** (p125) to watch the light play on the hoodoos.
- From **Sunset Point** hike into Bryce Amphitheater on the **Navajo Loop Trail** (p123); if time allows, add the **Queen's Garden Trail** (p124).
- Head to **Paria View** (p120) to watch the sunset.

Follow the tour for the one-day visit.

### Day Two

- Now that you've started to acclimate to the altitude, consider a day hike on the **Fairyland Loop Trail** (p127).
- If you're in *top* shape, consider hiking to the natural spring along the **Riggs Spring Loop Trail** (p133).
- In the afternoon, hike the **Rim Trail** (p125).

Follow the suggestions for the first two days.

### Day Three

- Give your feet a rest and take a half-day **horseback ride** (p133), which takes in the spectacular **Wall of Windows** and the **Silent City**.
- After lunch, head to the **Mossy Cave Trail** (p129) and play by the waterfall.
- In Tropic, enjoy a patio dinner at **Bryce Canyon Inn & Pizza** (p138).

### Day Four

- Backpackers should trek part of the **Under-the-Rim Trail** (p130); drop in via the Sheep Creek or the Agua Canyon Connecting Trails.
- Or, rent a bike and head to **Red Canyon** (p141), where you can ride a stretch of the Thunder Mountain Trail.

# Grand Staircase–Escalante National Monument

### Along Hwy 12

- Depending on your direction, stop at the **Cannonville Visitor Center** (p155) or the **Escalante Interagency Office** (p155) to get oriented.

- Dip into **Kodachrome Basin State Park** (p165) for a hike.
- If you have time, continue into the monument to **Grosvenor Arch** (p157).
- As you drive along scenic **Hwy 12** (p165), stop often to take in the breathtaking scenery.
- Take a coffee break at the oh-so-cool **Kiva Koffeehouse** (p167).
- At **Calf Creek Recreation Area** (p167), dip your feet in the creek and perhaps take a short hike.

### Along Hwy 89

- Stop at the **Kanab Visitor Center** (p169) to get your bearings.
- Drive to the **Paria Valley Rd & Movie Set** (p171).
- If you have time on the way back, drive **Johnson Canyon Rd** (p156) to **Glendale** (p113) via Glendale Bench Rd.

### ONE DAY

### Along Hwy 12

Follow the half-day itinerary, but take more time and add the following:

- Check out the Anasazi village at **Anasazi State Park** (p168).
- In the afternoon, drive the **Burr Trail** (p158) near **Boulder** (p167) to see **Waterpocket Fold** (p175) at sunset.
- Catch dinner at **Hell's Backbone Grill** (p168).

### Along Hwy 89

Follow the half-day itinerary, but add the following:

- Drive partway north on **Cottonwood Canyon Rd** (p157), perhaps hiking **Lower Hackberry Canyon** (p160).
- Hike **Wire Pass** (p171) in the **Paria Canyon–Vermilion Cliffs Wilderness Area** (p171).
- Have dinner at Glendale's **Buffalo Bistro** (p113) or Kanab's **Rocking V Café** (p170).

# Capitol Reef National Park

### HALF A DAY

- Stop at the **visitor center** (p176) to see the incredible relief map, carved using dental instruments.
- Take the **Scenic Drive** (p179) to road's end at **Capitol Gorge** (p180).
- Have a picnic lunch in **Fruita** (p176).

### ONE DAY

Follow the half-day itinerary, but add these.

- **Fruit picking** (p177) at the visitor center, if it's offered.
- Hike the **Hickman Bridge Trail** (p181).

Follow the one-day itinerary.

- Take the **Capitol Gorge Trail** (p180) to see the **Pioneer Register** and **The Tanks**.
- Take the **Grand Wash Trail** (p180) through the 80-story-high canyon walls of **The Narrows**.
- For dinner, drive to Torrey for a steak at the **Rim Rock** (p190) or superb Southwestern cooking at **Café Diablo** (p190).

# Canyonlands National Park

**HALF A DAY**

If you've only got a few hours to spend in Canyonlands, it's a no-brainer: Head to **Island in the Sky** (p193).

- After stopping at the visitor center, drive directly to **Grand View Point** (p195).
- Return along the **Grand View Point Scenic Drive** (p194).

**ONE DAY**

Pack a picnic and follow the half-day itinerary, but this time with feeling.

- Take the **Grand View Point Scenic Drive** (p194) and choose from among several day hikes, but don't miss **Mesa Arch** (p196).
- Stop for a picnic at the **White Rim Overlook** (p195).
- Follow the northwest fork of the **Upheaval Dome Scenic Drive** (p195) to **Upheaval Dome** (p196), stopping at the **Green River Overlook** on the way.
- On your way to Moab, stop at **Dead Horse Point State Park** (p206).

**TWO DAYS**

Follow the one-day itinerary, pick up another picnic lunch (try the **Red Rock Bakery**, p239, in Moab), then:

- Drive south to **The Needles** (p199). Along the way, stop at the cheesy **Hole 'n the Rock** (p220) if you like spelunking and '50s-kitsch home decor.
- Stop at the visitor center, but skip the video; it's the same as at Island in the Sky.
- Take the **Big Spring Canyon Overlook Drive** (p200) and be sure to take all four **day hikes**.
- If you're feeling ambitious, take the long hike to **Chesler Park** (p203).
- Another option is a side trip to **Canyon Rims Recreation Area** (p222).

# Arches National Park

**HALF A DAY**

- Get up early, beat the heat, and arrive at the **visitor center** (p209) by 8am.

- Take the **Scenic Drive** (p210), which passes all the major sights.
- Be sure to get out of the car at **The Windows** (p213) to stroll beneath a few arches.
- Pick a few easy day hikes, but don't skip **Landscape Arch** (p215).

ONE DAY

Arrive early, and bring lunch.
- At the visitor center, book a guided hike in the **Fiery Furnace** (p212) if it's offered.
- Take the **Scenic Drive** (p210), doing any day hikes that appeal to you, but don't skip the short ones, particularly **Landscape Arch** (p215).
- If it's July or August, go straight to the park's most famous arch, **Delicate Arch** (p214), before the heat becomes unbearable. Have a tailgate picnic afterward.

TWO DAYS

Follow the one-day itinerary.
- If you booked it the first day, start Day Two with the **Fiery Furnace guided hike** (p212).
- Do any day hikes you missed. Perhaps save the trail to **Landscape Arch** (p215) for today and continue hiking to **Dark Angel** and **Double O Arch**.
- If you have little kids, stop hiking early and go to **Butch Cassidy King World Water Park** (p239) in Moab.
- Spend the evening shopping and wandering around **Moab**.

# Southwest Peaks & Canyons

In the heat of summer, here's a weeklong journey that hits southwest highlights and keeps things cool(er).

ONE WEEK

- On Days One and Two, go to **Zion** and follow the two-day itinerary.
- On Day Three, stay in Zion and choose between **tubing** (p90) and **horseback riding** (p90), driving **Kolob Terrace Rd** (p71) or, for the adventurous, doing the **overnight Narrows hike** (The Narrows: From the Top, p82; make sure to reserve your permit ahead).
- On Day Four, if you're not in The Narrows, check out **Snow Canyon** (p107) and then head up into the refreshingly high **Pine Valley Mountains** (p108) for a wilderness hike. Sleep in Pine Valley or **St George** (p102).
- On Day Five, visit Zion's **Kolob Canyons** (p70) off I-15, then drive north and check out the easy vista hikes on **Hwy 14** (p112) and continue to **Cedar Breaks National Monument** (p112). Spend the night in **Cedar City** (p108) and enjoy a night at the **Shakespearean Festival** (p109).
- On Days Six and Seven, head to **Bryce Canyon** and follow the two-day itinerary.

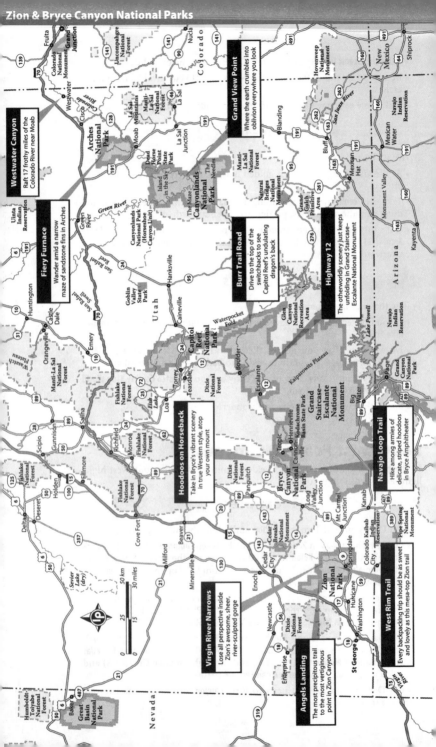

# Zion & Bryce Canyon National Parks

**Westwater Canyon**
Raft 17 frothy miles of the Colorado River near Moab

**Fiery Furnace**
Wander amid a narrow maze of sandstone fins in Arches

**Grand View Point**
Where the earth crumbles into oblivion everywhere you look

**Burr Trail Road**
Drive to the top of the switchbacks to see Capitol Reef's undulating dragon's back

**Highway 12**
The otherworldly scenery just keeps unfolding in Grand Staircase-Escalante National Monument

**Hoodoos on Horseback**
Take in Bryce's vibrant scenery in true Western style, atop your own mount

**Navajo Loop Trail**
Hike among armies of delicate, striped hoodoos in Bryce Amphitheater

**Virgin River Narrows**
Lose all perspective inside Zion's awesome, sheer, river-sculpted gorge

**Angels Landing**
The most precipitous trail to the most vertiginous point in Zion Canyon

**West Rim Trail**
Every backpacking trip should be as sweet and lovely as this mesa-top Zion trail

*Words can never do justice to America's most remote and dramatic desert. So enough bruised sunsets and purple prose – here are the pictures. Enjoy!*

# ZION & BRYCE CANYON **HIGHLIGHTS**

*In fact, southern Utah's national parks are even better in person, unobstructed by frames, with views that stretch to the horizon. You'll feel firsthand the embrace of the sheer canyon walls and the lure of their exposed rims. You'll hear coyotes howl beneath the continent's clearest, most star-clustered night sky. Then there's the fleeting magic when the evening sun breaks beneath clouds to set cliff faces on fire, while those puffs and streaks of cumulus vapor dance like the northern lights.*

*Oh, right, no sunsets. Well, we just couldn't help ourselves.*

CHECKERBOARD MESA Count this among Zion's more striking slickrock wonders.

RICHARD CUMMINS

CANYON TREE FROG These little fellas can give quite a concert.

KARL LEHMANN

'THE SUBWAY' Only canyoneers can get to this station, the Left Fork of North Creek.

RALPH LEE HOPKINS

THE WATCHMAN For the best light show on Earth, don't miss a sunset in Zion Canyon.

# ZION **HIGHLIGHTS**

REDROCK Zion's geological wonders have been 250 million years in the making.

THE NARROWS Hike in the Virgin River through its famous thousand-foot gorge.

BRYCE CANYON A rainbow arches over equally colorful geological formations.

NAVAJO LOOP TRAIL Trek inside a sandstone maze.

KEVIN LEVESQUE

RALPH HOPKINS

# BRYCE CANYON **HIGHLIGHTS**

SILENT CITY HOODOOS Winter in Bryce is a quiet, ethereal time.

RALPH HOPKINS

BRYCE AMPHITHEATER Row upon row of magically striped hoodoos march back in time.

HORSEBACK RIDING Saddle up for a classic Western ride.

PINK CLIFFS The moon looms large in America's clearest skies.

ISLAND IN THE SKY  The desert seems endless from Grand View Point, Canyonlands.

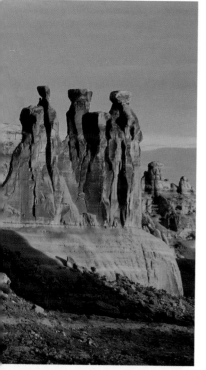

PACK TRIPS  Trek with llamas in the remote wilderness of the Grand Staircase-Escalante National Monument.

ARCHES NATIONAL PARK  Got a secret? Don't tell the Three Gossips.

THE CASTLE Capitol Reef's rock is both impossibly grand and delicately beautiful.

THE CONFLUENCE The mighty Green and Colorado Rivers finally meet in Canyonlands.

# SOUTHERN UTAH **HIGHLIGHTS**

CANYONLANDS NATIONAL PARK Beneath Mesa Arch, sunset inspires silent reveries.

WALL STREET Climb one of southern Utah's many challenging walls.

EMILY RIDDELL

PICTOGRAPHS Ancestral Puebloans left their marks throughout the Southwest.

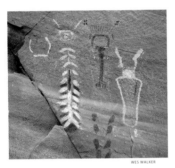

WES WALKER

DELICATE ARCH A paraglider gets a unique view of this marvelous formation in Arches National Park.

EDDIE BRADY

# Mama, Don't Take My Kodachrome

Here's a one-week jaunt for people who want color, color and more color. Bring lots of film.

### ONE WEEK

- On Days One and Two, go to **Zion** and follow the two-day itinerary.
- On Day Three, take either Hwy 89 or I-15 to **Hwy 14** (p112) for vista hikes and then **Cedar Breaks National Monument**. That night, enjoy theater in **Cedar City** (p108) or push on to sleep in or near **Bryce Canyon**.
- On Day Four, do the one-day **Bryce Canyon** itinerary.
- On Day Five, drive east on **Hwy 12** (p165), making sure to do a hike at **Kodachrome Basin State Park** (p165) and to drive the **Burr Trail** (p158). Spend the night in **Torrey** (p188).
- On Day Six, arrive at **Capitol Reef** and do the one-day itinerary.
- Day Seven allows a morning in Capitol Reef, but then you've got to get to the airport from here. It's a four- or five-hour drive to Las Vegas, Salt Lake City or Grand Junction.

# Keeping the Kids Happy

We know who's boss. This is a week of instant gratification for all ages, with a minimum amount of driving.

### ONE WEEK

- On Day One, go to **Zion** and do the one-day itinerary. Perhaps add the ghost town of **Grafton** (p65).
- Day Two is also devoted to **Zion**. Depending on ages and interests, take your kids **horseback riding** (p90), **tubing** (p90) the Virgin River and/or day hiking **The Narrows** (p77).
- On Day Three, do the easy trails at **Snow Canyon** (p107) in the morning and go swimming at **Sand Hollow Aquatic Center** (p104) in the afternoon. Visit the **Dinosaur Discovery Site** (p104) and spend the night in **St George** (p102).
- On Day Four, go to **Kolob Canyons** (p70) and hike to the **Timber Creek Overlook** (p80). Continue to **Cedar City** (p108) and visit **Iron Mission State Park** (p109) and perhaps the **Shakespearean Festival** (p109).
- On Day Five, enjoy the vistas and easy hikes along **Hwy 14**, including **Cedar Breaks** (p112). If there's time, visit accessible **Red Canyon** (p141) on Hwy 12 and spend the night near **Bryce Canyon**.
- Spend Days Six and Seven at **Bryce Canyon**. Follow the two-day itinerary and be sure to get in another horseback ride and, if you can, a **moonlight hike** (p134).

# Southeast Circle

If you want to base a four- to seven-day trip around Moab, here's one way to organize it.

## FOUR DAYS

- Spend Day One in Canyonlands National Park at **Island in the Sky** (p193), following the one-day itinerary. On the way there, stop at **Arches** and book the **Fiery Furnace guided hike** (p212) for Day Four.
- On Day Two, follow the Canyonlands Day Two itinerary and go to **The Needles** (p199).
- On Day Three, take a **river trip** (p228; reserve well in advance). A half-day trip isn't enough; take a *full-day* trip.
- On Day Four, follow the **Arches** one-day itinerary, including the Fiery Furnace guided hike you previously reserved.

## ONE WEEK

Follow the itinerary for the first four days, and add some of the following.

- Head into the La Sal Mountains, either by taking a full-day **guided horseback ride** (p232) or by driving the **La Sal Mountain Loop Rd** (p221).
- Take one of the other scenic drives, such as the one to the **Canyon Rims Recreation Area** or **Potash Rd** (p222).
- Rent a bike and head to a **mountain biking trail** (p225) that suits your experience level.
- If you don't like biking, canoe or kayak the **Moab Daily** (p230) on a flatwater paddle.
- Take a two-hour **guided Jeep tour** (p224) to see what all the fuss is about.
- Beat the heat at the **Butch Cassidy King World Water Park** (p239).
- Souvenir shop in **Moab**.
- Splurge on a few good meals: Try **Center Café** (p238), **Desert Bistro** (p238) or, if you feel like dressing up, **Sorrel River Ranch** (p238).

# Ascending the Grand Staircase

Here's one way to see much of what southwest Utah has to offer: Travel through time from the oldest to the youngest rock layers. This option also offers some of the best views.

## TWO WEEKS

### Week One

- On the first day, drive from Las Vegas straight to the **North Rim of the Grand Canyon** (p172). Stop at **Pipe Spring National Monument** (p173) on the way, but make sure to catch sunset from the Grand Canyon Lodge.
- To do it right, hike at least partway down the **North Kaibab Trail** (p172) or do an overnight hike all the way to the floor of the Grand Canyon.
- Next, head to **Kanab** (p169) and from here go to the **Paria Movie Set** (p171) and the **Paria Canyon–Vermilion Cliffs Wilderness Area** (p171); hike **Wire Pass** and/or **North Coyote Buttes** (p174).
- Take another day to drive **Cottonwood Canyon Rd** (p157) in **Grand Staircase–**

**Escalante National Monument**; hike **Lower Hackberry Canyon** (p160) and **Grosvenor Arch** (p157).

- Though technically a detour from the Grand Staircase, take another day to explore **Hwy 12** (p165) east to **Boulder** (p167); check out the **Calf Creek Recreation Area** (p167) and drive the **Burr Trail** (p158).
- Return down Hwy 12 and head to **Bryce Canyon**.

### Week Two

- Spend two days in **Bryce Canyon**, either following the easier two-day itinerary or going straight for an overnight hike on the **Under-the-Rim Trail** (p130).
- Take a day to enjoy **Hwy 14** (p112) and **Cedar Breaks** – the Grand Staircase's whipped topping. Spend the night in **Cedar City** (p108).
- Time to head back down the staircase. Go straight to **Zion**, where you'll have three or four days to play with.
- Rest for one day, have a fine meal in **Springdale** (p97) and end with at least one overnight adventure, like hiking **The Narrows** (p82) or the **West Rim Trail** (p83).

# Slickrock Junkies

For hikers, bikers and climbers who want the best of slickrock country, east to west, this is the trip. You'll have to move fast past some great stuff in order to leave time for the trails and climbs.

**TWO WEEKS**

### Week One

- Start in **Moab** and plan for at least four days. Mountain bikers must, of course, start with the **Slickrock Trail** (p226) but also do **Klondike Bluffs** (p227), and there's more.
- Take a day or two to hike **Arches**, a slickrock wonderland, but fit in the little-visited **Corona Arch Trail** (p232) outside Moab.
- Climbers should head first for **Wall Street** (p232) for top-roping and to meet fellow climbers. See if you're up for **Indian Creek**.
- You're here, so spend at least half a day seeing **Island in the Sky** (p193) in Canyonlands.
- Spend at least two days in **The Needles** (p199), biking some of the 4WD roads, such as the **Confluence Overlook** (p203), and hiking: try the **Slickrock Trail** (p201) and **Chesler Park Loop** (p203).
- On the seventh day, drive to **Capitol Reef**, stopping at **Goblin Valley State Park** (p190) on the way, just because it's so weird.

### Week Two

- In **Capitol Reef**, take a day for the **Scenic Drive** (p179) and a hike to the **Navajo Knobs** (p182).
- Next, get a taste of **Grand Staircase–Escalante National Monument** by driving

partway along **Hole-in-the-Rock Rd** (p157) to more bizarreness at **Devils Garden**.

- If you're itching to ride, stop at **Red Canyon** (p141) and tackle the **Thunder Mountain Trail** (p142).
- Don't linger too long, because you need to leave three or four days for **Zion**. Good climbers should tackle one or two of Zion's famous **big wall climbs** (p89).
- At least drive through Zion's east side on **Hwy 9** (p68), though hikers should stop at **Observation Point** (p79) and **The Subway** (p86).
- Hikers and climbers shouldn't miss the slickrock in **Snow Canyon** (p107), which could fill a day or more.
- Bikers should take a few days to explore **Gooseberry Mesa** (p90), the **Hurricane Cliffs** (p90) and **Green Valley Loop** (p104), among other slickrock trails.
- Finally, if you're serious about slickrock, reserve a hiking permit for the **North Coyote Buttes** in the **Paria Canyon–Vermilion Cliffs Wilderness Area** (p171) and end your trip here. It'll blow away everything you've seen so far.

# The Grand Circle

If you want to see it all, plan for at least three weeks, though four is best. You *could* drive the route in a fortnight if you never stop for more than a day, but you'll want a few big adventures, and you'll need some downtime between them.

**FOUR WEEKS**

### Weeks One & Two

- Take three to four days in **Zion**, following the four-day itinerary.
- Take a day or two to visit the **Grand Canyon's North Rim** (p172), stopping at **Pipe Spring National Monument** (p173).
- Take four or five days to explore **Grand Staircase–Escalante National Monument**: take a day along **Hwy 89** (p168), a day to drive through the monument on **Cottonwood Canyon Rd** (p157), then two or three days to explore the areas off **Hwy 12** (p165).
- Take three days to enjoy **Bryce Canyon**; spend one on a side trip to **Cedar Breaks** (p112).

### Weeks Three & Four

- Allow yourself three days in **Capitol Reef**.
- Then drive to **Moab**, where **biking** (p225), **rafting** (p228) and the **La Sal Mountains** (p232) deserve at least three days.
- Plan on two days at **Arches**.
- Take two to three days to explore Canyonlands' **Island in the Sky** (p193).
- Take two to three days to explore **The Needles** (p199).

*For such a dry, brittle, barren place, there's a surprising sensuality to southern Utah's landscape. Water's signature is everywhere.*

# ACTIVITIES

Determined rivers have left behind both majestic cliffs and slot canyons in their progress through ancient hardened seas, whose layers can be ticked off like the colorful lines on a child's growth chart. To follow a wash through a narrow canyon and run your hands over the carved sandstone walls is to witness a river's hydraulics frozen in time. It's easy to become addicted, to want to explore deeper, farther, higher – and you can.

It's possible, one supposes, to 'see' southern Utah only through the windows of a vehicle. There is certainly plenty of roadside scenery. But more than most places in the world, this land should be experienced firsthand to fully appreciate it. It's not just a matter of beholding sights most others will never see. It's about leaving the literal and figurative safety of your car and the modern world behind. There's no place in the US quite like this, and few elsewhere in the world. And you don't need cliff-hanging, death-defying determination to enter it. Just follow any trail. All too quickly, the desert will close around you, revealing a vision of the Earth so old and surreal it defies understanding.

## HIKING & BACKPACKING

Hiking is the main and most accessible activity at all the national parks. It involves little more than walking, but with preparation and a purpose – and this is the one thing to remember about hiking in southern Utah: be prepared. This is wild desert unlike what most people have ever experienced, and designating certain parcels as 'national parks' has not tamed it.

Detailed throughout this guide are hiking and backpacking opportunities for people of all ages and abilities. Every park offers one or two rewarding wheelchair-accessible trails, plus a bewildering variety of more moderate to difficult trails. **Zion** may have the best overall selection of trails for both day hikers and backpackers. Most trails in Zion Canyon either follow the Virgin River or climb its steep walls; the park's best-known hike, The Narrows, is literally *in* the river. **Bryce Canyon** presents the opposite configuration: Easy hikes are along the rim, while longer hikes drop steeply into its amphitheater of hoodoos. **Grand Staircase–Escalante National Monument** (GSENM) is a paradise for primitive backpackers, though it also provides plenty of easy to moderate trails – some very accessible, others along rough dirt roads. While slender **Capitol Reef** and **Arches** both offer lots of easy to moderate trails just off their main scenic drives, Arches is not recommended for backpacking. **Canyonlands** tends to the extremes: Short trails off the main roads let you dip your toes, but to really get into it, be ready for a major hiking or backpacking trek. All the national parks dispense maps and trail descriptions.

However, park boundaries seem almost arbitrary in this unending landscape, and hiking is just as good outside of the national parks and monuments. If you tire of red rock, try the **Pine Valley Mountains** outside St George, **Dixie National Forest** on the Aquarius Plateau north of Hwy 12, or the **La Sal Mountains** outside Moab. On the Utah–Arizona border, the **Paria Canyon–Vermilion Cliffs Wilderness Area** is among the most fantastical places on Earth, while state parks like **Coral Pink Sand Dunes** and **Goblin Valley** feature unusual spectacles that are worth a detour.

## When to Hike

Though southern Utah is a year-round destination, variations by location and season are extreme. As the majority of parks and other sights are in the desert, spring and fall are often the best times to hike. Summer – the height of tourist season – can be the worst, as temperatures routinely top 100°F. One summer strategy is to hike the big canyons only very early or late in the day, planning your hike for the side that will be in shade.

Elevation also plays a factor. At more than 8000ft, Bryce stays a bit cooler, as do other spots in the mountains. However, certain roads and trails at higher elevations may be closed to all but cross-country skiers until April or May, and sometimes June.

Camping in summer can be dreadful if you don't find shade, while in spring and fall overnight temperatures may drop to freezing (even when days are warm). At higher elevations, nighttime temperatures drop well below freezing.

Year-round, the weather is variable and often intense. When it rains, it rains hard and all at once. In fact, early summer is called 'monsoon season' because of these rainstorms, which send flash floods coursing through canyons. Whatever the season, always hike with caution and awareness.

For local weather updates, go to www.wrh.noaa.gov and click on the map for southern Utah.

### COOLEST PLACES

It's the desert – you know it's gonna be hot. Cool off in one of these refreshing spots:

✔ Swimming holes on the **Virgin River** (p73)

✔ **Cedar Breaks National Monument** (p112)

✔ **Pine Valley Mountain Wilderness Area** (p108)

✔ **La Sal Mountains** (p221)

✔ Lazy paddles on the **Green River** (p231)

✔ **Calf Creek Recreation Area** (p167)

## Difficulty Level

Hikes in this guide are rated by difficulty level. While such determinations are always subjective, they're particularly hard to quantify here. Heat, elevation and trail grade are only a few of the variables hikers should consider when deciding how difficult a trail will be. When in doubt, assume trails will be harder and take longer than you think.

**Easy**: Generally level and easy to navigate, these trails are often paved, accessible to wheelchairs and suitable for young children.

**Moderate**: Trails involve some elevation gain and may be slightly rocky or rough, but can be done by anyone of average fitness.

**Difficult**: These are strenuous trails involving steep climbs, tricky route finding and/or long distances.

## Day Hikes

The majority of hikes described in this guide are day hikes, taking anywhere from 30 minutes to eight hours. Durations do not account for breaks. On steep trails that lead from canyon floors to rims, or vice versa, a general guide is that it takes twice as long to ascend as to descend. For people who want to test themselves, or who don't have time for a full hike, it's always possible to tackle just the first few miles of a day or backcountry hike. Hike descriptions detail sights and viewpoints en route.

For an explanation of how to prepare for desert hikes, see Hiking Safety, later in this chapter.

### FARTHEST HORIZONS

Folks who want to see it all should head to these high places:

✔ **Lava Point** (p72), in Zion National Park

✔ **Hwy 14 overlooks** (p112)

✔ **Hwy 89** (p168) scenic viewpoints, looking north

✔ **Head of the Rocks** (p166), on Hwy 12

✔ **Burr Trail** (p158), atop the switchbacks

✔ **Grand View Point** (p194), at Canyonlands' Island in the Sky

✔ **Dead Horse Point State Park** (p206)

## Backcountry Hikes

People can and do spend weeks off trail in the southern Utah desert, but it's something to build up to, once you know the desert. Backcountry hikes in this guide lean toward the easier ones, usually involving one to three overnights. When you're ready for more, park rangers and local outfitters can help you find the challenge you seek. In general, Zion, Bryce Canyon and Capitol Reef offer a good selection of easy to moderate backpacking trips, while Canyonlands and Grand Staircase are famous for their difficulty.

The most important consideration on any backcountry hike is water. Will there be any on your route, and of what quality and quantity? Southern Utah has been suffering an extended drought since 2000, so don't trust blue lines and circles on a map. Always check with rangers or knowledgeable locals before trekking into the unknown.

Also, see the boxed text 'Desert Etiquette' (p33) for advice on minimizing your impact on the desert.

## Hiking Guides

The number of hiking guides to southern Utah grows each year, and many have a particular focus. Park visitor centers are usually stocked with good regional guides.

*Hiking Zion & Bryce National Parks,* by Erik Molvar and Tamara Martin, is a very good general hiking guide to the southwest region. A few details are now out of date (like permit regulations and water sources), but it has useful maps and elevation charts.

*Exploring the Backcountry of Zion National Park – Off Trail Routes,* by T Brereton and J Dunaway, covers some of Zion's easier canyoneering routes and its less-visited backpacking areas; it's particularly useful for experienced hikers.

*Hiking the Escalante,* by Rudi Lambrechtse remains one of the definitive guides to this region within GSENM. *Hiking the Southwest's Canyon Country,* by Sandra Hinchman is a good general guide.

Consider reading a general guide to desert hiking safety as well, such as *Desert Hiking Tips,* by Bruce Grubbs.

For an online resource, the American Hiking Society (www.americanhiking.org) is a national umbrella group of hiking clubs that has a useful 'trail finder' on its website.

## Hiking Safety

As a rule, the desert is not conducive to life, which generally has to use every trick in the book to survive. Willfully entering a desert means taking extra precautions to make sure you return safely. This is true whether you plan to be gone an hour or a week. The desert has a way of compounding simple errors in judgment very quickly, and consequences range from unpleasant to grave.

One of the most obvious dangers is falling, and people fall to their deaths every year in southern Utah. Cliff edges are sheer and trails along them very exposed; rocks can be loose; slickrock, when wet, is indeed slick. Watch your children carefully at all times. There are no guardrails.

Flash floods are another ever-present danger. No matter how dry a streambed looks, or how sunny it is overhead, a sudden rainstorm miles away can cause a creek to 'flash' in minutes, sending down a huge surge of rock- and log-filled water that sweeps away everything in its path. Always check the weather before hiking a canyon.

Most hikers would consider themselves lucky to see a rattlesnake, but not if they surprised one sunning on a rock. Don't reach blindly over ledges or beneath boulders.

Getting lost is another danger. Bring a map. For short national park trails, park maps are usually adequate. But route-finding skills never hurt; trails across slickrock usually require following cairns – small hiker-stacked piles of rocks. Bring and know how to use a compass, and be familiar with prominent landmarks. If you bring a topographical map, know how to read it.

Respect the sun and heat. *Always* wear sunscreen and a wide-brimmed hat. The rule of thumb is to drink a gallon of water a day; on the hottest days, or on a strenuous hike, this is a minimum, not a maximum. Always carry more water than you think you'll need; if your bag isn't too heavy when you start your hike, it will be too light by the end. If you'll be gone more than a few hours, bring a water purifier or purification tablets. If you need to, you'll want the ability to drink whatever water you find, and all stream and groundwater needs to be treated. Keep an extra gallon or two of water in your car.

But water is not enough. Bring food too, particularly salty foods. While dehydration can lead to heat exhaustion and heat stroke, drinking water and not eating can lead to hyponatremia, an equally debilitating condition that is common in the parks. One of the symptoms of severe dehydration and hyponatremia is impaired judgment, which can lead to poor choices that worsen your situation. For more on these conditions, see Health & Safety (p54).

Another risk facing hikers is their own exuberance. Respect your limits. Remember that even in the middle of a national park, you're in a remote place. Don't act foolishly by, for instance, jumping off rocks. Breaking an ankle or leg is easy – many people do, particularly young men. Depending on where you are when you're injured, it could be several hours to several days before a park rescue team can find you and get you to a hospital. Needless to say, if

## DESERT ETIQUETTE

The desert is an exceedingly fragile environment, easily damaged by feet, tires and fires and slow to heal. Even relatively small environmental changes can have long-lasting ramifications, as the margin between life and death is so thin for desert plants and animals.

Visitors to southern Utah should consider themselves its caretakers. Enjoy the desert, but leave it at least as healthy as it was when you arrived. Now that much of southern Utah is to varying degrees protected for public enjoyment, one of the greatest threats to the desert is us, the public.

While in the desert, follow these simple guidelines. For more information, contact **Leave No Trace** (☎ 800-332-4100; www.lnt.org).

✔ Stay on the trail, whether hiking, biking or driving. If it's muddy, either don't go or be willing to get dirty – it's better than creating wider, braided trails.

✔ If there is no trail, stay on slickrock, gravel or sand; never step or ride on plants or cryptobiotic soil (p275).

✔ Pack it in, pack it out: Bring resealable plastic bags to contain used wrappers and toilet paper; consider using a human-waste containment bag if camping.

✔ If camping, place your tent on established sites or durable surfaces, like bare dirt or slickrock.

✔ Protect all water sources and riparian areas: Camp 200ft from any water, never wash yourself or dishes in creeks or springs and use minimal or no soap.

✔ Backcountry fires are usually prohibited and should be avoided even when allowed. Use a camp stove.

✔ Never touch, move or take any cultural or archaeological artifacts; do not enter ruins.

you're not in a national park, they won't even come looking. For some typical rescue stories, see 'What Not to Do: An Expert Shares Stories' (p88).

### Hiking Rules & Permits

Hiking and backcountry use rules at the national parks and monuments are virtually the same. With minor exceptions, these are the guidelines for trail use:

- Day hikes on maintained trails do not require a permit.
- All overnight backcountry hikes require a permit; some permits are free, while others cost ($5 to $20).
- Pets are prohibited on all trails, whether day use or backcountry (Zion's Pa'rus Trail is the one exception). For more on pets, see p46.
- Bicycles are forbidden on all day-use or backcountry trails (again, Zion's Pa'rus Trail is the exception); however, bicycles are allowed on roads, including 4WD tracks.
- It's illegal to touch, disturb, take or deface any cultural sites or artifacts or to pick wildflowers or otherwise harm plants or animals.

For backcountry camping and use, further rules apply:
- Group limits apply to backcountry use; these vary, so always ask.

| NAME | TYPE | LOCATION START | DISTANCE R/T | DURATION R/T | CHALLENGE | ELEVATION CHANGE | FEATURES | FACILITIES | DESCRIPTION | PAGE |
|---|---|---|---|---|---|---|---|---|---|---|
| Angels Landing | Day hike | The Grotto | 5mi | 3½–4½ hrs | difficult | 1488ft | | | An exciting trail that is extremely exposed but worth the effort. | 78 |
| Cable Mountain | Day hike | Zion Ponderosa Ranch | 7.2mi | 3–3½ hrs | moderate | 70ft | | | Peaceful mesa-top jaunt ends with amazing Zion Canyon views. | 75 |
| Canyon Overlook | Day hike | Zion–Mt Carmel Tunnel, east end | 1mi | 30 min–1 hr | easy–moderate | 163ft | | | Short, varied, kid-friendly hike with marvelous canyon views. | 74 |
| Emerald Pools | Day hike | Zion Lodge | 1.2–2.5mi | 1–2 hrs | easy–moderate | 69–400ft | | | Perennial favorite for all ages; lovely pools and trickling waterfalls. | 74 |
| Hidden Canyon | Day hike | Weeping Rock | 2mi | 1½–2½ hrs | moderate–difficult | 850ft | | | Not ready for Angels Landing? Try this. | 76 |
| La Verkin Creek | Day hike/overnight | Lee Pass, Kolob Canyons Rd | 14.5mi | 8 hrs or 2 days | moderate–difficult | 800ft | | | Spring and fall are best for this hike past a desert river, giant arch and narrow canyons. | 84 |
| The Narrows: From the Bottom | Day hike | Riverside Walk | 10mi | 8 hrs | moderate–difficult | 300ft | | | Should be required of all Zion visitors, but hike prepared. | 77 |
| The Narrows: From the Top | Day hike/overnight | Chamberlain's Ranch | 16mi one way | 12 hrs or 2 days | moderate–difficult | 1220ft | | | Have a true adventure along the Virgin River, with solitude to boot. | 82 |
| Northgate Peaks | Day hike | Wildcat Canyon, Kolob Terrace Rd | 4.4mi | 2 hrs | easy | 110ft | | | This great, overlooked family hike ends at very cool lava rock promontory. | 81 |
| Observation Point | Day hike | Weeping Rock | 8mi | 4–5½ hrs | difficult | 2150ft | | | Very tough ascent, but worth every step; try in the late afternoon. | 79 |
| Pa'rus Trail | Day hike | Zion Canyon Visitor Center | 3.5mi | 1½ hrs | easy | 50ft | | | Fully accessible hike for all ages is the easiest way to take in Zion Canyon. | 72 |
| Riverside Walk | Day hike | Temple of Sinawava | 2mi | 1 hr | easy | 50ft | | | Enjoy a taste of the Virgin River Narrows along this paved walk. | 73 |
| The Subway | Day hike | Wildcat Canyon, Kolob Terrace Rd | 9.5mi one way | 6–8 hrs | difficult | 1850ft | | | One of Zion's most transcendent experiences; for canyoneers only. | 86 |
| Taylor Creek Middle Fork | Day hike | Kolob Canyons Rd | 5mi | 2½–3 hrs | moderate | 450ft | | | At trail's end, Double Arch Alcove is a meditative destination. | 80 |
| Timber Creek Overlook | Day hike | Kolob Canyons Rd | 1mi | 30 min | easy | 100ft | | | The easiest way to take in the ragged finger canyons of the Kolob. | 80 |
| Trans-Park Connector | Overnight | La Verkin Creek Trail | 15.5mi one way | 2 days | moderate–difficult | 1000ft | | | The only way for backpackers to span north and south Zion. | 85 |
| Watchman | Day hike | Zion Canyon Visitor Center | 2.7mi | 1½–2 hrs | easy–moderate | 368ft | | | Best at sunset for its lower canyon views. | 75 |
| Weeping Rock | Day hike | Weeping Rock | 0.5mi | 30 min | easy | 98ft | | | Don't miss this delicate, beautiful hanging garden. | 73 |
| West Rim | Day hike/overnight | Lava Point, Kolob Terrace Rd | 14.5mi one way | 9 hrs or 2 days | moderate–very difficult | 3600ft | | | Best high-country backpack, with views that keep coming. | 83 |

*See legend under Hiking in Bryce*

# HIKING IN BRYCE

| NAME | TYPE | LOCATION START | DISTANCE R/T | DURATION R/T | CHALLENGE | ELEVATION CHANGE | FEATURES | FACILITIES | DESCRIPTION | PAGE |
|---|---|---|---|---|---|---|---|---|---|---|
| Bristlecone Loop | Day hike | Rainbow Point | 1mi | 30 min–1 hr | easy | 100ft | [icons] | [icon] * | Stroll the plateau's southernmost tip for views of the Grand Staircase. | 128 |
| Fairyland Loop | Day hike | Fairyland Point | 8mi | 4–5 hrs | difficult | 900ft | [icon] | | Long hike away from crowds leads past castlelike formations, though not as spectacular as Bryce Amphitheater. | 127 |
| Mossy Cave | Day hike | Hwy 12 | 0.8mi | 30 min–1 hr | easy–moderate | 150ft | [icons] | | Hike beside running water to a waterfall and cave. | 129 |
| Navajo Loop | Day hike | Sunset Point | 1.4mi | 1–2 hrs | moderate–difficult | 521ft | | | Drops past Thor's Hammer, the Silent City and other prominent hoodoos. | 123 |
| Navajo Loop–Queen's Garden Combination | Day hike | Sunrise or Sunset Point | 2.8mi | 2–3 hrs | moderate | 521ft | [icons] | | Bryce's most popular hike offers great variety in short time. | 124 |
| Peekaboo Loop | Day hike | Bryce, Sunrise or Sunset Point | 5–6.6mi | 3–5 hrs | difficult | 500–900ft | [icons] | [icon] | This all-day hike through Bryce Amphitheater offers lots of variety. | 124 |
| Queen's Garden | Day hike | Sunrise Point | 1.6mi | 1–2 hrs | moderate | 320ft | [icons] | | Gentlest descent into the canyon passes myriad hoodoos. | 123 |
| Riggs Spring Loop | Day hike/overnight | Rainbow Point | 8.8mi | 4–5 hrs or 2 days | difficult | 1675ft | [icons] | [icons] | This strenuous day hike drops off plateau's southern tip through three ecological zones. | 133 |
| Rim Trail | Day hike | Bryce Point or anywhere along rim | 5.5mi one way | 2–3 hrs | easy–moderate | 550ft | [icons] | [icons] ** | Half-day hike along canyon rim features stellar overlook of hoodoos. | 125 |
| Under-the-Rim | Overnight | Bryce Point | 22.9mi one way | 2–3 days | moderate–difficult | 1315ft | [icons] | [icon] | Bryce's premier backcountry hike passes few hoodoos but promises wonderful solitude. | 130 |

* wheelchair accessible spur to Yovimpa Point
** wheelchair accessible between Sunset and Sunrise Points

[icon] View  [icon] Restrooms  [icon] Great for Families  [icon] Drinking Water  [icon] Waterfall  [icon] Picnic Sites  [icon] Swimming  [icon] Ranger Station  [icon] Bicycling  [icon] Wheelchair Accessible  [icon] Wildlife Watching  [icon] Backcountry Campsite

# HIKING IN GRAND STAIRCASE & CAPITOL REEF

| NAME | TYPE | LOCATION START | DISTANCE R/T | DURATION R/T | CHALLENGE | ELEVATION CHANGE | FEATURES | FACILITIES | DESCRIPTION | PAGE |
|---|---|---|---|---|---|---|---|---|---|---|
| **GRAND STAIRCASE–ESCALANTE** | | | | | | | | | | |
| Boulder Mail Trail | Overnight | Boulder | 16mi one way | 2–3 days | difficult | 700ft | | | Following an old mail route, this trail passes myriad slickrock wonders in Phipps–Death Hollow. | 161 |
| Escalante Natural Bridge | Day hike | Hwy 12 | 4mi | 2–3 hrs | easy | negligible | | | Follow the Escalante River to this towering arch. | 159 |
| Lower Calf Creek Falls | Day hike | Calf Creek Recreation Area | 6mi | 3–4 hrs | moderate–difficult | negligible | | | Red-rock canyon hike along a year-round running creek. | 158 |
| Lower Hackberry Canyon | Day hike | Cottonwood Canyon Rd | 2–6mi | 1–3 hrs | easy | negligible | | | Easy, pleasant hike through a sculpted, narrow gorge. | 160 |
| Phipps Wash | Day hike | Hwy 12 | 4mi | 2–4 hrs | moderate | negligible | | | Hike down a wash to two arches; route-finding may be necessary. | 159 |
| Slot Canyons of Dry Fork/Coyote Gulch | Day hike | Off Hole-in-the-Rock Rd | 1–4mi | 1–3 hrs | easy–moderate | 200ft | | | Shimmy through narrow slot canyons. | 159 |
| **CAPITOL REEF** | | | | | | | | | | |
| Capitol Gorge | Day hike | Scenic Drive | 2mi | 45 min–1½ hrs | easy | 40ft | | | Towering canyon features Indian petroglyphs, historical sites and waterpockets. | 180 |
| Cohab Canyon | Day hike | Gifford Homestead | 1.75mi one way | 1–2 hrs | moderate–difficult | 400ft | | | This hidden canyon high in the rocks overlooks Fruita. | 182 |
| Grand Wash | Day hike | Scenic Drive | 2.2mi one way | 45 min–1½ hrs | easy | 200ft | | | Pass between sheer 80-story canyon walls just 15ft apart. | 180 |
| Hickman Bridge | Day hike | Hwy 24 | 2mi | 1–2 hrs | easy–moderate | 200ft | | | This trail passes giant domes and a towering arch, ending with views to Fruita. | 181 |
| Lower Muley Twist Canyon | Overnight | Burr Trail | 15mi | 1–2 days | moderate–difficult | 850ft | | | Twist through an 80-story red-rock canyon just 10ft wide, then return across grasslands. | 185 |
| Rim Overlook–Navajo Knobs | Day hike | Hwy 24 | 9mi | 4–6 hrs | difficult | 1494ft | | | Ascends to Rim Overlook, then climbs higher still for 360-degree panoramas. | 182 |
| Upper Muley Twist Canyon | Overnight | Burr Trail | 15.7mi | 1–2 days | moderate | 830ft | | | This trail features arches, sculpted sandstone narrows and long views of Waterpocket Fold. | 183 |

**Legend:**

| | | | |
|---|---|---|---|
| View | Waterfall | Swimming | Bicycling |
| Restrooms | Picnic Sites | Ranger Station | Wheelchair Accessible |
| Great for Families | Drinking Water | Wildlife Watching | Backcountry Campsite |

| NAME | TYPE | LOCATION START | DISTANCE R/T | DURATION R/T | CHALLENGE | ELEVATION CHANGE | FEATURES | FACILITIES | DESCRIPTION | PAGE |
|---|---|---|---|---|---|---|---|---|---|---|
| **CANYONLANDS (ISLAND IN THE SKY)** | | | | | | | | | | |
| Aztec Butte | Day hike | Scenic Drive | 2mi | 1–1½ hrs | moderate | 225ft | 🪧🏜️ | | Skitter up slickrock to an ancient Native American granary. | 196 |
| Grand View Point | Day hike | Scenic Drive | 2mi | 1–1½ hrs | easy | 50ft | 🪧🏜️ | | No place in Canyonlands offers such a sweeping view; watch for passing condors. | 197 |
| Mesa Arch | Day hike | Scenic Drive | 0.5mi | 30 min | easy | 100ft | 🪧🏜️ | | Island in the Sky's most famous arch is gorgeous at sunrise. | 196 |
| Upheaval Dome | Day hike | Scenic Drive | 0.8–1.8mi | 1–1½ hrs | easy–moderate | 50–200ft | 🪧 | 🚻 | Marvel at Island in the Sky's geologic mystery. | 197 |
| **CANYONLANDS (THE NEEDLES)** | | | | | | | | | | |
| Cave Spring | Day hike | Scenic Drive | 0.6mi | 30–45min | easy–moderate | 50ft | 🪧🏜️ | | Past an abandoned cowboy camp, this trail climbs ladders up slickrock. | 201 |
| Chesler Park Loop & Joint | Day hike/ overnight | Elephant Hill Trailhead | 11mi | 1–2 days | moderate–difficult | 520ft | 🪧 | ▲ | Popular backcountry trek passes grasslands and pinnacles and threads through narrow fractures. | 203 |
| Pothole Point | Day hike | Scenic Drive | 0.6mi | 45 min | easy | 20ft | 🪧 | | Stop by natural potholes to spot tiny swimming organisms. | 201 |
| Roadside Ruin | Day hike | Scenic Drive | 0.3mi | 15–30 min | easy | 20ft | 🪧🏜️ | | Loop past desert vegetation and an ancient Native American granary. | 200 |
| Slickrock | Day hike | Scenic Drive | 2.4mi | 1½–2 hours | easy–moderate | 70ft | 🪧 | | Semiloop trail with views of The Needles and La Sal and Abajo Mountains. | 201 |
| **ARCHES** | | | | | | | | | | |
| Balanced Rock | Day hike | Scenic Drive | 0.3mi | 15–20 min | easy | 20ft | 🪧🏜️ | | This precariously poised boulder is perched atop a narrow rock spire. | 213 |
| Delicate Arch | Day hike | Scenic Drive | 3mi | 2–3 hrs | moderate–difficult | 480ft | 🪧🏜️ | 🚻 | Arches' premier hike ascends slickrock to the iconic Delicate Arch. | 214 |
| Landscape Arch | Day hike | Scenic Drive | 2.1mi | 30 min–1 hr | easy–moderate | 50ft | 🪧🏜️ | 🚻 | A short walk to one of the world's longest spans, with side hikes to smaller arches. | 215 |
| Park Avenue | Day hike | Scenic Drive | 1mi one way | 30–45 min | easy–moderate | 320ft | 🪧🏜️ | 🚌🚻🅿️ | Sheer sandstone monoliths call to mind New York City skyscrapers. | 212 |
| Sand Dune & Broken Arches | Day hike | Scenic Drive | 2.4mi | 15 min–2 hrs | easy–moderate | 140ft | 🪧🏜️ | | This trail passes the Fiery Furnace fins, ambles across grasslands, threads through an arch and crosses slickrock. | 213 |
| The Windows | Day hike | The Windows Section, Scenic Drive | 0.6mi | 30 min–1 hr | easy | 140ft | | 🚻🅿️ | Walk beneath giant arches that frame stunning views. | 213 |

*See legend under Hiking in Grand Staircase & Capitol Reef.*

- Certain other backcountry activities, like canyoneering in Zion and driving 4WD roads in Canyonlands, require a day-use permit.
- Human waste must be carried out or buried in a 6- to 8in hole; consider using human-waste disposal bags.
- No dispersed camping is allowed within 200ft of streams or trails, nor within a quarter mile of springs.
- No open fires are allowed in the backcountry; use a gas stove. The exceptions are Canyonlands and Grand Staircase–Escalante, which allow fires under certain restrictions.

## EXTREME SPORTS
Bored? Need a thrill? Try these:

✔ **Climb** (p89) Prodigal Son, Spaceshot or one of Zion's other big walls

✔ Raft **Cataract Canyon** (p230), on the Colorado River

✔ 4WD **Elephant Hill Loop** (p200), in The Needles

✔ Mountain bike the **Slickrock Trail** (p226)

✔ Hike to **Angels Landing** (p78), in Zion Canyon

✔ Canyoneer **Paria Canyon** (p171) to Lees Ferry, Arizona

## ROCK CLIMBING
Some of the country's best rock climbing lies in southern Utah, though many routes are for moderate to expert climbers. **Zion** is famous for big wall climbs, while the surrounding area, particularly **Snow Canyon State Park**, offers dozens of bolted and sport routes. You'll find great climbing in **Arches**, **Canyonlands** and **Capitol Reef** (restrictions apply) and several popular routes for all abilities around **Moab**. Climbers might be interested to read others' adventures at www.rocknrun.net.

Note that climbing in summer can get exceptionally hot. When the air temperature reaches 100°F, the cliff-face could top 115°F, and the rocks hold the heat all night. Spring and fall are better times to rock climb; if you do climb in summer, start early in the morning.

Some parks enforce seasonal closures of certain routes to protect nesting or breeding wildlife. All prohibit power drills, discourage excess bolting and ask climbers to use subdued colors for hangers and slings.

For a comprehensive overview of climbing in southwest Utah, refer to *Rock Climbs of Southwest Utah & the Arizona Strip*, by Todd Goss.

## CANYONEERING
While Europeans have been wild about canyoneering for years, it's just now starting to catch on seriously in the US. **Zion** and its environs are the sport's epicenter in southern Utah, but you'll also find fantastic slot canyons along the **Escalante River** in GSENM and in the **Paria Canyon–Vermilion Cliffs Wilderness Area**. Ask outfitters in **Moab** about slot canyons in that region.

One reason canyoneering is so popular is that it's relatively easy to learn, at least compared to rock climbing. In addition to outfitters mentioned in the destination chapters, the **American Canyoneering Association** (ACA; ☎ 435-590-8889; www.canyoneering.net), based in Cedar City, offers lots of information and runs a multitude of courses. Their three-day Basic Canyoneering course is $300. For more informal advice, visit **Tom's Utah Canyoneering Guide** (www.canyoneeringuse.com/utah/index.htm). In terms of books, *Canyoneering 1, 2* and *3*, by Steve Allen, are three top-notch guides that cover GSENM and the San Rafael Swell. Michael Kelsey, who apparently never rests, has written several canyoneering guides, including the comprehensive *Slot Canyon Guide to the Colorado Plateau*. Another all-around guide is *Canyoneering*, by John Annerino.

Bear in mind that the recent flood of inexperienced canyoneers has been largely responsible for an increase in the number of rescues at Zion and elsewhere. Rappelling, it turns out, is a particularly easy way to put yourself into situations you're not experienced enough to get out of. Canyoneers must also be especially mindful of flash floods. Being inside the cogs and wheels of Earth's geological machinery is very cool until they turn on.

## MOUNTAIN BIKING & CYCLING

The fat-tire crowd already knows about **Moab**, which has been a mountain biking mecca for 20 years. The original **Slickrock Trail** is here, among many others. What mountain bikers might not know, however, is that southwest Utah offers equally good slickrock trails in places outside Zion and St George, such as **Gooseberry Mesa**. And even though mountain biking is prohibited on national park trails, it is permitted on dirt or 4WD roads. In Canyonlands, **White Rim Rd**, in Island in the Sky, and the labyrinth of 4WD roads in **The Maze** are awesome experiences; in Capitol Reef, the **Cathedral Valley Loop** is recommended.

**Cycling** the national parks' main paved roads is an excellent way to take in the sights, although touring the region by bike is a hardy endeavor and best done with the support of an outfitter or tour operator. Companies offering bike rentals and guided trips are positioned near all the national parks.

The nationwide **Adventure Cycling Association** ( ☎ 406-721-1776, 800-755-2453; www.adventurecycling.org) arranges tours and provides information on cycling routes. *Above and Beyond Slickrock*, by Todd Campbell, is the regional biking bible.

Mountain bikers must follow all of the guidelines in 'Desert Etiquette' (p33), particularly the rule to stay on the trail.

## HORSEBACK RIDING

What, come out West and not ride a horse? Well, saddle up, pardner!

The same concessionaire runs horseback rides at Zion and Bryce Canyon: **Canyon Trail Rides** ( ☎ 435-679-8665; www.canyonrides.com). At each national park, they offer one- or two-hour rides and half-day rides. Costs range from $30 to $55 per person.

Several outfitters can get you on horseback for rides around **Capitol Reef** and into the **Grand Staircase** and **Box–Death Hollow Wilderness Area**. Nor will **Moab** outfitters and ranches disappoint; they can take you into the desert and La Sal Mountains, and some even run trips that combine horseback riding with river running – though not at the same time.

## FOUR-WHEEL DRIVING

Southern Utah boasts dirt roads aplenty, and a 4WD vehicle is useful on all of them. It also has many dirt roads – some of which are legendary – that are *only* manageable via 4WD. Yet if there's one piece of equipment that can get the inexperienced into trouble faster than a static canyoneering rope, it's a 4WD vehicle. A rental Jeep or SUV is not a magic bullet; sometimes it's just a means for getting as far from help as possible.

Before heading into the desert, know the capabilities of your vehicle. If you don't have the winches and experience to free a stuck vehicle, don't take chances on unknown roads. And before heading out, get current road and weather conditions. GPS is delightful, but it's useless in a muddy wash with a storm coming. If you've never driven back roads in Utah before, take a guided tour first – it's a good reality check.

All roads in **Grand Staircase–Escalante National Monument** qualify as 4WD roads; the main roads are good for beginners, as they're fairly straightforward and see a fair bit of traffic. Dozens of rough spurs and tracks branch off these roads, but unless you're an expert who's been here before, avoid them. **Dixie National Forest**, north of Hwy 12, has some good, mountainous 4WD roads, and **Capitol Reef** offers several great roads, including the **Cathedral Valley Loop** and **Burr Trail**.

By far the most and best-known 4WD roads are around **Moab** and in **Canyonlands**. At Island in the Sky, the 100-mile **White Rim Rd** is an epic adventure, while The Needles contains more than 50 miles of 4WD roads, including the challenging **Elephant Hill Loop**. **The Maze** is unbelievable, but it's only for hardcore, experienced adventurers. Around Moab, check out **Kane Creek Rd** and, if you dare, **Hell's Revenge**, among others.

*4WD Adventures: Utah*, by Peter Massey and Jeanne Wilson, is a very good, detailed 4WD guide, with useful maps, GPS coordinates and even a good history section.

See 'Desert Etiquette' (p33) for the essential Leave No Trace guidelines, and see 'OHVs & the BLM' (p223) for some cautionary history. Remember, nothing ruins the desert faster than car tires, and a single off-road joyride leaves harmful scars that can last decades.

> ## WEIRDEST ROCKS
>
> The competition is stiff, but for some of the strangest bits of sandstone you'll ever see, you can't miss at these places:
>
> ✔ **Goblin Valley State Park** (p190)
>
> ✔ **Devils Garden** (p157), on Hole-in-the-Rock Rd
>
> ✔ **Bryce Canyon Amphitheater** (p120)
>
> ✔ **Kodachrome Basin State Park** (p165)
>
> ✔ **The Needles** (p199) section of Canyonlands
>
> ✔ **Arches National Park** (p208)
>
>

## RAFTING & BOATING

Folks with desert river fantasies should head to Moab. The Virgin River through Zion is too shallow for any watercraft, except for the few days each year when kayakers are allowed. If you want to raft, aim for the Green or Colorado Rivers, which offer a wide range of experiences, from mellow canoes to jet boats to large rubber rafts that bob like balsa chips in the raging rapids.

Moab hosts an almost overwhelming number of outfitters and types of trips. For the calmest trips, you can rent equipment and paddle the **upper portion of the Green River** or the **Moab Daily**, a section of the Colorado along Hwy 128. More adventurous trips through Canyonlands require a permit, and the easiest way to get one is to join a guided trip. For a one-day whitewater trip, try **Westwater Canyon**; their multiday trips take you down the Green or Colorado, past the Confluence and into **Cataract Canyon**, the ultimate in white-water.

## SWIMMING & TUBING

Shocking but true – swimming options are limited in southern Utah. Though great for rafting, the Colorado and Green Rivers near Moab are lousy places to swim; even at their mellowest, the currents are dangerously strong for swimmers. The **Virgin River** through Zion is better. While generally shallow and cold, it does offer lots of swimming holes and warms up just enough in summer to enjoy a dip. Tubing is prohibited within the park, but outfitters in Springdale rent inner tubes for popular local floats.

## FISHING

Although Utah is an angler's paradise, offering scads of mountain lakes and rivers and oodles of stocked reservoirs, few options exist in southern Utah, and the national parks are notoriously terrible for fishing.

The mountains surrounding Zion harbor several good stocked reservoirs (mostly trout), including **Kolob Reservoir**; **Navajo Lake** and **Duck Creek** on Hwy 14; and the reservoir in the **Pine Valley Wilderness**. North of Hwy 12 outside Boulder, **Boulder Mountain** is a popular fly-fishing destination.

Wherever you fish, including the national parks, you'll need a Utah fishing license. Also familiarize yourself with each spot's particular restrictions. These vary and can be pretty strict, limiting the type of bait or lure and the catch, sometimes to only one fish.

Visit the website of the **Utah Division of Wildlife Resources** (www.wildlife.utah.gov) for fishing regulations. A one-/seven-day Utah fishing license is $12/32, available at businesses near good fishing spots. Or get one online through the Utah Travel Council (www.utah.com).

## WINTER ACTIVITIES

Several places offer **cross-country skiing** and **snowshoeing**. Perhaps the most popular is **Bryce Canyon**, which features 10 miles of cross-country trails, plus 20 more in the surrounding forest. Park officials keep the main road plowed in winter, and when snows are deep enough, the visitor center loans snowshoes for free. Cross-country skiing is also popular in the mountains north of Zion along **Hwy 14**, and visitors can ski the scenic amphitheater rim at **Cedar Breaks National Monument**. The **La Sal Mountains** outside Moab feature great cross-country skiing and even a hut-to-hut system.

The only downhill skiing is at **Brian Head Ski Resort**, north of Cedar City – that said, it's pretty good.

## WATCHING WILDLIFE

Southern Utah is home to some fabulous wildlife. Zion hosts mountain lions, bighorn sheep and nesting peregrine falcons, while Bryce is notable for its 'towns' of endangered Utah prairie dogs. Bighorn sheep have been reintroduced to Canyonlands, and reintroduced California condors now soar over the entire region. Almost anywhere it's possible to see coyotes and eagles, rattlesnakes and bats – though you have to be very, very lucky. Most of these desert species are very secretive, extremely rare or both.

More common are tame mule deer, proud cawing ravens and begging squirrels and chipmunks. Refrain from feeding these animals; they can carry disease, and if they become dependent on handouts, they will not survive in the wild.

Perhaps the most satisfying activity is **bird-watching**, as Utah is perched amid a major migratory flyway; ask at national park visitor centers for bird-watching lists.

## RANGER PROGRAMS

Every national park sponsors ranger talks and programs that cover topics of main interest to visitors – geology and wildlife, ecology and human history, and more. Zion and Bryce boast the widest range of talks and hikes, while all host evening campground talks. Arches offers a ranger-led hike into the Fiery Furnace, and Bryce features popular stargazing and full-moon hikes.

## PHOTOGRAPHY TIPS

Nothing is more disappointing than coming home from the desert and tearing through your just-developed film to find 10 rolls of washed-out horizons, with tiny friends and family squint-smiling in the distance.

You're not alone. Even the best photographers can't get the whole desert in their pictures. But you can improve the quality and composition of your photos, whether your camera is a top-shelf digital masterpiece or a disposable throwaway.

If you do have a digital camera, bring extra batteries or a charger; the instant gratification of your LCD preview screen will run the battery down fast.

For print film, use 100 ASA film for all but the lowest light situations; this is the slowest film, and it will enhance resolution. Color slide film is the best, though it's more expensive.

A zoom lens is extremely useful; most 35mm cameras have one. Use it to isolate the central subject of your photos. A common composition mistake is to include too much landscape around the person, animal or rock feature that's your main focus. Sacrifice background for foreground, and your photos will be more dramatic and interesting.

Morning and evening are the best times to shoot. The same sandstone bluff can turn four or five different hues throughout the day, and the warmest hues will be at sunset.

As a rule, don't shoot into the sun or include it in the frame; shoot what the sunlight is hitting. This is especially important when photographing people, who will turn into blackened silhouettes with the sun behind them. On bright days, move your subjects to the shade for close-up portraits.

As for other equipment, a tripod is useful for low-exposure dusk shots but is cumbersome on hikes, and some digital cameras have waterproof cases that are worth the investment for canyoneers and river runners.

And that endless horizon? Move people out of the way and shoot it at sunset's last gasp. Even then, the photo in your memory is always better.

Night skies here are among the darkest in North America – don't miss the chance to admire them.

## CLASSES

Of the national parks, only Zion and Bryce host instructional organizations, and both are relatively new. Started in 2002, the **Zion Canyon Field Institute** offers a large selection of interesting classes geared toward visitors. Launched in 2004, Bryce's **High Plateaus Institute** is more academic and scientific, though it's open to any interested visitors. In Moab, the **Canyonlands Field Institute** is a private organization that runs educational tours in the region. All the national parks sponsor a **Natural History Association** that visitors may contact for news and upcoming events. See Useful Organizations on p50 for contact information.

## KIDS' ACTIVITIES

All the national parks in this guide offer **junior ranger programs** (www.nps. gov/learn), which center largely on activity books that kids complete to get a special certificate and badge. However, Zion's Junior Ranger program, at its kid-friendly **Nature Center**, is much more involved; it's a drop-off program at which children join instructor-led activities, hikes and games. Capitol Reef recently opened its own kid-focused **Ripple Rock Nature Center**.

Beyond these offerings, of course, are the parks themselves, which feature enough easy trails and bizarre formations to rate high on most kids' interest meters. Refer to Day Hikes in each destination chapter, which highlight the best trails for kids. **Horse trail rides** in Zion and Bryce are winning activities, as is **tubing** outside Zion, and families can pick fruit in **Fruita** in Capitol Reef. **Goblin Valley** and **Coral Pink Sand Dunes State Parks** are particularly good for kids, as they're allowed to run free.

Outside the parks, **St George** and **Moab** provide surefire diversions such as water and amusement parks. And throughout the region, you'll find touristy **chuckwagon dinners**, featuring cowboy shootouts and entertainment (in particular, see Cedar City, Kanab and Moab).

COURTESY OF ZION NATIONAL PARK CAT10164

*They don't call it the Grand Circle for nothing. There's a lot to see in southern Utah, and few people have the time or stamina to do it all in one trip.*

# PLANNING THE TRIP

When you're going will have a tremendous impact on what activities are possible (or enjoyable), what roads are open and how crowded it will be. For your trip to be a success, you'll need to do some research.

Reservations are recommended for busy weekends and for the hotels and activities you don't want to miss. However, southern Utah is rarely so crowded that you can't find a bed somewhere (though it may be 15 or 30 miles down the road), and there's so much to explore, you'll never lack for awesome experiences. If you can, plan for some flexibility. One of the best things about the region is that you're always stumbling across the unexpected, and you should feel free to pursue each intriguing side canyon. We guarantee they'll be the ones you remember most.

## WHEN TO GO

Southern Utah's national parks are open year-round, and great trips are possible in any season. High season varies a bit regionally, but it extends roughly from the beginning of April to the end of October at lower elevations and from Memorial Day to Labor Day at higher elevations. By contrast, winter visitation drops so low that many businesses serving the national parks curtail their hours or close altogether, though that's no reason to stay away. What you miss out on in winter is more than outweighed by the quiet you gain.

### Seasonal Highs & Lows
#### SPRING
Spring is unpredictable, bringing both rain and sun. At lower elevations, spring begins in March, when daytime temperatures average in the 60s and with nights still just above freezing. By May, days are in the 80s, nights in the 50s. At higher elevations, snow can linger in quantity through May. Spring wildflowers begin to bloom in April and continue through June.

#### SUMMER
By June, the average daytime temperature tops 90°F, and July and August average around 100°F; nights are in the mid to upper 60s. However, Bryce's daytime average is in the low 80s, and rarely tops 90°F. Everywhere, July and

August are 'monsoon' season, when sudden, short thunderstorms may appear (often in the afternoon), interrupting the plans of canyoneers and making dirt roads impassable.

### FALL

Many say fall is the best season in the desert. September is still pretty hot, averaging about 90°F during the day and 60°F at night, but days are usually clear, water in the rivers and canyons remains warm, and foliage at high elevations begins to change color. This spectacular display continues through late October at lower elevations; by then, temperatures have dropped to the mid-70s during the day and to 50°F at night. Snow starts to close mountain roads in October. In November, the weather cools considerably, with days in the 60s and nights in the mid-30s.

### WINTER

At lower elevations, winter is pretty mild; from December through February, days remain in the 50s and nights around 30°F. On clear days, temperatures can reach into the 60s and be quite lovely. However, storms can bring snow and ice, making driving hazardous just about anywhere. At higher elevations, winter storms, snow and cold are more serious. Daytime highs at Bryce average around 40°F, while nighttime temperatures drop to 10°F or lower.

## Coping with Crowds

Crowds in southern Utah are about as localized as summer thunderstorms. They strike all at once and for a short time in a single place, sometimes wreaking flash floods of commotion and traffic on certain roads or scenic corridors. These tourist squalls are easier to predict than the atmospheric kind and so are easier to avoid. And given the region's immensity, you can make a quick escape even if caught by surprise.

Summer is high season, so you're guaranteed a quieter time if you visit in spring or fall, when crowds are typically limited to weekends. In winter, southern Utah is a lonely place.

As a general rule, crowds exist in inverse relation to effort. Scenic drives are the most crowded stretches, followed by easy trails just off these roads, and then by the less-traveled moderate to difficult trails. Finding solitude in high season is simply a matter of working harder than everyone else.

The scenic drives in **Arches** and **Bryce** suffer the most congestion. **Zion** attracts more visitors, but its shuttle handles them so smoothly that its main scenic drive *feels* less crowded. **Capitol Reef** and **Canyonlands** receive significantly fewer visitors. With few paved roads and no services, **Grand Staircase–Escalante National Monument** is the least crowded by default. One strategy for driving a popular scenic road is to do so very early or late in the day (which incidentally provides the prettiest light). Or, ride a bicycle, which, other benefits aside, exempts you from the fight for parking.

Of the towns covered in this guide, **Moab** draws the most crowds. Many would say it's overrun, but there's a reason: It's a hub for a huge variety of activities and is the liveliest place in southern Utah. That said, if finding solitude is your main goal, avoid it, as well as **St George**, **Cedar City** and **Springdale**, which also get quite busy in high season. Instead, investigate the small towns along **Hwys 12 and 89**, which are near the national parks and are surrounded by many lesser-known but still amazing sights.

## Special Events

**Cedar City** (aka 'Festival City USA') is southwest Utah's special-events epicenter. Befitting its nickname, the town hosts major festivals year-round, including a **Paiute Pow-Wow**, the **Utah Summer Games** and a **Western rodeo**. Beginning in June, its main attraction is the three-month-plus **Shakespearean Festival**, which brings Tony Award–winning theater to the region.

**St George** boasts its own rodeo, the **World Senior Games**, and the **St George Marathon**, which descends from the neighboring Pine Valley Mountains.

If you're westwardbound to celebrate all things cowboy, don't miss Kanab's **Western Legends Roundup** in late August.

Giving Cedar City a run for its money is **Moab**, which is packed with events from spring to fall, many of which celebrate the outdoor activities that have made the city famous. April ushers in its huge **Jeep Safari**, October welcomes the **Fat Tire Bike Festival**, and in between are bike races, an arts festival, a rodeo and more.

For more on these and other events, see the destination chapters.

## GATHERING INFORMATION

More information on the national parks and monuments is available on the National Park Service website: www.nps.gov. The lone exception is Grand Staircase–Escalante, which is administered by the Bureau of Land Management (BLM; www.ut.blm.gov).

---

### PETS IN THE PARKS

Pets are allowed in the national parks, but under a lot of restrictions. They are not allowed on any trails (Zion's Pa'rus Trail is the lone exception) or at scenic viewpoints. They are not allowed on any park shuttles. They *are* allowed in campgrounds and outside of cars on main roads, but they must remain on a leash at all times. Within the parks, they can be left alone inside RVs during the day, but they cannot be left in cars. Considering summertime temperatures, this is best for the pet's health anyway.

Some hotels allow pets, though many do not. Those that do charge extra, anywhere from $10 to $25. Most parks are near kennels, where dogs and cats can be boarded for a day or overnight; see the destination chapters, or contact the parks for referrals.

---

**Arches** ( ☎ 435-719-2299; www.nps. gov/arch)
**Bryce Canyon** ( ☎ 435-834-5322; www. nps.gov/brca)
**Canyonlands** ( ☎ 435-259-7164, 435-719-2313; www.nps.gov/cany)
**Capitol Reef** ( ☎ 435-425-3791; www.nps. gov/care)
**Cedar Breaks National Monument** ( ☎ 435-586-9451; www.nps.gov/cebr)
**Grand Staircase–Escalante National Monument** ( ☎ 435-826-5499; www. ut.blm.gov/monument or http://gsenm. az.blm.gov)
**Pipe Springs National Monument** ( ☎ 928-643-7105; www.nps.gov/pisp)
**Utah State Parks & Recreation** ( ☎ 801-538-7220; www.stateparks.utah.gov)
**Zion** ( ☎ 435-772-3256; www.nps.gov/zion)

### Suggested Reading

The Southwest provides rich soil for writers, if for no one else. Any list of suggested reading can only skim the surface of the great books that tackle this complex land. While most of the books mentioned in this section deal specifically with Utah, others focus broadly on the Southwest region, which includes Utah, Arizona, New Mexico and Nevada's Great Basin.

For outdoor activity guidebooks, see the Activities chapter.

## TRAVEL, ENVIRONMENT & NATURE WRITING

For a good general introduction to the region and the people who have made their name writing about it, pick up the Travelers' Tales anthology *American Southwest* (2001) and/or the anthology *Words from the Land* (1995), edited by Stephen Trimble.

Terry Tempest Williams is Utah's fierce angel of the desert. A Mormon, a naturalist and an environmentalist, she excels at evoking a desert sensibility and at connecting the personal with the political in our relationship to the land. *Red: Passion & Patience in the Desert* (2001) is a thoughtful, provocative companion on any road trip, while *Coyote's Canyon* (1989) is a beautiful dance of photos and text.

Provocative, passionate and cranky to boot, Edward Abbey's *Desert Solitaire* (1968), about his experiences as a ranger at Arches, is a classic must-read. See also 'The Bard of Moab' (p216).

In *Run, River, Run: A Naturalist's Journey Down One of the Great Rivers of the American West* (1975), naturalist Ann Zwinger describes her journey down the Green River from Wyoming to the confluence with the Colorado, dispensing history, insight and observations of beauty.

Much is made of Everett Ruess, a writer and artist who loved the desert so much he simply vanished into it in 1934 at age 20. *Everett Ruess: A Vagabond for Beauty* (1983), by WL Rusho, is the definitive take on his story.

*Cadillac Desert: The American West & Its Disappearing Water* (1986), by Marc Reisner, is an exhaustively researched, compelling account of the West's most critical issue: balancing development with its most precious resource.

## FICTION

A great deal of Southwest fiction focuses on Arizona and New Mexico, particularly when it concerns Native American tribes. Oddly enough, one early book set in southern Utah is *A Study in Scarlet* (1887), Sir Arthur Conan Doyle's first Sherlock Holmes mystery. Half the book is set in Utah's 'Great Alkali Plain,' and Doyle's descriptions of the 'arid and repulsive desert' typify the era's attitude toward the region.

Famous Western novelist Zane Grey used Arizona and southern Utah as backdrops for his romanticized cowboy tales; *Riders of the Purple Sage* (1912) is his most famous. It's a galloping read.

Edward Abbey's *The Monkey Wrench Gang* (1975) is a mostly fictionalized, raucous tale of 'eco-warriors' and their plan to blow up Glen Canyon Dam before it is built and floods the canyon.

## NATIVE AMERICANS

Perhaps the best introduction to Native American tribes in the Southwest is Stephen Trimble's *The People* (1993), which stitches together tribal histories and modern realities through the voices of Native Americans. It includes an excellent chapter on southern Utah Paiutes and a great bibliography.

*Guide to Rock Art of the Utah Region* (2000), by Dennis Silfer, is an authoritative overview of our current knowledge about prehistoric Indian cultures, and it offers detailed descriptions and explanations of Utah rock-art sites.

*Those Who Came Before* (1983), by Robert and Florence Lister, takes a look at the archaeological record found in the Southwest's national parks and monuments. In Utah, it only covers Capitol Reef, Arches and Canyonlands, but it's very informative, with striking photographs.

## EARLY EXPLORATION

To learn more about the 1776 Domínguez–Escalante expedition, and to read

Escalante's diary, track down *Pageant in the Wilderness* (1950), by Herbert Bolton; it is one of the first authoritative accounts.

To read about one-armed explorer John Wesley Powell's famous trip down the Colorado, pick up a modern reprint of his very readable *Exploration of the Colorado River of the West* (1875). For more context on Powell and the groundbreaking work he did, read the fascinating *Beyond the Hundredth Meridian* (1953), by Wallace Stegner.

### REGIONAL & MORMON HISTORY

The history of Utah and that of the Mormons are inextricably linked. Great Western writer and Utah resident Wallace Stegner beautifully captures the early history of both in two books: *The Gathering of Zion: The Story of the Mormon Trail* (1964) and *Mormon Country* (1942). With elegant, spare prose and uncommon insight, he paints a compelling portrait of an amazingly resilient and determined people.

Another excellent Mormon history – this one by a Mormon who joined the 'cotton mission' – is *I Was Called to Dixie*, by Andrew Karl Larson.

The Zion Natural History Association's *The History of Southern Utah & Its National Parks* (1950), by AM Woodbury is an oddly fascinating book. It's as much a period piece as a source of reliable history and was written by a man who lived through the founding of southern Utah's national parks.

The best all-in-one description of southern Utah, spanning from its geologic beginnings to its present-day realities, is *The Redrock Chronicles* (2000), by TH Watkins, who doesn't let his love for the desert glaze his sharp eye.

## ACCESS FOR ALL

The national parks exist for the enjoyment of all, offering opportunities for those in wheelchairs or with hearing, visual or other disabilities to experience the wilderness. The National Park Service publishes an *Accessibility Guide* with helpful information and details about facilities at specific parks.

All national parks described in this guide have wheelchair-accessible visitor centers, at least one accessible campsite in their main campgrounds, and a few viewpoints and/or trails that are wheelchair accessible. Other trails may be accessible to wheelchairs with assistance, all of which are indicated in trail descriptions.

The lodges at Zion and Bryce offer ADA-compliant wheelchair-accessible rooms, and their shuttles are wheelchair accessible. Contact the parks for information on ranger talks and programs for the hearing impaired.

Accommodations outside the parks are required to reserve at least one room for wheelchair-using guests, though few are fully ADA-compliant. More often, these are ground-floor rooms with wider doorways, less furniture, and handles around the tub and toilet. Always ask what 'accessible' means when making reservations. Hotels with ADA-compliant rooms tend to be newer and more expensive; some are noted in this guide.

**Access Utah Network** ( ☎ 801-533-4636, 800-333-8824, 711 TDY; www.accessut.org) is a state agency that provides accessibility information for all Utah parks and can refer you to other helpful organizations.

The nonprofit, Salt Lake City–based **Splore** ( ☎ 801-484-4128; www.splore.org) specializes in providing outdoor activities – such as rafting, rock climbing and canoeing – for people with disabilities and special needs, and it offers a scholarship program.

An equally expansive, well-researched history of southern Utah is *The Proper Edge of the Sky* (1992), by Edward Geary, who stitches together in telling detail the ongoing relationship of people and the land.

Jon Krakauer's *Under the Banner of Heaven* (2003) is perhaps the most high-profile book ever written on Utah. It's a compelling exposé of extremist polygamist groups, and even Mormons agree the author does a fair job. However, it's worth noting that polygamy, which was banned a century ago by the Mormon Church, and Krakauer's book are less-clear windows into everyday mainstream Mormonism.

Still, polygamy is practiced in Utah, and another take on the subject is *The Secret Story of Polygamy* (2002), by Kathleen Tracy, who is remarkably evenhanded, even though her goal is to uncover the abuse polygamy can hide.

In its own way, *Mountain Meadows Massacre* (1950), by Juanita Brooks, is more revealing than either of the books on polygamy. In it, this celebrated Mormon author unflinchingly examines one of the darkest incidents in Mormon pioneer history (p245).

### GEOLOGY

*Roadside Geology of Utah* (1990), by Halka Chronic, is an invaluable companion for geology buffs, aspiring and otherwise. It's clear, concise, detailed and, best of all, uses examples from the formations you'll pass along the road. By the end of your trip, you'll never confuse your Wingate and Entrada sandstones again!

Among the piles of slick picture books, *Canyons of Color: Utah's Slickrock Wildlands* (1995), by Gary Paul Nabhan and Caroline Wilson, stands out: It pairs great photos and illustrations with eloquent writing and clear descriptions of geology.

Those interested in just southeast Utah might pick up *Canyonlands Country* (1993), by Donald Baars.

*Basin & Range* (1981), by John McPhee, is as much about the journey through as the geology of the Great Basin, which covers much of western Utah and Nevada.

### NATURAL HISTORY

*Wildflowers of Zion National Park,* by Stanley Welsh, is an excellent pocket-size guide that covers the most common wildflowers travelers encounter.

*Utah Wildlife Viewing Guide,* by Jim Cole, is a good general wildlife guide, while *A Naturalist's Guide to Canyon Country,* by David Williams, comes as close as possible to an all-in-one compendium – covering geology, birds, mammals, insects, reptiles, trees, wildflowers and more. Its primary focus is southeast Utah.

Also look for excellent topical field guides from such respected publishers as Peterson, Golden, the National Geographic Society and the Audubon Society. Every national park bookstore has a selection.

## Internet Resources

In addition to the national and state park websites listed elsewhere in this chapter, the following web resources enable good pretrip preparation:

**Public Lands Information Center** (www.publiclands.org) Provides information on all types of public lands in the US, arranged by state. A great resource.

**Utah Travel Council** (www.utah.com) This state-sponsored tourism website has everything to plan your trip.

**American Park Network** (www.americanparknetwork.com) Publishes guides to many national parks, including all the ones in Utah.

**Church of Jesus Christ of Latter-Day Saints** (www.mormon.org) The Church's official website has a good FAQ page that can answer many of your questions about the Mormon faith.
**Great Outdoor Recreation Pages** (www.gorp.com) This is a general outdoor resource and national retailer.
**Lonely Planet** (www.lonelyplanet.com) On Lonely Planet's Thorn Tree bulletin board, you can ask fellow travelers for their tips and share your own.

## Maps

The best backcountry hiking maps are United States Geological Survey (USGS) 1:24,000-scale (7.5-minute) topographical maps, available at most national park visitor centers, good public land offices and better bookstores throughout southern Utah. To purchase in advance, contact the **USGS** ( ☎ 888-275-8747; www.usgs.gov).

**National Geographic** (www.nationalgeographic.com) publishes a series of waterproof, tear-resistant 1:37,700-scale topographic maps that cover the national parks, and each park's natural history association (see below) publishes a similar 1:37,700-scale map. Based on USGS maps, both are widely available at national park visitor centers and elsewhere.

Both **BLM** (www.blm.gov) and **USFS** (www.fs.fed.us) offices give away or sell maps that cover lands under their jurisdiction. These are not great maps for general use, but they are indispensable if you're hiking on public lands outside the national parks, which can be a patchwork of jurisdictions and private landholdings.

As far as road atlases, Rand McNally's *Utah* state map is perfectly adequate, while AAA publishes an *Indian Country Guide Map* that covers southern Utah, northern Arizona and the Four Corners area, which is better for folks doing the Grand Circle.

## Useful Organizations

All the national parks have supporting natural history associations that put out a slew of park information, sell books and maps, and sometimes sponsor events and classes.

**Bryce Canyon Natural History Association** ( ☎ 435-834-4600; www.brycecanyon.org)
**Canyonlands Natural History Association** ( ☎ 435-259-6003, 800-840-8978; www.cnha.org) Covers Arches as well.
**Capitol Reef Natural History Association** ( ☎ 435-425-3791)
**Zion Natural History Association** ( ☎ 435-772-3264, 800-635-3959; www.zionpark.org)

County and other regional travel bureaus are also very helpful.
**Garfield County Travel Council** ( ☎ 435-676-1160, 800-444-6689; www.brycecanyoncountry.com) Covers Bryce and Hwy 12.
**Grand County Travel Council** ( ☎ 435-259-8825, 800-635-6622; www.discovermoab.com) Covers Moab and everything north.
**Iron County Tourism Bureau** ( ☎ 435-586-5124, 800-354-4849; www.scenicsouthernutah.com) Covers Cedar City and Hwy 14.
**Kane County Office of Tourism** ( ☎ 435-644-5033, 800-733-5263; www.kaneutah.com) Covers Kanab and Hwy 89.
**Wayne County Travel Council** ( ☎ 435-425-3365, 800-858-7951; www.capitolreef.org) Covers Capitol Reef and Hwy 24.
**St George Area Convention & Visitors Bureau** ( ☎ 800-869-6635; www.utahsdixie.com) Covers southwest Utah around St George.
**Zion Canyon Visitors Bureau** ( ☎ 888-518-7070, www.zionpark.com)

Backpackers will have a longer list than this, but try to pack light. If you forget something, southern Utah has plenty of camping supply stores and outfitters to fix you up. These are the essentials:

✔ Sunscreen

✔ Hat (wide-brimmed is best)

✔ Day pack and/or roomy fanny pack that holds two water bottles

✔ Water bottles (several and sturdy)

✔ Bandanna (for wiping brow and swatting flies)

✔ Sunglasses

✔ Hiking boots (for backpackers; sturdy and waterproof)

✔ Flashlight (with spare batteries)

✔ Camera (with spare batteries)

✔ Binoculars (not essential but useful)

✔ First-aid kit

✔ Water purifier or water purification tablets

✔ Resealable plastic bags (stores toilet paper, snacks or camera on river hikes)

✔ Fleece sweater (for cool evenings)

✔ Nylon shorts (they dry quickly)

✔ Rain poncho (for summer thunderstorms)

✔ Whistle (to signal for help)

If you want to volunteer at or donate to the national parks, contact the non-profit **National Park Foundation** ( ☎ 202-238-4200; www.nationalparks.org); more than 100,000 people volunteer nationwide annually.

If you're interested in learning more about some of the environmental issues facing southern Utah and/or want to get involved, contact the **Utah Wilderness Coalition** ( ☎ 801-486-2872; www.uwcoalition.org), **Southern Utah Wilderness Alliance** (SUWA; ☎ 801-486-3161; www.suwa.org), Utah chapter of the **Sierra Club** ( ☎ 801-467-9297; http://utah.sierraclub.org) or **Great Old Broads for Wilderness** ( ☎ 907-385-9577; www.greatoldbroads.org). Remember, you don't need to be an old lady to be a Great Old Broad (p163).

## WHAT'S IT GOING TO COST?

The cost of a trip in southern Utah varies considerably depending on how and when you travel, but it's usually not as cheap as people think.

The area is ill-served by public transportation, so renting a car is usually a necessity. Rentals can run from $30/day for the cheapest, no-frills compact to $60/day and up for a 4WD SUV; rates between different companies and airports can vary by sometimes twice as much, so call around. Then there's gas, and given the distances between sights, you'll burn a lot; plan on $5-15 a day, depending on your itinerary.

Accommodations and food are the biggest variables under your control. If you make your own meals and take advantage of free dispersed camping on public lands, you could live on $15 a day. A more reasonable budget is $25-30 a day, which allows camping at established campgrounds (usually $10-15 a site, though some charge $20-25) in and around the national parks. The minute you start eating at diners and buying espresso, however, add $10 to your daily ration.

Acceptable low-end accommodations cost $30-40 a night, with steady year-round rates, though such places are rarely beside the parks (eg, Moab offers few, St George has plenty). In high season in towns closest to the parks, even the cheapest beds rise to $50 or more a night. Mid-range places run $60-90, the better hotels and park lodges clock in at $100-130, and upscale B&Bs and ranches climb to $170 or more. Discounts start to appear in early spring and late fall, while winter (outside of holidays) sees the best rates. Expect top-end rates to fall the farthest, some by as much as half. For the nicest accommodations at the best prices, look for B&Bs on quiet highways in small towns.

If you're eating out for all your meals, it will cost a minimum of $20 a day, not counting the occasional splashy steak dinner. If money is no object, there are just enough fine restaurants in southern Utah that you can spend lavishly if you wish.

Finally, factor in park fees, the cost of any necessary backcountry permits, rental equipment or hiker shuttles, and the cost of guided tours or lessons. Hiking may be free, but invariably the more involved and active you want to be, the more you'll spend.

### National Parks Passes

Except for Grand Staircase–Escalante, every national park and monument in this guide charges a fee to enter, and entry is valid for seven days. If you're staying for more than a week or visiting several national parks, consider purchasing an annual **National Parks Pass**. It costs $50 and covers admission for you and everyone in your vehicle for a year from the date of purchase (this includes all national parks, monuments and historical sites administered by the NPS – more than 400 in all). Or consider a **Golden Eagle Passport** ($65), which provides access for a year to *all* public lands that charge a fee, whether run by the NPS, BLM, USFS or Fish & Wildlife Service. Neither pass covers campground fees.

If you're a US citizen or resident who is 62 or older, you're eligible for a **Golden Age Passport**. A onetime $10 fee grants the user unlimited free access to any NPS-managed area.

If you're a US citizen or resident with a permanent disability, you're eligible for a free **Golden Access Passport**, which, like the Golden Age Passport, grants the user unlimited free access.

Passes are available at all national park and monument entrance stations. Upon entry, be prepared to present your pass along with a picture ID (such as a driver's license).

## ACCOMMODATIONS

Of the national parks listed in this guide, only Zion, Bryce and the Grand Canyon's North Rim offer on-site lodges. Run by **Xanterra Parks & Resorts** ( ☎ 888-297-2757 in US, 303-297-2757 outside US; www.xanterra.com), these lodges are worth the splurge. Rooms book up fast, so reserve at least four to six months in advance. For campground reservations in the national parks, contact the **NPS** ( ☎ 800-365-2267; reservations.nps.gov).

You'll find plenty of accommodations in towns just outside the parks. Weekends and big festivals are the busiest times, occasionally filling every room. At any time, make reservations if park proximity or a certain standard of quality are important. Towns with the most accommodations are St

George, Cedar City, Springdale, Kanab and Moab, while a few good options exist in towns along Hwy 12 like Torrey, Boulder, Escalante and Tropic.

The **Utah Hotel & Lodging Association** ( ☎ 801-359-0104, 866-733-8824; www.utahhotel-lodging.com) publishes a free annual accommodations guide to the state.

**Free Room Reservations** ( ☎ 800-578-3379; www.freerooms.com) is a reservation service that covers the entire Southwest.

Note that in this guide, room rates do not include Utah's 11.5% hotel tax. Just about every hotel and motel offers air conditioning, nonsmoking rooms, a TV and a phone.

## BRINGING THE KIDS

National parks are kid-friendly destinations. **Zion** and **Bryce** are particularly attractive to families, as each offers convenient lodges with kid-centric meals and activities and lots of easy, accessible hikes that please everyone. Both parents and children will find lots of impromptu companionship on their journey. Plus, Mormon culture is very family-oriented; most businesses welcome kids, and most towns have the necessary baby and toddler supplies. See **Kids' Activities** (p42) for a list of fun things to do.

One thing to remember is that children are particularly vulnerable to the heat; they dehydrate faster, and symptoms can turn severe more quickly (see Health & Safety, p54). Make sure your kids drink plenty of water, whether they've been active or not, and never let your children, whether toddlers or teens, run loose on exposed trails or near cliff edges. Even short falls can be deadly. It's a sad fact that as many kids as adults are injured each year in the parks.

### ALCOHOL + UTAH = HUH?

It's a misconception that you can't get a drink in Utah. You can get just as drunk here as anywhere in the US.

Understanding Utah's arcane liquor laws – now that's hard. After a while, you feel like you're listening to John Travolta in *Pulp Fiction* explaining hash in Amsterdam.

Grocery stores can sell only beer, and only beer that's no more than 3.2% alcohol. If it's over 3.2%, it's called 'stout' or 'hard' beer and can be sold only in a state-approved liquor store, which is the only place to buy packaged wine and spirits to carry out. Most towns only have one such liquor store, if any, and they're usually in nondescript, unadvertised locations. You must be 21 to buy alcohol, and it's never sold on Sundays.

Depending on their liquor license, restaurants can sell wine, beer and spirits with their food, but you must ask to see the drink list; they're not supposed to offer it. A place with a 'tavern' license can sell only 3.2% beer, but you must order food to go with it; you can't have just a drink.

A 'private club' serves a full range of liquor, and you don't need to order food to enjoy it. But you must be a member to enter. Temporary, two-week memberships are usually $5 and allow five guests; if you ask at the door, someone inside will often sponsor you as their guest to avoid the cover charge.

At any establishment, you can have only one drink in front of you at a time. Sometimes called 'Utah's slammin' rule,' this means you must finish a drink before ordering another; in the case of pitchers of, say, margaritas, there must be three people present to order one.

And so on. And no, we're not making this up.

An increasing number of outdoor activity guidebooks are geared toward families. *The Sierra Club Family Outdoors Guide,* by Marilyn Doan, is comprehensive, and it's useful for parents who are new to the outdoors themselves. Lonely Planet's *Travel with Children* is another good general resource.

*Best Hikes with Children: Utah,* by Maureen Keilty, offers thoughtful general advice and covers the entire state, though southern Utah's national parks are particularly well represented.

## HEALTH & SAFETY

In any emergency, dial ☎ 911. Unfortunately, when you're injured while hiking in southern Utah, calling may not be an option; cell phones often don't work outside the major interstate corridors, and canyon walls block signals. When visiting this region, you'll need to be more self-sufficient and prepared for the unexpected than usual. The desert offers innumerable ways to come to a bad end, and people discover new ways all the time.

The **National Park Service** (www.nps.gov/public_health) has good information on disease and water issues. Also see 'Hiking Safety' (p32).

### Falls & Jumping

Nothing focuses one's attention like the edge of a 2000ft-high crumbling sandstone cliff. The consequences of a fall are self-evident and keep most people from taking unnecessary risks. The more pernicious danger is carelessness in less dire circumstances. The vast majority of park rescues involve young men fracturing their legs while having fun leaping off rocks, jumping into shallow, murky pools or falling while bouldering. Some mishaps can be chalked up to youth, but it's also true that one's sense of scale can get thrown out of whack. In the shadow of that 2000ft-high cliff, a 15- or 20ft boulder looks like nothing, and a trail with a sheer drop of 50ft isn't scary at all. But these translate into falls of two to four stories and should be treated with appropriate respect.

### Water Purification

All groundwater in the desert, whether a river, seasonal stream or sandstone seep, should be considered unsafe to drink and treated accordingly. Giardiasis and cryptosporidiosis are common intestinal diseases that stem from drinking untreated water. Symptoms include diarrhea, abdominal cramps, gas, headaches and fatigue. Giardiasis can be treated, but there is no effective treatment for cryptosporidiosis; both can last for anywhere from a few weeks or months to several years, though neither is typically life threatening.

The most reliable way to destroy the offending organisms is to boil water for at least 10 minutes. Water purification tablets and portable water filters (0.5 microns or smaller) are also effective, as is bleach and iodine.

Drinking water provided at park campgrounds and visitor centers is reliably safe.

### Altitude Sickness

The rim at Bryce Canyon ranges in altitude from 8000 to 9000 feet above sea level, and Cedar Breaks National Monument rises above 10,000 feet. A common complaint at such high elevations is altitude sickness, characterized by shortness of breath, fatigue, headaches, dizziness and loss of appetite. You can avoid it by drinking plenty of water and taking a day or two to acclimatize before attempting any long hikes. If symptoms persist, return to a lower elevation.

## Sunburn

You can sunburn fast in the desert, sometimes in less than an hour, even on a cloudy day. Apply sunscreen (SPF 30 or higher) religiously every morning and reapply during the day, and don't forget the kids. Always wear a hat, preferably one with a wide brim.

## Dehydration, Heat Exhaustion & Hyponatremia

You don't need to do much to become dehydrated in the desert – just stand around. If you do engage in an activity, expect water and salts to leave your body at a vastly accelerated rate.

It's very important to both drink water and eat salty foods when hiking in the desert. The rule is a gallon of water a day per person. Though that may sound like a lot, you'll drink that and more if you're active. Keep a few extra gallons of water in the car. Eating is just as important, however, and is the half of the equation many people forget. Always carry high-energy bars, trail mix or something else to munch.

Symptoms of heat exhaustion, which occurs when you lose water faster than you're drinking it, include nausea, vomiting, fatigue, headaches, stomach cramps, blanching and cool clammy skin. Treat heat exhaustion by drinking, eating, resting in the shade and cooling the skin with a wet cloth.

Heat stroke, which can be fatal, is an advanced stage of heat exhaustion. It occurs when your internal cooling mechanism breaks down and your body temperature rises dangerously. Other symptoms include flushed dry skin, a weak pulse and poor judgment. Some victims may act uncharacteristically silly. To treat a victim, move them to the shade, remove clothing, cover with a wet cloth or towel, fan vigorously and seek immediate help. Hospitalization may be necessary.

Hyponatremia (low sodium blood level) occurs when you drink a lot of water but don't eat. The water essentially flushes all nutrients from your body. Symptoms are identical to heat exhaustion (as is its potential to be life threatening), and treatment is the same.

## Snake Bites & Scorpion Stings

Despite southern Utah's abundance of venomous snakes, spiders and scorpions, fatalities are rare. There are no particular first-aid techniques for spider or scorpion bites; some (like tarantula bites) are merely painful, while others (like black widow and scorpion bites) contain venom. Doses are generally too small to kill adult humans, but children do face a risk of serious complications. Don't treat with ice, and if you're hiking, return immediately; reactions can be delayed for up to 12 hours, and you may indeed want to call poison control and seek medical help.

If bitten by a snake, seek immediate help. Snakebites don't cause instantaneous death, and medical centers usually stock the necessary antivenins. If you're bitten on a limb, a light constricting band above the bite can help. Keep the affected area below the level of the heart, and move it as little as possible. What you should *not* do is wrap the limb in a tight tourniquet, slash or suck the wound, put ice on it or take any alcohol or drugs. Simply stay calm and get to a hospital.

## Hypothermia

While generally associated with winter hiking at altitude, hypothermia is as real a danger in the desert in any season. It occurs when your body's internal temperature drops too low, causing a rapid physical and emotional breakdown; symptoms include shivering, loss of coordination, weakness, slurred speech and disorientation or confusion.

In southern Utah, hypothermia often strikes people hiking narrow canyons, where they must wade or swim pools that are frigid even in summer. One such place is The Narrows in Zion, where hikers spend most of their time immersed in the Virgin River. It's also a danger for desert campers from fall to spring, when overnight temperatures routinely drop to freezing, even following mild days. To help avoid hypothermia, don't canyoneer in cotton clothes (which dry slowly and provide no insulation when wet), and eat lots of high-energy food.

To treat hypothermia, replace wet clothing with dry clothing, warm the victim with your own body and give them hot liquids and food. Put them in a sleeping bag, if available, and get in with them.

## DANGERS & ANNOYANCES

Crime is not a particular issue in any of the national parks, or even throughout southern Utah, but let common sense prevail: lock your car, and put valuables in the trunk, especially when parking at trailheads.

### Weather

Overall precipitation is low, but when it does rain, it can wreak havoc. Most common from late June to early September, short, heavy thunderstorms can cause flash floods and turn dirt roads into impassable mud slicks, though they dry quickly. Even the lightest rain leaves the desert slickrock and hard clay roads treacherously slippery and too dangerous for any vehicle, including 4WDs. Long inured to the desert's unpredictability, the weather service often covers itself by forecasting a 20% to 30% chance of showers, which tells you nothing. Always check with rangers before hiking canyons or driving dirt roads, and watch the skies. Then, of course, there's the summer heat, which routinely hovers above 100°F.

In winter, higher elevations get socked with snow and lower elevations with freezing rain, occasional snow and freezing nighttime temperatures, which can turn blacktop roads icy.

### Allergies

The desert used to offer respite from pollen and allergy attacks, but the increasing abundance of nonnative species is changing this. Springtime is now allergy season, and in May the abundant cottonwood trees pollinate, releasing millions upon millions of tufted seeds that dust the ground like snow. If you're sensitive, avoid campgrounds near rivers during this month.

### Vertigo

Anyone who suffers from acrophobia will find plenty to suffer from in southern Utah. Some hikes and overlooks are so dizzying that even those not normally bothered by heights experience queasiness, sweaty palms and panic. This is vertigo, and you should respect it. Just back away and sit down, and you'll soon return to normal.

### Insects & Animals

Southern Utah is awash in critters that, if bothered, can inflict a fair bit of pain, including rattlesnakes, scorpions, tarantulas, black widows, wasps and even centipedes. Avoid shoving your hand beneath logs and rocks or into piles of wood, where scorpions and other biting insects like to hide, and shake out your boots in the morning. Spiders rarely bite unless harassed, which is also true of rattlesnakes, who like to warm themselves on trails or rock ledges, particularly in late afternoon. See Health & Safety (p54) for what to do if one of these bites or stings you. Such large predators as falcons, eagles, condors and mountain lions rarely if ever interact with humans; for more on mountain lions, see p79.

One animal to watch for when camping is the ringtail cat. This cousin to the raccoon has been known to unzip tents and backpacks to get at food. If you can, keep your food sealed in lockable containers, as stringing food is just a dinner invitation for squirrels.

## GETTING THERE

Depending on their itinerary, travelers can approach southern Utah from different directions. The most common method is to fly into Salt Lake City, Las Vegas or Grand Junction, Colorado, and rent a car. From Salt Lake City, you can also take regional flights to airports in St George, Cedar City or Moab. Taking an Amtrak train or Greyhound bus is possible but inconvenient, and you'll still need to hire a shuttle or rent a car to get to a national park.

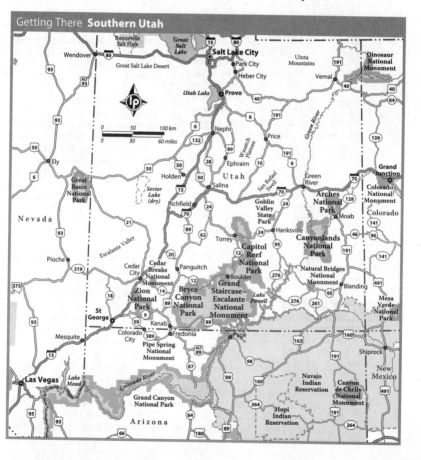

Getting There **Southern Utah**

## Zion & Bryce Canyon

### AIRPLANE

**Salt Lake City International Airport** (☎ 801-575-2400; www.slcairport.com) and Las Vegas' **McCarran International Airport** (☎ 702-261-5743; www.mccarran.com) are served by most major US and international carriers.

From Salt Lake City, Skywest Airlines (☎ 435-634-3000, 800-453-9417; www.skywest.com) has several daily flights to **St George Municipal Airport** (☎ 435-673-3451) and **Cedar City Regional Airport** (☎ 435-867-9408; www.cedarcity.org/airport.html).

If you need a shuttle from any of these airports, contact **St George Shuttle** (☎ 435-628-8320, 800-933-8320; www.stgshuttle.com), with daily vans, or **Red Rock Shuttle** (☎ 435-635-9104), with on-demand service.

### TRAIN

The nearest **Amtrak** (☎ 800-872-7245; www.amtrak.com) train stop is at Milford, 45 miles north of Cedar City on Hwy 130. Arrange with Cedar City shuttle companies to pick you up.

### BUS

**Greyhound** (☎ 800-231-2222; www.greyhound.com) runs several buses a day along the I-15 corridor between Salt Lake City and Las Vegas. Buses stop at St George but not Cedar City.

### ORGANIZED TOURS

For a wide range of tours that cover all of southern Utah, contact **Western Leisure Inc** (☎ 801-467-6100; www.western-leisure.com) or **Passage to Utah** (☎ 801-519-2400, 800-677-0553; www.passagetoutah.com); both are based in Salt Lake City.

For more local tours and companies, see the destination chapters.

### CAR

To get to Zion National Park from Las Vegas, take I-15 to St George, which is about 120 miles and 1½ hours, and from St George, take Hwy 9 to Zion, another 43 miles and 40 minutes. From Salt Lake City, take I-15 to St George, about 305 miles and 4½ hours away.

---

## HOW FAR IS IT?

Judging how long it will take to drive from point A to point B in southern Utah is an art form. Some highways drive like dirt roads, some dirt roads like highways, and slow-moving trucks and RVs can impede your progress for miles uphill. While this guidebook does list driving times, most southern Utah road savvy is only gained through hard-won experience. When in doubt, always plan for it to take longer than you think.

As a rule, if a dirt road is noted as 'good' and passable to passenger cars, you can usually drive an average of 30mph on it, but numerous rough sections and washes will force you to slow to 20mph or even 10mph. On most blacktop roads you can average 55mph, but you'll need to slow to 40mph or 30mph through small towns (unless you're fond of speeding tickets) and on sometimes very long, mountainous sections. Only on the interstates can you be assured of making good time; I-15 and I-70 allow speeds up to 75mph.

---

To get to Bryce Canyon National Park from Las Vegas, drive to St George via I-15, then take Hwy 9 to Hwy 89 north to Hwy 12 east; St George to Bryce is about 132 miles and 2½ hours away. From Salt Lake City, take I-15 to Cedar City, about 250 miles and 3½ hours away; then take Hwy 14 to Hwy 89 north to Hwy 12 east; Cedar City to Bryce is about 80 miles and 1½ hours.

Another option is to drive from Los Angeles to St George via I-15, which is about 410 miles and six hours.

## Car Rental

Most major car rental companies have offices at Salt Lake City and McCarran International Airports.

In St George and Cedar City, you can rent cars from **Avis** ( ☎ 800-230-4898; www.avis.com), **National** ( ☎ 800-227-7366; www.nationalcar.com) and **Enterprise** ( ☎ 800-261-7331; www.enterprise.com).

### RV & Camper Rental

**Cruise America** ( ☎ 800-327-7799; www.cruiseamerica.com) rents recreational vehicles (and motorcycles) nationwide and has offices in Las Vegas.

In St George, **Canyonlands RV Rentals** ( ☎ 435-688-2525, 800-597-3370; www.rentrvutah.com; 1333 E 100 South) rents trailers and RVs, and they'll shuttle you to and from Las Vegas.

### Road Conditions

For winter driving conditions on highways across Utah, contact the **Utah Department of Transportation** (UDOT; ☎ 511, outside Utah 866-511-8824; www.udot.utah.gov); online, visit the public page for the road conditions link; reports are updated twice daily November through April. Each national park provides updates on roads within its boundaries. For conditions on dirt roads outside the national parks, contact the federal agency in charge of that area. Most often it's the county BLM or USFS office; see the destination chapters. For conditions in Grand Staircase–Escalante National Monument, call ☎ 435-826-5499.

## Arches, Canyonlands & Moab

If you're driving to Arches or Canyonlands, Moab is the closest town.

### AIRPLANE

The nearest airport is **Canyonlands Airport** ( ☎ 259-7421; www.moabairport.com), 16 miles north of Moab via Hwy 191. **Salmon Air** ( ☎ 800-448-3413, 435-259-0566; www.salmonair.com) operates daily commuter service to Moab from Salt Lake City, a 75- to 90-minute flight. For a list of charter-flight operators, contact the airport.

Major air carriers serve Salt Lake City (SLC; 235 miles northwest) and Grand Junction, Colorado (GJT; 115 miles northeast). Commuter flights link Moab to Salt Lake City only, not Grand Junction.

If you need a shuttle, make a reservation with either **Bighorn Express** ( ☎ 888-655-7433; www.bighornexpress.com), with scheduled van service, or **Roadrunner Shuttle** ( ☎ 259-9402; www.roadrunnershuttle.com), with on-demand service.

### BUS & TRAIN

**Greyhound** ( ☎ 564-3421, 800-229-9424; www.greyhound.com) and **Amtrak** ( ☎ 872-7245, 800-872-7245; www.amtrak.com) both serve Green River, 53 miles northwest of Moab. From there, call the shuttle services listed under Airplane, above.

### CAR

To reach Moab from Salt Lake City, drive south on I-15 to US 6 to I-70 east to US 191 south, a 4½-hour, 235-mile drive. Most major car rental companies have offices in Grand Junction, Colorado. In Moab, there's **Thrifty Car Rental** ( ☎ 435-259-7317, 800-847-4389; http://moab.thrifty.com; 711 S Main St or Canyonlands Airport).

Arches is 5 miles north of Moab via US 191, while Canyonlands has three distinct sections; see Orientation in the Canyonlands chapter.

From Bryce Canyon, there are two routes. For the scenic route (6-7 hours), take Hwy 12 east to Torrey; turn east on Hwy 24 through Hanksville and north to I-70 east. Turn south on US 191 to Moab. For a slightly faster route (5-6 hours), take Hwy 12 west to US 89 north to I-70 east to US 191 south.

*Zion Canyon is among a handful of America's most dramatic natural wonders, those that inspire rhapsody no matter how often they are visited.*

# EXPERIENCING ZION

However, if you were to arrive at Zion National Park after seeing every other national park and monument in the Grand Circle, what would strike you most would probably not be the canyon's towering red-and-white cliffs – although, sheer as God's bookends, they certainly make an impression. Instead, you would be drawn to the impossibly delicate beauty these torn mountains protect – the weeping rocks, grottos and hanging gardens, the lush riverbanks, the meadows of mesa-top wildflowers. Southern Utah, Zion suggests, only *appears* forever desolate and barren. But here along the deceptively gentle Virgin River is a vision of this desert at its most heavenly.

Zion Canyon is not unlike a sandstone version of Yosemite Valley in the Sierra Nevada. Entering along the canyon floor, a visitor's first response is awe, followed by a desire to surmount these massive walls. Indeed, hiking and climbing are two of Zion's prime activities, and the adrenaline thrill of peeking your nose over a 2000ft sandstone lip is irresistible. Zion also offers an adventure Yosemite lacks: descending into its dozens of slot canyons, the mightiest of which is the one the Virgin River has carved, called The Narrows.

About 2.5 million people come to experience Zion's beauty and majesty each year. Since the vast majority of visitors arrive between May and September, you'd think Zion would feel more like an amusement park than a spiritual oasis, but it doesn't. Yes, a few trails are perpetually busy, and having a certain tolerance for humans improves your peace of mind, but what were once the park's biggest aggravations – car noise and parking – have been solved by its shuttle system. And solitude is generally just a few thousand feet away, straight up.

## WHEN YOU ARRIVE

Zion National Park is open year-round. Park entrance fees vary depending on which of the three roads you use to enter the park. The main entrance to Zion Canyon is from the south via Hwy 9; here, the fee is $20 per vehicle, $10 per person on foot or bicycle. To the northwest, at the Kolob Canyons entrance off I-15, it's $10/5 per vehicle/person, but this fee is good only for the Kolob Canyons area. If you want to visit Zion Canyon as well, you'll need to pay the full $20/10 fee. It's free to drive from Hwy 9 along Kolob Terrace

Rd to the middle of the park, but you must pay the full entrance fee if you want to park to picnic or hike; rangers patrol this road and will check to see if you've paid.

All entrance fees are valid for seven days, and all park passes (p52) are accepted.

## ORIENTATION

Zion comprises a relatively tidy 147,000 acres between I-15 to the northwest and Hwy 9 to the south. No roads within the park directly connect the north section with the south section. You'll have to either hike between them or drive around (about 50 minutes).

Three roads access the park. To the northwest, Kolob Canyons Rd branches east off I-15 and continues past an entrance gate and visitor center. To the south, Hwy 9 links I-15 with Hwy 89, passing the park's main visitor center, all its services and Zion Canyon Scenic Drive. Both I-15 and Hwy 9 are open year-round. The middle road, Kolob Terrace Rd, leads about 35 miles north from Hwy 9 to Hwy 14 near Cedar City. The road lacks any services or facilities, is paved only halfway and is closed by snow in winter.

The town of Springdale sits on Hwy 9 just outside the park's South Entrance. This attractive, friendly community offers lots of hotels and restaurants and just about every service a visitor might need. Springdale is about 3 miles long, but its center is a very walkable quarter-mile stretch about a mile southwest of the park.

Other small towns line Hwy 9 farther west, including Rockville, Virgin, La Verkin and Hurricane, the largest. However, if you can't find what you need in Springdale, your best bet is St George (p102), the largest city in southern Utah; it lies on I-15 about 40 minutes southwest of both the Zion Canyon and Kolob Canyons entrances. Cedar City (p108), another sizable town on I-15, lies about 15 minutes north of Kolob Canyons.

Things east of Zion are pretty quiet, though a few towns dot Hwy 89; the largest, Kanab (p169), is about 40 minutes from the park.

See the Zion map (Map 1) on pp144-5.

## INFORMATION

The **Zion Canyon Visitor Center** ( ☎ 435-772-3256; www.nps.gov/zion; ☽ 8am-7pm summer, 8am-6pm spring & fall, 8am-5pm winter) is the central source for park information. Outside are exhibits to help you plan your itinerary, plus drinking water and restrooms; inside you'll find an orientation video, bookstore and information desk with maps, brochures, updated weather and river conditions, and campground information. It also houses Zion's **Backcountry Desk** ( ☎ 435-772-0170;

## HIGHLIGHTS

✔ Standing knee-deep in the **Virgin River Narrows** (p77)

✔ Lounging in the shade beneath the great cottonwood at **Zion Lodge** (p93)

✔ Sitting with the angels on the pinpoint of **Angels Landing** (p78)

✔ Admiring the sunset from the **West Rim Trail** (p83)

✔ Getting gossip and great coffee at the **Mean Bean** (p97)

✔ Swimming the brisk pools in **The Subway** (p86)

✔ **Driving Hwy 9** (p68) through the tunnel to Zion's slickrock east side

## SIZE MATTERS

Henry Ford's Model T was only 20 years old when engineers started blasting the Zion–Mt Carmel Tunnel, so forgive them for not anticipating today's internal-combustion behemoths.

If your vehicle is 7ft, 10in wide or 11ft, 4in high or larger, it must be 'escorted' through the tunnel, as vehicles this big cannot safely stay in their lane. Motorists requiring an escort must pay a $10 fee on top of the park entrance fee, good for two trips by the same vehicle in a seven-day period. When you arrive at the tunnel, rangers will stop oncoming traffic as you drive down the center of the road. Between April and October, rangers are stationed at the tunnel from 8am to 8pm daily; at other times, ask at the entrance stations.

Vehicles prohibited at all times include those more than 13ft, 1in tall, single vehicles more than 40ft long and combined vehicles more than 50ft long, as well as semitrucks, commercial trucks and trucks carrying hazardous materials.

⏲ 7am-7pm summer, 7am-6pm spring & fall), which dispenses backcountry permits and information; its permit window opens an hour before the main visitor center each morning.

At the park's northwest entrance, the **Kolob Canyons Visitor Center** (☎ 435-586-0895; ⏲ 8am-4:30pm summer & winter, 7am-4:30pm spring & fall) is much smaller, but you can get all of the same parkwide information and backcountry permits.

For more information prior to arriving, the **Zion Canyon Visitors Bureau** (☎ 888-518-707; www.zionpark.com) maintains a good website with links to area businesses.

### Bookstores

The **Zion Natural History Association** (ZNHA; ☎ 435-772-3264, 800-635-3959; www.zionpark.org) runs the excellent bookstore in the Zion Canyon Visitor Center, offering stacks of hiking, nature and outdoor guides, park and regional histories, children's books, and books on geology, natural history, dinosaurs and more. You'll also find topographical maps, posters, games, videos, souvenirs and limited hiking and camping gear. Become a ZNHA member to receive a 20% discount.

The **Human History Museum** (p69) includes a smaller version of the visitor center bookstore. Springdale does not have a dedicated bookstore, though **Zion Rock & Mountain Guides** (p89) has a notable selection of activity-specific guides.

Nearby **Pipe Spring National Monument** (p173), about 60 miles south in Arizona, also offers a high-quality bookstore, with many titles you won't find at Zion.

### POLICIES & REGULATIONS

Zion's hiking and backcountry use regulations include those listed for all the parks in the Activities chapter; see individual activities for activity-specific regulations. Backcountry use requires a permit (p82).

Campfires are allowed only in fire grates in Watchman and South Camp-grounds. Wood gathering is not permitted in the park; buy all firewood in Springdale.

Bicycles and pets are permitted on only one trail, the Pa'rus Trail (p72). Bikes are allowed on park roads but may not be ridden through the Zion–Mt Carmel Tunnel. For more on pets, see p46.

As at all national parks, you are not allowed to feed wildlife or to touch or deface any cultural artifact or site.

# GETTING AROUND

How you get around Zion depends on the season. Between April and November, access to Zion Canyon is restricted to the Zion Park Shuttle. Passenger cars are permitted between December and March, when the shuttle does not operate.

## Car

During shuttle season, it's still possible to drive through Zion on Hwy 9, which offers several parking lots and turnouts. However, the Zion–Mt Carmel Tunnel has vehicle size restrictions; if you're driving an RV, see 'Size Matters.' If you need to rent a car, see St George (p102).

### PARKING

Winter visitation is low enough that parking in Zion Canyon is almost never an issue. In summer and on busy weekends in spring and fall, parking lots along Hwy 9 can fill up by 10am and remain full till 4pm or 5pm. The visitor center provides a large lot with RV spots and a one-hour area, while the Human History Museum has a much smaller lot with all-day and one-hour spaces. You'll also find limited parking at the Nature Center and about a dozen spaces on Hwy 9 near Canyon Junction.

If it's after 10am, save yourself time and hassle by parking in Springdale and taking the town shuttle to the park. Most hotels are near shuttle stops, and you'll find tons of free shuttle parking along the town's main road (park inside the solid white line) and at Zion Canyon Giant Screen Theatre, beside the park entrance.

## Zion Park & Springdale Shuttles

From April 1 to October 31, the park service operates two free, linked shuttle loops: The Zion Park Shuttle makes nine stops along Zion Canyon, from the visitor center to the Temple of Sinawava (a 90-minute round-trip); the Springdale Shuttle makes six regular stops and three flag stops along Hwy 9 from the park entrance to the **Majestic View Lodge** (p95), the hotel farthest from the park. Park visitors take the Springdale Shuttle to **Zion Canyon Giant Screen Theatre** (p99) and walk across a footbridge to a kiosk where rangers collect fees. The visitor center and the first Zion Canyon Shuttle stop lie just on the other side. It really couldn't be easier.

The wheelchair-accessible shuttle buses can accommodate large backpacks and carry up to two bicycles or one baby jogger. Pets are not allowed. All shuttle stops feature a shaded wood bench with a posted schedule and route description.

In summer the shuttles operate from 5:45am to 11pm; in spring and fall from 6:45am to 10pm. Shuttles run every 6 to 10 minutes between 9am and 8pm and every 15 to 30 minutes early and late in the day. At the very busiest times, you may have to stand, though rarely for your whole ride.

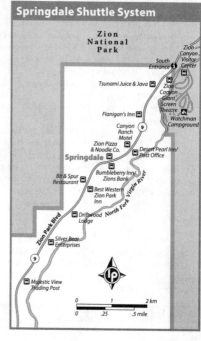

**Springdale Shuttle System**

### Hiker Shuttles

The hiker shuttle business has become fiercely competitive. In 2004, the number of companies tripled to three.

**Red Rock Shuttles** ( ☎ 435-635-9104)
**Zion Canyon Transportation** ( ☎ 877-635-5993)
**Zion Rock & Mountaineering Guides** ( ☎ 435-772-3303)

Each operates vans to trailheads on the east side of the park, ending at Chamberlain's Ranch at the trailhead for The Narrows (p82), as well as vans to trailheads along Kolob Terrace Rd, ending at Lava Point for the West Rim Trail (p83). All destinations are a 60- to 90-minute ride. Rates depend on demand, and there's sometimes a two-person minimum. Typical high-season fares are $25 per person to a busy trailhead like The Narrows and $35 for other trails, and companies offer one or two regular morning runs. However, for the right price, they'll go wherever and whenever you want.

Reservations are required. It's best to book your shuttle as early as possible and confirm your arrangements the day before your trip.

### Organized Tours
**Red Rock Shuttle & Tour** ( ☎ 435-635-9104) and **Southern Utah Scenic Tours** ( ☎ 435-867-8690, 888-404-8687; www.discover-the-west.com) offer Zion tours, as well as combination

---

## SHUTTLING ALONG

It's worth remembering what Zion was like before shuttle service was inaugurated in 2000. Now, on even the busiest weekends, the park is quiet. Wildlife approaches the road, undisturbed. The air is cleaner. Hikers can ride to as many trails as they like, strangers chat across the aisle – everyone's happy...

Fade to 1999. The park is like Disney World, only you can't leave your car. Vehicles inch forward, and every parking lot is full. So you keep moving, circling in your air-conditioned cage, muttering increasingly vivid curses at those out there enjoying themselves.

*Brrrr!* It's like a bad dream.

Now other national parks would like to know: How did Zion manage it, and can they replicate its success? Unfortunately, the key may be circumstantial. Zion Canyon lies along a single short road, as does Springdale. The geometry is a line. Given an ample number of buses, moving people efficiently is easy – and that's how Zion has made it look.

More math: In all, there are 30 quiet propane buses and 21 trailers, and each bus and trailer holds 68 people – enough passengers to fill some 28 cars. And the buses expel less than a quarter of the pollution. According to Ron Terry, Zion's chief of Interpretation & Visitor Services, visitor response has been 90% positive, and there hasn't been a single complaint about frequency.

Imagine that. A public bus system where people never wait long enough to complain.

Not only that, some shuttle drivers turn their rides into de facto park tours, dispensing historical facts and humorous anecdotes. They don't have to, mind you – the park is running a transport system, not a tour service. But even the shuttle drivers are having a good time.

And if a happy bus driver isn't a modern miracle, what is?

tours of Zion, Bryce and the Grand Canyon's North Rim. Trips start at $100 per person.

**ATV Wilderness Tours** ( ☎ 888-656-2887; www.atvadventures.com/atv2/) and **Outback Zion Safaris** ( ☎ 866-946-6494; www.zionjeeptours.com) offer guided ATV or Jeep tours of the region. Rates start at around $50 per person.

# SIGHTS

All sights within Zion National Park, including the Human History Museum and the Zion Nature Center, are described under **Driving Tours** (p66). Below are a few worthwhile diversions to occupy an afternoon in and around nearby Springdale, which also hosts lots of attractive shops and fine-art galleries, restaurants and a big-screen theater.

## Springdale & Around
### ZION CANYON ELK RANCH

This **agricultural ranch** ( ☎ 435-619-2424; 792 Zion Park Blvd; ☿ sunrise to sunset; free admission) offers kids of all ages a chance to feed and pet elk, buffalo, Texas longhorn steers, horses and miniature donkeys. The animals roam free in a large paddock, and if you ask, you can roam free with them; a bag of feed

---

### WHEN KIDS GET BORED

It's amazing how jaded a four-year-old can be, and let's not even talk about your eight-year-old. Here are some alternatives to 'yet another dumb trail.'

✔ Feed the animals at **Zion Canyon Elk Ranch** (this page)

✔ Play games with other kids at the **Zion Junior Ranger Program** (p91)

✔ Enjoy quality swim time at the **Sand Hollow Aquatic Center** (p104)

✔ Ride a horse (p90) in Zion Canyon (ages seven and up)

✔ Take an **inner tube** (p90) down the Virgin River

---

is $2. Don, the gregarious owner, will be happy to share his family's Mormon pioneer history. He just asks that whatever you do, don't call his place a 'zoo' – because zoos are not allowed in Springdale!

### PUBLIC PARKS

Springdale has two public parks where kids and dogs can run wild; both are open dawn to dusk and feature nice lawns, shaded picnic tables, grills and bathrooms. **Springdale River Park**, about 2 miles from the park entrance on Zion Park Blvd, includes a pretty riverside trail. **Springdale Town Park**, on Lion Blvd next to the Town Hall, boasts perhaps the most scenic playground in America, not to mention a baseball diamond, volleyball and tennis courts and a large gazebo.

### GRAFTON GHOST TOWN

Originally settled in 1859, Grafton never amounted to much. Today, what remains is the well-maintained cemetery, the restored 1886 adobe meeting-house, the general store and some pioneer cabins on adjacent private land. The evocative ghost town achieved its 15 minutes of fame in 1969 as the setting for the bicycle scene in *Butch Cassidy & the Sundance Kid*.

To get there: In Rockville, take Bridge Rd, cross the bridge and turn right on Grafton Rd. In half a mile, the main road bears left and becomes gravel. A mile farther, bear right at the dead end sign. After another 2 miles, you'll pass the cemetery on your left, then drive a quarter mile farther to the ghost town. Park at the red gate.

### LA VERKIN OVERLOOK

On Hwy 9 between Virgin and La Verkin, a 1.5-mile gravel-and-dirt road leads to La Verkin Overlook, which offers a fantastic 360-degree view of the surrounding 40 sq miles, from Zion to the Pine Valley Mountains. Various trails lead along the ridge above the Virgin River. It's a great sunset perch.

## DRIVING TOURS

Three roads access Zion National Park: **Kolob Canyons Rd** to the northwest, **Kolob Terrace Rd** in the middle and, to the south, **Hwy 9**, known within the park as **Zion–Mt Carmel Hwy**. Branching off Hwy 9 is **Zion Canyon Scenic Drive**, which pierces the heart of Zion Canyon and is the prime destination for most visitors. If you have time for only one activity at Zion, touring this road is a good choice.

All four roads promise worthwhile scenic drives, and each is quite different. The busiest is Zion–Mt Carmel Hwy, a winding, narrow route that is just as scenic as Zion Canyon Scenic Drive and includes the famed Zion–Mt Carmel Tunnel. Kolob Terrace Rd is the longest and least-visited route, yet it contains some of the park's best vistas. Kolob Canyons Rd is so short it hardly counts as a drive, but it does offer a spectacular detour off I-15.

**ZION CANYON SCENIC DRIVE**
Route: Hwy 9 to the Temple of Sinawava
Distance: 12.4 miles round-trip
Speed Limit: 35 mph

This spur road forks off Hwy 9 within the park and leads 6.2 miles into Zion Canyon. From November through March, cars can drive freely from the South Entrance to the Temple of Sinawava. But from April through October, Zion Canyon Scenic Drive is closed to private vehicles, and all visitors must ride the **Zion Canyon Shuttle** (p63), which as a result constitutes most visitors' first impression of Zion. And that's not such a bad thing. It means you don't have to drive, park or worry about distracted drivers crashing into you. You can just sit back and watch – often straight up through the skylights. Expect a 90-minute round-trip by shuttle, 60 minutes if you drive your own car.

Officially, the scenic drive begins where cars are restricted, at Canyon Junction, although shuttle riders usually start at the visitor center. For a description of sites between the South Entrance and Canyon Junction, see **Zion–Mt Carmel Hwy (Hwy 9)** (p68). The following description is organized by shuttle stops.

### Canyon Junction

This is the intersection of Hwy 9 and Zion Canyon Scenic Drive. You'll find a few parking spaces just past the junction. Prominent signs warn drivers not to continue up this road during the months the shuttle is in operation, so it's no use playing dumb.

The shuttle stop also marks one end of the **Pa'rus Trail** (p72), which leads to the visitor center and accesses wading spots along the Virgin River.

### Court of the Patriarchs

Halfway to the Court of the Patriarchs, you'll pass a **1995 landslide** that buried the road and dammed the river. It took several days to dig through the debris, during which Zion Lodge guests were 'trapped on vacation,' as one shuttle driver likes to quip. The prominent stone riprap now holding back the slide is the same means the park uses to keep the river in its current course. Left free, it would flood and meander, ruining park facilities and making visitation an annual act of improvisation.

This shuttle stop marks the shortest trail in the park, a 50yd uphill walk to an overlook of the **Three Patriarchs**. Named by a Methodist minister in 1916, the trio of peaks features (from left to right) Abraham, Isaac and Jacob, while crouching in front of Jacob is Mount Moroni. Though many people skip it, this is a nice spot, especially at sunset.

Across the road from the shuttle stop is access to the **Sand Bench Trail**, an alternate route to **Emerald Pools** (p74). Watch your step, as this route is used for horse rides.

## Zion Lodge

**Zion Lodge** (p93) houses the park's only café and restaurant, plus it has bathrooms, a gift shop and a wide grassy lawn shaded by a giant cottonwood tree – the perfect place for a posthike ice cream and nap.

Across the road from the lodge is the corral for **horse rides** (p90) and the **Emerald Pools trailhead** (p74). Heading north from the lodge, the easy half-mile **Grotto Trail** leads past The Grotto shuttle stop, beyond which hikers can complete a 3-mile loop, crossing the road and returning south on the modestly uphill, mile-long **Kayenta Trail**, followed by the Emerald Pools Trail.

## The Grotto

This shuttle stop features a large, shady picnic area with lots of tables, restrooms, and drinking water. From the picnic area, the Grotto Trail leads south to Zion Lodge. Across the road, the Kayenta Trail leads south to Emerald Pools, while the **West Rim Trail** (p83) heads north toward Angels Landing (p78). Those who'd rather admire Angels Landing than climb it should stroll the flat first quarter mile of the West Rim Trail to a stone bench for the perfect vantage.

## Weeping Rock

The only facilities at this shuttle stop are chemical toilets, but it accesses a trio of great trails: the easy and bucolic **Weeping Rock Trail** (p73), the moderately strenuous **Hidden Canyon Trail** (p76) and the Papa Bear of workouts, the **Observation Point Trail** (p79). There's a lot to see at this big bend in the river, a great example of what's called an incised meander. Pause to admire Angels

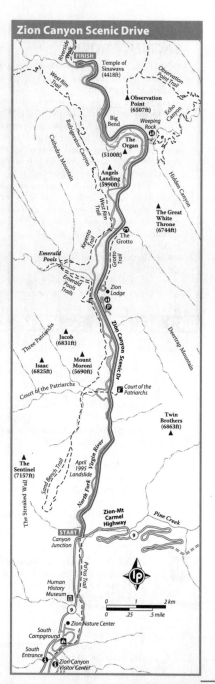

Zion Canyon Scenic Drive

## SACRIFICE ROCK

The National Park Service does its best to protect and preserve the natural and cultural resources under its care. But when it comes to the strange peckings and etchings left by ancestral inhabitants, there's only so much they can do. Ancient Native Americans couldn't have imagined us – we camera-toting moderns – or they wouldn't have left so much of their sacred writing in the wide open beside busy trails and roads.

Zion rangers only advertise one rock art site, the South Gate Petroglyphs, a handful of intriguing designs and animals a few steps from the road near the South Entrance. What strikes one most, however, is not the petroglyphs themselves but the overwhelming amount of modern graffiti surrounding them. 'Jayrod' may indeed rock, but did he need to let everyone know right here, for all eternity?

In the national parks it's illegal, not to mention thoughtless and selfish, to damage or otherwise deface any ancient cultural site, including petroglyphs. For some, that's not incentive enough to curb the ageless and universal urge to communicate – across time, with each other, with laughing friends. The varnished sandstone slabs are like tablets, and the ground is littered with pens.

But don't. In this regard, the national parks are no different than a museum, and rock art sites are both priceless artifacts and spiritual places for modern-day tribes whose ancestors created them.

Indeed, vandalism is why some have dubbed this site 'sacrifice rock.' For due to an accident of location, it could not be protected from ourselves.

Landing, The Organ, Cable Mountain, The Great White Throne and the looming Observation Point.

### Big Bend
There are no facilities and no trailheads at this shuttle stop. Rock climbers get out here on their way to some of Zion's famous walls, while others just soak up the view, which is a different vantage of the features seen from Weeping Rock.

### Temple of Sinawava
At the end of the road you'll find restrooms, water fountains and the start of the **Riverside Walk** (p73). It's at this point that Zion Canyon begins to close in (or open up, depending on your perspective), and interpretive signs do a good job of explaining how the seemingly soft and gentle Virgin River could have carved this 1500ft gash.

### ZION–MT CARMEL HIGHWAY (HWY 9)
**Route: South Entrance to East Entrance**
**Distance: 12 miles one way**
**Speed Limit: 35 mph**

Open year-round to private vehicles, this road features the marvelous Zion–Mt Carmel Tunnel and leads to Zion's altogether different and evocative east side. Drivers should expect delays on either end of the tunnel, which has vehicle size restrictions (p62) and is closed to bicycles and pedestrians.

This scenic drive starts at **South Entrance**, a ranger-staffed gate where you pay your fees and get your maps.

## Zion Canyon Visitor Center & Watchman Campground

The turn for the **Zion Canyon Visitor Center** (p61) and **Watchman Campground** (p92) is on the right, just past the South Entrance. Beside the visitor center you'll find the first stop for the **Zion Canyon Shuttle** (p63), trailheads for the **Pa'rus Trail** (p72) and **Watchman Trail** (p75) and a 100yd interpretive walk along the Virgin River.

In addition to being the font for all park information, the visitor center is a model of environmental architecture. Cooling towers harness summer winds to cool water and funnel colder, heavier air into the building, while passive solar walls are positioned to catch the winter sun. Despite its lack of air-conditioning or heating units, the building remains pleasant year-round. A computer display inside charts the building's energy use.

## Zion Nature Center & South Campground

A quarter mile farther is the signed turnoff for **South Campground** (p92) and the **Zion Nature Center**, home to Zion's Junior Ranger Program (p91). Housed in a gymlike building with flora and fauna exhibits, the Nature Center is open to the public Memorial Day to Labor Day. A grassy riverside picnic area beside the center makes a great place to chill out during the midday heat.

## Human History Museum

Less than a mile into the park is the **Human History Museum** ( ☎ 435-772-0168; ⏰ 8am-6pm; free admission), established in the old visitor center in 2002. This air-conditioned oasis presents a handful of well-done permanent exhibits about the history of Zion Canyon and its birth as a national park. Temporary exhibits cover topics from fire management to oral histories of early pioneers. The building itself is part of an original Mormon homestead settled by the Crawford family. One of the family's sons, JL Crawford, was born here and served as Zion's first park ranger. Now in his 90s, Mr Crawford is still active in the park!

The museum screens a 22-minute film every half hour from 8:30am to 5:30pm. While the small screen doesn't exactly overwhelm the senses, this film is a much better introduction to Zion than Springdale's *Treasure of the Gods*. Featuring beautiful photography, it escorts you through the seasons, and you can trust that its history is accurate.

The museum also offers a bookstore (a slimmed-down version of the visitor center's), restrooms and water, half-hour ranger talks at 11:25am and 2:25pm, and daily weather, trail and campground updates.

Just past the museum on Hwy 9 are a few turnouts that overlook The Streaked Wall. In spring, if you have binoculars, scan the rim for nesting peregrine falcons.

## Canyon Junction

Less than a mile farther is Canyon Junction, where **Zion Canyon Scenic Drive** (p66) forks left. This shuttle stop marks one end of the **Pa'rus Trail** (p72) and is a popular access point for dips in the Virgin River.

## Zion–Mt Carmel Tunnel

Past Canyon Junction, Hwy 9 climbs a 3.5-mile series of long switchbacks. This scenic stretch offers amazing views of **The Great Arch** from several large turnouts.

Rangers are stationed at either end of the two-lane tunnel to manage traffic, which is restricted to one-way traffic when an oversized vehicle must be escorted through. When delays occur, they can last from five to 20 minutes.

At the time of its completion in 1930, the 1.1-mile tunnel was the longest tunnel in the US. Even before the national park was established in 1919, local officials considered building a road through Zion to be an important way to spur tourism. At first considered impossible, construction on the road began construction in 1927. Engineers blasted into the side of the cliff, creating six 'galleries,' and the tunnel was excavated in either direction from these points. For many years after the tunnel was completed, drivers were allowed to stop at these galleries to admire the views, but modern cars and increased traffic eventually made this unsafe.

At the tunnel's east entrance is a small parking lot with pit toilets and the trailhead for the **Canyon Overlook** (p74).

### From the Tunnel to the East Entrance

It's about 5 miles from the east end of the tunnel to the park's East Entrance. The road here passes vast undulating fields of slickrock that would resemble a moonscape were the moon made of sandstone and not – as we all know – cheese. The rock looks liquid, and brittle slabs ooze right up to the road. Make use of scenic turnouts, as the highway is too narrow and winding to allow proper sightseeing while driving.

After about 3.5 miles, you'll get your first glimpse of **Checkerboard Mesa**, a huge sloping face of yellow-and-white slickrock etched like a badly scoured pot. It's another mile to the official Checkerboard Mesa viewpoint.

About a quarter mile past this viewpoint is the ranger-staffed East Entrance, which has no facilities except toilets. This also marks the trailhead for the **East Rim Trail**, a hardy 8-mile route that connects with Zion Canyon via the **Observation Point Trail** (p79). This route sees little use since Stave Spring dried up.

About a mile past the gate is the park boundary, where the speed limit returns to 55mph.

### KOLOB CANYONS ROAD
**Route: Visitor center to Kolob Canyons Viewpoint**
**Distance: 10 miles round-trip**
**Speed Limit: 35 mph**

At Zion's northwest entrance, this short road off I-15 only accesses the Kolob Canyons area. Just off the highway is the **Kolob Canyons Visitor Center** (p62); pull over and walk inside to pay your fee or show your pass. This tiny visitor center provides a few small exhibits, updated parkwide information, restrooms and the only drinking water for this section of the park. It also sells a descriptive pamphlet ($1) for Kolob Canyons Rd that describes Zion's geology, flora and fauna; numbered markers along the road correspond with the pamphlet.

The road is fairly steep, ascending 1100ft in five winding miles; thus, it's not a favorite cycling route. After 1.8 miles you'll reach a signed turnout for the trailhead to the **Taylor Creek Middle Fork** (p80) and your first good views of the finger canyons and Zion's highest point, 8726ft Horse Ranch Mountain. A mile farther is another spacious scenic turnout with even broader views. As the road affords a high vantage point, these rough-hewn cliffs appear shorter than those in Zion Canyon, but they are every bit as tall and have an equivalent flair for the dramatic.

Three-quarters of a mile farther is the signed turnout for Lee Pass, the trailhead for **La Verkin Creek Trail** (p84).

About a mile farther you'll reach the end of the road, marked by a large parking area and chemical toilets. This is the trailhead for the **Timber Creek Overlook** (p80), a relatively short and easy hike to a grand overlook of the plateau to the south. A hundred yards along this trail is a picnic area in the scrub forest.

## KOLOB TERRACE ROAD
### Route: Hwy 9 to Lava Point
### Distance: 22 miles one way
### Speed Limit: 35 mph

It's free to drive Kolob Terrace Rd through the park's narrow waist – most likely because the NPS can't be bothered to staff entrance gates on a road that's often closed from late October to late May, lacks water and visitor services (except for chemical toilets at the trailheads and campground) and serves mainly as a 4WD 'through road' for locals bound for Cedar City. That said, if you do stop to picnic or hike, be ready to show your park pass or entrance receipt to patrolling rangers.

The road branches off Hwy 9 in the tiny burg of Virgin, just shy of 14 miles west of Zion's South Entrance. Look for a brown NPS sign and a green street sign for Kolob Rd, which becomes Kolob Terrace Rd once it crosses the park boundary, after about 6.5 miles. The road leaves and reenters the park several times. If you miss the signs, one way to tell is by the color of the road – red inside the park, gray asphalt outside. Respect private property boundaries; landowners are not known for their tolerance of stray hikers.

Just inside the park are two trailheads for canyoneering routes: at 6.8 miles, the **Right Fork trailhead**, and at 7.2 miles, the **Grapevine trailhead**.

A quarter mile farther is the turnoff for **Smith Mesa Rd**. This well-graded dirt road (passable to cars when dry, impassable to all when wet) leaves the park after a mile as it winds along the top of Smith Mesa. The first few miles offer nice views back toward Tabernacle Dome, South Guardian Angel and Cougar Mountain.

A half mile past the Smith Mesa turnoff is the trailhead for the left fork of North Creek, the lower end of the famed canyoneering route called **The Subway** (p86).

After going 12.5 miles from Hwy 9, and having ascended about 3000ft, you'll reach the **Hop Valley trailhead** (see the Trans-Park Connector, p85), where series of turnouts offer splendid views. Just south is **Spendlove Knoll**, while north is **Firepit Knoll** – cinder cones that are reminders of the volcanism that once dominated this region. At one point, so much lava coursed south over the Lower Kolob Plateau that it blocked the Virgin River, creating an enormous lake. Eventually, the river eroded the sandstone at the edge of the lava to establish its present course.

### ✔ TIP

Time your return journey on Kolob Terrace Rd for sunset. The views are even better on the way back, so why not appreciate them in the best light?

This point in the road is also about as far as snowplows go in winter; only those with snowshoes or cross-country skis can go farther then.

Three miles past the Hop Valley trailhead is the **Wildcat Canyon trailhead**, the starting point of The Subway (p86) and the **Northgate Peaks Trail** (p81). Just past this turnoff is one of the largest scenic turnouts along the road, offering picnic benches.

About 4.5 miles past the Wildcat Canyon trailhead, some 20 miles from Hwy 9, is the junction with a graded gravel road to **Lava Point**, which reaches the viewpoint and primitive campground in 1.8 miles and the **West Rim trailhead** (p83) in 2.4 miles. Don't make this journey without visiting Lava Point, a onetime fire lookout (though the tower was removed in 2000). At 7890ft, it's one of Zion's highest and best vantage points, offering a virtual diorama of the park, with views south to Arizona on clear days.

Beyond the Lava Point junction, Kolob Terrace Rd continues as a paved road for 3.5 miles to **Kolob Reservoir**, a popular spot among local anglers that also offers free dispersed camping. Visit in fall to appreciate the spectacular aspen stands. Beyond the reservoir, the road reverts to dirt and leads to Hwy 14 a few miles east of Cedar City; lingering snow and runoff make this stretch wet and hazardous through late June.

## FESTIVALS & EVENTS

Events at Zion and in Springdale tend to be local affairs, but they're still fun. An early kickoff to the season is **St Patrick's Day** in mid-March, the highlight of which is the hilarious and highly competitive green Jell-O sculpture competition. **July 4** heralds a parade and fireworks, and the festivities continue during Utah's **Pioneer Day**, on July 24. In August is the lively **Zion Canyon Jazz & Arts Festival**, and in November the **Butch Cassidy 10k Marathon**. Contact the **Zion Canyon Visitors Bureau** ( ☎ 888-518-7070; www.zionpark.com) for information.

## DAY HIKES

Zion seems to have been cut and crafted with hikers in mind. Its wealth of experiences and scenery rivals that of any national park, and most of it is accessible on day hikes. Even backcountry routes like the West Rim and La Verkin Creek Trails are doable in a single (admittedly long) day, and hikers can reach the famed Narrows in an afternoon.

Though each of Zion's three areas offers day hikes for all abilities, Zion Canyon boasts the lion's share of trails, and they tend to be more crowded. Most canyon trails are paved to some degree, even the steepest; route-finding is rarely an issue, and every trailhead features a signboard with a map.

See the Activities chapter for desert hiking safety tips. Don't come unprepared, no matter how short your planned hike.

The following trail descriptions are organized in approximate ascending order of difficulty.

### Zion Canyon

Trails in Zion Canyon can be roughly divided into two categories: level paths that follow the river, and steep trails that climb the canyon walls. Durations for steep trails are listed below as ranges, as these can vary considerably. One rule of thumb is that it usually takes twice as long to hike up as to hike down.

The Zion Canyon Shuttle stops at every trailhead, and bus drivers usually announce the trails at each stop. Note that a few trails begin on the east side of the park.

**PA'RUS TRAIL**
Distance: 3.5 miles round-trip
Duration: 1½ hours
Challenge: Easy
Elevation Change: 50ft

This paved, wheelchair-accessible trail is one of two routes that start from the visitor center (the other is the Watchman Trail). It's also the only trail in Zion open to bicycles and dogs (which must remain on a leash). Thus, the Pa'rus (PAH-roos) Trail is one of Zion's busiest pedestrian thoroughfares. From dawn to dusk you're sure to meet someone along this pleasant path, which links arms with the Virgin River down the middle of the lower canyon.

But don't come for convenience alone. With some distance between them, the canyon walls are stately and majestic rather than awesome and overpowering. The trail is the perfect place to contemplate the **Towers of the Virgin**, **The Streaked Wall**, **Bridge Mountain** and **The Watchman**. Four footbridges cross the Virgin River, and numerous dirt paths lead to it.

This may be the best trail for a post-sunset hike. In the waning light, you can watch the canyon walls fade to silhouettes while stars crown the peaks, and you don't have to worry about getting lost or even walking back. Just take the trail from the visitor center or South Campground to the Human History Museum (about 1 mile) or to trail's end, at Canyon Junction, and hop a shuttle to return.

## WEEPING ROCK TRAIL

**Distance: 0.5 mile round-trip**
**Duration: 30 minutes**
**Challenge: Easy**
**Elevation Change: 98ft**

For a trail that's over almost before it's begun, this one is surprisingly memorable. The enormous, cool alcove at trail's end contains the park's largest **hanging garden** and, if you trust the shuttle drivers, the greatest plant diversity in Utah. But mainly, it's memorable because of the tender, delicate beauty of the weeping rock itself, the vibrant green life clinging to it, and the romantically framed view of Zion Canyon. Interpretive signs explain much of the bustling, blooming foliage.

The short paved trail is steep; those in wheelchairs can make it with assistance. The trailhead is at the Weeping Rock shuttle stop.

## RIVERSIDE WALK

**Distance: 2 miles round-trip**
**Duration: 1 hour**
**Challenge: Easy**
**Elevation Change: 50ft**

Starting from the Temple of Sinawava shuttle stop, at the end of Zion Canyon Scenic Drive, this paved path serves as a crowded on-ramp to the river highway. Shadowed from the slanting sun by towering walls, the wheelchair-accessible (with some assistance), kid-friendly trail ends amid the slippery cobblestones of the **Virgin River**. Accessing seeps, hanging gardens and swimming holes, it's a must on any visit to Zion.

Interpretive signs explain the geology and ecology of the river corridor, and various spur trails lead to the river itself. The trail ends at a raised cul-de-sac with steps leading down to a rocky fan at river's edge. Wear shoes you don't mind getting wet (but avoid sandals), because you won't be able to resist the river, which beckons all to enter.

Those with thoughts of hiking The Narrows should turn to p77, though even a brief stroll past the first mysterious bend is a perfect finish to this sweet taste of what makes Zion special.

## MERALD POOLS TRAIL

**stance: 1.2 miles round-trip to the Lower Pool;**
**2.5 miles round-trip to the Middle & Upper Pools**
**Duration: 1–2 hours round-trip**
**Challenge: Easy to Lower Pool; Moderate to Middle & Upper Pools**
**Elevation Change: 69ft to Lower Pool; 150ft to Middle Pools;**
**400ft to Upper Pool**

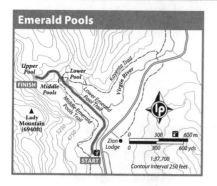

**Emerald Pools**

This interconnecting series of three trails and four pools is extremely popular for good reason: Each pool is its own bucolic oasis. Water seeps from the sandstone in sparkling waterfalls, and the sometimes bright green pools are rimmed with life, including hundreds of full-throated canyon tree frogs, who many an evening make of each grotto a concert hall.

The trailhead begins across the road from Zion Lodge. The easiest section is the Lower Pool Trail, which is well paved and level overall, though not flat; wheelchairs can make it with assistance. At the **Lower Pool**, waterfalls cascade over a stained overhang, misting the trail and you as you pass beneath.

From here the dirt trail climbs steps toward the two **Middle Pools**, which feed the waterfalls below. Be careful, as this unassuming spot causes more than its share of injuries, particularly to kids. Though chains are in place to keep people away from the slippery lip, the curious inch out anyway.

Between the Middle Pools, a steep, rocky .3-mile spur leads to the **Upper Pool**, the loveliest of all. Visitors look straight up the sheer-walled skirts of Lady Mountain, which shelters this sandy grotto and is polite enough to ignore your stares.

To make it a loop, return on Middle Pools Trail.

### CANYON OVERLOOK
**Distance: 1 mile round-trip**
**Duration: 30 minutes–1 hour**
**Challenge: Easy–Moderate**
**Elevation Change: 163ft**

Though rough and uneven in spots, this dirt trail is manageable for people of all ages and fitness levels. Starting from the east end of the Zion–Mt Carmel Tunnel, it's a convenient, popular stop that offers something for everyone, including views down dark, narrow **Pine Creek Canyon**, overhangs that shelter seeps and fern gardens, and a gorgeous weathered slickrock patio.

The final sweeping canyon viewpoint is wide enough for visitors to spread out comfortably as they admire the distant **Towers of the Virgin**. Watch small children near the edge, which overlooks an adrenaline-boosting 700ft drop.

If the small parking lot by the tunnel is full, try parking areas just up the road.

## WATCHMAN TRAIL
**Distance: 2.7 miles round-trip**
**Duration: 1½–2 hours**
**Challenge: Easy–Moderate**
**Elevation Change: 368ft**

Once the midday heat has worn off, this relaxed, relatively easy trail offers a good pre- or postdinner leg stretch. It starts at the visitor center from the same trailhead as the Pa'rus Trail (p72).

At first a dusty path along the Virgin River, the trail gently ascends to a small canyon at the base of **Bridge Mountain**. Continue your ascent on several long switchbacks past moderate drop-offs to the top of a foothill, where the trail emerges to wide views. The pungent scent of sagebrush and spring blooms of prickly pear cactus make this an enjoyable ramble.

A loop trail skirts the foothill, leading to several prime overlooks of the angular **Watchman**, the **Towers of the Virgin** and the town of Springdale. Rising alone to the south are the ragged **Eagle Crags**, which locals like to claim all of Zion will someday resemble.

## CABLE MOUNTAIN TRAIL

**Distance: 7.2 miles round-trip**
**Duration: 3–3½ hours**
**Challenge: Moderate**
**Elevation Change: 70ft**

If, as Greta Garbo once vamped, you 'vant to be alooone,' take any of the quiet East Rim trails. The route to **Cable Mountain** is one of the easiest, and for those who want to make a full day of it, it can be combined with a hike to **Deertrap Mountain**. Both are mainly plateau hikes that end at almost indescribable viewpoints over Zion Canyon.

To reach the trailhead, drive to the **Zion Ponderosa Ranch** (p96), a lodge on the east side of the park that allows public access to park trails. Enter the ranch and head straight; the road quickly becomes gravel and dirt. In a half mile, turn left (on Buck Rd) at the signed junction for Cable Mountain. After 0.6 mile, turn left at an unsigned junction, and in 100yd turn right onto West Pine Rd. In a half mile, this road dead ends at a locked gate for the national park. There is no parking area, so try not to block the gate.

The clear dirt trail threads through fire-scarred ponderosa pines (from a proscribed burn in 2004) and in a quarter mile reaches a signed junction with a trail to **Echo Canyon**. After a steady half-mile ascent through scrub forest, you'll reach a signed junction with the East Rim Trail. Stave Spring is nearby, though it's been dry for several years – don't count on any water anywhere on the East Rim. A mile farther you'll reach the signed trailhead for Deertrap Mountain, another 2 miles from this point.

### BEST HIKES FOR FAMILIES

Six hikes that will please everyone ages five to 65:

✔ **Weeping Rock** (p73)

✔ **Canyon Overlook** (p74)

✔ **Emerald Pools** (p74)

✔ **Riverside Walk** (p73)

✔ **Northgate Peaks** (p81)

✔ **Pa'rus Trail** (p72)

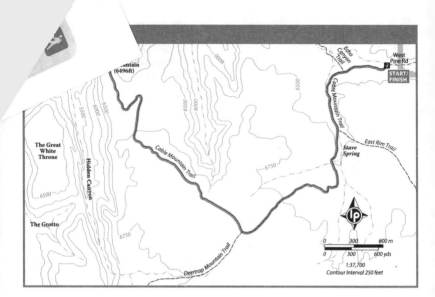

The trail to Cable Mountain soon tops out and descends a final mile to the **historic cable works**, once used to haul down lumber. The wooden structure seems in imminent danger of collapse, so don't climb on it. Instead, enjoy the panorama, which extends north to the pink cliffs and Cedar Breaks, and peer over the crumbling rim for as much vertigo as your stomach can handle.

### HIDDEN CANYON TRAIL
**Distance: 2 miles round-trip**
**Duration: 90 minutes–2½ hours**
**Challenge: Moderate–Difficult**
**Elevation Change: 850ft**

For fit hikers, this is the perfect warm-up to Zion's more challenging hikes; for beginning hikers, it serves as a good test of your abilities and your comfort with heights. (Overheard halfway up the trial: `I'm not used to, like, real air.') Either way, it's best tackled in early morning, when the difficult initial ascent is in shade.

From the Weeping Rock shuttle stop, the largely paved trail to Hidden Canyon (and Observation Point) leads right, quickly ascending a series of long switchbacks that put your legs and lungs to work.

After half a mile, the trail to **Observation Point** branches left, while you bear right up a series of even steeper zigzags to an unprotected point with vertiginous views. Onward, the trail skirts a slickrock ledge as it threads in and out of a draw. Chains are bolted into the rock at the most exposed points. Make use of them – from the thin ledges, it's nearly a thousand feet straight down.

Fifty yards beyond the ledges, you'll reach the mouth of **Hidden Canyon**. There is no trail on the slickrock here; watch for cairns and steps cut into the rock.

You can extend the hike by up to a mile round-trip by entering the scenic narrow canyon, which is sandy, rocky and crowded with bigtooth maples. Its left wall is as sheer as a loaf of country bread cut in half. A quarter mile in on your right, you'll reach a **standing arch**. Farther on, the canyon narrows, a series of increasingly large rock falls make hiking difficult, and then impo only those with climbing experience should continue past the arch.

## THE NARROWS: FROM THE BOTTOM
### Distance: Up to 10 miles round-trip
### Duration: Up to 8 hours
### Challenge: Moderate–Difficult
### Elevation Change: 300ft

Hiking The Narrows is the quintessential Zion experience, and tons of people day hike it from the bottom rather than attempt the more adventurous overnight from the top (p82). From this direction, you can still reach the narrowest and most spectacular section, and if you trek the entire 5 miles to Big Springs (as far as day hikers are allowed), you'll outpace all the dabblers and running kids and be left with nothing but the meditative rushing river for a companion.

Even better, you don't need a permit to day hike The Narrows from the bottom. If time is short, or if the overnight permits are booked, this route still allows you to enjoy this rare and unforgettable journey in a desert river.

Preparation and timing are the keys to a successful Narrows adventure. See the **backcountry Narrows hike** (p82) for a more complete description, but note: The hike is mostly in the rocky river itself, sometimes through deep pools that require swimming, and day hiking from the bottom means forging upstream. Folks clad in Tevas and clutching a water bottle will not travel well or far.

Nor will people who get caught in a flash flood. Always check conditions with a ranger before hiking The Narrows.

The trail begins at the end of the **Riverside Walk** (p73). At river's edge you'll find a bin that contains rough walking sticks, but don't rely on the bin, as it often holds little more than kindling. Around the first bend is **Mystery Falls**, the exit point for Mystery Canyon. You may catch canyoneers on their last rappel here.

As you hike, the canyon walls seem to grow and press in on you, so it's often easier to focus on the intricacies of erosion rather than the entirety of it. Each alcove, bowl, hollow, crack and arch seems its own secret place. Ravens glide low over the water, and you can sometimes hear waterfalls spilling down from inside the rock.

It's about 2.5 miles to the junction with **Orderville Canyon**, which makes an intriguing detour. From its top, Orderville is another popular canyoneering route, and you can access about a mile of it from this direction.

Beyond Orderville, you'll enter **Wall Street**, where the sheerness, nearness and height of the cliffs shatter whatever remains of your

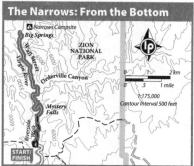

**The Narrows: From the Bottom**

perspective. After this section, the canyon opens slightly again, the water gets periodically deeper (usually requiring your first swims), and your fellow hikers thin out.

After the 4-mile point, you'll negotiate a series of huge boulders, and the canyon, though gorgeous, grows somewhat less otherworldly. At 5 miles you'll reach **Big Springs**, a fern-fringed rush of water much larger than anything so far. The last Narrows campsite lies just beyond this point, and day hikers are required to turn around.

While it can take up to eight hours to do the full round-trip to Big Springs, set aside a minimum of five hours so you'll at least have time to reach memorable Wall Street.

### ANGELS LANDING
**Distance: 5 miles round-trip**
**Duration: 3½–4½ hours**
**Challenge: Difficult**
**Elevation Change: 1488ft**

This is another classic Zion experience you'll never forget. By the time you reach Scout Lookout, sweaty and exhausted, you'll realize that Angels Landing isn't the tremendous mountain of rock it looks like from the trailhead; it is instead a cake, and the Virgin River has eaten all but the tiniest sliver, and left it for you.

That sliver – a final half mile of angled, narrow slickrock – is at times no more than 5ft or 6ft wide and some 1500ft above the canyon floor on either side. Anyone with a fear of heights should stop at the wide saddle of Scout Lookout. Others arrive here only to experience their first bout of vertigo, which has led some to dub this 'Chicken-Out Point.' However, the ability to continue usually has more to do with peer pressure, the threat of shame and the nearness of one's shoetops than with any act of bravery.

The trailhead is across the road from The Grotto shuttle stop. From here to Scout Lookout, you'll trace the end of the **West Rim Trail** (p83), so bear right and follow signs for the West Rim. You'll initially meander along the river toward Angels Landing, which juts into the sky like a ship's prow. The trail ascends gradually but relentlessly, growing ever steeper as you begin long, wide, paved switchbacks up the canyon wall. The last switchback crosses beneath a rock overhang. Beyond it, the trail levels out, thankfully, and runs deep into narrow, slightly cooler **Refrigerator Canyon**.

You'll ascend a few more switchbacks before reaching **Walters Wiggles**, one of the park's engineering marvels. This set of 21 short stonework zigzags lifts you straight up a cleft in the rock like an elevator. You'll emerge at **Scout Lookout**, which offers unbelievable vistas and a place to gather strength for the final scrabble to Angels Landing.

As you'll notice with some dismay, the trail, such as it is, keeps climbing. It's so steep, in fact, that it's possible to lose track of it, which can be a harrowing realization. Thankfully, chains are bolted into the rock for much of the way, its links more highly polished than the brass bottoms of the showgirls fronting Las Vegas' Riviera casino. If you do wander off course, carefully retrace your steps and look for the next length of chain.

Trail's end is abundantly clear and wide enough to sit and take in the stunning 360-degree view of nearly all of Zion Canyon. If you can, relax and rest. You've earned it.

## OBSERVATION POINT

**Distance: 8 miles round-trip**
**Duration: 4–5½ hours**
**Challenge: Difficult**
**Elevation Change: 2150ft**

This popular trail is one of the most difficult day hikes in Zion. Because it's so strenuous, the trail is rarely crowded. It makes a good late-afternoon hike, as the setting sun casts the canyon in gorgeous light, and by then the steepest ascent, out of Echo Canyon, lies in blessed shade.

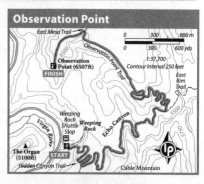

Starting from the Weeping Rock shuttle stop, the trail is mostly paved all the way to the mesa top, where it becomes dirt. For the first half mile, it follows the **Hidden Canyon Trail** up long, steep switchbacks, then branches left at a signed junction. The switchbacks continue for another half mile until you make a final turn north and enter **Echo Canyon**.

The trail levels out briefly, and for a moment the sandstone walls close around you; towering above is the flat face of **Cable Mountain**, truly a sight to behold. Then, before you realize it, you're climbing again. The upper reaches of Echo Canyon open on lovely slickrock slopes, while below, the serpentine slot canyon closes as tight as a zipper.

At the 2-mile point, you'll reach a junction with the **East Rim Trail**, which also leads to Cable and Deertrap Mountains. After this, a long series of tough switchbacks pull you up the mountain without relief. Though wide, the trail

## MOUNTAIN LIONS

Rangers estimate that about 20 mountain lions reside in Zion National Park. To verify that number and determine familial relationships, they are conducting a DNA tracking program. How do you get a mountain lion's DNA? Since the park service frowns on shooting and killing, rangers set 'hair traps' – such as Velcro patches – where mountain lions frequent, and they collect the big cats' scat.

The best chance for visitors to spot a mountain lion (also called a cougar or puma) is to visit the taxidermy display in the **Zion Nature Center** (p69), though sightings of the elusive animal are becoming more frequent. This is partly due to the shuttle, which has lowered noise levels in the park, but it's mostly due to the ongoing drought, which drives animals to the Virgin River. In 2003, a mountain lion killed a deer near the base of the Watchman Trail, and paw prints turn up many places.

As of 2004, there has never been a documented mountain lion attack on humans in the park, though there have been several outside of it. If, by luck or misfortune, you encounter a mountain lion up close, the best strategy is to be aggressive: shout, wave your arms and throw things. Don't run, as that will trigger a chase. If the lion does attack, fight back. Unlike a bear, it will not grow bored if you play possum.

is very exposed, but having a mountain on one side makes it less dizzying for some than the trail to Angels Landing. In spring, purple penstemon and crimson paintbrush dot the slickrock.

After about a mile, you'll reach the mesa top, and the trail is mostly level as it skirts the rim. For the final half mile, you'll traverse a piñon-juniper forest (passing a signed junction with the East Mesa Trail) to footpaths that crisscross the point. From this perch at 6508ft, you can peer 600ft down to the knife-edge of **Angels Landing** and 2150ft down to the **Virgin River**. The raven's-eye view down the canyon also includes a nice perspective of **Red Arch Mountain**. To the west, you're level with **Cathedral Mountain**. In the recent geologic past, it would have been a simple wade to this peak – now, just the thought of it makes your palms sweat.

### Kolob Canyons

Zion's northwest section includes only three maintained trails. Those who want a challenge should consider day hiking La Verkin Creek Trail (p84).

### TIMBER CREEK OVERLOOK
**Distance: 1 mile round-trip**
**Duration: 30 minutes**
**Challenge: Easy**
**Elevation Change: 100ft**

This short dirt trail gets a bit steep and rocky, but it is quite easy. It starts at the end of Kolob Canyons Rd and is the natural destination for first-time visitors to this section of Zion. About 100yd along the trail, you'll find picnic benches nestled beneath the Gambel oaks and junipers.

The view at trail's end encompasses the ragged, fingerlike **Kolob Canyons** to the east and the flat mesas of the **Lower Kolob Plateau** to the south. From here, **Zion Canyon** is a wispy haze, unrecognizable as the mighty trench and inspiration of majestic homilies that it is.

### TAYLOR CREEK MIDDLE FORK
**Distance: 5 miles round-trip**
**Duration: 2½–3 hours**
**Challenge: Moderate**
**Elevation Change: 450ft**

This trail follows the Taylor Creek Middle Fork through classic piñon-juniper forest. You'll pass two teetering pioneer cabins, but the real payoff is at the end: **Double Arch Alcove**, a natural amphitheater where the seep-stained red rock glows and echoes with dripping water and swirling wind.

Signed trailhead parking is about 2 miles from the visitor center. The trail quickly drops to creek level, and trail and water continually crisscross like strands of DNA. In places, informal spurs obscure the main trail; pay particular attention at streambed crossings. Though the creek is small, expect to get a little wet and muddy and to be harassed by bugs.

After about a mile, you'll reach the 1930 **Larson cabin** and a sign identifying the Taylor Creek Trail. As the trail enters a finger canyon between **Tucupit** and **Paria Points**, the walls narrow, and your steady ascent grows steeper still. A mile farther you'll reach the **Fife cabin**, which, like its predecessor, is too fragile to enter; respect the chicken wire on the windows and doors.

The last half mile leads to Double Arch Alcove for a cool, refreshing ⅃ before your return trip.

## Kolob Terrace

Most of the trails along this scenic road are considered backcountry routes, but this one is notable exception.

**NORTHGATE PEAKS TRAIL**
**Distance: 4.4 miles round-trip**
**Duration: 2 hours**
**Challenge: Easy**
**Elevation Change: 110ft**

An overlooked gem, this trail offers an easy hike to one of Zion's best views. And since this area sees so little traffic, the trail remains largely uncrowded.

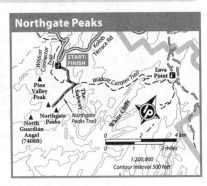

On Kolob Terrace Rd about 28.5 miles from Hwy 9, the trailhead is signed 'Wildcat Canyon,' the main route from this point. Look for the dirt path at the end of the parking area. For about a mile, you'll wander through an open meadow of scrub and burnt pines from a 1996 wildfire. At the first junction, stay straight, following the sign for the **West Rim Trail** (the endpoint of the Wildcat Canyon Trail). The Wildcat Connector Trail branches right and connects with the **Hop Valley Trail** (p85).

A hundred yards farther, you'll reach the signed Northgate Peaks Trail junction; turn right. The ponderosa pines, manzanita and oodles of spring wildflowers are a welcome rest for rock-weary eyes. You soon crest a rise to a final Y junction. Here, the trailhead for the canyoneering route **The Subway** (p86) branches left. Keep going straight.

The appropriately named **White Cliffs** tower to the east as you gently ascend and descend to a lava rock outcrop at trail's end – a convenient perch from which to admire the stunning terrain. On either side, seemingly close enough to touch, are the pale, crosshatched **Northgate Peaks**. Front and center is **North Guardian Angel**, sporting an arch so deep it's more of a cave. Framed amid these in the distance is the heart of Zion Canyon, including **East and West Temples** and **Deertrap Mountain**, on the East Rim.

## BACKCOUNTRY HIKES

Despite its accessibility, Zion's backcountry sees relatively little use, at least compared to other major national parks. Thus, the backcountry remains a place where hikers can enjoy the park's ethereal and overwhelming beauty in contemplative solitude, even on jam-packed weekends when the Zion Canyon Shuttle is standing room only.

One thing Zion doesn't have much of is multiday routes. About the longest trip you can take within park borders is the four-day trans-park journey. Most trails require only a single overnight to complete.

The **Backcountry Desk** (p61) in the Zion Canyon Visitor Center is the main information resource, offering up-to-the-minute weather reports, water-level and temperature reports for the Virgin River, and information on water availability at backcountry springs. You can also peruse three-ring binders with exhaustive descriptions (and often photos) of every backcountry trail and campsite, climbing route and slot canyon.

For desert hiking safety advice, turn to Health & Safety (p54). It bears reminding that one reason the Zion backcountry is so quiet is that it can be a hot, dry, extremely remote place – preparation is essential.

## Permit Information

Another reason Zion's backcountry is so refreshingly human-free is that there are firm use restrictions. You need a permit for any overnight in the backcountry, and the most popular trails allow camping only at a few designated sites. You also need a permit to through-hike The Narrows and to canyoneer any slot canyon; all canyons but The Narrows must be completed in one day.

About half of the available permits for any route can be reserved **online** (www.nps.gov/zion; $5), while the remaining permits are distributed in person on a first-come, first-served basis up to one day ahead. Trying to get a next-day walk-in permit on a busy weekend for the most popular routes is like trying to get tickets to a rock concert; lines can form at the Backcountry Desk by 6am or earlier.

Online reservations, which you can make about two months ahead, are a safer bet. Four months in advance, a permit lottery is held for the two most sought-after routes: The Subway and Mystery Canyon. The Narrows is the third-most popular permit. Do check the list of routes in the lottery, as it's likely to grow.

Note that a reservation is not the permit itself, which you must pick up in person at the Backcountry Desk. If you're a frequent (at least once a year) park visitor, you can join Zion Express Permits, which allows you to purchase an actual permit online.

Permit fees (which are in addition to the reservation fee) are as follows: one to two hikers, $10; three to seven hikers, $15; eight to 12 hikers, $20.

## Backcountry Camping

Trails limited to designated campsites include the West Rim, La Verkin Creek, Hop Valley and The Narrows. Dispersed camping is allowed within certain restricted areas on the East Rim, the Southwest Desert and sections of the Wildcat Canyon Trail; check specific boundaries with backcountry rangers.

While campsites can only be reserved online for one night, you can arrange multinight stays in person at the Backcountry Desk. Designated backcountry campsites are primitive, offering only a numbered marker and a cleared area.

## Backcountry Trails

Most backcountry routes are one way, so they require vehicles positioned at each end or a shuttle ride to the trailhead; see Hiker Shuttles (p66) for local companies. The Backcountry Desk also provides an informal ride-share board.

### THE NARROWS: FROM THE TOP
Distance: 16 miles one way
Duration: 2-day backpacking trip, or 12-hour day hike
Challenge: Moderate–Difficult
Elevation Change: 1220ft

If there's one hike that's made Zion famous, it's this waltz down the Virgin River through the thousand-foot sheer gorge known as The Narrows. Overnight camping promises the best experience, though you can hike from the top in one very strenuous, long day. You can also day hike The Narrows from the **bottom** (p77), the only approach that doesn't require a permit.

Twelve campsites line the river; only two take groups larger than six (12 maximum). The best time to hike is June through September, when the river is lowest and warmest. In summer, under optimum conditions, you at least need sturdy river shoes (preferably 5.10 canyoneers with neoprene socks), a waterproof backpack (trash-bag liners are fine) and a walking stick – ideally two – to negotiate slippery rocks and swift currents. Also bring nylon hiking shorts and a fleece jacket for warmth.

The rest of the year, wetsuits or dry suits are necessary and are available for rent from Springdale outfitters. Overnight hikers are also required to use human-waste disposal bags, which are given free to permit holders.

Flash floods occur year-round, and river closures can happen at any time, particularly in July and August, the region's 'monsoon'

**The Narrows: From the Top**

season. Before hiking, always check with rangers about current weather and water conditions.

The trail begins at **Chamberlain's Ranch**, on the east side of the park, 90 minutes from the South Entrance; ask a ranger for driving directions. Past the ranch gate, a dirt road leads to the river, where you'll find an NPS trailhead marker.

From here, the trail is the river. The first 9 miles are the quietest and easiest, and the lonely river and undulating walls cast a mesmerizing spell. **Deep Creek** is the first major confluence, doubling the river's volume. The following 2-mile stretch to **Big Water** features most of the campsites, secretive side canyons and faster water, sometimes waist deep and involving swims.

Past Big Water are the 5 miles open to day hikers, and meeting people for the first time is a little like being woken from a dream. In 2 miles you'll reach well-known **Wall Street**, and your company will steadily increase till you're just one of the crowd on the **Riverside Walk** (p73). For more on this final 5 miles, see the description under Day Hikes (p77).

---

## WEST RIM TRAIL

**Distance: 14.5 miles one way**
**Duration: 2-day backpacking trip, or 9-hour day hike**
**Challenge: Moderate from Lava Point; Very Difficult from The Grotto**
**Elevation Change: 3600ft**

This is Zion's most popular high country trail, affording spectacular views that at sunset will leave you speechless. Better yet, it's uncrowded; you can sometimes hike for two days and count the number of fellow hikers on one hand.

You can approach this hike from either direction, but note: The West Rim Trail leads from one of Zion's highest points to one of its lowest. Beginning in Zion Canyon at The Grotto requires a brutal, unrelenting, 6-mile ascent of nearly 3000ft. A few see this as a worthy challenge. Most prefer to *descend* from Lava

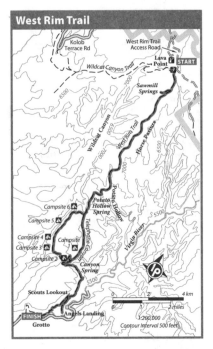

**West Rim Trail**

Point, at the end of **Kolob Terrace Rd** (p71), and that's how this description is presented.

First, take in the panoramic view from **Lava Point** itself, then walk to campsite 2 in the adjacent campground, where **Barney's Trail** drops to the West Rim Trail access road. Turn right; the trailhead parking area is a half mile farther.

After dropping again to the top of **Horse Pasture Plateau**, the trail descends oh-so-gently for about 5 miles. In about a mile, you'll reach the spur trail to the semireliable **Sawmill Spring**. Abundant trailside wildflowers include arrowleaf balsamroot, desert phlox, larkspur and Uinta groundsel. Scars remain from a 1996 wildfire.

The first big view west opens up at around 4 miles, stretching for what seems forever across the valley of the left fork of North Creek. A mile or so farther you'll descend into the grassy meadows of **Potato Hollow**, where a spur leads to a good-sized spring. So long as it's running, this is the best place to get water and a perfect shady spot for lunch.

The hike up and out of Potato Hollow is your only real workout, and it's mitigated by the increasingly dramatic views west. After about 2 miles, you'll reach the junction with the **Telephone Canyon Trail**, a shorter route to Cabin Spring, but don't take it. The next 2-mile stretch is an incredible experience and is the primary reason for this trail's enduring popularity.

**Campsites 3 through 6** are spread along this edge of the mesa; reserve one of these blessed perches if you can. However, it can get windy, so bring rope for your tent, and never build a campfire.

About a mile and a half before Cabin Spring (also called West Rim Spring), the trail descends steeply and, except for a half-mile stretch midway down, keeps descending sharply all the way to The Grotto.

**Cabin Spring** is a major junction. From here, short spur trails lead to the spring itself (a trickle) and **campsite 2**. Telephone Canyon connects here, and **campsite 1** is not far along it. Though both campsites are very nice, the views don't quite compare.

About 12.5 miles from Lava Point, you'll reach **Scout Lookout** and the junction for **Angels Landing** (p78). Those with the legs and stomach for it should scoot out for a look. Beyond the junction, it's a 2-mile drop to the canyon floor and your shuttle ride to the visitor center.

### LA VERKIN CREEK TRAIL TO KOLOB ARCH
**Distance: 14.5 miles round-trip**
**Duration: 2-day backpacking trip, or 8-hour day hike**
**Challenge: Moderate as backpack, Difficult as day hike**
**Elevation Change: 800ft**

This is a spring or fall trail. From late May through mid-July, biting goat flies hound hikers along La Verkin Creek, and throughout summer, temperatures are discouraging. It's a strenuous day hike year-round due to length, sand and elevation changes; an overnight is both easier and allows time to explore the highly recommended Willis Creek area.

The trailhead is just south of the Lee Pass parking area on **Kolob Canyons Rd** (p70). For the first 2 miles or so, you'll descend an open ridge with fine views of the finger canyons, which seem the unnatural result of an ax-wielding madman.

Eventually, you'll skirt the spire of **Shuntavi Butte** and descend more steeply through piñon-juniper forest along **Timber Creek**. The trail then turns east to the north bank of **La Verkin Creek**, a permanent, vigorous stream lined with the most convenient **campsites** (numbers 6 through 19).

Along La Verkin Creek, the trail is sandy and slow-going. Ponderosa pines provide shade, while orange butterfly weed makes a lovely appearance.

After about 6.25 miles, you'll reach the signed **Kolob Arch Trail** junction. Just beyond it lies the signed junction for the **Hop Valley Trail**, used mainly as a trans-park connector.

Past this, La Verkin Creek Trail continues for 4.5 miles, steadily narrowing, then turning up **Willis Creek**, a steep defile with towering sheer walls that open up near the park boundary. Don't leave the park limits, as private property owners have been known to run off stray hikers at gunpoint.

The half-mile spur to **Kolob Arch** is as far as day hikers should travel. Some scrambling and route-finding is required. When you reach a sign advising against further travel up canyon, look high on the west wall for Kolob Arch. Though at 310ft, its opening may be the largest in the world, the distant arch is so dwarfed by massive walls that it at first seems strangely anticlimactic. Spend some time watching the sun dress the rock in ever-shifting shadows, however, and it soon makes a satisfying destination after all.

## TRANS-PARK CONNECTOR

**Distance: 15.5 miles one way**
**Duration: 2-day backpack**
**Challenge: Moderate–Difficult**
**Elevation Change: About 1000ft**

The most popular way to traverse Zion is to trek north to south over four days. Hikers spend the first night on **La Verkin Creek Trail** (p84), the second night on the **Wildcat Canyon Trail** or at **Lava Point** (p84) and the third night on the **West Rim Trail** (p83). La Verkin Creek and the West Rim were already described in this chapter, so following is a brief explanation of how to link them.

From La Verkin Creek Trail, head south on the 6.7-mile **Hop Valley Trail**, which begins with amazing views. You'll descend about 1000ft on long, hot, sandy stretches, emerging on **Kolob Terrace Rd**.

The 4-mile **Wildcat Connector Trail** links Hop Valley with the 4.7-mile **Wildcat Canyon Trail** to Lava Point. Together, the Wildcat trails comprise an uneven ascent of nearly 2000ft. Two sites offer dispersed camping if you'd rather not press on to Lava Point in one day.

There's very little water along this route. The only absolutely reliable source is La Verkin Creek; other springs are seasonal. Check with rangers for current conditions. Spring is your best bet for water, while fall brings spectacular colors.

## THE SUBWAY
**Distance: 9.5 miles one way**
**Duration: 6–8 hours**
**Challenge: Difficult**
**Elevation Change: 1850ft**

The left fork of North Creek – better known as The Subway – is arguably Zion's best all-around hike, and it is unquestionably the hardest backcountry permit to get. Day hiking from the bottom up (permit also required) limits access to less than half of this popular route – so unlike The Narrows, only the descent from the top is recommended. That description follows.

The Subway is officially a canyoneering route. While it's easy by canyoneering standards – involving four or five short rappels of 20ft or less – you still need to know what you're doing. If you don't have any rappelling experience, get some first (p89). The last of these rappels is Keyhole Falls, just above the titular Subway section, and it is the barrier to day hikers headed upstream.

Like all of Zion's canyons, The Subway is prone to flash floods. Always check with rangers before starting.

The trail starts at the Wildcat Canyon trailhead on **Kolob Terrace Rd** (p71). At first, it follows the **Northgate Peaks Trail** (p81); turn there for a description. Once you reach the signed spur to The Subway, the real adventure, and route-finding, begins.

Very quickly, the dirt trail emerges on slickrock. Sidehill right, watching for cairns and a park service 'boot' sign. Also look below for where the trail reenters the trees. This strategy of following cairns, sidehilling right and looking below should keep you on course as you traverse several slickrock sections.

In about a mile, you'll reach a viewpoint. Wooded **Russell Gulch**, which you've been following, narrows into a technical slot canyon to the right, while across the drainage is a rise with two nipplelike peaks. Cross the rise between these points to an amazing bowl of sculpted slickrock on the other side.

Make sure to cross and not descend Russell Gulch. If you're unsure which drainage you're in, simply avoid using your ropes until you are sure. Remember, The Subway is not a slot canyon.

At the base of the slickrock bowl, the trail bears left and soon reaches a cleft in the cliff face and a steep, downhill scrabble. You've now entered the left fork drainage.

Just as quickly, you arrive at your first obstacle: an oversized boulder that you can rappel or down climb. Above all, do not jump.

Once in the left fork, you can't get lost, and the hiking is fairly level, alternating between sand and rocks, cold pools of increasingly clear water (some swimming involved) and short rappels. The sculpted canyon is full of surprises, beauty and camera-worthy moments.

Below **Keyhole Falls** and **The Subway**, the canyon walls widen as the creek tumbles scenically over low slickrock ledges. Eventually, the slickrock gives way to boulders, and you're forced to meander in and out of the streambed. On the west side of the river, below a large sandstone buttress with a lava

## FLASH FLOODS

Whenever you hike a narrow canyon, you need to watch for signs of a flash flood. A two-week drought is meaningless once a single raincloud arrives; in fact, in that situation, the ground is so hard, it absorbs very little rainwater, and creekbeds fill in a hurry. Here are some telling signs of imminent danger:

✔ Any buildup of clouds or the sound of thunder

✔ Sudden changes in water clarity from clear to muddy

✔ Rising water levels or floating debris

✔ A rush of wind and/or a low roar that sounds like thunder

If you witness any of these signs, do the following immediately:

✔ Do not run down canyon; you can't beat a flash flood.

✔ Get to higher ground anywhere; even a few feet could save your life.

✔ If there is no higher ground, get behind a rock fin, which will break the initial, debris-filled wave.

✔ Wait. Water levels usually drop within six to 24 hours.

On the other hand, so long as you're not in-canyon, a flash flood is an awesome event to witness. In Zion Canyon, there are many safe places to watch the Virgin River, and when Pine Creek flashes, you can watch from the east end of the Zion–Mt Carmel Tunnel. Even rangers act like schoolkids.

outcrop, you'll find 30 or so **dinosaur tracks** on an unusual white rock slab. Look carefully, as they're easy to miss.

The next sandstone buttress indicates the location of a big cliffside spring, which signals the approach of trail's end. Keep to the west side of the river, and look for signs for the **Left Fork trailhead**. Here, the steep trail climbs atop the plateau and then meanders amiably to the parking lot.

## OTHER ACTIVITIES

Besides hiking, the two most popular activities in Zion are canyoneering its slot canyons and rock climbing its massive sandstone walls – both world-class experiences. There are also opportunities for cycling, horseback riding, swimming and tubing, though the Virgin River is not normally deep enough for boating – and it is *not* a successful spot for anglers.

Zion also offers a wide selection of classes and ranger programs for all ages.

### Canyoneering

If there's one sport that makes Zion special, it's canyoneering. Rappelling a hundred feet over the lip of a sandstone bowl, swimming icy pools, tracing a slot canyon's sculpted curves, staring up at a ragged gash of blue sky – canyoneering is beautiful, dangerous and sublime all at once. And it's easy, deceptively easy, to learn.

As such, canyoneering has become the fastest-growing activity at Zion, with usage in the park's slot canyons tripling in the past five years. This increased impact in designated wilderness areas has spurred the park service to set day-use limits on once-unrestricted canyons and to tighten limits on others. At the same time, a rise in the number of inexperienced and reckless canyoneers has led to a concurrent rise in the number of backcountry rescues.

As park officials continue to search for the right balance between use, safety

## WHAT NOT TO DO: AN EXPERT SHARES STORIES

In spring 2004, a group of teenage boys were fooling around atop Angels Landing. One boy edged out farther and farther, 150ft beyond where he should have been, and slipped. His friends turned only in time to see his head disappear out of sight.

The boy fell 900ft and died, and Dean Wood is the climber the park service called to retrieve his body. An expert climber and canyoneer who co-owns **Zion Rock & Mountain Guides** (opposite), Dean has worked with the park's search-and-rescue team since 1996, and he agreed to share his advice for staying safe in Zion's backcountry, along with a few stories of adventure gone awry.

Here are Dean's five simple rules:

✔ Don't jump off rocks.

✔ Don't get lost.

✔ Don't lose track of your kids.

✔ Don't forget how far you are from help.

✔ Know how to use your equipment.

'Jumping incidents are the biggest volume rescue in the park. This spring we had a Boy Scout who was jumping off a waterfall in the upper Narrows. You can walk around it, but this is one of the things I guess they do when they do this hike. It was his third jump actually. He jumped once, came back up, jumped twice, came back up. Did the third jump and did a tib-fib compound fracture, put his tibia right out his leg. It happened at 1 o'clock, took them five or six hours to get someone downriver to notify the park, and we didn't get there till dark, at which point we couldn't carry him out. So another group of 12 came in, and we spent the night. So you know, a simple little accident now is involving up to 20 people. Takes us till noon the next day to get him out, and then a helicopter to fly him to a hospital. And he was lucky. It could have been a broken femur with arterial bleeding, and you can die from that.

'With canyoneers, it's a very common thing where they don't know the terrain and start dropping into things you shouldn't be dropping into. One couple was trying to find The Subway, didn't have a valid route description and went into Russell Gulch. They're hand lining, it's vertical, they don't have enough rope, and he slips down the last 20ft and hits his head. At that point his girlfriend can either go back and get help or go down to him. She goes down and same thing happens. Now they're ledged out. Can't go down, can't go up. They were forced to stay there for three days, rationing water and trail mix, until the park service put two and two together and finally found them.

'Another two guys were going to do Mystery Canyon. Don't quite know where Mystery is. So they drop into another canyon just thinking they're going to find Mystery. The canyon keeps going and going and no way out, so they try to climb back up. They have ascenders and everything, but one guy doesn't have the skills and doesn't know how to use them. His buddy hikes out and gets help. When we return with the helicopter next morning, he's on this ledge, hanging there with a rope and ascenders. It was a comedy rescue, just comedy.'

And, as Dean likes to emphasize every time, 'Totally preventable.'

and conservation, the next few years may see further changes to canyoneering regulations.

Raw beginners should take a course before attempting any slot canyon. Since guided trips are prohibited in the park, courses are held outside Zion, after which students can try out their newfound skills in the park. Among the easiest canyoneering routes are the left fork of North Creek (known as **The Subway**, p86) and **Orderville Canyon**, which ends at The Narrows. In terms of equipment, these require only about 50ft of rope or webbing (basically flat rope), a submersible daypack, canyoneering shoes and, in every season but summer, a wetsuit or dry suit. From mid-June through September, water in the canyons is usually just warm enough to swim in shorts. Quick-drying nylon shorts are best.

For people who know how to use a harness (and who can ascend and belay others), **Pine Creek Canyon** and **Mystery Canyon** are two gorgeous, very popular routes. They offer moderate challenges, with seven or eight rappels of 50ft to 100ft. Pine Creek features easy access, while Mystery Canyon lets you be a rock star – the last rappel drops you into the Virgin River in front of admiring crowds day hiking The Narrows.

Zion contains dozens more slot canyons beyond these. All require permits, and most will eventually be listed on the online reservation system. These canyons are the park's most sought-after backcountry experience, so it's best to reserve your dates as soon as possible. For more on permits, see p82.

Springdale is home to two operations that can teach you and suit you up for canyoneering (providing harnesses, helmets, canyoneering shoes, dry suits, fleece layers, waterproof packs and more) and that offer hiker shuttles. Both have excellent reputations and tons of experience at Zion.

**Zion Rock & Mountain Guides** ( ☎ 435-772-3303; www.zionrockguides.com; 1458 Zion Park Blvd; ☯ 8am-7pm) rents the full range of river hiking, canyoneering, rock climbing and camping gear; it also sells climbing, canyoneering and camping equipment and has a great selection of region-specific guides. You could rent gear separately or through rental packages, which include river footwear ($12/18 day/overnight), a full dry suit ($35/48) and rock climbing ($15/22.50). Zion Rock is the only place that rents static canyon ropes. Custom guided trips and a range of half-, one- and multiday canyoneering and climbing courses begin at around $100 per person; pricing varies depending on group size.

**Zion Adventure Company** ( ☎ 435-772-1001; www.zionadventures.com; 36 Lion Blvd; ☯ 8am-8pm) has made its name outfitting groups of hikers for The Narrows, and this thorough, efficient operation has opened a second location at **Zion Outdoor** ( ☎ 435-772-0990; 868 Zion Park Blvd; ☯ 9am-9pm), which also sells camping, clothing and some climbing gear. Rental packages include footwear ($16/25 day/overnight) and a full dry suit ($35/55). As with Zion Rock, all canyoneering gear can be rented separately, and the shop offers a range of guided trips and classes, for beginners and experts, in both canyoneering and climbing. Rates begin at around $100 and are dependant on group size.

## Rock Climbing

Zion Canyon contains some of the most famous big wall climbs in the country, including Moonlight Buttress, Prodigal Son, Touchstone and Space Shot. These are epic, aided climbs that draw the best of the best for their challenge and beauty. And though the number of mapped routes in the park has doubled in the last seven years, Zion still offers experienced climbers the thrill and bragging rights of a first ascent. Climb with a local, and be prepared for many stops while he or she stares at an opposing cliff face, pondering a new route.

This is all well and good for experts and those ready to tackle their first big wall or bivouac, but Zion doesn't offer much for beginners or for those who prefer sport climbs and bolted routes, which the park lacks. Those folks will find better opportunities outside Zion, at such places as **Snow Canyon State Park** (p107) near St George.

While day climbs in Zion do not require a permit, all overnights and bivouacs do (for more on permits, see p82). Zion's Backcountry Desk also keeps an ever-growing binder of climber-written route descriptions.

Both outfitters listed under Canyoneering offer recommended rock climbing courses for beginners and intermediates, but Zion Rock has a wider selection of climbing gear for sale, as well as route books that are even more up-to-date than the park service's.

## Cycling & Mountain Biking

In the park, cycling is allowed only on Zion Canyon Rd and the Pa'rus Trail, both of which are very pleasant and popular. In fact, the lack of cars on Zion Canyon Rd from April through October makes cycling a great way to see the canyon. As at all national parks, mountain biking is prohibited, but nearby areas provide lots of single-track slickrock trails on a par with any in southern Utah (even Moab). Try **Gooseberry Mesa**, **Hurricane Cliffs** and **Rockville Bench**; Springdale bike shops can provide directions and point you to more trails. Just remember, summer is hot, hot, hot; spring and fall are the most enjoyable times for biking.

**Zion Cycles** ( ☎ 435-772-0400; www.zioncycles.com; 868 Zion Park Blvd; ☼ 9am-9pm) is a full-service rental and repair shop. Rentals start at $10/22/35 by the hour/half day/full day. It also rents tandem bikes ($14/30/40), kids bikes ($5/10/15) and kids trailers ($5/10/15). Tune-ups run $25 to $60.

**Springdale Cycle Tours** ( ☎ 435-772-0575, 800-776-2099; www.springdalecycles.com; 1458 Zion Park Blvd; ☼ 9am-6pm) is another full-service rental and repair shop that operates a satellite **rental hut** ( ☼ 9am-1pm, 3-6pm) in front of Sol Foods Market, right beside the park. Bike rentals start at $25/35 for a half/full day. It also rents tandem bikes ($30/40), kids bikes ($7/10) and kids trailers ($7/10). It started as a guided tour company and still offers a range of all-day tours that include lunch; rates begin around $100 per person and vary by group size.

## Horseback Riding

**Canyon Trail Rides** ( ☎ 435-679-8665, 435-772-3810; www.canyonrides.com) is Zion's official horseback riding concessionaire, operating from a corral across the road from Zion Lodge. Every day from March through November, it offers four one-hour rides ($30) and two three-hour rides ($55). There's a 220lb weight limit, and children must be seven years old. Both rides follow the **Sand Bench Trail**, which runs along the Virgin River.

You can ride your own horse as well. In Zion Canyon, the only trail open to horses is the Sand Bench Trail; otherwise, horses are allowed on most trails in the backcountry. Permits are not required for day trips; maximum group size is six animals. The only overnight stock camp is on the **Hop Valley Trail**. For more about regulations and overnight permits, contact the Backcountry Desk (p61).

## Swimming & Tubing

Though generally too cold for swimming, the Virgin River warms to between 55°F and 65°F from June through September. The river is fairly swift and shallow (generally no more than knee-deep), but there are numerous deeper swimming holes.

Tubing is prohibited within Zion but is quite popular outside the park. Floats stretch about 2.5 miles and last from 90 minutes to two hours. Tubing season runs from mid-May through August.

Two places in Springdale rent inner tubes. Right on the river, **Zion Canyon Campground** ( ☎ 435-772-3237; www.zioncamp.com; 479 Zion Park Blvd) rents tubes ($10) but doesn't provide return transportation. **Zion Tubing** ( ☎ 435-772-8823; wwwziontubing. com; 180 Zion Park Blvd; ⏰ 8am-8pm), inside Tsunami Juice & Java (p98), rents tubes alone ($12) or with return transportation ($14).

## Kayaking

Kayaking is allowed in Zion when the Virgin River runs above 140cfs (cubic feet per second). This happens only a couple of days a year, usually once or twice during the spring snowmelt and occasionally after a late summer storm. Less than a dozen people get to enjoy this sport of opportunity every year, but bring your kayak and you might get lucky. There are no rentals.

## Watching Wildlife

Desert wildlife tends to be secretive, so while Zion is home to mountain lions, bighorn sheep, ringtail cats, rattlesnakes and nesting peregrine falcons, few visitors ever see them. More common, and spotted frequently near Zion Lodge, are mule deer and wild turkeys. Then, of course, there are lizards, which skitter seemingly at your every step.

## Ranger Programs

Federal budget cuts in recent years have curtailed ranger programs at Zion, but a decent slate of daily talks and walks cover such popular topics as geology, water and erosion, native animals and plants, and history. The visitor center posts a list of each week's upcoming ranger programs.

## Classes

Launched in 2002 by the national park and the Zion Natural History Association, the **Zion Canyon Field Institute** ( ☎ 435-772-3264, 800-635-3959; www.zionpark.org) offers a variety of excellent one- and multiday seminars and classes year-round, the majority between April and October. All involve accompanying an expert naturalist outdoors, and some require strenuous hiking. This is your chance to hike The Narrows or Angels Landing with a geologist, or to go on a nighttime prowl for such elusive fauna as mountain lions, bats and ringtail cats. Photography classes are popular, and other subjects include rock art, edible plants, botanical illustration, archaeology and much more. Prices run $30 to $80 per day; class sizes are usually limited to 12 to 14 people.

## Kids' Activities

Zion sponsors a drop-off **Junior Ranger Program**, open to children age six to 12. The program runs from Memorial Day to Labor Day and is based at the Zion Nature Center, near South Campground. There are two sessions daily: one from 9 to 11:30am, the second from 1:30 to 4pm; arrive half an hour early to register. There's a onetime $2 fee per child, after which the child can attend as many programs as he or she wants. Parents must return to pick up their kids between programs; children cannot be left all day.

Programs vary daily, but all involve indoor and outdoor activities, including half-hour hikes. They cover all the topics of the adult ranger programs, but use games, observation and hands-on activities to bring them to life. Each session is usually divided into two age groups: six to eight, and nine to 12. Kids earn a pin for completing one program and a patch for completing two.

There is no drop-off program for children ages five and under, though they can join the Junior Ranger Helper program by completing an activity sheet, for which they earn a sticker. They (and their parents) are also free to tour the nature center, whose displays include a mountain lion, various raptors, a beaver, tons of bugs and butterflies, and touch tables with skulls, horns and lots of cool creepy things.

## SLEEPING

Many national parks lie far from the nearest attractive, sizeable town, necessitating all sorts of practical and logistical considerations – but not Zion. Tourist-friendly Springdale borders the park, a stone's throw across the Virgin River. You can literally walk from a few Springdale businesses into the park or vice versa, and shuttles both in town and in the park make getting around a breeze.

This is especially helpful, as Zion itself boasts just one lodge and two basic campgrounds, all of which book up quickly and far in advance on weekends and in summer. So if you find yourself shut out of the park, don't despair: Springdale has many options.

### Camping

#### INSIDE THE PARK

Just inside Zion's South Entrance are the park's two main campgrounds, Watchman and South. They are adjacent to each other and to the visitor center, and they are virtually identical in terms of ambience. Facilities vary slightly, but neither one has showers, laundry facilities or a general store; these are available in Springdale. During high season, you can **reserve** ( ☎ 800-365-2267; http://reservations.nps.gov) sites at Watchman up to five months in advance, while South Campground is first-come, first-served only. At both, there is a maximum stay of 14 days.

Folks with allergies should note that in May the campgrounds' cottonwoods pollinate in potentially unbearable abundance.

**Watchman Campground** (170 sites; tent $16, electrical hookup $18, river site $20, group site $3 per person; ☯ year-round) Towering cottonwoods provide ample shade for the pretty, well-spaced sites at Watchman. Sites along the Virgin River come at a premium and provide electricity, but your most important request should be shade. The cottonwoods don't protect every inch of ground, and the last thing you want is to come home to a nylon oven. Since individual sites can't be reserved in advance, the best strategy is to check in at the **Watchman kiosk** ( ☯ 7:30am-9pm) about a half hour after the 11am official checkout, when the most sites will be available. Rangers do their best to honor requests. Facilities at Watchman include restrooms (but no showers), drinking water, picnic tables, fire grates, some electrical hookups, a dump station and recycling bins. Watchman accepts reservations from April 2 to October 31; the rest of the year it's first-come, first-served. Regular sites allow up to two vehicles, four tents and eight people; campsites are also available for organized groups of nine to 40.

**South Campground** (141 sites; tent $16; ☯ mid-Mar–Oct) There are no electrical hookups or group sites at South Campground, but it does have a dump station and all the other same facilities and amenities as Watchman. It's also just as pretty, with popular riverside sites; however, these sites are also beside the busy Pa'rus Trail (p72), so consider how much company you want. South is entirely first-come, first-served, and on busy weekends it's full by late morning.

**Lava Point Campground** (6 sites; free; summer only) The free primitive campground at Lava Point is an attractive loop of six sites at the end of Kolob Terrace Rd. The first-come, first-served sites include a pit toilet, picnic tables and fire grates, but no water. It's only open after Kolob Terrace Rd opens, usually in late spring, and closes when snow arrives in fall.

As small as it is, Lava Point is rarely full – few are willing to take a chance on it, as it's more than an hour from the South Entrance. If it is full when you arrive, drive a little farther on Kolob Terrace Rd to Kolob Reservoir, where you'll find free dispersed camping (and pit toilets) on what is technically public water department land.

**Zion Canyon Campground** ( ☎ 435-772-3237; www.zioncamp.com; 479 Zion Park Blvd; tent by day/week $20/120, RV hookup $24/144; 🅟 ) On the Virgin River in Springdale, a half mile from Zion's South Entrance, this extensive campground provides 85 tent sites, 115 RV sites and full facilities, including a coin laundry, convenience store, pizza parlor, inner tube rentals ($10) and public showers ($3). Camp-sites can be dusty and close together, but most are shaded. Rates are based on two people.

**Zion River Resort** ( ☎ 435-635-8594, 800-838-8594; www.zionriverresort.com; tent $30, RV hookup $38-43, cabin $60-70, teepee $35; 🅟 🖳 ) Ten miles east of Hurricane on Hwy 9, this is a pristine, friendly RV park along the Virgin River with a slew of attractive amenities. It offers only eight tent sites compared to 114 RV sites; the clean camping cabins (no linens) have air-conditioning. You'll also find a coin laundry, convenience store, barbecue gazebo, showers (50¢), cable TV and wireless Internet.

**Mukuntuweep** ( ☎ 435-648-3011; www.xpressweb.com/zionpark; tent $15, RV hookup $19, cabin $25) A half mile from Zion's East Entrance, this dusty campground will do in a pinch, though it's nothing special; the cabins are beat up. Facilities include a coin laundry and showers ($1/3 guests/nonguests), while across the street is a gas station, a passable **Mexican restaurant** ( 🕑 8am-6pm Mon-Thu, till 9pm Fri-Sun; items $8-9) and a gift shop that is a throwback to old-style Americana. Get your cap rifles, rubber tomahawks and coonskin caps here.

**Mosquito Cove** If you can't find a tent site anywhere, Mosquito Cove is a free primitive campsite on BLM land along the Virgin River; it's a rowdy, crowded local hangout. At the Rockville town sign on Hwy 9, drive 3 miles west and look for an unsigned dirt road on the left. You'll immediately enter a maze of dirt tracks and will most likely see others already camping.

## Lodging
The **Zion Canyon Visitors Bureau's website** (www.zionpark.com) lists information and links to most but not all area accommodations.

The only lodging within the park is the **Zion Lodge** ( ☎ 435-772-3213, 888-297-2757, reservations 303-297-2757; www.zionlodge.com; summer rates: hotel $125, cabin, $133, ste $147; 🕑 year-round; 🅟 ✖ 🖳 ). The original building, built in the 1920s, burned down in 1966. Today you'll find modern buildings with nostalgic, chocolate brown, shingle-roofed exteriors. The complex includes 81 motel rooms (including six suites) and 40 cabins. All accommodations are grouped together within easy walking distance of the main lodge and restaurant.

Motel rooms feature two queen beds, while cabins offer two double beds and a gas-log fireplace. All match the standard of a top-quality chain, with national park touches, such as historic photos of Zion, wood shutters, Mission-style headboards and roomy wood porches with, needless to say, great views. All rooms have private bathrooms, efficient air-conditioning, phones, alarm clocks and hair dryers, but no TVs. Motel rooms toward the back are farther from foot traffic and so are quieter.

Springdale has a few more luxurious digs, but you can't deny the attractiveness of the lodge, which includes a restaurant and café, a morning espresso window, a gift shop and free Internet for guests, not to mention the park and its shuttle at your fingertips. The lodge lawn's signature cottonwood is the closest thing Zion has to a social center, and everyone eventually gathers there to rest and linger in the shade.

Lodge rates are based on double occupancy (extra person $10), and youth 16 and under are free; however, rollaways/cribs ($10/5) are not allowed in the cabins, which only sleep four. Rates in winter (December 1 to March 10, except holidays) drop by about $50 and include breakfast.

You can **reserve** online (no fee), by email (reserve-zion@xanterra.com) or by phone up to 23 months in advance. It also doesn't hurt to try for a **same-day reservation** ( ☎ 928-638-2631).

Finally, if you have a lodge reservation, you're allowed to drive your car to and park at the lodge when Zion Canyon Rd is otherwise closed to private vehicles. You'll receive a red display pass in the mail that rangers at the entrance gate must authorize.

### SPRINGDALE

Springdale tries hard to make itself an ideal base for travelers, and it succeeds admirably. Hotels are uniformly clean and well maintained, and enjoy marvelous views of the canyon. But rooms aren't cheap, and during high season (April 1 to November 1) finding a bed for under $50 is nearly impossible. Confirmed budget travelers should camp or look to St George.

During the research for this guide, a wave of expansion and building was sweeping Springdale. Expect changes in facilities and rates. The rates below are for high season; winter welcomes 10% to 40% discounts.

Note that the lower the number on Zion Park Blvd, the closer the hotel is to the park entrance; all are close to shuttle stops.

### Budget

**El Rio Lodge** ( ☎ 435-772-3205, 888-772-3205; www.elriolodge.com; 995 Zion Park Blvd; 1/2 beds $48/53; ⚑ ⚑ ) The friendly owners run one of the best deals in town. Their 10 plain rooms are clean and in good condition. Each has a TV and microwave but no phone. El Rio books up with Europeans and backpackers.

**Terrace Brook Lodge** ( ☎ 435-772-3932, 800-342-6779; www.terracebrooklodge.com; 990 Zion Park Blvd; 1/2 beds $50/63, family unit $80-94; ⚑ ⚑ ⚑ ) This is another good deal. Its basic, pleasant rooms leave nothing to complain about, and they have TVs and phones. The tiny pool is off-street.

### Mid-Range

**Under-the-Eaves Bed & Breakfast** ( ☎ 435-772-3457, 866-261-2655; www.under-the-eaves.com; r $75-95, ste $145; 980 Zion Park Blvd; ⚑ ⚑ ) This historic home is now run by a very engaging British couple, Steve and Deb, who have infused their wit, spirit and art throughout. Rooms vary considerably, from the functional Hikers Room ($75) to the charming Garden Cottage ($95) – a refurbished 1920s Zion cabin – to the Eaves Suite ($145), a palatial, top-floor roost with funky decor and great views. Breakfast (included) is a riotous good time.

**Red Rock Inn** ( ☎ 435-772-3139; www.redrockinn.com; 998 Zion Park Blvd; r $92-96, ste $150; ⚑ ⚑ ) The five romantic rooms feature nice art, rich color schemes, pretty quilts and jetted tubs for one; the spacious suite includes a private hot tub. An opulent breakfast basket is delivered to your door, to be enjoyed on your terrace or up the hill in a desert garden. The sophisticated owners are knowledgeable, longtime Springdale residents.

**Harvest House** ( ☎ 435-772-3880; www.harvesthouse.net; 29 Canyon View Drive; r $90-110; ⚑ ⚑ ) This modern B&B has four spacious, bright, comfortable rooms. Two have a balcony, and all share an outdoor hot tub. Breakfast is included.

**Canyon Ranch Motel** ( ☎ 435-772-3357; www.canyonranchmotel.com; 668 Zion Park Blvd; 1 bed $64-82, 2 beds $74-92; ⚑ ⚑ ⚑ ) Detached, good-sized cottages, each with two averagely decorated rooms, surround an attractive green lawn with lots of shade and swinging benches. Some have full kitchens (add $10). The pool area is very nice.

**Pioneer Lodge** ( ☎ 435-772-3233, 888-772-3233; www.pioneerlodge.com; 838 Zion Park Blvd; r $72-82 midweek, $82-92 weekends, ste $131-171; ❄ ⚼ ✕ ) Despite much-needed renovations, decor in the 40 rooms still leans heavily on nondescript pine paneling. Aim for the popular second-floor 'canyon view' rooms, which share a massive deck.

**Bumbleberry Inn** ( ☎ 435-772-3224, 800-828-1534; www.bumbleberry.com; 897 Zion Park Blvd; 1/2 beds $68/78, minisuite $90; ❄ ⚼ ✕ ) Dressed in bumbleberry hues, these 47 chain-quality rooms have their fans, particularly for the quiet rear rooms with good views. There's also a racquetball court.

Other properties to consider include the following:

**Zion Park Motel** ( ☎ 435-772-3251; www.zionparkmotel.com; 855 Zion Park Blvd; r $70, ste $130; ❄ ⚼ ✕ ) It looks tired from the outside, but rooms are very clean; two suites are great for large families.

**Driftwood Lodge** ( ☎ 435-772-3262, 888-801-8811; www.driftwoodlodge.net; 1515 Zion Park Blvd; r $82, minisuite $120; ❄ ⚼ ✕ ) The exterior is like a brick bunker, but the decent chain-quality rooms are acceptable.

**Quality Inn** ( ☎ 435-772-3237, 800-424-6423; www.zioncamp.com; 479 Zion Park Blvd; r $68, ste $90; ❄ ⚼ ✕ ) Part of Zion Canyon Campground, the Quality Inn is new, meticulously clean and spacious.

## Top End

**Desert Pearl Inn** ( ☎ 435-772-8888, 888-828-0898; www.desertpearl.com; 707 Zion Park Blvd; poolside from $103, riverside from $115; ❄ ⚼ ✕ ) The artfully modern, romantic Desert Pearl is Springdale's most stylish property. The 61 amenity-laden rooms are dressed in sage hues, with suede sofas, handwoven Oaxacan bedspreads, pressed-tin coffee tables, wet bars, vaulted ceilings and more. The large bathrooms have bidets, balconies have Adirondack chairs, and the pool and hot tub patio is a flagstone masterpiece. There are also ADA-compliant accessible rooms. Look for a new building and individual cottages soon.

**Flanigan's Inn** ( ☎ 435-772-3244, 800-765-7787; www.flanigans.com; 428 Zion Park Blvd; standard $100, garden $110, deluxe $120, ste $120-210; ❄ ⚼ ✕ ) Flanigan's is another top-notch property. Large, attractive rooms with vaulted ceilings feature bold color schemes and real art, a comfortable couch and an array of lovely aromatherapy bath products. Caveats: The bathrooms are small, as is the pool area. Then again, its on-site **Deep Canyon Adventure Spa** ( ☎ 800-765-7787; www.deepcanyonspa.com; 1-hour massages & treatments $80-90) is a Sedona-worthy indulgence.

**Majestic View Lodge** ( ☎ 435-772-0665, 866-772-0665; www.majesticviewlodge.com; 2400 Zion Park Blvd; r $120, ste $200; ❄ ⚼ ✕ ) This hotel epitomizes the varnished-log-furniture-and-antlers school of Western design, so much so it achieves genuine kitsch. But underneath the decor are 66 surprisingly comfortable, modern rooms. The complex includes a restaurant, saloon and free wildlife museum, which reflects an authentic passion: The hotel's owner shot and stuffed 90% of the animals.

**Best Western Zion Park Inn** ( ☎ 435-772-3200, 800-934-7275; www.zionparkinn.com; 1215 Zion Park Blvd; r $105-115, ste $115-180; ❄ ⚼ ✕ ▢ ) For those on business, or who prefer the comforting dependability of a good chain, the 120 rooms here offer lots of amenities, including ADA-compliant accessible rooms, concierge service, the town's only liquor store, restaurants, in-room data ports, basketball courts, two pools and much more.

**Cliffrose Lodge** ( ☎ 435-772-3234, 800-243-8824; www.cliffroselodge.com; 281 Zion Park Blvd; garden $110-120, riverfront $130, ste $135-165; ❄ ⚼ ✕ ) The 40 rooms are nice enough but not worth the price by themselves. You're really paying to be a walkable quarter mile from the park and to enjoy the five gorgeous acres of secluded lawns and gardens, with a pretty pool and kid's playground.

**Novel House Inn** ( ☎ 435-772-3650, 800-711-8400; www.novelhouse.com; 73 Paradise Rd; r $105-125; ⬚ ⬚ ) At this B&B, the 10 rooms are named after and decorated in the style of famous novelists; they are well executed and romantic, if a trifle formal. Breakfast is included; small children are discouraged.

### ROCKVILLE
B&Bs in Rockville, 4.5 miles west of Zion, offer quiet retreats away from the Springdale hubbub.

**Serenity House** ( ☎ 435-772-3393, 800-266-3393; www.serenity-house.com; 149 E Main St; r $40-50; ⬚ ⬚ ) The two plain but nice rooms in the owners' friendly home are a great deal; sharing a bath nets a discount. The organic breakfast emphasizes fresh breads, orchard fruit and jams.

**Dream Catcher Inn** ( ☎ 435-772-3600, 800-953-7326; www.dreamcatcherinn.com; 225 E Main St; r $70-100; ⬚ ⬚ ) The six pretty rooms feature floral wallpaper and private baths. Children are welcome. A full breakfast is served in the dining room.

**Lyon's Inn** ( ☎ 435-772-6881; www.lyonsinn.com; 125 E Main St; r $65-105; ⬚ ⬚ ) The four rooms are decorated in different contemporary styles. It includes a big lawn and an outdoor hot tub.

### HURRICANE
Hurricane (pronounced locally as HER-uh-cun) is a fallback choice. It offers chains (with rates from the $50s to the $70s), including Motel 6, Best Western, Super 8, Days Inn and Comfort Inn. The exception is **Pah Tempe Hot Springs** ( ☎ 435-635-2879; 825 N 800 E), a hot spring on the Virgin River with rooms for rent; it has been closed indefinitely but hopes to reopen by late 2005.

### OUTSIDE THE EAST ENTRANCE
**Zion Ponderosa Ranch Resort** ( ☎ 435-648-2700, 800-293-5444; www.zionponderosa.com; all rates are per person: tent $69, cabin $105, cabin ste $145, children 3-11 $69; ⬚ ⬚ ⬚ ⬚ ) This all-inclusive resort is the ideal destination for activity-hungry families. 'All-inclusive' means everything – three meals a day and more activities than you can name, including canyoneering and climbing, hiking and biking, ATV tours and horseback rides, basketball, tennis, swimming, a separate kids camp and much, much more. Cabins are attractive and comfortable, and they share separate, new, spotlessly clean bathroom facilities. Rates vary depending on group size, and guests can rent a handful of homes (from $130 to $250 per person).

The turnoff for the resort is about 2 miles from park's East Entrance and about 5 miles north of Hwy 9.

## EATING
Zion Lodge is the only place within the park that serves or sells food, and unfortunately, its quality does not match its unparalleled surroundings. Thankfully, Springdale offers a multitude of choices, from quick-and-easy to fine dining, though the town is too relaxed to ever be formal.

### INSIDE THE PARK
**Red Rock Grill** ( ☎ 435-772-3213; ☷ in summer: breakfast 6-10am, lunch 11:30am-2:30pm, dinner 5-10pm, lounge 11:30am-10pm) The lodge's dining room is on the 2nd floor, and the best thing about it is the spacious deck, where you can soak up the magnificent red cliffs. Large windows bring the view inside, where the decor is classic park lodge, with lots of wood and large photos of the canyon.

Besides the view, the meals have convenience to recommend them. Breakfast is a basic buffet (adult/child $8.50/4.50), where the eggs, potatoes, sausages, blintzes and French toast sit in soggy institutional steam trays. only way to get pancakes is off the kids menu. With an hour's notice, can make a pack lunch for the day.

Lunch (items $6 to $7.50) isn't quite as bad, but your choices are no fa than the standard sandwiches, burgers and wraps.

Dinner (reservations required; entrées $12 to $21) at least reaches for something higher, but the kitchen doesn't quite bring it home. Vegetables and sides tend to be overcooked and underflavored, which describes some of the entrées as well. The salmon disappoints, while the trout is better, showing that, with luck, a good meal can be had. The menu covers a wide range of steaks, prime rib, fish, chicken and pastas. There's a wine list, liqueur-spiked coffees and a range of can't-miss chocolate-and-ice-cream desserts.

You could be excused if you missed the 'lounge,' a tiny alcove of seats behind the hostess station; the bartender and bar are inexplicably hidden in the back. Still, sitting here, you can get a beer or a hard drink and some light bar food.

Attached to the lodge, the **Castle Dome Café** (most items $3-6, whole pizza $11-15; ⏰ 11am-5pm) meets the official travel writer's definition of fast food: very basic, very cheap and very fast, with no pretensions otherwise. The cash-only café serves sandwiches, burgers, pizza, salads, soups and rice bowls of vaguely Asian flavors. Most importantly, it sells ice cream and soft-serve yogurt ($1.50 to $2.50), which you can enjoy under the lodge's giant cottonwood tree. Yum!

## SPRINGDALE

**Mean Bean** ( ☎ 435-772-0654; 932 Zion Park Blvd; items under $6; ⏰ 6:30am-5pm) If you want to know what's happening in Springdale (or the world), talk to enthusiastic Joe at the Mean Bean. His great coffee and good company draws everyone – from park rangers to climbers to shopkeepers – and his expanded menu now includes sandwiches, breakfast burritos and soon even beer.

**Zion Pizza & Noodle Company** ( ☎ 435-772-3815; www.zionpizzanoodle.com; 868 Zion Park Blvd; pizza $10-14, pasta $11; ⏰ 4-10pm) The inventive pizzas have attitude, and the pastas are good. Either way, this unpretentious, friendly joint is always jumping. Order from the counter, take a number, and a server will bring the food. Utah microbrews make any seat the perfect spot.

**Oscar's Café** ( ☎ 435-772-3232; 948 Zion Park Blvd; mains $6-14; ⏰ 8am-10pm, breakfast till 11am) The outdoor patio at popular Oscar's can become a regular United Nations of languages. The menu emphasizes Mexican standards, sandwiches and garlic burgers, but the specials get the chef's best efforts; always go for fresh fish tacos ($14) and huge rib-eye steaks ($27).

**Bit & Spur Restaurant & Saloon** ( ☎ 435-772-3498, 1212 Zion Park Blvd; mains $10-14, specials $18-24; ⏰ 5pm-midnight, dinner 5-10pm) A local institution and the liveliest spot in town, the Bit rates among southwest Utah's best restaurants. Mexican dishes like chile verde, enchiladas and flautas get gourmet treatment, and Southwest-influenced fish and rib-eye steak specials are worth the splurge. Walls are hung with wild art, and it has the only bona fide bar in Springdale (with – gasp! – a pool table). When live music happens, be here.

---

## BEST SUNSET PATIOS

✔ Front porch at the **Bit & Spur**

✔ Second-floor patio at Zion Lodge's **Red Rock Grill**

✔ Back patio at **Sol Foods Deli**

✔ Front porch at **Zion Pizza & Noodle**

✔ Back porch at **Pentimento**

**Spotted Dog Café** ( ☎ 435-772-3244; 428 Zion Park Blvd; mains $12-25; ✸ 7-11:30am, 5-10pm) Some prefer the Spotted Dog, at Flanigan's Inn, to the Bit & Spur. Its menu is certainly broader and its quality high. The gourmet, Western-style cooking includes buffalo and elk meatloaf, blackened ahi tuna, local trout and top sirloin, and there is a full bar. They also serve a recommended breakfast.

**Pentimento** ( ☎ 435-772-0490; 1515 Zion Park Blvd; dinner mains $9-20; ✸ 7-11am, 4-10pm) This upscale newcomer in the Driftwood Lodge offers a simple, classic menu done well – with generous rib-eye steaks, rack of lamb and lasagna. The twice-whipped potatoes are divine, and the homemade pies are hard to skip. They also serve breakfast ($3 to $7).

**Dolce Vita Bistro** ( ☎ 435-772-0481; Paradise Rd; crepes $9-10, salads $13; ✸ 4-10:30pm Thu-Sun) Behind Zion Pizza & Noodle, this evokes a relaxed bistro atmosphere, with glass- and slate-topped tables, a lighter menu emphasizing fancy crepes and salads, and board games for amusement. Live music occurs regularly.

**Pioneer Restaurant** ( ☎ 435-772-3009; 828 Zion Park Blvd; breakfast & lunch $4.50-8, dinner $7-16; ✸ 7am-closing; breakfast till 11:30am) The dusty Pioneer got a facelift in 2003, and the gal looks good. Thankfully unchanged is the petrified wood fireplace and the perfect country diner food. Breakfast is still the best meal, with chicken-fried steak slathered in gravy, fresh hash browns and the requisite meat and egg variations.

**Switchback Grille** ( ☎ 435-772-3700; 1149 Zion Park Blvd; lunch items $6-13, dinner mains $14-30; ✸ breakfast 7-11am, lunch 11am-2:30pm, dinner 5-9:30pm) Breakfast and lunch are served in the cafeteria-style café, while dinner is in a more formal, white-tablecloth dining room. It's good, all-American fare: sandwiches, burgers, wood-fired pizza, pasta, steak, ribs and fish, with one of the largest wine lists in town.

**Majestic View Lodge Restaurant** ( ☎ 435-772-0665, 866-772-0665; www.majesticviewlodge. com; 2400 Zion Park Blvd; lunch $6-8, dinner mains $15-25; ✸ 7am-10pm) With its antler chandeliers and mounted animal heads, this restaurant lets you know what's cooking. The fare is neither fancy nor refined, but it's an opportunity to dine on elk and buffalo in addition to plain old beef.

**Bumbleberry Restaurant** ( ☎ 435-772-3224; 897 Zion Park Blvd; breakfast $5-8.50, sandwiches $5-7.50, dinner mains $9-13; ✸ 7:30am-9pm in summer, breakfast till 11:30am) The meals at this affordable family restaurant are not special, but their delectable bumbleberry pie is. A warm slice with ice cream ($3.50) is an après-hike favorite.

To put together a pack lunch or to just get something quick and easy, here are several good choices: **Sol Foods Market & Deli** ( ☎ 435-772-0277; 95 Zion Park Blvd; items $6-8; ✸ 8am-9pm, till 6pm in winter) features a decent cafeteria-style deli – with falafel and gyros, fish and chips, burgers and wraps – and a fantastic back patio that hosts occasional musical happenings. **Springdale Fruit Company Market** ( ☎ 435-772-3222; 2491 Zion Park Blvd; sandwiches $5; ✸ 8am-8pm in summer, closed Nov-Mar) makes great focaccia sandwiches and fruit smoothies ($3) and provides a pretty picnic area amid its orchards. **Zion Park Gift & Deli** ( ☎ 435-772-3843; 866 Zion Park Blvd; sandwiches $5.50, subs $10.50; ✸ 8am-9:30pm Mon-Sat) makes generous sandwiches and whole subs and equally generous ice cream cones ($2 to $3). **Tsunami Juice & Java**

( ☎ 435-772-3818; 180 Zion Park Blvd; wraps $6; ⌚ 8am-8pm) specializes in fat but not filling wraps for the trail (get sauce on the side), plus good fruit smoothies ($4).

Rounding out the ethnic choices in town are the following basic places:

**Thai Sapa** ( ☎ 435-772-0510; 145 Zion Park Blvd; mains $9-12; ⌚ 11am-10pm Thu-Mon, 4:30-10pm Tue-Wed) Serving a mix of Thai, Chinese and Vietnamese dishes, Thai Sapa is located in the Zion Canyon Giant Screen Theatre complex.

**Panda Garden** ( ☎ 435-772-3535; 805 Zion Park Blvd; entrées $6.25-12, specials $13-19; ⌚ noon-11pm) This typical Chinese restaurant has a mile-long menu.

**Roberto's Baja Tacos** ( ☎ 435-772-6901; 445 Zion Park Blvd; plates $8-12; ⌚ 11am-11pm) More Mexican can be found at Roberto's, housed in an old gas station.

## ENTERTAINMENT

Springdale is no Moab, but it offers a few options to occupy an evening. Live music doesn't occur often, but best bets are the **Bit & Spur** (p97), **Dolce Vita Bistro** and **Sol Foods Market**.

Springdale's arts community is very active. Two groups to contact about readings and events are **The Mesa** ( ☎ 435-772-0300; www.themesa.org), a nonprofit artist-in-residence program that has brought the likes of jazz musician Stanley Crouch to town, and the Zion Canyon Arts and Humanities Council, aka **Z-Arts!** (www.zionarts.homestead.com).

**OC Tanner Amphitheater** ( ☎ 435-652-7994; www.dixie.edu/tanner; 300 Lion Blvd; adult/18 & under $9/5) Run by Dixie State College, this 2000-seat outdoor amphitheater set beneath gorgeous red cliffs hosts a live concert every Saturday at 8pm from mid-May through August. The schedule includes the symphony, bluegrass, country, folk and cowboy music; come join the locals for picnics and dancing.

**Zion Canyon Giant Screen Theatre** ( ☎ 888-256-3456, 435-772-2400; www.zioncanyontheatre.com; 145 Zion Park Blvd; adult/children 11 & under $8/5) Four times a day you can catch the 40-minute film *Zion Canyon: Treasure of the Gods* on the theater's six-story screen, Utah's largest. Much of the history is pure hokum, and some of the scenery is from other national parks, but it's stunningly beautiful nonetheless. Other IMAX-type films are shown, as are Hollywood releases at 8pm.

**Bumbleberry Playhouse** ( ☎ 866-478-4854, 435-772-3611; www.bumbleberry.com/playhouse.html; 897 Zion Park Blvd; adult/children 6-14 $17.50/10) Five nights a week in summer, the Bumbleberry puts on a nostalgia-heavy variety show.

## SHOPPING

There are gift stores aplenty in Springdale, from funky clothing boutiques to jewelry stores to souvenir shops to gem-and-rock stands with chainsaw bears out front. If you need camping or outdoor gear, check the outfitters under Canyoneering (p87).

What sets Springdale apart are its fine art galleries. The nationally recognized **Worthington Gallery** ( ☎ 435-772-3446, 800-626-9973; www.worthingtongallery.com; 789 Zion Park Blvd; ⌚ 9am-9pm) showcases 20 artists from Springdale and Utah, emphasizing simply unbelievable pottery and a few notable Southwestern painters, like Jim Jones and Willamarie Huelskamp.

Michael Fatali is the local photography rock star, capturing Zion in rich Cibachrome majesty. He lives in Rockville, but Springdale boasts his **Fatali Gallery** ( ☎ 435-772-2422; www.fatali.com; 868 Zion Park Blvd; ⌚ 4-10pm). With equal talent but a different approach, photographer David Pettit is on display at the **Driftwood Gallery** ( ☎ 435-772-3206; 1515 Zion Park Blvd; ⌚ 7am-10pm). You'll have to decide if either deserves the 'next Ansel Adams' encomium.

Those in search of authentic, high-quality Native American art and jewelry should head for **Tribal Arts Zion** ( ☎ 435-772-3353; www.tribalartszion.com; 291 Zion Park Blvd; ⌚ 10am-sunset). Tribes from all over the Southwest are represented, and the knowledgeable staff can field any questions.

## AUTOMOBILE REPAIR

**Chevron** ( ☎ 435-772-3677; 1593 Zion Park Blvd; ☺ 7am-10pm) includes a full-service garage, while **Canyon Tire & Food Mart** ( ☎ 435-772-3963; 962 Zion Park Blvd; ☺ 7am-10pm) has a full-service tire center.

## GROCERIES

New owners are turning **Sol Foods Market & Deli** ( ☎ 435-772-0277; www.solfoods.com; 95 Zion Park Blvd; ☺ market 8am-10pm, deli 8am-9pm, winter 10am-6pm) into Springdale's only true grocery store. The produce section is still weak, and meat and fish are frozen, but it has almost everything else you need. It also offers a decent camping supply section, including firewood.

**Zion Park Market** ( ☎ 435-772-3843; 855 Zion Park Blvd; ☺ 8am-9pm Mon-Sat), a sort of grocery/convenience store, has a little bit of everything, including basic camping supplies. If for no other reason, come for the ultra-cool walk-in soda and beer fridges!

It ain't cheap, but the organic **Springdale Fruit Company Market** ( ☎ 435-772-3222; 2491 Zion Park Blvd; ☺ 8am-8pm in summer, closed Nov-Mar) stocks all the high-quality fruit and vegetables you crave, as well as fresh-baked goods, fancy local condiments, soy milk and Tom's toothpaste. Its fruit orchards produce peaches and apples beginning in July.

## INTERNET ACCESS

The Springdale **Library** ( ☎ 435-772-3676; 898 Zion Park Blvd; ☺ 10am-6pm Mon, Wed & Fri, 10am-9pm Tue & Thu, 10am-5pm Sat) provides Internet terminals (30 min/$1). In 2006, the library will move to Lion Blvd beside the Town Hall. International visitors: When you return home, send the library a postcard for its world map!

Two other places with Internet access ($1/5 min) are **Sol Foods Market & Deli** and **Best Western Zion Park Inn**.

## LAUNDRY

**Zion Park Laundry** (855 Zion Park Blvd; $1.50 wash, 10 min/25¢ dry, soap 50¢; ☺ 7am-8pm, last load 7:45pm) is run by the adjacent Zion Park Market, which dispenses quarters. If you plan to do laundry on Sunday, remember to get quarters from the market on Saturday.

## LIQUOR

Springdale's only state-run liquor store is inside the Best Western Zion Park Inn's **convenience store** ( ☎ 435-772-3200, 800-934-7275; 1215 Zion Park Blvd; ☺ 8am-9pm, no liquor sales on Sun).

## MEDICAL SERVICES & EMERGENCIES

In an emergency, dial ☎ 911 or ☎ 435-772-3322. For Washington County police, fire and ambulance, call ☎ 800-624-9447. For poison control, call ☎ 800-456-7707.

**Zion Canyon Medical Clinic** (☎ 435-772-3226; 120 Lion Blvd; ⏲ 9am-5pm Tue-Sat in summer; 1 day only in winter) is a walk-in urgent care clinic. The nearest 24-hour emergency room is in St George (p102).

## MONEY

**Zions Bank** (☎ 435-772-3274; 921 Zion Park Blvd; ⏲ 9am-4pm Mon-Fri) offers currency exchange and provides a 24-hour ATM.

## PET BOARDING

**Doggy Dude Ranch** (☎ 435-772-3105; www.doggyduderanch.com; day/overnight $20/25) boards dogs and takes them on riverside walks. It's on Hwy 9, about a quarter mile west of the Springdale Fruit Company Market.

## POSTAL SERVICES

Springdale's **Post Office** (☎ 435-772-3950; 624 Zion Park Blvd; ⏲ 7:30-11:30am & noon-4pm Mon-Fri, 9am-noon Sat) also sells phone cards and posts a community bulletin board.

**Zion Canyon Visitor Center** (p61) offers a mail drop and a stamp machine, while **Best Western Zion Park Inn** (p95) has a FedEx drop box.

## PUBLIC SHOWERS

Three places in Springdale provide public showers: **Zion Canyon Campground** (p93; $3); **Tsunami Juice & Java** (p98; $4) and **Zion Rock & Mountain Guides** (p89; $3).

## TRASH & RECYCLING

Paper, glass and aluminum recycling are offered at **Sol Foods Market** (p98), the **Zion campgrounds** (p92) and **Zion Lodge** (p93).

# AROUND ZION

## ST GEORGE
**Map 3, p147 / pop 54,000 / elevation 2880ft**

St George – like its doppelganger, Las Vegas – is one of the fastest-growing cities in the country. Rather than sin and casinos, however, St George is known for retirees and golf courses – by some estimates, half the city qualifies for a senior discount. But these are *active* retirees, and this explains a lot: the care showered on the city's Mormon history, the bustling RV parks, the plethora of paved walking trails, the thriving strip malls and chain businesses, the dearth of nightlife...

Southern Utah's largest city, St George is a major gateway to Zion National Park and contains the area's only truly budget lodgings. Basing all or part of a visit here puts you within easy striking distance of Snow Canyon State Park, Pine Valley Wilderness, Cedar City and Cedar Breaks National Monument. And that's not bad at all.

### Orientation

St George is on I-15 just north of the Arizona border, 120 miles and 90 minutes from Las Vegas, and 305 miles and 4½ hours from Salt Lake City. The town lies about 40 minutes from Zion's South Entrance, 25 minutes from the Kolob Canyons entrance on I-15, and 45 minutes from Cedar City.

St George itself began life as a typical Mormon pioneer plat: it's a firm grid of numbered streets whose numbering radiates from a centerpoint and follows the compass. The center is the intersection of Main and Tabernacle Sts. The city's main commercial streets are St George Blvd and Bluff St, which with I-15 form a triangle that encompasses most of town. The street-numbering system is very logical, and in no time you'll read '100 S 300 W' and know exactly where you are, or need to be.

### Information

Northbound on I-15, 2 miles south of St George, is a **Utah Welcome Center** (☎ 435-673-4542; ⏰ 8:30am-5:30pm, later in summer) with statewide information.

The main source for town information is the **Chamber of Commerce** (☎ 435-628-1658; www.stgeorgechamber.com; 97 E St George Blvd; ⏰ 9am-5pm Mon-Fri, 10am-2pm Sat). Also useful is the city's Convention & Visitors Bureau website (www.utahsdixie.com). The **Interagency Information Center** (☎ 435-688-3246; 345 E Riverside Dr; ⏰ 7:45am-5pm Mon-Fri, 9am-5pm Sat) provides information on USFS and BLM lands, state parks and the Arizona Strip. It sells topographical and other maps and has a great selection of guides and regional histories.

Other services include the **library** (☎ 435-634-5737; 50 S Main St; ⏰ 9am-9pm Mon-Thu, 9am-6pm Fri-Sat), with Internet access ($1/hr); the **post office** (☎ 435-673-3312; 180 N Main St); **Dixie Regional Medical Center** (☎ 435-251-1000; 700 S & River Rd); **police** (☎ 435-634-5001; 175 E 200 N); the region's main 24-hour emergency medical services (☎ 911); and **Zions Bank** (☎ 435-673-4867; 40 E St George Blvd; ⏰ 9am-5pm Mon-Fri), with currency exchange and a 24-hour ATM.

**Little Professor Books** (☎ 435-674-9898; 15 N Main St; ⏰ 9am-6pm Mon-Sat) is a convenient general-interest bookstore.

### Sights

St George boasts an interesting Mormon history. The chamber publishes a good self-guided walking tour of the historic district, or you can take a guided tour with **Historic St George Live!** (☎ 435-634-5942; www.stgeorgelive.org; adult $2, children 12

& under free), which offers tours at 9am and 10:30am Tuesday through Saturday from Memorial Day to Labor Day.

### HISTORIC MORMON SITES

All of the following offer free admission and guided tours:

The 1877 **Mormon Temple** was Utah's first. The temple itself is closed to non-Mormons, but not its remodeled visitor center (☎ 435-673-5181; 440 S 300 E; 🕑 9am-9pm). The pretty **Mormon Tabernacle** (☎ 435-628-4072; Tabernacle & Main St; 🕑 9am-6pm) *is* open to the public and hosts free music programs.

St George's **Daughters of Utah Pioneers (DUP) Museum** (☎ 435-628-7274; 145 N 100 E; 🕑 10am-5pm Mon-Sat) is the best of its kind outside Salt Lake City. Its two floors are crammed with pioneer articles, furniture, newspapers, photographs, cutlery, quilts, guns and everything else.

The 1871 **Brigham Young Winter Home** (☎ 435-673-2517; 67 W 200 N; 🕑 9am-7pm) was the Mormon leader's seasonal headquarters for several years.

Just north of St George in Santa Clara, the 1863 **Jacob Hamblin Home** (☎ 435-673-2161; Santa Clara Dr; 🕑 9am-5pm, till 7pm in summer) is more evocative of the Mormon pioneer experience and mission, as reflected through Hamblin's extraordinary life.

### PIONEER CENTER FOR THE ARTS

This collection of historic buildings contains the small yet satisfying **St George Art Museum** (☎ 435-634-5942; 47 E 200 N; 🕑 6-8pm Mon, 11am-6pm Tue-Sat, till 8pm Fri; free admission). The focus is on local and Western art of all media, in both modern and traditional styles.

# DINOSAURS AT JOHNSON'S FARM

It's the third millennium, and there's nothing left to discover, right? That a Utah alfalfa farmer should, in the middle of a city of 50,000 people, unearth one of the world's largest and most important dinosaur sites – well, in the words of its discoverer, Sheldon Johnson, 'It just doesn't happen.'

It was spring 2000, and Johnson was leveling some 'useless' land. He turned over a sandstone slab with his backhoe and immediately recognized the three-toed dinosaur tracks on the underside. Curious, he turned over another, and another, and still another, and 'they all have it,' he says.

Having survived to age 74 by wits and hard work, his obvious first thought was, 'Is it possible someone's pulling a practical joke on me?'

Telling the story today, Johnson laughs, wonder still clouding his voice: 'It was unbelievable.'

In fact, no one would believe him. The Smithsonian yawned, and the state's paleontologist brushed him off, later admitting that 'we get kooks calling all the time.'

Finally, a local scientist came over, and he was stunned. The footprint molds were clearer than any he'd ever seen. As it turns out, the age, size and complexity of the site makes it one of the richest on earth. Rare and unique paleontological finds are being made practically every other month, and scientists have only scratched the surface. 'They will be excavating this site for the next 20 years,' Johnson declares.

Ever gracious, Johnson donated the land to the city of St George, which is now charged with protecting the site (p104). But he still comes by often, as much to take a grandfatherly interest in the children who visit as to make sure the city is doing right by his find.

'I hope this inspires kids long after I'm gone,' Johnson says. 'That's why we call it a discovery site, not a museum – because there's so much left to discover.'

### DINOSAUR DISCOVERY SITE

St George's oldest residents have turned out to be Jurassic-era dinosaurs. A new **museum** ( ☎ 435-674-5757; 2200 E Riverside Dr; ☼ 9am-5pm Mon-Sat; adult/child $2/1) is being built to house the growing collection of tracks and other evidence first discovered here in 2000 (p103). One day this will rank as one of the country's most important dinosaur sites. To get here, take 700 S to Riverside Drive.

### ROSENBRUCH WORLD WILDLIFE MUSEUM

More than 300 species are evocatively displayed in this **museum** ( ☎ 435-656-0033; www.rosenbruch.org; 1835 Convention Center Dr; ☼ noon-9pm Mon, 10am-6pm Tue-Sat; adult/children 3-12 $8/4), which is a tribute to wildlife and the art of taxidermy. Faux storms provide atmosphere, while the bug room is gnarly.

### SILVER REEF GHOST TOWN

This abandoned 19th-century silver mining town is at exit 23 off I-15, 13 miles northeast of St George, near Leeds. The restored Wells Fargo building houses a small museum and **art gallery** ( ☎ 435-879-2254; ☼ 9am-5pm Mon-Sat). In an adjacent building, accurate dioramas of the old town and mine provide a good feel for what it was like.

## Activities

A network of easy, paved walking and biking trails crisscross St George. Eventually, all will be connected, and the trail along the Virgin River will be extended to Zion. Pick up maps at the chamber. For good views, visit the red-rock gardens at **Pioneer Park** on Skyline Drive.

Run by a local expert, **Paragon Climbing** ( ☎ 435-673-1709; www.paragonclimbing.com) offers beginning and intermediate rock climbing courses (from $80/half day) and guided mountain biking ($35 to $45/hour).

### MOUNTAIN BIKING

First-rate slickrock mountain biking abounds around St George, particularly at **Gooseberry Mesa** and the **Green Valley Loop** (also called Bearclaw Poppie Trail).

Two good bike shops, with full-day rentals for $35, are **Red Rock Bicycle Company** ( ☎ 435-674-3185; 446 W 100 S; ☼ 9am-7pm Mon-Sat) and **Bicycles Unlimited** ( ☎ 435-673-4492, 888-673-4492; www.bicyclesunlimited.com; 90 S 100 E; ☼ 8am-7pm Mon-Sat), which also sells topographical maps.

### SWIMMING

In Santa Clara, the modern, indoor **Sand Hollow Aquatic Center** ( ☎ 435-634-5938; 1144 N Lava Flow Dr; ☼ 1-9pm Mon-Fri, noon-6pm Sat; adult/children 3-17 $6/5.50) is as good as any water park and offers the perfect summer escape. Extensive facilities satisfy everyone, from Olympic hopefuls to teens and even toddlers.

### GOLF

The following courses are open to the public. The first three charge $16/27 for nine/18 holes in winter; Sunbrook charges $23.50/43. Prices drop in summer. You can reserve tee times up to two weeks in advance.

**Dixie Red Hills** ( ☎ 435-634-5852; 1250 N 645 W), nine holes/par 34
**Southgate** ( ☎ 435-628-0000; 1975 S Tonaquint Dr), 18 holes/par 70
**St George Golf Club** ( ☎ 435-634-5854; 2190 S 1400 E), 18 holes/par 73
**Sunbrook** ( ☎ 435-634-5866; 2366 Sunbrook Dr), 27 holes/par 36 each nine

## Festivals & Events

Avoid St George around Easter, when it serves as Utah's spring-break capital.

Mid-September ropes in the **Dixie Roundup** (☎ 435-628-8282), a PRCA rodeo, and the scenic **St George Marathon** (www.stgeorgemarathon.com), which descends from the Pine Valley Mountains. October welcomes the **World Senior Games** (www.seniorgames.net).

## Sleeping

Lodgings are plentiful and affordable in St George. Troll St George Blvd and Bluff St near I-15 for the most choices.

Nearly every chain hotel known to humankind is represented, including Motel 6, Super 8, Budget Inn, Quality Inn, Claridge Inn, Fairfield Inn, Days Inn, Comfort Inn, Travelodge, Econo Lodge, Best Western, Ramada Inn, Comfort Suites and Holiday Inn. All offer the comfort of knowing exactly what you'll get.

### CAMPING

Flocks of snowbirds fill St George's many RV parks every winter. Folks in tents are better off at Snow Canyon State Park (p107) or in Springdale (p93).

**Settler's RV Park** (☎ 435-628-1624, 800-628-1624; www.settlersrv.com; 1333 E 100 S; tent $20, RV hookup $26) is the most convenient RV park in town, providing more than 150 RV sites, a handful of tent sites and full facilities, including laundry, showers, a game room, pool and more.

### BUDGET

Prices are more attractive than the rooms at most budget motels in St George. Ask to see your room first, but be prepared for stains and scuffs. Those below are among the best and offer acceptable levels of cleanliness. A dozen others also have rooms in the $30s midweek and the $40s on weekends.

**Sullivan's Rococo Inn** (☎ 435-628-3671, 888-628-3671; 511 S Airport Rd; s $31-40, d $45-50; 🞉 🞊 🗙) If the owner spruced up the rooms, this inn could charge another $15 for the views alone. On a bluff by the generally quiet municipal airport, the scruffy hotel offers a valentine to St George every sunset.

**Dixie Palm Motel** (☎ 435-673-3531; 185 E St George Blvd; r midweek $34-45, weekend $40-70; 🞉 🗙) It may not look like much from the outside, but regular maintenance and attention put this ahead of the pack. The 15 good rooms include refrigerators and microwaves.

**Ancestor Inn** (☎ 435-673-4666, 800-864-6882; 60 W St George Blvd; r midweek $30-35, weekend $35-40; 🞉 🞊 🗙) The 60 rooms are dull but well kept; 20 feature kitchenettes.

Other acceptable but rough-around-the-edges choices include:

**Chalet Motel** (☎ 435-628-6272; 664 E St George Blvd; r midweek/weekend $38/44; 🞉 🗙)

**Sands Motel** (☎ 435-673-3501; 581 E St George Blvd; 1/2 beds $35/40; 🞉 🗙)

**Sun Time Inn** (☎ 435-673-6181, 800-237-6253; 420 E St George Blvd; d midweek/weekend $40/70) Overpriced on weekends.

### MID-RANGE

**Best Inn & Suites** (☎ 435-652-3030, 800-718-0297; 245 N Red Cliffs Dr; d midweek/weekend $50/60; 🞉 🞊 ▢ 🗙) This attractive chain is well positioned for fast getaways out of town. It provides a coin laundry.

**Singletree Inn** (☎ 435-673-6161, 800-528-8890; 260 E St George Blvd; d $50 -60; 🞉 🞊 ▢ 🗙) This independent is very clean and comparable to the chains.

**Coronada Vacation Village** (☎ 435-628-4436; 559 E St George Blvd; d midweek/weekend $50/75; 🞉 🞊 🗙) Though faded and worn, rooms are bigger than most, with full kitchens and eat-in areas. Weekly rates are a better deal.

**Best Western Coral Hills** (☎ 435-673-4844; www.coralhills.com; 125 E St George Blvd; r midweek/weekend $71/85; 🞉 🞊 🗙) This location of the dependable Best Western chain provides two nice pools along with its comforting level of amenities.

**Greene Gate Village** ( ☎ 435-628-6999, 800-350-6999; www.greenegatevillageinn.com; 76 W Tabernacle; r $80-180, add $20 on weekends; 🏃 🖴 ✂ ) This complex of 14 rooms in nine historic buildings (which can be rented in their entirety) is an attractive B&B option. All rooms feature lovely antiques, TVs, refrigerators and private modern bathrooms; full breakfast is included. Grounds include a relaxing pool and picnic area.

**The Seven Wives Inn** ( ☎ 435-628-3737, 800-600-3737; www.sevenwivesinn.com; 217 N 100 W; r $95-250; 🏃 🖴 ✂ ) This is another eclectic and historic B&B property. Of its 13 named rooms, Sarah ($250) is playfully idiosyncratic and worth a splurge, with a retro gas pump and a private hot tub inside a Model T Ford. Ada ($225) is a pretty, separate cottage with a half kitchen. All rooms include a private bath and full breakfast. The inn also offers a midweek five-course dinner by reservation only ($35).

## Eating

St George may seem a culinary purgatory of bland chains, but you'll find a handful of saving graces.

**The Bean Scene** ( ☎ 435-574-6434; 511 E St George Blvd; 🕑 6am-7pm Mon-Fri, 7am-4pm Sat, 8am-1pm Sun; sandwiches $4.50) What, you say, a bohemian coffeehouse in St George? With a bona fide art gallery, Saturday night happenings, steamed espresso and a chill vibe, what else would you call it?

**Jazzy Java** ( ☎ 435-674-1678; 285 N Bluff St; 🕑 6am-5pm Mon-Fri, 7am-4pm Sat, 8am-2pm Sun; items $2.50-8) St George's other funky coffeeshop features a larger food selection, with real breakfasts of pancakes and eggs and a good range of sandwiches and salads.

**Bear Paw Coffee Company** ( ☎ 435-634-0126; 75 N Main St; 🕑 7am-3pm; items $7-9) This recommended breakfast place will satisfy everyone with its wide-ranging menu, but Belgian waffles are a specialty.

Those in need of let's-sit-down-and-eat, family-friendly sustenance can head to **Ancestor Square** at Main and St George Blvd, which serves easy and cheap pizza, pasta, Mexican and Chinese (closed Sun).

Or, head to **Chuck-A-Rama** ( ☎ 435-673-4464; 127 N Red Cliffs Dr; 🕑 11am-9pm Mon-Sat, 11am-8pm Sun; lunch/dinner $7/9), a surprisingly good all-you-can-eat buffet that's always elbow to elbow with Mormon families and seniors. It's a Utah institution.

**Irmita's** ( ☎ 435-652-0161; 500 S Bluff; 🕑 11am-3pm Mon, 11am-8pm Tue-Sat; plates $6) This family-run shack with palm-frond umbrellas out front dishes up the city's best Mexican. The salsa bar will cure what ails you.

**Alvaro's** ( ☎ 435-656-5746; 471 N 1680 E; 🕑 24hr; items $2.50-6) This is authentic Mexican fast food with an all-night drive-through window. For some, that makes it indispensable.

**Samurai 21** ( ☎ 435-656-8628; 245 N Red Cliff Dr; 🕑 11:30am-2:30pm & 4:30-10pm Mon-Sat, 4:30-9pm Sun; hibachi, teriyaki & sushi $15-20) Come for the grillside hibachi show, regular dining or the sushi bar. This above-average Japanese restaurant shimmers like an oasis in a land of Applebee's.

**Sullivan's Rococo Steak House** ( ☎ 435-628-3671; 511 S Airport Rd; 🕑 11:30-3pm Mon-Fri, 5-10pm nightly; prime rib $22-28, steak & seafood $18-31) Sullivan's boasts first-class city views to go with its succulent prime rib and grilled steaks. Romantic carnivores will leave sated.

**Scaldoni's** ( ☎ 435-674-1300; www.scaldonis.com; 929 W Sunset Blvd at Valley View; 🕑 11:30am-10pm Mon-Sat, 5-9pm Sun; dinner entrées $11-28) This classic upscale Italian restaurant works hard to conjure romance in its strip-mall setting. The well-reviewed menu runs from filet mignon, cioppino and veal marsala to the requisite pastas. There is also a full bar.

**Painted Pony** ( ☎ 435-634-1700; 2 W St George Blvd, Ancestor Square; ⏰ 11:30am-10pm Mon-Sat; sandwiches $8, dinner entrées $17-25) The Pony offers fine dining by any standard, and it's almost revolutionary in St George. Nuances of presentation and preparation grace most dishes, which, like the decor, feature a Southwestern flare. Drawing raves are the rib-eye steak, pan-roasted escolar and the grilled portobello sandwich.

## Entertainment

Classic Broadway musicals are alive and kicking. If in doubt, check out the **St George Musical Theater** ( ☎ 435-628-8755; www.sgmt.org; 37 S 100 W), which offers performances year-round, or the outdoor **Tuacahn Amphitheater** ( ☎ 435-652-3300, 800-746-9882; www.tuacahn.org), 10 miles northwest in Ivins, which hosts musicals in summer and a variety of other performances year-round.

From October to May, Dixie College ( ☎ 435-652-7994; www.dixie.edu/concerts) hosts a Celebrity Concert Series at the **Fine Arts Center Theater** ( ☎ 435-628-3121; 225 S 700 E).

There are also several **cinema complexes** ( ☎ 435-673-1994) in town.

## Getting There & Away

**St George Municipal Airport** ( ☎ 435-673-3451; 444 S River Rd) sits on a bluff above town.

**Skywest Airlines** ( ☎ 435-634-3000, 800-453-9417; www.skywest.com) operates five flights daily to and from Salt Lake City and two flights to Los Angeles. Commercial service will expand when the new airport is completed.

**Greyhound** ( ☎ 435-673-2933, 800-231-2222) leaves from the McDonald's at 1235 S Bluff. Buses follow I-15, with connections at Salt Lake City ($54, six hours) and Las Vegas ($30, two hours).

**St George Shuttle** ( ☎ 435-628-8320, 800-933-8320; www.stgshuttle.com) runs daily vans to Las Vegas Airport ($25) and Salt Lake ($55). You can also try **Red Rock Shuttle** ( ☎ 435-635-9104), which advertises the same destinations, as well as Brian Head, Utah (from $65).

## Getting Around

**SunTran** ( ☎ 435-673-8726) is St George's new public transit system. Its three routes run 6am to 8pm Monday through Friday and 8am to 6pm Saturday. The fare is $1, and buses include bike racks. Signs mark the flag stops.

If you need a rental car, **Avis** ( ☎ 435-627-2002) and **National** ( ☎ 435-673-5098) operate from the airport, and **Enterprise** ( ☎ 435-634-1556, 652 E St George Blvd) is in town.

If you need a taxi, call **Taxi USA** ( ☎ 435-656-1500).

## SNOW CANYON STATE PARK

In this beautiful canyon, red-and-white sandstone flows like lava, and lava lies broken like sheets of smashed marble. Small and accessible, Snow Canyon is a human-scale, amusement-park version of southwest Utah: Short easy trails lead to tiny slot canyons, cinder cones, lava tubes and vast fields of undulating slickrock. It provides instant gratification for the under-10 set and is gorgeous no matter what your age.

You'll also find great **rock climbing**, particularly for beginners, with more than 150 traditional bolted and sport routes, plus top roping. Recommended 1- to 3-mile **hiking** routes include Jenny's and Johnson Canyons, Petrified Dunes and Hidden Pinyon. **Cycling** is popular on the main road through the park, a 17-mile loop from St George.

The only catch is that summer is blazing hot, so plan your activities for early morning, or come in spring or fall, when the park is at its busiest.

Outside of summer, the scenic campground is great. The park provides showers, and campers can **reserve** ( ☎ 800-322-3770; tent/RV $14/17) about 20 of its

33 sites. Day use is $5 per vehicle. For further information, contact the **park** (☎ 435-628-2255).

From St George, take Hwy 18 north 1.5 miles to Snow Canyon Parkway and follow signs past Ivins' gated retirement communities to the main entrance.

For the record, it does snow here.

## PINE VALLEY MOUNTAIN WILDERNESS AREA

At 70 sq miles, this is Utah's second-largest wilderness area, and it is wilderness the way God intended it – mountainous, forested and garlanded in rushing streams. The mountains rise sharply, and the highest point, Signal Peak (10,365ft), remains capped by snow till July.

In midsummer, when the pulsating painted desert is liquefying your brain, Pine Valley offers quiet, temperate, but still-challenging hiking. Many hikes begin as strenuous climbs. The 5-mile **Mill Canyon Trail** and the 6-mile **Whipple Trail** are the most popular routes, each linking up with the 35-mile **Summit Trail**. *Loving the Laccolith,* by Bridget McColville, is the best hiking guide.

A small trout-stocked reservoir attracts local anglers.

The wilderness area is usually open May 15 to October 1; day use is $2 per vehicle. Its popular campgrounds ($8 to $11) provide water but not showers; bring mosquito repellent. Most are first-come, first-served, though you can **reserve** (☎ 877-444-6777) a few sites. The ranger station in St George (p102) can provide further information and free backcountry camping permits.

A few miles outside the wilderness area is the bucolic, tiny town of Pine Valley, first settled in the 1850s. The **Pine Valley Chapel** (Forest Rd & E Main St; � 10am-6pm Mon-Sat, noon-6pm Sun) was built in 1868 by Ebenezer Bryce, and free guided tours spotlight Bryce's unique handiwork.

In theory, the **Pine Valley Heritage Center** (☎ 435-574-2463) on E Main St provides information Monday through Saturday, but it's unreliable and often closed.

The only lodging option is **Pine Valley Resort** (☎ 435-574-2544, 435-574-3500; www.pinevalleyutahresort.com; 960 E Main St; r $80, cabin $60), which features four attractive lodge rooms and six rustic camping cabins. The **café** (☐ 7am-9pm Wed-Sat, 7am-7pm Sun) serves good, no-frills country cooking, while the **general store** (☐ 8am-8pm) sells basic camping supplies, canned goods and ice cream. You'll also find public showers ($2) and horseback and hayrides.

From St George, take Hwy 18 to Central and head east to Pine Valley (about 32 miles); the wilderness area lies a few miles farther, within the Dixie National Forest.

## CEDAR CITY

**Map 4, p148 / pop 21,500 / elevation 5800ft**

Southern Utah's second-largest town, Cedar City serves as a pleasant stopover for travelers headed to Zion, Bryce, Cedar Breaks or Brian Head, particularly in summer, when cooler temperatures and the nationally acclaimed Shakespearean Festival provide welcome diversions.

### Orientation & Information

Cedar City is on I-15, 55 miles from (and 3000ft higher than) St George, 180 miles from Las Vegas and 260 miles from Salt Lake City. Bryce Canyon and Zion's South Entrance are about 90 minutes away, while Zion's Kolob Canyons section lies just 20 miles south on I-15. Most Cedar City businesses front Main St.

Offering free Internet access, the **Cedar City & Brian Head Tourism & Convention Bureau** (☎ 435-586-5124, 800-354-4849; www.scenicsouthernutah.com; 581 N Main St; ☐ 8am-5pm Mon-Fri, also 9am-1pm Sat in summer) shares space with the **Chamber of Commerce** (☎ 435-586-4484; www.chambercedarcity.com) and a Daughters of Utah Pioneers Museum.

## THE PLAY'S THE THING

Southern Utah's main event is Cedar City's annual Shakespearean Festival, which has been held at SUU every year since 1962. In 2000 it won the Tony Award for Outstanding Regional Theater. While the top-quality plays are indeed the thing, the entire city vibrates with activity and excitement, transforming a simple night at the theater into a true event whose warm glow lingers long after the lights have faded.

In summer (late June to September), the festival presents three of the bard's plays plus three stage classics. In the extended fall season (mid-September to mid-October), it presents two more theatrical chestnuts. Summer performances are preceded by a free Greenshow, a mini-Renaissance Fair's worth of fiddles and mallet drums, songs and dancing, fair maidens hawking fruit tarts and vaudeville jokes in English accents. The festival also offers free seminars on the plays, Renaissance feasts, backstage visits, child care during performances and much more.

Shakespeare's plays are performed in the roofless Adams Memorial Theater, a reproduction of London's original Globe Theater, while other plays are performed in nearby Randall Jones Theater. **Reservations** ( ☎ 435-586-7878, 800-752-9849; www.bard.org; tickets $20-42) are highly recommended, as most shows sell out. On the day of each performance, the festival makes available 66 last-row gallery bench seats ($12 to $16), with excellent if slightly obstructed views. Arrive when the box office opens, at 10am, for the best chance at getting one.

The **Dixie National Forest Cedar City Ranger Station** ( ☎ 435-865-3200; 1789 N Wedgewood Lane; 8am-5pm Mon-Fri) provides information on the trails and campgrounds along Hwy 14. The **BLM** ( ☎ 435-586-2401;176 E DL Sargent Dr; 7:45am-4:30pm Mon-Fri) manages most of the land west of I-15, known for its herds of wild horses.

Other services include the modern **library** ( ☎ 435-586-6661; 303 N 100 E; 9am-9pm Mon-Thu, 9am-6pm Fri-Sat), with free Internet access; **post office** ( ☎ 435-586-6701; 333 N Main St); **Valley View Medical Center** ( ☎ 435-868-5000; 1303 N Main St); **police** ( ☎ 435-586-2956; 10 N Main St); and **Zions Bank** ( ☎ 435-586-7614; 3 S Main St; 9am-5pm Mon-Fri, 9am-1pm Sat), with currency exchange and a 24-hour ATM.

**Mountain West Books** ( ☎ 435-586-3828; 77 N Main St; 9am-7pm Mon-Fri, 9am-6pm Sat) is a good general-interest bookstore.

## Sights & Activities

**Iron Mission State Park** ( ☎ 435-586-9290; 635 N Main St; 9am-6pm, closed Sun in winter; $2 per person, $6 per family) is an attractive museum focused on Mormon pioneers and their early attempts at mining. Also on display are scores of brightly painted 19th-century stagecoaches and buggies, a garden of rusting farm equipment and a model-train diorama of historic Cedar City.

Founded in 1897, **Southern Utah University** (SUU; ☎ 435-586-7700; www.suu.edu; 351 W Center) features a pleasant, green campus that hosts an annual Shakespearean Festival. It also contains the intimate **Braithwaite Fine Arts Gallery** ( ☎ 435-586-5432; noon-7pm Mon-Fri; free admission), which is currently open only during the school year.

Popularly called the Rock Church, the **Mormon Tabernacle** (75 E Center) was built in 1931 from locally quarried rock; free tours are offered in summer, though hours are unreliable.

Wonderful opportunities for hiking and biking abound. At the foot of 300 E, the recommended 8-mile, unpaved **C Trail** is a strenuous hike or bike. **Canyon**

**Park** (400 E at College Ave) marks the start of the paved **Canyon Walking Trail**, which leads past painted cliffs for several miles along Hwy 14. Hwy 14 itself offers lots of great trails (see p112), as does nearby **Brian Head Resort** (Hwy 143 north of Cedar Breaks; ☎ 435-677-3101; www.brianhead.com), which is a ski resort in winter and a premier mountain biking destination in summer.

**Cedar Cycle** ( ☎ 435-586-5210; www.cedarcyle.com; 38 E 200 S; ☺ 9am-5pm Mon-Fri, 9am-2pm Sat) rents mountain bikes ($20 to $30/day), does repairs and can point you to more trails.

## Festivals & Events

Cedar City has been dubbed Festival City USA for good reason. Its events calendar is looong. Contact the tourism bureau to find out what's happening while you're here. Highlights include the **Utah Summer Games** ( ☎ 435-586-7872) – the state's largest amateur sporting event – a Renaissance fair, a film festival, a Paiute Powwow, a vintage car show and a Western rodeo and stampede.

## Sleeping

### CAMPING

**Cedar City KOA** ( ☎ 435-586-9872; 1121 N Main St; tent/RV $23/31, 1-/2-room cabin $43/60; ⊋ ▢ ) This typically clean, full-service KOA provides showers, a public laundry, pool, playground, grocery store and movie theater.

You'll find several USFS campgrounds nearby on Hwy 14 (p112).

### BUDGET

Cedar City budget lodgings look worse on the outside than they do inside; competition keeps the level of maintenance high. Rates vary widely but tend to be high too, particular during the Shakespearean Festival and other event weekends.

The recommendations below are all decent, kept up and clean, and most rooms include refrigerators.

**Cedar Rest Motel** ( ☎ 435-586-9471; 479 S Main St; r $36-45; ⊠ ⊠ )

**Best Value Inn** ( ☎ 435-586-6557, 888-315-2378; 323 S Main St; r $45-52; ⊠ ⊋ ⊠ )

**Super 7 Motel** ( ☎ 435-586-6566; 190 S Main St; s/d from $45/55; ⊠ ⊠ )

You'll find a Motel 6 and a Super 8 at exit 59 off I-15.

### MID-RANGE

Cedar City's mid-range options are chain, or chain-equivalent, hotels. All provide a swimming pool, reliable cleanliness and inoffensive decor. In addition to the choices listed below, Cedar City hosts Rodeway Inn, Comfort Inn, Days Inn, Quality Inn and Holiday Inn.

**Abbey Inn** ( ☎ 435-586-9966, 800-325-5411; www.abbeyinncedar.com; 940 W 200 N; midweek/weekend $86/100; ⊠ ⊋ ⊠ ) Richer decor and a full breakfast make this a better choice.

**Stratford Court Hotel** ( ☎ 435-586-2433, 877-688-8884; www.stratfordcourthotel.com; 18 S Main St; r from $90; ⊠ ⊋ ▢ ⊠ ) Includes coin laundry.

**Best Western El Rey Inn** ( ☎ 435-586-6518, 800-688-6518; www.bwelrey.com; 80 S Main St; r $70-100; ⊠ ⊋ ▢ ⊠ ) Rooms include data ports.

**Ramada Limited** ( ☎ 435-586-9916, 800-272-6232; 281 S Main St; r from $60; ⊠ ⊋ ⊠ ) This is a Ramada 'Limited,' so it's a bit cheaper.

**Crystal Inn** ( ☎ 435-586-8888, 888-787-6661; www.crystalinns.com; 1575 W 200 N; r from $70; ⊠ ⊋ ▢ ⊠ ) Includes an attached restaurant.

### TOP END

To do Cedar City right, you should stay in one of its ever-growing number of plush, romantic B&Bs. All are completely nonsmoking and serve a full breakfast, and most discourage children under 12. Stop by the visitor center for a full list, or visit the website www.lodgingcedarcity.com. Reservations are essential.

**Big Yellow Inn** ( ☎ 435-586-0960; www.bigyellowinn.com; 234 S 300 W; r $100-190; 🅿 🖳 ⊠ ) This beautiful Georgian Revival–style home features 11 eclectic, sumptuously furnished, exceedingly comfortable rooms, all with private bath; the tastefully opulent decor ranges from Western to Oriental to full-on Victoriana. A house across the street offers five more rooms ($100). Public areas are just as memorable and include a dining room, library and fully equipped guest office.

**Garden Cottage B&B** ( ☎ 435-586-4919, 866-586-4919; www.thegardencottagebnb.com; 16 N 200 W; r $100-110; 🅿 ⊠ ) A lovely nostalgic air infuses the five charming rooms here, which feature private baths, antiques, handmade lace and embroidery, floral wallpapers, hardwood floors, quilts and historic photos of the owner's Mormon forebears. When in bloom, the gardens are a stunning fantasia.

**Bard's Inn B&B** ( ☎ 435-586-6612; www.bardsbandb.com; 150 S 100 W; r $80-95; 🅿 ⊠ ) An easy walk to the Shakespearean Festival, the seven attractive rooms here boast beautiful antiques, if somewhat more modest decor.

**Baker House B&B** ( ☎ 435-867-5695, 888-611-8181; www.bakerhouse.net; 1800 W Royal Hunte Dr; r $110-160; 🅿 ⊠ ) The five rooms in this Queen Anne Victorian–style home are another luxurious choice; all feature king beds, Jacuzzis and fireplaces and are designed to the Victorian nines.

## Eating

It would be nice if Cedar City offered fine dining to go with its pampering B&Bs and first-rate theater – alas, it does not. Instead, it relies on diners and uninspired American-style restaurants to feed the masses. Main St hosts numerous affordable choices that will keep you from going hungry; most are open daily. Below are the town's few highlights.

**Pastry Pub** ( ☎ 435-867-1400; 86 W Center; ☾ 7:30am-10pm Mon-Sat; items $3.50-6) This friendly gathering spot serves fresh baked goods, quesadillas, salads and sandwiches, plus good coffee and yummy espresso shakes ($3.25). During the Shakespearean Festival, it stays open till midnight.

**Blue Kat** ( ☎ 435-867-0041; www.bluekatco.com; 90 W Hoover; ☾ 7am-midnight Mon-Sat; pizza $7-12, sandwiches $7-8) This new restaurant and live music club is aiming to shake up Cedar City. It serves specialty pizzas with funky names and toasted sub sandwiches, which you can wash down with a real live beer.

**Sulli's Steakhouse** ( ☎ 435-586-6761; 301 S Main St; ☾ 6-10pm; entrées $13-27) It's not fancy or romantic, but the dinner-only menu covers the classic Italian and steak and seafood bases, and it offers a full bar.

Along Hwy 14 are two unpretentious and very popular Western steakhouses: **Rusty's Ranch House** ( ☎ 435-586-3839; ☾ 5-10pm Mon-Sat) is 2 miles east of Cedar City, and **Milt's Stage Stop** ( ☎ 435-586-9344; ☾ 5-10pm) is 5 miles east. Both serve dinner only ($12 to $20). Rusty's leans toward steaks and barbecue, while Milt's is more steaks and seafood.

Or, indulge in a bit of touristy fun at **Bar G Chuckwagon** ( ☎ 435-586-9700, www.bargchuckwagon.com; 3308 N Bulldog Rd; adult/children 9 & under $20/10), which dishes up a cowboy comedy and music show during its Old West chuckwagon dinners every night from May 30 to September 1. It's just outside Cedar City; reservations are required.

## Entertainment

The **Heritage Center** ( ☎ 435-865-2882; www.heritagectr.org; 105 N 100 E) hosts performances year-round, including a **Neil Simon Festival** ( ☎ 435-327-8673; www.simonfest.org) and the **American Folk Ballet** ( ☎ 435-586-7872) in summer. The pretty lobby displays rotating art exhibits.

The **Blue Kat** ( ☎ 435-867-0041; www.bluekatco.com; 90 W Hoover; ☾ 7am-midnight Mon-Sat) not only brings live jazz, folk, bluegrass and rock to Cedar City almost nightly – which is accomplishment enough – it actually *feels* like a late-night club. Cover charges range from free to $5. It's worth searching out.

## Getting There & Around

**Cedar City Regional Airport** ( ☎ 435-867-9408; www.cedarcity.org/airport.html; 2281 W Kittyhawk Dr) is a mile out of town, and **Skywest Airlines** ( ☎ 435-586-3033, 800-453-9417; www.skywest.com) flies to and from Salt Lake City daily (from $100 one way).

Greyhound no longer stops in Cedar City; the closest stop is Parowan, 20 miles away. The **St George Shuttle** ( ☎ 435-628-8320, 800-933-8320; www.stgshuttle.com) can take you from Cedar City to Salt Lake City ($55), but it doesn't go to St George.

The local **CATS bus system** ( ☎ 435-559-7433; ☒ 7am-5:30pm Mon-Fri, 10am-6:30pm Sat) runs a single route through town. The fare is $1.

If you need a rental car, **Avis** ( ☎ 435-867-9898) and **National** ( ☎ 435-586-4004) operate from the airport, while **Enterprise** ( ☎ 435-865-7636, 800-325-8007; 360 N Main) and **Speedy Rental** ( ☎ 435-586-7369; 650 N Main) are in town.

If you need a taxi, call the **Iron County Shuttle** ( ☎ 435-865-7076).

# HWY 14 EAST OF CEDAR CITY

As scenic drives go, Hwy 14 is one of the best. It leads 42 miles over the Markagunt Plateau, cresting at 10,000ft and offering unbelievable vistas of Zion National Park and Arizona to the south. Along the way you'll find several hiking trails, fishing lakes and lodges, and USFS campgrounds (all $10, with water). Stop by the Dixie National Forest Cedar City Ranger Station (p109) for maps and information. Though Hwy 14 remains open and plowed all winter, snow tires or chains are required between November and April.

Highly recommended trails with tremendous views, particularly at sunset, include the very short **Cascade Falls** and **Bristlecone Trails** and the 32-mile **Virgin River Rim Trail**, accessible at numerous points. A signed turnoff 24.5 miles east of Cedar City leads to acres of jumbled lava beds.

A half mile farther, pretty **Navajo Lake** features a small marina with boat rentals, trout fishing, a **lodge** (www.navajolakelodge.com), a store, and three campgrounds. These facilities are open Memorial Day through October.

Thirty miles east of Cedar City, **Duck Creek** hosts a seasonal USFS **ranger station** ( ☎ 435-682-2432; ☒ 10am-5pm Memorial Day to Labor Day), a campground, gas, a grocery store, diners, more fishing and several lodges. One rustic possibility is **Falcon's Nest Cabins** ( ☎ 435-682-256; www.falconsnestduckcreeklodging.com; cabin $75-90).

A couple of miles east of Duck Creek, a signed, passable dirt road leads about 10 miles to **Strawberry Point**, offering what some feel are the best views of all.

# CEDAR BREAKS NATIONAL MONUMENT

If southern Utah held a natural beauty contest, Cedar Breaks would be a finalist. In its wildly eroded and striped natural amphitheater, sculpted cliffs and hoodoos glow like neon tie-dye – a kaleidoscope of magenta, salmon, plum, rust and ochre. Geologists refer to Cedar Breaks as the icing on the Grand Staircase cake – it contains the same geologic layers as Bryce Canyon but is more than a thousand feet higher, rising to 10,450ft atop the Markagunt Plateau. As a visual feast, it is equally rich and buttery.

Snow typically closes this tiny park between October and late May, when plows finally clear Hwy 148. From Memorial Day to Labor Day, the **visitor center** ( ☎ 435-586-9451; www.nps.gov/cebr; ☒ 8am-6pm) is open, and rangers hold hourly geology talks throughout the day. Entrance is $3 per person, and national park passes are accepted. The pretty, first-come, first-served 28-site campground ($12) provides water and restrooms but no showers and is rarely full. The weather has something to do with that: Summer temperatures range from 40°F to 70°F, and brief storms can drop rain, hail and even snow.

Including **Point Supreme** at the visitor center, the park offers five viewpoints off Hwy 148 and just two 4-mile round-trip trails, which trace the rim; no park trails descend into the breaks. The best views are along the **Ramparts Trail**, which leaves from the visitor center. In a mile it reaches Spectra Point, and in another mile it ends at an unnamed promontory, dropping 400ft along the way. Ranking among the best trails in this guide, Ramparts offers indescribable views. Due to the elevation, it should be considered moderately difficult; you'll quickly get winded.

A mostly forested loop just back from the rim, the **Alpine Pond Trail** is beautiful but less dramatic. Experienced hikers might consider tackling the difficult and unmaintained 9-mile **Rattlesnake Creek Trail**, which skirts the edge of the park in the adjacent national forest and drops to the canyon floor.

Take Hwy 14 to reach Hwy 148 and Cedar Breaks, about 22 miles from Cedar City, 60 miles from Bryce and 70 miles from the Zion's East Entrance.

## GLENDALE & AROUND

Four small, historic Mormon towns dot Hwy 89 just north of its junction with Hwy 9 east of Zion: Mt Carmel Junction, Mt Carmel, Orderville and Glendale. Like Kanab, they're at a crossroads for the region's attractions, but few people ever stop, and that's part of their charm.

For regional information, contact the **East Zion Tourism Council** ( ☎ 435-648-2174; www.eastziontourismcouncil.org).

In Mt Carmel, the beautiful **Maynard Dixon Home & Studio** ( ☎ 435-648-2653; www.maynarddixon.com; ⏰ hours vary, May–Oct) is where Western artist Maynard Dixon (1875–45) lived and worked with his second wife, artist Edith Hamlin, from 1939 until his death in 1946. Docent-led tours ($20 per person) are by appointment only; the three buildings house works by Dixon and Hamlin, plus photos by his first wife, Dorothea Lange, and his friend Ansel Adams. If the red gate is open, you can take a self-guided tour ($5) of the grounds only. The home is at mile marker 84 on Hwy 89 and is easy to miss. The Maynard Dixon Country Art Show is held in August.

In Glendale, **Glendale Bench Rd** accesses Johnson Canyon and Skutumpah Rds in Grand Staircase–Escalante National Monument. To reach it, turn onto 300 North from Hwy 89; a faded 'Glendale Bench' sign marks the intersection.

In Glendale, the seven-room **Historic Smith Hotel** ( ☎ 435-648-2156, 800-528-3558; www.historicsmithhotel.com; 295 N Main St; r $44-80; ✷ ✕ ) offers a taste of true country hospitality. Rooms are comfortable, eclectic and homey, featuring bunk beds, antiques, quilts, handwoven rugs, family photos and old-fashioned needlepoint art. Children are welcome, the homemade breakfast is delicious, and owners Bunny and Rochelle are quite charming.

Next door, the unpretentious **Buffalo Bistro** ( ☎ 435-648-2778; 305 N Main St; ⏰ 1-8pm Thu-Mon; burgers $7, mains $17-28) conjures an Old West spirit with its breezy porch and outdoor grill sizzling with buffalo steaks, wild boar and Utah elk ribs, rabbit-and-rattlesnake sausage and, yes, rocky mountain oysters. For more, attend its riotously impolite Testicle Festival in late June.

If you just need a bed, Mt Carmel Junction offers a couple of options: The **Best Western Thunderbird Resort** ( ☎ 435-648-2203, 888-848-6358; www.bwthunderbird.com; r $88; ✷ ✿ ✕ ) features 61 dependable chain rooms and a bland restaurant, while the well-used **Golden Hills Motel** ( ☎ 435-648-2268, 800-648-2268; www.goldenhillsmotel.com; r $38-46; ✷ ✿ ✕ ) is just clean enough for the price.

*Graceful spires of pink, yellow, white and orange hoodoos stand like sentinels at the eroding escarpment that is Bryce Canyon National Park.*

## EXPERIENCING
# BRYCE CANYON

Though the smallest of southern Utah's national parks, Bryce is the most visually stunning, particularly at sunrise and sunset, when an orange wash sets the otherworldly rock formations ablaze with color, an awe-inspiring sight. Not actually a canyon, Bryce comprises the eastern edge of an 18-mile-long plateau, whose steep cliffs have eroded into jutting fins and spindly towers of pastel-hued limestone and sandstone. These eerie towers form horseshoe-shaped amphitheaters that drop 1000ft to the undulating high-mountain desert below. Down on the canyon floor, under the rim, you can hike among vanilla-scented cedar trees and towering pines.

The park's Pink Cliffs mark the top step of the Grand Staircase, the giant geologic terrace that begins in the Grand Canyon and tops out here and at the adjacent Aquarius Plateau. This region sits up high, roughly 6600ft to 9000ft above sea level, so summer temperatures are cooler – sometimes by as much as 20 degrees – than at lower-lying parks such as Zion. Temperatures climb into the 90s in July, and the air is very dry, but you won't have to worry about heatstroke the way you would elsewhere.

Crowds flock here from May to September, sometimes clogging the park's one main road and famous overlooks with busloads of tourists. You can disappear on a few less-traveled hiking trails under the rim, but if you really want to avoid people, consider visiting in winter, when the crowds disappear and Bryce becomes a wonderland, her rosy rock formations and pine forests robed in a blanket of powdery white snow. Though nighttime temperatures can drop below freezing for more than 200 consecutive nights, days are often mild and sunny, perfect for snowshoeing or cross-country skiing.

### WHEN YOU ARRIVE

As you approach, tune your radio to AM 1590 for current general park information. Bryce Canyon is open 24 hours a day, 365 days a year. Admission, good for seven days, costs $20 per car or $10 per person arriving by motorcycle, bicycle or foot.

Turn south from Utah Hwy 12 onto Hwy 63, and drive 3 miles to the park gate. At the entrance kiosk you'll receive a park brochure that includes a good driving map, general information about facilities, and details about the park's geology and wildlife. You'll also get a copy of the park newspaper, the *Hoodoo,* which gives up-to-date information about opening hours, ranger-led activities, hiking trails, backpacking and shuttle information.

## ORIENTATION

Compared with the vast landscape that surrounds it, Bryce is small (only 55 sq miles), its jagged boundaries stretching 16 miles long and only 4 miles across at its widest point. Shaped somewhat like a seahorse, the long, narrow park is an extension of the sloping Paunsaugunt Plateau and runs north-south, rising from 6600ft on the canyon floors to 7893ft at the visitor center and 9115ft at Rainbow Point, the plateau's southernmost tip.

The famed hoodoo amphitheaters line the eastern rim of the plateau. Sunrise, Sunset and Inspiration Points are 2 miles from the visitor center; Bryce Point is 4 miles. If you're tight on time, these are the sights to see – they're also the most crowded. Aside from lodging and dining at Bryce Canyon Lodge, and camping supplies and groceries at the general store (both near Sunrise Point), the park lacks commercial services.

En route to the park, just north of the entrance gate along Hwy 63, you'll pass the privately owned Ruby's Inn, a giant, garish motel complex that encompasses, among other things, a campground, post office, grocery store, restaurants and gas stations. Because Ruby's is so big and so near the park, Bryce's administration works closely with the resort, so expect to see references to it in park publications, particularly in descriptions of shuttle stops or places to rent equipment such as snowshoes.

See the Bryce Canyon map (Map 2) on p146.

### Entrances & Roads

The park's sole vehicle entrance is 3 miles south of Utah Hwy 12, via Hwy 63. Though the gate is always open, entrance kiosks are unmanned at night. The park's well-paved, 18-mile-long main road dead ends at the south end of the plateau. The route gets jammed on summer weekends, sometimes with more cars than available parking spots. To alleviate congestion between mid-May and late September, the park employs a system of voluntary shuttles (p116), which you can board either inside the park or just north of the entrance station, at the junction of Hwys 12 and 63.

## HIGHLIGHTS

✔ Seeing the hoodoos burst into color as the sun rises over **Bryce Amphitheater** (p121)

✔ Riding **horseback** (p133) on Peekaboo Loop Trail beneath the soaring Wall of Windows

✔ Oohing and aahing at the setting sun from **Paria View** (p120)

✔ Supping at **Bryce Canyon Lodge** (p138) and trading stories of the day's adventures

✔ Stargazing from **Inspiration Point** (p121) into the darkest skies over the continental US

## INFORMATION

Upon arrival at the park, stop at the **visitor center** ( ☎ 435-834-5322; www.nps.gov/brca; Hwy 63; ◷ 8am-8pm May-Sep, 8am-6pm Oct-Nov & Apr, 8am-4:30pm Jan-Mar), immediately adjacent to the entrance station, to pick up maps and books, check weather and road conditions, inquire about campground availability, talk to rangers, and watch an excellent orientation video. Park headquarters is here, as are first aid and telephones.

The nonprofit **Bryce Canyon Natural History Association** ( ☎ 435-834-4600, 888-362-2642; www.brycecanyon.org) aids the park service with educational, scientific and interpretive activities at Bryce Canyon. The association operates the bookstore, and trained staff members are on duty to answer questions in the visitor center. It also runs an excellent online shop that sells books, maps, videos, music and trip-planning packets tailored to individual traveler's needs.

Due to Bryce's high elevation, some visitors may experience altitude sickness. For basic remedies, see Health & Safety (p54).

## POLICIES & REGULATIONS
Bryce Canyon's hiking and backcountry use regulations include those listed for all the parks in the Activities chapter.

Pets must be kept on a leash and are not allowed at scenic overlooks, on trails or in public buildings. The nearest kennel, **Canyon Park Animal Retreat** ( ☎ 435-679-8548), is in Tropic, 7 miles east of Bryce.

It's particularly important not to feed wild animals. You not only risk contracting disease, you also endanger juvenile animals, which learn to beg rather than forage and then become dependent – come winter, these animals die when people aren't around to feed them.

## GETTING AROUND
Most people arrive at Bryce in their own cars. Unless you're on an organized tour, the only way to get around the park from fall through spring is in a private vehicle. But in summer, particularly on weekends, consider riding the park's free, voluntary shuttle buses, which stop at all of the park's major sights and trailheads.

### Car
The best way to see Bryce is by car. The park's main road is easily navigable and well maintained, with turnouts and parking areas clearly marked in the brochure you receive upon paying your fee. The maximum speed limit in the park is 35mph. Rangers do give traffic tickets, so avoid speeding.

Gasoline is not available in the park. The closest stations are 3 miles north, at Ruby's Inn, though the price is better in the town of Tropic, 7 miles east of the Hwy 12/63 junction.

If you're towing a trailer, you must leave it in either the trailer turnaround lot in summer or the visitor center parking lot in winter. (If you're camping, you can leave the trailer at your campsite.) No trailers are permitted south of Sunset Point.

### Shuttle Bus
If you're visiting during a peak period, such as a summer weekend, seriously consider riding the shuttle bus into the park, as parking lots at the major overlooks and visitor center fill up fast. Leave your car in the large lot at the shuttle terminus, just south of the Hwy 12/63 junction outside the park. If you do pay your fee and drive into the park only to find that parking lots are full, you can easily turn around and drive the five minutes back to the shuttle staging area. Make sure to bring your admission receipt with you on the bus to avoid having to pay again.

Tune your radio to AM 1610 as you approach the park to learn about current shuttle service and boarding instructions.

Shuttle information changes annually; check with rangers for current schedules. If the shuttle is operating during your visit, the *Hoodoo* newspaper will list current routes. Buses typically run every 10 minutes May through September, from the shuttle terminus north of the park to Ruby's Inn, the visitor center and the major Bryce Amphitheater overlooks as far south as Bryce Point. Depending on the park budget, there may be service to points south. If not, you'll have to take your own vehicle or join an organized tour.

## Organized Tours

Rangers lead seasonal hikes; ask at the visitor center for current schedules. To arrange a 2-hour tour, contact **Bryce Canyon Area Tours & Adventures** ( ☎ 435-834-5200, 800-432-5383; www.brycetours.com; PO Box 640025, Bryce, UT 84764; adult/child $26/12).

You can arrange a day trip on horseback (p133), but there are no overnight backcountry tours within the park. Commercial outfitters do not offer guided hiking in Bryce Canyon.

Several companies lead bicycle tours in and around Bryce Canyon, including **Backroads** ( ☎ 800-462-2848, 510-527-1555; www.backroads.com; 801 Cedar St, Berkeley, CA 94710-1800), **Rim Tours** ( ☎ 435-259-5223, 800-626-7335; www.rimtours.com; 1233 S Hwy 191, Moab, UT 84532) and **Western Spirit Cycling** ( ☎ 435-259-8732, 800-845-2453; www.westernspirit.com; 478 Mill Creek Rd, Moab, UT 84532).

## SIGHTS

Bryce Canyon's major sights are easily accessible along the park's scenic drive (p118).

The **Bryce Canyon Visitor Center** ( ☎ 435-834-5322; www.nps.gov/brca; Hwy 63; ⊙ 8am-8pm May-Sep, 8am-4:30pm Nov-Mar, 8am-6pm Apr & Oct) should be your first stop. A large dry-erase board on one wall of the center lists everything from campground availability to atmospheric conditions (including sunrise and moonrise), schedules of ranger-led programs and a calendar of events.

Be sure to watch the excellent 20-minute video, *Bryce Canyon: Shadows of Time*, which describes the park layout, discusses the geologic history of the Colorado Plateau, explains how hoodoos form, shows the park in various seasons and highlights park wildlife and plant life.

Excellent interpretive exhibits also show plant and animal life, as well as cross-sectional drawings of Earth's crust and various geologic displays that explain how Bryce connects with the Grand Canyon and Grand Staircase.

### WHY IS IT CALLED BRYCE CANYON?

Bryce Canyon takes its name from an early pioneer who settled in the valley east of the park. In 1870, Ebenezer Bryce traveled south from Salt Lake City with a group of Mormon pioneers who hoped to establish permanent settlements in the area. During Ebenezer's five short years here, he surveyed the 10-mile-long Tropic Ditch as a means to deliver water for crops and livestock. (Today, the ditch still provides water to the town of Tropic; park visitors can stroll beside it on the **Mossy Cave Trail**, p129.) People nicknamed the canyon behind Ebenezer's home 'Bryce's Canyon,' and the name stuck. Despite his engineering prowess, Bryce is remembered today mainly for having said of his namesake canyon, 'It's a hell of a place to lose a cow,' a statement you're bound to hear repeatedly during your visit. Of course, when you gaze from the rim into the maze of hoodoos, you'll understand exactly what he meant.

If you have children, you can pick up Junior Ranger Activity Guides and learn more about kids' activities (p134).

## DRIVING TOUR

The scenic drive winds south for 18 miles and roughly parallels the canyon rim, climbing from 7894ft at the visitor center to 9115ft at Rainbow Point, the plateau's southern tip at road's end.

It takes about 30 minutes to drive from the visitor center to Rainbow Point. As most sights lie on the east side of the road (or left side as you drive south), you may want head directly to Rainbow Point, then work your way back, stopping at the scenic overlooks and turnouts as you reach them.

The park speed limit is 35mph, though traffic may slow significantly on weekends in high season, when lumbering RVs clog lanes. Traffic generally eases the farther you drive into the park, as most visitors stick to Bryce Amphitheater's main overlooks, which are concentrated near the visitor center.

### BRYCE CANYON SCENIC DRIVE
**Route: Rainbow Point to visitor center**
**Distance: 18 miles one way**
**Speed Limit: 35mph**

First, drive past all the sights to road's end at Rainbow Point. While ascending the plateau, note the change in plant life as you move from the ponderosa pine community to the fir-spruce community. The higher you go, the cooler the temperatures and the greater the precipitation. In autumn, stands of aspen turn a brilliant gold.

Lightning strikes are very common at Bryce, as iron in the rock attracts electricity. If caught at an overlook during a sudden thunderstorm, immediately take shelter. The safest retreat is inside your vehicle.

While park officials do their best to keep the road to Rainbow Point plowed in winter, severe snowstorms may close the road. Check at the visitor center for current road conditions.

#### Rainbow Point & Yovimpa Point

First visit Rainbow Point, via a short, paved, wheelchair-accessible path at the far end of the parking lot. From the overlook, you'll get your first jaw-dropping glimpse of canyon country. On a clear day you can see more than 100 miles. Giant sloping plateaus, tilted mesas and towering buttes jut above the vast landscape, and interpretive panels explain what you're seeing. To the north, the park stretches out before you, only hinting at the hoodoos that lie ahead. On the northeastern horizon look for the **Aquarius Plateau** – the very top step of the Grand Staircase – which rises 2000ft higher than Bryce. You'll spot this vast, pink-edged plateau from many angles during your trip, especially if you take the Hwy 12 scenic drive (p165).

When ready, stroll to the other end of the parking lot to **Yovimpa Point.** Another short, paved, wheelchair-accessible trail leads to this point, one of the park's windiest spots. The southwest-facing view here differs from Rainbow Point, revealing more tree-covered slopes and less eroding rock. But on a clear day, it's no less spectacular. Look for **Molly's Nipple**, an eroded sandstone dome often mistaken for a volcano – you'll also spot this dome from many angles during your visit. Dipping below the horizon is the **Kaibab Plateau**, marking the Arizona border and the Grand Canyon.

If you want to take a short, easy hike, the .8-mile **Bristlecone Loop Trail** (p128) starts and ends at Rainbow Point. Yovimpa Point also offers a great tree-shaded picnic area.

## Black Birch Canyon

Just north of mile marker 16, at 8750ft, this small overlook demonstrates just how precipitously the cliffs drop from the road. It also offers your first up-close look at hoodoos – though these are modest in comparison to those at Bryce Amphitheater. There are no trailheads here, only a small lookout, so if the parking lot is full, don't sweat having to skip this stop. More glorious views lie ahead.

## Ponderosa Canyon

Higher than the previous stop, this point offers long vistas like those at Rainbow Point. Below, note the namesake giant ponderosa pines, some as much as 150ft tall. If you're thinking of waiting in the car because the view doesn't look like much, don't be deceived: This small amphitheater of hoodoos and burnt-orange cliffs is breathtaking, especially in morning light.

If you're feeling ambitious, descend a stretch of the moderately strenuous **Agua Canyon Connecting Trail,** a lightly traveled, steep trail that drops past woods into a brilliant amphitheater of hoodoos before joining the **Under-the-Rim Trail** (p130), 1.8 miles ahead.

## Agua Canyon

One of the best stops at this end of the park, this viewpoint overlooks two large formations of precariously balanced, top-heavy hoodoos that could – quite literally – fall at any time. That you can only see the tops of these giant spires, not their bases, ought to give you an idea of the precipitous drop-off at your feet. On the ridge above, note the distinct sedimentary lines between iron-rich red rock and the relatively pure white limestone. Clear days promise mesmerizing vistas of the purple and blue horizon.

## Natural Bridge

The parking lot here is the biggest since Rainbow Point, and with good reason: A stunning span of eroded, red-hued limestone juts from the edge of the overlook. Though called a bridge, it's technically an arch. A bridge forms when running water, such as a stream, causes the erosion. In this case,

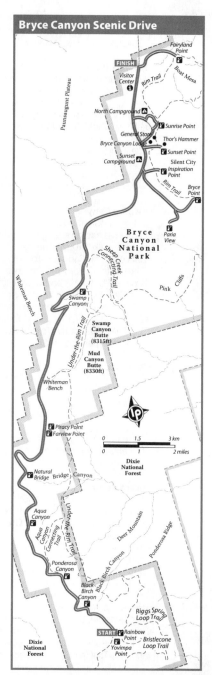

**Bryce Canyon Scenic Drive**

freezing and thawing of water inside cracks and crevices, combined with gravity, shattered rock to create the window.

Even if you're tight on time, squeeze this stop onto your agenda.

### Farview Point

As its name suggests, this stop offers a grand view of the tree-studded rises and benches, giant plateaus, blue-hued mesas and buttes that extend from the skirts of Bryce into the Grand Staircase as far as the eye can see. Navajo Mountain lies 90 miles away on the Arizona border, but even that's not the farthest visible point. On clear days you can see as far as 160 miles to Arizona's Black Mesas!

A short walk leads to another overlook at **Piracy Point**, and though it's not much different, the walk among the deep-green, cedar-scented pines is a great chance to stretch your legs before getting back in the car.

You'll also find toilets here, but no running water.

### Swamp Canyon

This overlook sits in a forested dip between two ridgelines that extend into the canyon as fins, dropping to hoodoo formations. From the turnout you can take a short walk through the trees and descend slightly to towering pink-orange cliffs of crumbling sandstone, one of the more intimate views along the drive. Trees extend from the rim into the canyon, as does red-barked manzanita. Amateur botanists and animal lovers like the variety of plant and animal life here; kids like the steep trail into the canyon.

This is also the jumping-off point for the scenic Swamp Canyon Trail, which drops into the canyon and follows a series of switchbacks about a mile to the **Under-the-Rim Trail** (p130). To do this hike, bear right at the fork in the trail below the parking area.

### Paria View

Three miles north of Swamp Canyon, turn right and follow signs to this viewpoint, 2 miles off the main road. If you're tired of RVs and buses, you'll be pleased to learn that this small overlook is for cars only – though it's reserved for cross-country skiers in winter, when the access road isn't plowed.

This is *the* place to come for **sunsets**. Most of the hoodoo amphitheaters at Bryce face east, making them particularly beautiful at sunrise, but not sunset. The amphitheater here, small by comparison but beautiful nonetheless, faces west toward the Paria River watershed.

### Bryce Point

If you stop nowhere else along the scenic drive, be sure to catch the stunning views from Bryce Point. You can walk the rim above **Bryce Amphitheater** for awesome views of the **Silent City**, an assemblage of hoodoos so dense, gigantic and hypnotic that you'll surely begin to see the shapes of people frozen in the rock. Be sure to follow the path to the actual point, a fenced-in promontory that juts out over the forested canyon floor, 1000ft below. Because it sticks out so far, you'll have an awesome, broad view of the hoodoos. This rivals any overlook in the park for majestic splendor and eye-popping color. (If you're in a wheelchair, you'll need someone with strong arms to maneuver the chair along the sometimes steep and bumpy path to the promontory, but if that's not possible, the views from the parking area are every bit as beautiful.) An interpretive panel explains how grottos and windows form.

Bryce Point marks the beginning of the 11-mile **Rim Trail** (p125). The **Peekaboo Loop Trail** (p124) also begins here.

## Inspiration Point

A short ascent up a paved path takes you to this overlook into **Bryce Amphitheater**. Inspiration Point sits lower than Bryce Point and provides much the same view, though seen from here, the **Silent City** is more compelling than from any other rim-top viewpoint. The hoodoos feel closer here, and you can make out more details on the canyon floor below. To the left, follow the sweep of trees along the rim to spot the next stops along the drive. Kids like scrambling up the hill to the right of the parking area to reach the fenced-in promontory. No trails lead into the canyon from here.

Inspiration Point is a great place to return for **stargazing** – Bryce Point sits up too high, in view of the too-bright lights farther north at Ruby's Inn.

## Sunset Point

While views here into **Bryce Amphitheater** are as good as they get, don't expect solitude. You're at the core of the park, near campgrounds, the lodge and all visitor services. Aside from great views of the Silent City, this point is known for **Thor's Hammer**, a big square-capped rock balanced atop a spindly hoodoo. Just left of the point, it stands apart from the other hoodoos and makes a terrific picture. This is the starting point for the **Navajo Loop Trail** (p123), the park's most popular hike. You'll also find restrooms, drinking water and picnic tables.

Don't be fooled by the name of this point. Because it faces east, sunrises are actually better here than sunsets.

## Sunrise Point

Marking the north end of Bryce Amphitheater, this northeast-facing point offers great views of hoodoos, the **Aquarius Plateau** and the **Sinking Ship**, a sloping mesa that looks like a ship's stern rising out of the water. Keep your eyes peeled for the **Limber Pine**, a spindly pine tree whose roots have been exposed through erosion, but which remains anchored to the receding sand nonetheless.

Within walking distance or a one-minute drive are the Bryce Canyon General Store, drinking water, restrooms, picnic tables and a snack bar; head north toward the campground on the loop road.

## Visitor Center & Fairyland Point

End your driving tour at the visitor center (p117) or, if you have time, head to **Fairyland Point**. To reach the point, drive a mile north of the entrance gate, then a mile east of the main road (the turnoff is marked only to northbound traffic – you won't see it on your way into the park). Fairyland is a less-visited spot where you can take in wooded views north toward the Aquarius Plateau and see hoodoos at all stages of evolution, from fin to crumbling tower. It's also the starting point of the **Fairyland Loop Trail** (p127).

# FESTIVAL & EVENTS

Just north of the park boundary, **Ruby's Inn** (☎ 435-834-5341, 866-866-6616; www.rubysinn.com) hosts several annual events not affiliated with the park. In February, over President's Day weekend, **Bryce Canyon Winterfest** includes everything from cross-country skiing and snowmobiling to archery and snow sculpting. In August, the **Bryce Canyon Rim Run** follows a 6-mile course along a portion of the canyon rim outside park boundaries. For more details, contact Ruby's Inn or the **Garfield County Tourism Office** (☎ 435-676-1160, 800-444-6689; www.brycecanyoncountry.com).

## DAY HIKES

Though you can see much of Bryce's spectacular rock formations from turnouts along the scenic drive, the best way to appreciate hoodoos is from the canyon floor. Towering above and around you in phantasmagoric splendor, the spires take on changing shapes and hues, casting their spell on your imagination.

You can also trek backcountry trails, particularly the **Under-the-Rim Trail** (p130), accessible by four connecting trails: Sheep Creek, Swamp Canyon, Whiteman Bench and Agua Canyon. Unless you make it an out-and-back hike, you'll have to arrange for pickup, hitchhike or take the park's shuttle buses (if operating). For more on the connecting trails, check with rangers. You can also day hike the backcountry **Riggs Spring Loop Trail** (p133).

As Bryce is a relatively small park, most trails are day hikes around and into Bryce Amphitheater, home to the highest concentration of hoodoos. Hikes range from easy walks on paved paths along the rim (with some stretches suitable for wheelchairs) to steep switchbacks up and down sometimes muddy, sometimes dusty, packed-earth trails. Farther south or north on the plateau, you won't see as many hoodoos – neither will you see as many people.

The trails are well maintained and often marked by cairns. The *Hoodoo* newspaper provides a hiking overview map. If you want more than a general trail guide and prefer something with topographic lines, buy a map at the visitor center. The large-scale *Bryce Canyon Hiking Map* ($2) is good for day hikes into the main amphitheater only, covering terrain from Fairyland Point to Bryce Point. If you plan on hiking the Under-the-Rim Trail, Riggs Spring or any trails at the park's south end, pick up the medium-scale *National Geographic Trails Illustrated Map* ($10), which shows the entire park, with brief trail descriptions and topographic lines.

Carry lots of water (1 quart for every two hours of hiking), particularly in summer. Don't expect to find water along trails, with few exceptions, depending on season and drought cycles (inquire with rangers). Though temperatures are often comfortable at Bryce, remember you're at 8000ft in a high-desert climate. The sun's rays aren't filtered as much as they are at sea level, and it's easy to get dehydrated. Wear extra sunscreen and a hat. Until you're acclimated to the elevation, expect to get winded quickly. Your pulse will also spike more readily than it does at sea level, so take it slow and pace yourself, especially ascending out of the canyon.

Loose rock and sand make trails slippery; ankle injuries are extremely common and can ruin your trip. Always wear well-fitting hiking boots with ankle support, and lace your boots all the way up.

In winter many of these trails are impassible due to snow; some are reserved for cross-country skiing and snowshoeing. Check with rangers at the visitor center.

---

### BEST HIKES TO ESCAPE THE CROWDS

✔ Fairyland Loop Trail (p127)

✔ Riggs Spring Loop Trail (p133)

✔ Sheep Creek Connecting Trail (p131)

✔ Agua Canyon Connecting Trail (p132)

✔ Under-the-Rim Trail (p130)

---

## NAVAJO LOOP TRAIL
**Distance: 1.4 miles round-trip**
**Duration: 1–2 hours**
**Challenge: Moderate–Difficult**
**Elevation Change: 521ft**

Short but spectacular, this hike packs a punch. From the trailhead at Sunset Point, you drop right into the canyon beneath towering rock formations that dwarf onlookers. Along the way you'll pass through **Wall Street**, a narrow canyon with steep rock walls that reveal only a sliver of sky above; beneath **Two Bridges**, a pair of small water-carved arches; and alongside **Thor's Hammer**, perhaps the park's most famous rock formation. It's a steep ascent and descent, but the trail is clearly marked and fairly wide. If you're in reasonably good shape you won't have a problem.

From the wide, fenced-in viewing area at Sunset Point, follow signs for the Navajo Loop. The trail drops immediately into a switchback, then forks about 100 yards ahead. The left fork leads past Thor's Hammer down a long slope to the canyon floor. Instead, bear right and descend into a more concentrated area of land features.

To the right of the trail, the Silent City looms large. If the spur trail through the tunnel on your right is open, take a quick jaunt to look down on these eerie pinnacles. After a series of 30 switchbacks, you'll emerge on Wall Street, where 100ft walls block much of the sunlight, keeping the canyon shady and cool. The giant Douglas fir trees that tower between the walls are more than 750 years old!

When you reach the canyon floor, turn left to continue the loop and ascend back to the rim. (You could also follow signs to the Queen's Garden Connecting Trail for a more gradual ascent that will lengthen your hike by 30 to 60 minutes; see the Navajo Loop–Queen's Garden Combination, p124.) As you climb out of the canyon, follow a sign on your right to see Two Bridges. As you approach the rim, up several switchbacks and just past a tall spire called the Sentinel, Thor's Hammer will come into view on your right.

## QUEEN'S GARDEN TRAIL
**Distance: 1.6 miles round-trip**
**Duration: 1–2 hours**
**Challenge: Moderate**
**Elevation Change: 320ft**

This is the easiest trail into the canyon. The gentle descent over sloping erosional fins passes elegant hoodoo formations but stops short of the canyon floor – unless you add the Queen's Garden Connecting Trail, part of the Navajo Loop–Queen's Garden Combination (p124). The hike to Queen's Garden is not a loop, but an in-and-out hike.

From Sunrise Point, follow signs to the trailhead off the Rim Trail. Views of the amphitheater as you descend are superb – a maze of colorful rock spires extends to Bryce Point, and deep-green pines dot the canyon floor beneath undulating slopes seemingly tie-dyed pink, orange and white. As you drop below the rim, watch for the stark and primitive **bristlecone pines**, which at Bryce are about 1600 years old (specimens in California are 5000 years old). These ancient trees' dense needles cluster like foxtails on the ends of the branches.

After a series of switchbacks, turn right and follow signs to Queen's Garden. The short spur from the main trail passes through a tunnel and emerges on exceptionally beautiful hoodoo castles in striking whites and oranges amid rich-green pines. After looping around a high wall and passing through two more tunnels, bear right and follow signs to **Queen Victoria**. The trail's namesake monarch peers down from a white-capped rock, perched atop her throne, lording over her kingdom.

Return to the rim or link up with the Navajo Loop via the Queen's Garden Connecting Trail, which drops to the canyon floor.

---

### NAVAJO LOOP–QUEEN'S GARDEN COMBINATION
**Distance: 2.8 miles round-trip**
**Duration: 2–3 hours**
**Challenge: Moderate (Moderate–Difficult if done in reverse)**
**Elevation Change: 521ft**

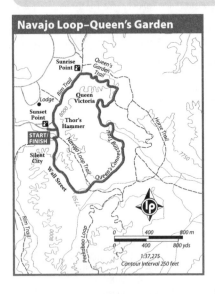

This is the most popular route in the park, enabling hikers to see some of Bryce's most famous features in a relatively short amount of time on fairly gentle terrain, despite the sometimes steep grade. Begin with the Navajo Loop to end on a gentle ascent through Queen's Garden.

Start at Sunset Point and follow the Navajo Loop Trail description (p123), but before forking right, detour left a short distance to see Thor's Hammer, then return to the right fork in the path. This descent past the Silent City and down through Wall Street is the more visually stunning of the two trails.

When you reach the trail junction on the canyon floor, rather than making a hard left and climbing to the rim, follow signs for the Queen's Garden Connecting Trail, which follows the canyon floor and ascends to the garden of spires. Another advantage of taking this trail is time spent on the canyon floor, where tall green pines provide shade and offer perspective to the dazzlingly tall hoodoos.

Back on the rim, stroll back to Sunset Point along the Rim Trail, gazing into the canyon for yet another perspective on the hoodoos.

---

### PEEKABOO LOOP TRAIL
**Distance: 5.5 miles round-trip from Bryce Point, 6.6 miles round-trip from Sunrise Point, 5 miles round-trip from Sunset Point**
**Duration: 3–5 hours**
**Challenge: Difficult**
**Elevation Change: 500-900ft, with multiple elevation changes**

If you're looking for an all-day hike that offers the most variety within Bryce Amphitheater, this is the one. Access to this 3.5-mile circular trail is via either the Navajo Loop (p123) or the Queen's Garden Connecting Trail (above). The following description starts from Bryce Point.

The Peekaboo Loop is also a horse trail, so expect to see occasional teams.

They move slowly, so you'll have plenty of advance warning. Stock animals have right of way – step off the trail and let them pass undisturbed. But views here are fantastic, among the best in the park, particularly the **Wall of Windows**, the **Silent City** and the **Fairy Castle**. You'll also find shady spots to rest, a picnic area and pit toilets (the latter are on the loop, just west of its intersection with the connecting trail to Bryce Point).

From Bryce Point follow signs to the Peekaboo Connecting Trail, just east of the parking area. Bear left at the fork 0.1 mile down the connecting trail. You'll pass through mixed conifers, then swoop out along a gray-white limestone fin beneath the Bryce Point overlook. Farther down the trail, the hoodoo columns take on a bright orange hue. After passing through a manmade tunnel, look for **The Alligator** in the white rock ahead. As you work your way down the switchbacks, watch for the Wall of Windows, which juts above bright-orange hoodoos atop a sheer vertical cliff face perpendicular to the canyon rim. The windows line the top of this wall.

At the loop trail junction, bear right. As you pass beneath healthy fir and spruce trees, you'll spot a few blackened snags – victims of electrical storms, not forest fires.

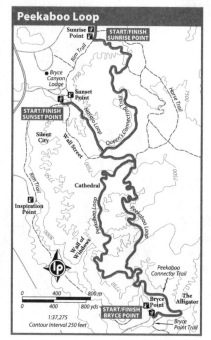

The iron-rich soil attracts lightning. Also look for ancient bristlecone pines; an inch of this tree's trunk represents 100 years' growth.

Climbing a saddle, you'll rise to eye level with the hoodoo tops before dropping over the other side to the cluster of delicate red spires at Fairy Castle. Midway around, just past the turnoff for the Navajo Loop, the trail climbs again to spectacular views of Silent City and passes beneath **The Cathedral**, a majestic wall of buttresslike hoodoos. The rolling trail skirts the Wall of Windows, threads through a tunnel and switchbacks down. Notice the rapidly changing views as you pass the huge Wall of Windows. The trail turns west and climbs, then drops again amid more hoodoos. As you approach the Bryce Point Trail, take the spur on your right to the lush green rest area near the horse corral for a cool-down or picnic before climbing out of the canyon.

This trail rises and falls many times. Be prepared for a workout. If you're afraid of heights, be forewarned that in places you'll pass sheer drops, though the trail is wide enough for a horse, so don't worry.

<br>

### RIM TRAIL

**Distance: 5.5 miles one way**
**Duration: 2–3 hours**
**Challenge: Easy–Moderate**
**(wheelchair accessible between Sunrise & Sunset Points)**
**Elevation Change: 550ft**

As its name suggests, this trail hugs the canyon rim, stretching from the south

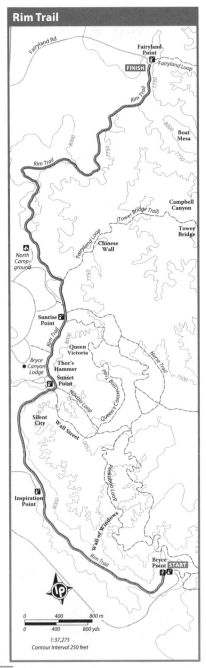

**Rim Trail**

end of Bryce Amphitheater at **Bryce Point** all the way to **Fairyland Point**, near the northern park boundary.

Sections of the trail are level, particularly between Sunrise and Sunset Points, where the path is paved. A low chain-link fence marks vertical drop-offs in many places. In other spots you'll ascend moderately steep, wooded rises to seek shade beneath the pines, watch wildlife or soak up vibrant displays of spring wildflowers. The colors in the rock pop out most when lit by the morning or afternoon sun.

You can join the trail anywhere along its 5.5-mile route – just keep in mind that unless the shuttle is running or you arrange to be picked up, you'll have to walk back. You'll find restrooms and drinking water at Sunset Point and the general store and snack bar (both open spring through fall) near Sunrise Point, the approximate midpoint of the trek. You can also duck into **Bryce Canyon Lodge** for lunch.

Remember that Bryce sits atop a sloping plateau. The north end of the Rim Trail is lower than the south end, so it's easier to walk from Bryce Point to Fairyland Point, though the trail rises and falls in a couple of spots, particularly in its climb from Sunrise Point to North Campground.

From **Bryce Point** to **Inspiration Point** the trail skirts the canyon rim atop white cliffs, revealing gorgeous formations, including the **Wall of Windows**. After passing briefly through trees, it continues along the ridgetop to Inspiration Point, 1.3 miles beyond Bryce Point.

The leg to Sunset Point drops 300ft in half a mile, wending its way along limestone-capped cliffs that yield to orange sandstone fins. Below the rim the **Silent City** rises in all its hoodoo-dense glory; the lower you go, the higher the rock spires rise up beside you.

At **Sunset Point** you may wish to detour along the Navajo Loop Trail (p123) for a taste of the canyon; you can reemerge on the Rim Trail farther ahead by adding the Queen's Garden Connecting Trail (p124). Otherwise, stay the course and look for **Thor's Hammer** as you continue the half-mile stroll along a paved, wheelchair-accessible path to **Sunrise Point** – the most crowded stretch of trail in the entire park. The views are worth it.

Past Sunset Point, crowds thin as the trail climbs 150ft toward North Campground. Fork left at the Fairyland Loop Trail junction, unless you'd like to follow the moderately difficult, 3-mile round-trip spur into the canyon (800ft elevation loss) to see the window-laced **Chinese Wall** and **Tower Bridge**, twin arches between chunky rock spires. Otherwise, watch for these features from the Rim Trail.

Topping out near North Campground, the path ambles across gently rolling hills on the forested plateau before rejoining the canyon rim at **Fairyland Point**, 2.9 miles from Sunrise Point. During the walk, you'll leave behind Bryce Amphitheater and arrive above Campbell Canyon and Fairyland Amphitheater. You'll find fewer formations at this end of the park, but giant **Boat Mesa** and her high cliffs rise majestically to the north.

**FAIRYLAND LOOP TRAIL**
**Distance: 8 miles round-trip**
**Duration: 4–5 hours**
**Challenge: Difficult**
**Elevation Change: 900ft, with multiple elevation changes**

This is a great all-day hike and a good workout, and unlike Bryce Amphitheater, Fairyland is spared the crowds. You'll find fewer hoodoos in this section of the park. The trail begins at Fairyland Point and circles the majestic 8076ft cliffs of flat-topped **Boat Mesa**, emerging on the rim near Sunrise Point. The last 2.5 miles of the loop follow the Rim Trail back to the trailhead. If you plan on taking the shuttle, be sure to check current routes and schedules: Buses don't always stop at Fairyland.

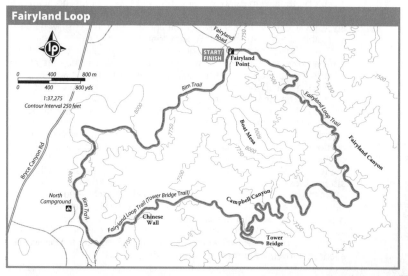

Fairyland Loop

From the point, the trail dips gradually below the rim – watch your footing on the narrow sections. To the south, **Boat Mesa** stands between you and views of the park. A short walk leads past ancient bristlecone pines, some clinging precariously to the ragged cliffs, their 1000-plus-year-old roots curled up like wizened fingers. Looping around hoodoos that rise like castle turrets and towers from a children's book, the trail soon drops to the canyon floor and a seasonal wash. Much of the north-facing terrain here holds its snowpack until May, sometimes June.

At **Fairyland Canyon**, 600ft below your starting point, towers of deep-orange stone rise like giant totem poles. The trail rises and falls before traversing a ridge toward **Campbell Canyon**. As you walk beneath Boat Mesa's great cliffs, notice how the formation comes to a point like the bow of a ship – you'll quickly understand how it got its name.

Zigzagging up and down, the trail eventually reaches a seasonal wash on the floor of Campbell Canyon. Keep an eye out for **Tower Bridge**, its three spires and two windows connected like a bridge. To reach the base of the formation, take the clearly marked dead-end spur from the wash. From Tower Bridge it's a 700ft climb in 1.5 miles to the Rim Trail, some of it strenuous. En route to your left, look for the long white **Chinese Wall** and its little windows. Also remember to turn around and look back at Boat Mesa and the changing vistas of canyon country.

This trail is difficult primarily because it meanders – in and out of the hoodoos, down into washes, up and over saddles etc. Carry plenty of water, and pace yourself.

### BRISTLECONE LOOP TRAIL
**Distance: 1-mile loop**
**Duration: 30 minutes–1 hour**
**Challenge: Easy (wheelchair-accessible spur to Yovimpa Point)**
**Elevation Change: 100ft**

If you plan to drive to Rainbow Point, this short hike is a must-do. Starting at 9115ft at the south tip of the Paunsaugunt Plateau, this is the highest trail at Bryce. It's an easy walk for almost anyone, and though the trail isn't wheelchair accessible, the spur to adjacent **Yovimpa Point** is.

The quick loop takes you through fir forests to high cliffs, from which you can see how Bryce Canyon – the top step of the Grand Staircase – fits into the surrounding landscape and larger Colorado Plateau. Along the way are places to rest and take in the marvelous vistas. On clear days you can see as far as 200 miles! Though you'll spot hoodoos rising from the forested canyon floor, first from the trailhead and again at the tip of the plateau, this walk doesn't focus on the brilliant pink spires.

Park at the Rainbow Point lot, 18 miles from the visitor center. From the overlook kiosk, the well-marked trail ducks into the woods. Bear left at the beginning of the loop. You'll quickly descend below the rim, cross the Under-the-Rim Trail (p130) and enter pine stands. Interpretive panels along the route discuss forest ecology.

When you arrive at the tip, stop in the wooden gazebo to get out of the sun (or escape a summer thunderstorm) and enjoy the view before continuing west to see the **ancient bristlecone pines**. This is the breeziest spot in the park, so carry a windbreaker and hold on to your hat. A short ascent leads back to the parking lot, but bear left when you reach the paved path to **Yovimpa Point**, a fenced-in overlook at the edge of sheer drop-offs.

**MOSSY CAVE TRAIL**
Distance: 0.8 mile round-trip
Duration: 30 minutes–1 hour
Challenge: Easy–Moderate
Elevation Change: 150ft

If you're visiting Bryce in the heat of summer, you can cool off in a **year-round waterfall** off Hwy 12 at the north end of the park and check out a small, damp cave with year-round moss, a rarity in this dry climate. If the trail is passable in winter, **Mossy Cave** is hung with icicles, a dramatic sight.

Though within the park, the trail lies outside the section requiring an entrance fee. From the Hwy 12/63 junction north of the park, turn east on Hwy 12 and drive just past mile marker 17 (about 2 miles) to a small parking area on the right. A placard at the trailhead shows the route.

Skirting the **Tropic Ditch**, the main water channel for the town of Tropic, the route takes you across two wooden footbridges into small Water Canyon. Take the right fork to reach the waterfall or the left fork to reach Mossy Cave; both are 0.4 mile from the parking lot.

Don't attempt to climb down the small cliffs to the base of the falls. Instead, at the second footbridge, hop off the path and walk up the wash alongside the creek. Beware of flash floods following rainstorms. Above the falls you can cross the creek and scramble up a short, steep trail to the small arches and windows in the salmon-colored rock.

Mossy Cave may be a slight disappointment after the waterfall, but if you're an amateur botanist or geologist, it's worth the detour. Stay out of the cave to avoid trampling the fragile mosses.

## BACKCOUNTRY HIKES

Only 1% of park visitors venture into the backcountry, virtually guaranteeing backpackers a peaceful trek. You won't encounter many hoodoo formations as you would on day hikes through the major amphitheaters, but you will get a keen sense of the park's three distinct plant and animal communities as you pass through forest and meadow, with distant views of rock formations.

Most backcountry trails are covered with snow from late October to March or April; even in May, water sources along the trail may be frozen. June and September are ideal, while in July and August you'll have to contend with thunderstorms and mosquitoes. At any time of year, bring a fleece jacket for the cool nights.

### Safety Issues

Beyond the usual safety preparations for hiking in the deserts of southern Utah (see Hiking Safety, p32), the primary safety concern is the elevation. You'll be hiking above 7000ft, so take it slow until you're acclimated.

When you pick up your permit, ask about availability of water along your route, which depends on the season and annual drought cycles. Rangers will tell you where to look. Plan to carry a gallon of water per person, per day. All water in the backcountry must be purified.

### Permit Information

A backcountry permit costs $5 for up to 14 days and covers everyone in your party. Permits are only available at the visitor center between 8am and two hours prior to sunset. You cannot place an advance order by telephone or email, but you can make reservations in person up to 48 hours in advance. Processing permits takes time; plan to arrive two hours before the close of the visitor center. In winter you must have an interview with the backcountry ranger to discuss hazards.

## Backcountry Camping

Hikers may camp only at designated backcountry campsites. Bryce offers 10 individual campsites, each with a six-person capacity, and two group sites, each with a 10-person capacity (register for a group site at the visitor center).

You'll be assigned a campsite once you purchase your backcountry permit. You may only stay at a particular site for a maximum of three nights.

## Backcountry Trails

Bryce features two backcountry trails: the **Under-the-Rim Trail** and the **Riggs Spring Loop Trail**. Due to its length and diverse terrain, the Under-the-Rim Trail is the premier overnight trek. This one-way trail 500ft to 1000ft beneath the rim roughly parallels the scenic drive. You'll neither hear nor see the road until you return to the rim.

The park's southernmost trail, the Riggs Spring Loop, can be done as a day hike from Rainbow or Yovimpa Points, offering an excellent 'backcountry sampler.' Because of the trail's gradual but steep grade, however, most hikers make this an overnight trek. Spend several nights to develop an intimate understanding of how Bryce's spectacular Pink Cliffs yield to the rolling green hills and canyons beyond the park.

Stay on trails at all times. Though it may not appear fragile, high-mountain desert vegetation is easily damaged. If you must leave the trail, step only on rocks, not soil.

**UNDER-THE-RIM TRAIL**
Duration: 3 days
Distance: 22.9 miles one way
Challenge: Moderate–Difficult
Elevation Change: 1315ft

Starting at **Bryce Point** and ending at **Rainbow Point**, this one-way hike can be done in two days, though three are recommended. In either direction you'll face a hefty ascent the last 3 miles. By hiking north to south, you'll have the sun at your back in the afternoon and Rainbow Point as the grand finale.

Running nearly the length of the park, the trail skirts beneath cliffs and through amphitheaters amid pines and aspens. You'll rise from the piñon-juniper community (6600ft to 7000ft), through the ponderosa pine community (7000ft to 8500ft) to the fir-spruce community (8500ft to 9100ft), touching the rim only at the trailheads.

Descending from the scenic drive, four connecting trails link up with the Under-the-Rim Trail, each near a backcountry campsite. These connecting trails allow hikers to approach any section as a day hike. You could also set up base camp at one of the sites and take day hikes in either direction. If you have the time, extend your trek south along the 8.8-mile Riggs Spring Loop Trail (p133).

This is a one-way hike, so consider leaving a car at one or both ends. Shuttle service (p116) to Rainbow Point isn't always available, though hikers have been known to catch rides back to Bryce Point without much difficulty.

### Day 1: Bryce Point to Swamp Canyon Connecting Trail
*(4–6 hours, 12.4 miles)*

From **Bryce Point** the trail descends steeply almost due east, then swings south. After a half mile you'll wind down to a ridge, where the color of the earth changes from gray to orange. Over the next half mile Rainbow Point comes into view above the ridge in the foreground.

As the trail traces a south-facing promontory, look north for a grand panorama of the Pink Cliffs. On the right (west) the Right Fork Yellow Creek forms a steep-sided drainage. Two miles in you'll pass the **Hat Shop**, whose gray boulder caps perch atop spindly conglomerate stands.

At the base of this descent, 2.9 miles from Bryce Point, is the **Right Fork Yellow Creek campsite**, a good spot in a clearing beside the creek, which runs most of the year.

From the campsite, follow the left (east) bank of the creek for half a mile, then cross it and bear south. Here the landscape is a semidesert, with little shade and plenty of pungent sage growing in the sandy soil. As the trail turns west, you'll pass the Yellow Creek group campsite on the left.

A quarter mile beyond the campsite, you'll reach **Yellow Creek**. The trail follows the creek and climbs toward the Pink Cliffs at the head of the creek, atop which – 1000ft above – sits Paria View. The trail soon crosses the creek; cairns point the way.

Another quarter mile brings you to the **Yellow Creek campsite**, in plenty of shade beside the creek – one of the better places in the park to watch the sunset.

From here you'll turn southwest up a short, steep hill. The trail undulates for about 2 miles, crossing a slope between two amphitheaters. After 1.5 miles the trail drops into Pasture Wash. Follow cairns to the south edge of the wash and look for a sharp uphill turn, where the trail visibly zigzags up and out of the wash. The view of (north to south) Swamp Canyon, Mud Canyon and Noon Canyon Buttes will reward your effort.

Descend into the valley to the junction with the Sheep Creek Connecting Trail, which climbs 2 miles to the scenic drive. A well-signed spur leads a half mile south to the **Sheep Creek campsite**, whose beauty is second only to the Yellow Creek site; you can usually find water here.

From the junction, the trail climbs 150ft – crossing from the Sheep Creek amphitheater to the Swamp Canyon amphitheater – then

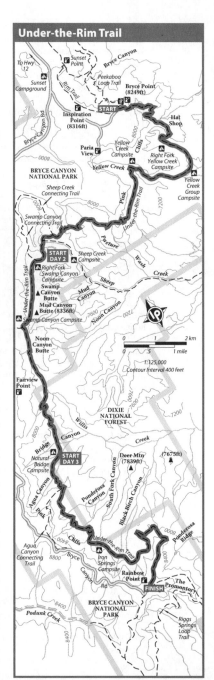

**Under-the-Rim Trail**

descends into Swamp Canyon amid a stand of large quaking aspens. On the left (southeast), in a clearing among large ponderosa pines, is the **Right Fork Swamp Canyon campsite**; water is sometimes available in upper Swamp Canyon, 100yd north of the campsite.

Three hundred feet past the site is the junction with the mile-long Swamp Canyon Connecting Trail, which climbs north to the scenic drive.

### Day 2: Swamp Canyon Connecting Trail to Agua Canyon Connecting Trail
*(1.5–2.5 hours, 4.3 miles)*

From the connecting trail junction, you'll climb steadily south, then turn west up switchbacks. Just beyond, at 8200ft, is the **Swamp Canyon campsite**. There's not much flat ground, and the site is near the trail, but it's cool in summer. You'll find water a quarter mile up the Whiteman Connecting Trail, which climbs 0.9 mile to the scenic drive.

Beyond camp the trail passes aspens and pines, then descends to the base of Farview Cliffs. From here you'll skirt **Willis Creek** for a mile until it turns southeast. You may find it difficult to distinguish the trail from other small creeks; bear south and west.

The trail ducks into Dixie National Forest for a quarter mile, then curves sharply east to climb an eroded sandstone slope southwest of Willis Creek. At the top, the sandy trail snakes around the east edge of a promontory for gorgeous views of the Pink Cliffs.

Descend to a southern tributary of Willis Creek and continue a half mile (you may need to cross several times if the water is running high) to the **Natural Bridge campsite**, which usually lacks water.

Onward half a mile, the trail traverses a sage-studded meadow toward Agua Canyon. Crossing this canyon may prove tricky: On older topo maps, the trail turns slightly west and cuts straight across the canyon, but due to floods you now need to hike up-canyon three-quarters of a mile, then switchback up the canyon's south ridge. When in doubt, follow the cairns. The switchbacks are snowed under till late spring. Atop this ridge, the Agua Canyon Connecting Trail climbs 1.6 miles to the scenic drive.

### Day 3: Agua Canyon Connecting Trail to Rainbow Point
*(2–3 hours, 6.2 miles)*

From the connecting trail junction, you'll skirt a pink promontory, descend into Ponderosa Canyon, then zigzag up and down to South Fork Canyon. Just past the head of the canyon, you'll reach the **Iron Spring campsite** on your right; the east-facing ridge leaves little room to spread out. Amid a grove of aspens 600ft up canyon (southwest) from the campsite, **Iron Spring** supplies year-round water. The turnoff for the spring lies 100yd north of the campsite.

The trail continues its undulating rhythm, dipping to cross both arms of Black Birch Canyon, where directional cairns are sometimes obscured by debris. After clambering over the lower slopes of a northwest-jutting promontory, you'll enter the southernmost amphitheater of Bryce Canyon's Pink Cliffs.

The trail traces the hammer-shaped ridge below Rainbow Point, climbing steadily and offering unsurpassed views. Ascend the final 1.5 miles up the back (south) side of the amphitheater to the rim. You'll cross the Riggs Spring Loop Trail just beneath the rim, 100yd east of the Rainbow Point parking lot. While the urge to peer over the rim is irresistible, use extreme caution, as the edges are unstable.

## RIGGS SPRING LOOP TRAIL
**Distance: 8.8-mile loop**
**Duration: 4–5 hours (or overnight)**
**Challenge: Difficult**
**Elevation Change: 1675ft**

This trail loops from the tip of the Paunsaugunt Plateau, descending beneath the spectacular Pink Cliffs through spruce, fir and aspen forests, then through ponderosa pines to a desert habitat of sagebrush and scrub oak that stretches all the way to the Kaibab Plateau and northern Arizona. Make the loop clockwise, not counterclockwise.

Starting at **Rainbow Point,** follow the Bristlecone Loop Trail to the turnoff for the Under-the-Rim Trail and follow signs to the Riggs Spring Loop Trail.

The trail descends the Pink Cliffs onto **The Promontory**, a ridgeline that juts out from the plateau in a sweeping arc south. **Molly's Nipple** rises to the southeast, while **Navajo Mountain** looms on the horizon 90 miles to the east-southeast.

After dropping off The Promontory along forested slopes, you'll double back north for sublime views of the Pink Cliffs, then descend to **Coral Hollow campsite**. This shady site lies beneath oak and pine trees 3.6 miles from, and 1200ft below, Rainbow Point; there is no water here.

From Coral Hollow you'll loop below Yovimpa Point on a gradual descent through pines to Mutton Hollow. **Riggs Spring campsite** (7480ft) sits amid pines at the base of this hollow. Of the three camps on this loop, this one is most idyllic. You'll almost always find water at Riggs Spring, hemmed in by a log fence. This marks the lowest point along the trail.

Onward, the increasingly steep trail climbs past towering ponderosa pines en route to **Yovimpa Pass**, which lies atop a plateau at 8360ft. The higher you get, the better the views of the approaching cliffs. Perched atop this plateau, the **Yovimpa Pass campsite** provides little shade but often has water.

The last 1.6 miles of the trail skirt the edge of the plateau through woods before rejoining the rim at **Yovimpa Point**. Intermittent breaks in the forest reveal panoramas of the Grand Staircase and the rosy-hued hoodoos below Rainbow Point.

## OTHER ACTIVITIES

When your feet grow tired of hiking, you can explore the amphitheaters on horseback or perch beside a meadow to bird-watch. Rangers lead walks and talks, and at night the sky glows with the light of a million stars.

### Horseback Riding

Horses are permitted in the park on specific trails, most notably the Peekaboo Loop Trail (p124). If you don't have the energy to hike this fantastic trail, or if you have little ones (under the age of seven) who can't walk that far, book a half-day trail ride. Alternatively, you can descend the canyon on a two-hour round-trip ride below the Queen's Garden Trail (p123).

The only outfitter permitted to operate in the park is the excellent **Canyon Trail Rides** ( ☎ 435-679-8665; www.canyonrides.com; PO Box 128, Tropic, UT 84776; 2-hour ride $40, half-day $55), which operates out of Bryce Canyon Lodge. It uses both horses and mules (mules offer a smoother ride). For horseback rides into Dixie National Forest or BLM lands around Bryce, call **Scenic Rim Trail Rides** ( ☎ 435-679-8761, 800-679-5859; www.brycecanyonhorseback.com; Ruby's Inn, 1000 S Hwy 63; 1-1/2-hour rides $19/22, half-day $45, all day $75-90).

If you want to bring your own horse to Bryce, you must coordinate with

Canyon Trail Rides. Contact the park for regulations. There are no overnight backcountry campgrounds suitable for stock animals.

## Watching Wildlife

Bryce Canyon is home to 59 mammal species, 11 reptile species, four amphibian species and more than 1000 insect species. As many as 175 bird species pass through annually, though large, highly adaptable **ravens** are the only birds that make the park their year-round home. If you're lucky, you might also spot **California condors** or a **peregrine falcon**. Keep an eye to the ground for the threatened **Utah prairie dog**, which looks like a cross between a chipmunk and a cat.

The Ecosystem chapter offers a rundown of many of Bryce's resident species. For more information, pick up books and wildlife charts at the visitor center, or visit the wildlife page on the park website (www.nps.gov/brca/wildlife.html).

## Ranger Programs

From early summer until fall, rangers lead rim walks, hikes amid the hoodoos, short geology lectures, campfire programs, kids' ecology walks and astronomy talks, complete with telescopes. Check the *Hoodoo* newspaper or ask at the visitor center for current schedules, or visit the park website for general information. If you time your visit to coincide with the full moon (and clear skies), don't miss the **Moonlight Hike**, a two-hour stroll among the hoodoos; register at the visitor center on the day of the hike, but book early due to limited capacity.

## Classes

In 2004 the **Bryce Canyon Natural History Association** (☎ 435-834-4600, 888-362-2642; www.brycecanyon.org) founded the **High Plateaus Institute** to offer scientific courses about the park. Geared mostly to the academic community, but for all ages, the institute provides in-depth studies of Bryce's unique geology. Call for a list of current offerings.

## Kids' Activities

When you arrive at the park, stop by the visitor center to pick up a **Junior Ranger Activity Guide**. Once kids complete certain activities, they can return to the visitor center to receive a special certificate and badge from a ranger. The visitor center also sells coloring books specific to Bryce, as well as bookmark magnifying glasses and 3-D View-Master reels.

## Winter Activities

Bryce freezes 235 nights a year and receives an average 100in of snowfall each winter. The good news is that visitors then are scarce, and the dry, light snow is perfect for **snowshoeing** and **cross-country skiing**. Ten miles of Bryce's dedicated ski trails connect with 20 additional miles through Dixie National Forest. Rent skis at **Ruby's Inn** (☎ 435-834-5341, 866-866-6616; www.rubysinn.com; half-day $7, all day $10), 3 miles north of the park.

When more than 12in of snow covers the ground, rangers at the visitor center loan snowshoes for free on a first-come, first-served basis. If the visitor center runs out, Ruby's rents them for about the same price as cross-country skis (see above). Ruby's also operates **snowmobile trips** north of the park.

## SLEEPING

The park is home to two campgrounds and a lodge. However, most visitors stay at lodgings just north of the park near the Hwy 12/63 junction in **Bryce,** or 7 miles east, in the town of **Tropic** (p137 ). (Bryce is not an actual town but simply the name given to open range north of the park.)

If nearby lodgings are full, consider staying in or around **Panguitch** (p140), 24 miles west of the park, or **Kodachrome Basin State Park** (p165), 19 miles east.

## Camping

Bryce's two campgrounds are extremely popular. Open year-round, North Campground accepts **reservations** ( ☎ 877-444-6777; www.reserveusa.com) in summer. Open late spring through fall, Sunset Campground is available on a first-come, first-served basis only.

If you're unable to secure a reservation and don't arrive early enough to get a site at Sunset, you could spend a night at nearby Ruby's Inn Campground, then head back early in the morning to grab a spot at Sunset.

For a complete list of campgrounds in Dixie National Forest, which surrounds Bryce Canyon, visit www.fs.fed.us/dxnf. The Powell and Escalante Ranger Districts are closest to Bryce.

### INSIDE THE PARK

**North Campground** (107 sites; tent or RV $10, plus $9 reservation fee May 15–Sep 30; ☉ year-round) Just off the scenic drive near the visitor center, this popular campground is divided into four loops. Loop A is for RVs only and provides many pull-through spots. Loops B and C accommodate both tents and RVs: Loop B sits up high amid tall trees, while Loop C is closest to the canyon rim (sites 59 through 61 have canyon views, though little privacy). For tents only, Loop D sits on a hill amid small to medium-sized trees. All sites include campfire rings, and you'll also find showers, a coin laundry and a general store (summer only).

**Sunset Campground** (101 sites; $10; ☉ late spring–fall) Just south of Sunset Point, this first-come, first-served campground offers more shade than North but has few amenities beyond flush toilets (for laundry, showers and groceries, visit North). Inquire about availability at the visitor center, and secure your site early. Loop A allows RVs, though it has few pull-through spots (generators are allowed 8am to 8pm). Loops B and C are reserved for vehicles under 20ft: Loop B offers less shade, while Loop C's sites vary widely in quality; for shade and privacy, try for sites on the outer ring.

### OUTSIDE THE PARK

**Ruby's Inn Campground** ( ☎ 435-834-5341, 866-866-6616; www.brycecanyoncampgrounds.com; 3 miles north of visitor center; 200 sites; tent sites $16-26, teepees $27-36, RV sites $30-40, cabins $46-53; ▣ ) This crowded campground just outside Bryce boasts lots of amenities, including flush toilets, showers, drinking water, a coin laundry, electrical hookups, a dump station, restaurant, general store and even a hot tub. You'll have a choice of sites and accommodations, including cabins (no bath) and teepees. Though horrendously commercial, this is the easiest place to camp outside the park.

Dixie National Forest offers several campgrounds within a short drive of the park. The ranger stations in Panguitch and Escalante can provide maps and information.

**King Creek** (Powell Ranger District ☎ 435-676-8815; www.fs.fed.us/dxnf; group reservations ☎ 877-444-6777; www.reserveusa.com; 3 miles west of Hwy 12/63 junction, then 7 miles south via unpaved USFS Rd 087; 37 sites; $9; ☉ mid-May–Oct 1) Near Bryce's western boundary, this woodsy, well-maintained, first-come, first-served campground is adjacent to Tropic Reservoir and the Sevier River (bring bug spray). It's also popular with ATV riders (bring earplugs). Amenities include flush toilets, drinking water and a dump station.

**Red Canyon** (Powell Ranger District ☎ 435-676-8815; www.fs.fed.us/dxnf; Hwy 12, 10 miles west of Hwy 12/63 junction; 37 sites; $9; first-come, first-served;  mid-May–Oct 1) One of the best-maintained campgrounds in the national forest, Red Canyon includes beautiful hiking trails and doesn't allow ATVs. Amenities include showers, flush toilets, drinking water and a dump station.

Also worth a look, **Pine Lake** (Escalante Ranger District ☎ 435-826-5400; www.fs.fed.us/dxnf; group reservations ☎ 877-444-6777; www.reserveusa.com; 11 miles north of Hwy 12/63 junction, then 6 miles east on unpaved Clay Creek; 33 sites; $9; Jun-Sep) sits in a pretty pine forest near a reservoir. Powerboats aren't allowed, but expect ATVs. There's no trash collection, and amenities are limited to vault toilets and drinking water.

**KOA of Cannonville** ( ☎ 435-679-8988; www.koa.com; Hwy 12, 5 miles east of Tropic; 80 sites, 5 cabins; tent $20, RV hookup $28, cabin $46; Mar-Dec; ) Particularly good for families with kids, this KOA provides lots of amenities (flush toilets, drinking water, dump station, electrical hookups etc), including spotlessly clean bathrooms and showers.

## Lodging
### INSIDE THE PARK
Built in the 1920s, **Bryce Canyon Lodge** ( ☎ 435-834-5361; reservations ☎ 435-772-3213 in summer, ☎ 888-297-2757 in winter; www.brycecanyonlodge.com; r $108-136, cabins $126; closed Nov 1–Mar 31; ) exudes rustic mountain charm. If you can secure a reservation, it's worth every penny. Flanked by hickory rocking chairs, a stone fireplace dominates the lobby, where orange-hued, wood-paneled walls and ceiling echo the color of canyon hoodoos. Ranging from modern hotel units to freestanding cabins, most rooms are in satellite buildings. Hotel rooms are in discrete, two-story wood-and-timber buildings and feature new furnishings, a private balcony or porch, and bathrooms tiled in attractive stone. Cabins have peaked roofs with exposed raw-bark timbers, gas fireplaces, private baths and small porches. Some cabin furnishings are a bit dated, but you can't beat the romance of sleeping beneath open eaves with a fire glowing in the corner.

All accommodations include two queen beds; none have air-conditioning or TV. Evening programs are held in the lodge auditorium, which boasts a 30ft cathedral ceiling and giant fireplace. You'll also find a gift shop but no bar.

### OUTSIDE THE PARK
Except for a few notable exceptions, lodging here is nothing special. Expect

## BRYCE & THE UNION PACIFIC RAILROAD

In the early 1920s, the Union Pacific Railroad saw vast profit potential in bringing tourists to the majestic, but still-inaccessible canyons of southern Utah and northern Arizona. They funded and built great lodges laden with modern comforts at the Grand Canyon, Zion, Cedar Breaks and Bryce Canyon. Trains arrived at Cedar City, and guests were shuttled via motor coach on a loop the railroad dubbed the Grand Circle Tour. In trip brochures, the railroad wrote of Bryce, 'There bursts upon [the visitor's] amazed eyes what is probably the most astonishing blend of exquisite beauty and grotesque grandeur ever produced by the forces of erosion. It is not to be described, however imperfectly, except in the language of fancy.' Bryce Canyon Lodge stands as a reminder of that long-lost era of luxury rail travel in America.

motel rooms with fiberglass tub–shower combinations and plastic drinking cups by the sink. A coffeemaker is a luxury in southern Utah.

For more character, book a cabin or B&B. Rates drop in the fall and spring; most properties close in winter.

## Bryce

**Best Western Ruby's Inn** ( ☎ 435-834-5341, 866-866-6616; www.rubysinn.com; 1000 S Hwy 63; r $100-130; ✖ ⬜ ⬛ ) A gargantuan motel complex a mile north of the park entrance, Ruby's has 369 standard rooms with amenities like coffeemakers, hair dryers, ironing boards and irons; all rooms include two beds, either queen- or king-size. The facilities are the major attraction. Open to nonguests, the sprawling property includes a grocery store (camping supplies, books, clothing and souvenirs), two gas stations, a post office, coin laundry, a pool and hot tub, showers, a foreign-currency exchange, gift shops, email kiosks and wireless Internet, one-hour film processing and a liquor store (a rarity around here). The tour desk can book helicopter tours and horseback riding. Ruby's also rents bicycles and ATVs. In summer there's a nightly rodeo (except Sunday).

Also run by Ruby's, **Bryce View Lodge** ( ☎ 435-834-5180, 888-279-2304; www.bryceviewlodge.com; r $65) sits across the highway. Geared to budget travelers, its 130 standard rooms are older and smaller than Ruby's with fewer amenities, but you'll have free access to all the facilities across the street, including the pool and hot tub.

**Bryce Canyon Resort** ( ☎ 435-834-5351, 800-834-0043; www.brycecanyonresort.com; Hwy 12/63 junction; r $65-85, cabins $55-105; ⬛ ✖ ) Four miles from the park, this is a great alternative to Ruby's. Remodeled rooms include new furnishings and extra amenities, while economy rooms are standard and have neither air-conditioning nor phones. Some units have kitchenettes. There's also a small campground and **restaurant** (p138).

Also worth a look, **Bryce Canyon Pines** ( ☎ 435-834-5441, 800-892-7923; www.brycecanyonmotel.com; Hwy 12, 4 miles west of Hwy 12/63 junction; r $65-85; closed Nov-Mar; ✖ ✖ ⬛ ) has clean, plain motel rooms, a **restaurant** (p138) and a small campground.

## Tropic

**Bryce Country Cabins** ( ☎ 435-679-8643, 888-679-8643; www.brycecountrycabins.com; 320 N Main St; cabins $65; ✖ ✖ ) These six cozy cabins on the west side of town feature peaked roofs, knotty pine walls, TVs, coffeemakers, small porches and lots of charm – among the best simple accommodations near Bryce.

**Bryce Canyon Inn** ( ☎ 435-679-8502, 800-592-1468; www.brycecanyoninn.com; 21 N Main St; r $55-65, cabins $75-90; ✖ ✖ ) In addition to regular motel rooms, you can opt for a cabin with knotty pine walls and ceiling, a refrigerator, coffeemaker and TV. The 18 cabins here are larger, but closer together, than those at Bryce Country Cabins. There's also an on-site pizzeria (p138).

**Stone Canyon Inn** ( ☎ 435-679-8611, 866-489-4680; www.stonecanyoninn.com; 1220 Stone Canyon Lane; r $99-149; closed Dec-Jan; ✖ ✖ ) The top choice for savvy travelers, Stone Canyon sits hidden on the outskirts of Tropic and has five rooms with ultra-comfortable beds, high-thread-count sheets and gorgeous views. Delicious breakfasts include homemade breads and imaginative entrées. The charming, urbane innkeeper, who designed and built the inn, also guides tours on foot, horseback or ATV.

**Bullberry Inn** ( ☎ 435-679-8820; www.bullberryinn.com; 412 S Hwy 12; $65-85; ✖ ✖ ) Built in 1998, this well-run, farmhouse-style inn has boasts great views of the surrounding landscape and is an excellent alternative to a motel. The affable owners make their own bullberry jam, which they serve with breakfast.

If these B&Bs are booked, try **Bryce Trails B&B** ( ☎ 435-679-8700, 866-215-5043; www.brycetrails.com; 1001 W Bryce Way; r $80-120;  ⊠  ☒ ).

You can also find rooms at **Bryce Valley Inn** ( ☎ 435-679-8811, 800-442-1890; www.brycevalleyinn.com; 199 N Main St; r $65-80;  ☒ ) and **Bryce Pioneer Village** ( ☎ 435-679-8546, 800-222-0381; www.bpvillage.com; 80 S Main St; r $55-75;  ☒ ), which sits on 14 acres of land and includes an **RV campground**.

## EATING

### INSIDE THE PARK

**Bryce Canyon Lodge** ( ☎ 435-834-5361; breakfast & lunch $7-11, dinner $15-22;  ⊗ 6:30-10:30am, 11:30am-3:30pm, 5:30-9:30pm; closed Nov-Mar) Windows line the walls of the comfortable, casual dining room at Bryce Canyon Lodge, which serves three meals a day. At breakfast and lunch, expect well-prepared standard American fare. At dinner the ambitious menu sometimes tries too hard to be gourmet and ends up being heavy-handed. Stick to simple dishes. This is by far the best place to eat in or around the park. Reservations are necessary for dinner. Beer and wine; no liquor.

**Bryce Canyon General Store & Snack Bar** ( ☎ 435-834-5361; dishes $3-5;  ⊗ 8am-8pm summer, 8am-6pm spring & fall; closed Nov-Mar) In addition to foodstuffs and sundries, the general store near Sunrise Point sells hot dogs, cold drinks, packaged sandwiches, chili, soup and pizza.

### OUTSIDE THE PARK

Nobody comes to Bryce for the food. A typical dinner: chicken-fried steak, canned gravy, frozen peas, gluey pie and watery coffee, all served at a snail's pace. If you're a vegetarian, travel with a cooler of vegetables – otherwise, subsist on iceberg lettuce and soggy fries.

**Bryce Canyon Pines** ( ☎ 435-834-5441; Hwy 12, 4 miles west of Hwy 12/63 junction; breakfast & lunch $5-8, dinner $10-16; closed Nov-Mar;  ⊗ 6:30am-9:30pm) Marked only by a yellow 'Restaurant' sign, the Pines serves three meat-and-potatoes meals daily. It's known for its homemade soups and pies, which are heavy but pretty good.

**Bryce Canyon Resort** ( ☎ 435-834-5351; Hwy12/63 junction; breakfast & lunch $5-9, dinner $6-14;  ⊗ 7am-9pm) The only Mexican restaurant near Bryce features fajitas, burritos and burgers. It also serves breakfast and runs a small sports bar (beer and wine only; no margaritas).

**Foster's Family Steakhouse** ( ☎ 435-834-5227; Hwy 12, 2 miles west of Hwy 12/63 junction; dinner mains $9-18;  ⊗ 7am-10pm summer, 4-9pm spring & fall; closed Nov-Mar) The beef-heavy menu at this diner-cum-steakhouse is satisfactory, despite the thin-cut steaks and iceberg-lettuce salad bar.

**Ruby's Inn** ( ☎ 435-834-5341; 1000 S Hwy 63; breakfast & lunch $5-10, dinner $12-29;  ⊗ 6:30am-10pm, till 9:30pm in winter) Ruby's operates two restaurants: a full-service dining room and buffet off the lobby, and a diner that serves pizza, burgers and fried food. Both serve mediocre assembly-line cooking that's overpriced but convenient. Expect a wait at dinner.

**Bryce Canyon Inn & Pizza** ( ☎ 435-679-8888; 21 N Main St, Tropic; dishes $5-12;  ⊗ 7:30-9pm Mon-Sat, 2-9:30pm Sun, no breakfast in spring; closed Nov-Mar) Good pizza at lunch and dinner, as well as outdoor seating, make this Tropic's top spot for simple dining.

**Hoodoo's** ( ☎ 435-679-8600; 141 N Main St, Tropic; lunch & dinner $7-16;  ⊗ 11:30am-10pm summer, 11:30am-8pm spring & fall; closed Nov-Mar) If you want a full, hot meal in Tropic, Hoodoo's serves steaks and fish, as well as burgers and sandwiches. There is beer but no wine.

## GROCERIES & SUPPLIES

If you need anything beyond basic supplies, don't count on finding it near Bryce; bring it with you, or shop in a metropolitan area en route. In the park, the **General Store** ( ☎ 435-834-5361; ⏱ 8am-8pm summer, 8am-6pm spring & fall; closed Nov-Mar) carries a good variety of essentials, from coffee to toothpaste. **Ruby's Inn** ( ☎ 435-834-5341; 1000 S Hwy 63; ⏱ 7am-10pm) carries groceries, sundries, clothing and camping supplies.

## INTERNET ACCESS

**Ruby's Inn** ( ☎ 435-834-5341; 1000 S Hwy 63) offers free high-speed wireless Internet access for guests and nonguests with a computer and wireless card; otherwise, you can rent time at a terminal for $1 per five minutes.

## LAUNDRY

The park's **General Store** ( ☎ 435-834-5361; ⏱ 8am-8pm summer, 8am-6pm spring & fall; closed Nov-Mar) provides coin-operated laundry facilities during store hours. North of the park, **Ruby's Inn** ( ☎ 435-834-5341; 1000 S Hwy 63) offers a 24-hour coin laundry; buy soap at the inn's general store.

## LOST & FOUND

Stop by the visitor center or call ☎ 435-834-4303.

## MEDICAL SERVICE & EMERGENCIES

In an emergency, dial ☎ 911 or ☎ 435-676-2411. The nearest clinic and emergency room are at **Garfield Memorial Hospital** ( ☎ 435-676-8811; 200 N 400 E, Panguitch).

## POSTAL SERVICE

**Ruby's Inn** ( ☎ 435-834-5341, ext 7188; 1000 S Hwy 63, Bryce, UT 84764) runs a year-round post office. **Bryce Canyon Lodge** ( ☎ 435-834-5361; Bryce Canyon, UT 84717) operates a post office April through October.

## SHOWERS

The park's **General Store** ( ☎ 435-834-5361; ⏱ 8am-8pm summer, 8am-6pm spring & fall; closed Nov-Mar) provides coin-operated hot showers during store hours. **Ruby's Inn** ( ☎ 435-834-5341; 1000 S Hwy 63) offers hot showers at its campground.

# AROUND BRYCE CANYON

## PANGUITCH

**pop 1623 / elevation 6666ft**

Founded in 1864, Panguitch was, until recently, a center for the local ranching and lumber communities. Now tourism is the number-one industry. A popular stopping place for travelers, the town enjoys pleasant summer weather and is crisscrossed by scenic byways – Hwy 89 to the north and south, Hwy 143 to the west and Hwy 12 to the east. Panguitch is the Garfield County seat and has long been the gateway to Bryce Canyon National Park (24 miles east). In summer the town hosts a number of festivals. June welcomes the Quilt Walk Festival, in honor of the region's pioneer history, and Chariots in the Sky, a huge hot-air balloon festival. July's Pioneer Days include a rodeo. The Garfield County Fair takes place in August.

### Orientation & Information

The main drag through town, Hwy 89 comes in on Main St from the north, then turns east on Center St. South of Center, Main becomes Hwy 143 leading to Panguitch Lake.

The **Garfield County Tourism Office** ( ☎ 435-676-1160, 800-444-6689; www.brycecanyoncountry.com; 55 S Main St, ✆ 9am-5pm) provides regional travel and event information. Also stop by the **Dixie National Forest Powell Ranger Station** ( ☎ 435-676-8815; www.fs.fed.us/dxnf; 225 E Center St).

Other services include the **library** ( ☎ 435-676-2431; 25 S 200 E), **post office** ( ☎ 435-676-8853; 65 N 100 W), **hospital** ( ☎ 435-676-8811; 224 N 400 E) and **police** ( ☎ 435-676-8807; 45 S Main St).

### Sights

The **Paunsaugunt Wildlife Museum** ( ☎ 435-676-2500; www.brycecanyonwildlifemuseum.com; 250 E Center St; adult/child 6-12 $4/2.50; ✆ 9am-8pm May-Oct) is town's best attraction, showcasing more than 400 mounted animals from the West and around the world, as well as a butterfly and giant bug room.

Panguitch once hosted a brick factory and boasts a number of **red-brick houses**. The information booth provides a self-guided tour pamphlet.

### Sleeping

#### CAMPING

Most private campgrounds close in winter. **Big Fish KOA** ( ☎ 435-676-2225, 800-562-1625; www.koa.com; 555 S Main St; tent $19, RV hookup $23, cabin/shared bath $44; 🏊 ) offers complete facilities. Both **Hitch-n-Post** ( ☎ 435-676-2436; 420 N Main St) and **Paradise Campground** ( ☎ 435-676-8348; 2153 N Hwy 89), 2 miles north, provide tent/RV sites for $16/18.

**Showers** are available at the Big 4 Travel Center (see opposite).

#### LODGING

**Red Brick Inn** ( ☎ 435-676-2141, 866-732-2745; www.redbrickutah.com; 11161 N 100 W; d $79; ❌ ) Panguitch's only B&B is lovingly tended by on-site owners who have an expansive worldview. The individually decorated rooms are cozy and comfortable, and there's an outdoor hot tub.

Panguitch and the area around the Hwy 89/12 junction (7 miles south) feature a good selection of budget and mid-range accommodations, which are uniformly clean and well kept (with a few exceptions). Summer rates are quoted below, but if you pull into town without a reservation, rates may be higher. Properties that remain open in the off-season (November to March) reduce rates significantly.

Two of the cheapest motels are the **Big 4 Travel Center** ( ☎ 435-676-8863; 445 E Center St; r $38; ✕ ✖ ), which is essentially a truck stop, and the **Bryce Canyon Motel** ( ☎ 435-676-8441; 308 N Main St; r $40; ☽ Apr-Oct), whose otherwise clean rooms need updating.

**Purple Sage** ( ☎ 435-676-2659, 800-241-6889; www.purplesagemotel.biz; 132 E Center St; r $35-65; ☽ Mar-Oct; ✕ ✖ ) Perhaps the most comfortable motel in Panguitch. Rooms feature pillow-top mattresses and new furnishings, and there's an outdoor hot tub.

**Horizon Motel** ( ☎ 435-676-2651, 800-776-2651; www.horizonmotel.net; 730 N Main St; r $55-60; ☽ Mar-Nov; ✕ ✖ ) An old-fashioned motel showing pride of ownership, the Horizon has several rooms with refrigerators and microwaves.

**Canyon Lodge** ( ☎ 435-676-8292, 800-440-8292; www.colorcountry.net/~cache; 210 N Main St; r $45-50; ☽ Mar-Oct; ✕ ✖ ) This immaculately kept, 10-room motel also offers a hot tub and massage.

**Color Country** ( ☎ 435-676-2386, 800-225-6518; www.colorcountrymotel.com; 526 N Main St; r $45-60; ✖ ▣ ) Color Country boasts the best pool in town, an outdoor hot tub and well-kept rooms.

Other properties with standard rooms worth a look include **Hiett Lamplighter** ( ☎ 435-676-8362, 800-322-6966; www.lamplighterinn.biz; 581 N Main St; r $40-60; ✕ ✖ ), **Blue Pine** ( ☎ 435-676-8197, 800-299-6115; fax 676-2128; 130 N Main St; r $48-55; ✕ ✖ ), **Adobe Sands** ( ☎ 435-676-8874, 800-497-9261; www.adobesands.com; 390 N Main St; closed Nov-Apr; ✖ ) and **Bryce Way Motel** ( ☎ 435-676-2400, 800-225-6534; fax 676-8445; 429 N Main St; r $45-55; ✖ ). The **Best Western New Western** ( ☎ 435-676-8876, 800-528-1234; 200 E Center St; r $65-85; ✕ ✖ ▣ ) is unnecessarily expensive but still recommended.

## Eating

Panguitch's selection of restaurants, unlike that of its lodgings, is neither wide nor notable.

Surprising enough, town does offer a 24-hour diner, the **Big 4 Travel Center** ( ☎ 435-676-8863; 445 E Center St; dishes $4-15). The **C-Stop Pizza & Deli** ( ☎ 435-676-8366; 561 E Center St; pizzas $5-14; ☽ 10:30am-10pm, shorter winter hours) serves pizza and sandwiches. **Foy's Country Corner Café** ( ☎ 435-676-8851, 80 N Main St; dishes $5-12; ☽ 7am-9pm Mon-Sat) and **Flying M Restaurant** ( ☎ 435-676-8008, 580 Main St; dishes $5-12; ☽ 7am-10pm, till 9pm in winter) are run-of-the-mill family diners. **Cowboy's Smokehouse BBQ** ( ☎ 435-676-8030; 95 N Main St; dinner mains $18-28; ☽ 11:30am-9pm Mar-Oct) sometimes serves good steaks and house-smoked meats, but the quality is erratic. **Grandma Tina's** ( ☎ 435-676-2377; 523 N Main St; dishes $5-15; ☽ 7am-10pm summer, closed Mon-Wed in winter) serves good Italian sausage and vegetarian pasta dishes.

## Getting There & Away

Hwy 89 is the main route through town. There is no scheduled bus, air or train service to Panguitch.

## RED CANYON

If you're heading to Bryce Canyon from the west, Red Canyon provides your first arresting view of magnificent rock formations. Aptly named, the canyon's iron-rich limestone towers are saturated a deep red. Legend has it that outlaw Butch Cassidy once rode trails in this area, and one of the toughest hiking routes (the Cassidy Trail) bears his name.

## Orientation & Information

Red Canyon is on Hwy 12, 1.5 miles from the Hwy 89 junction south of Panguitch, and 15 miles from Bryce Canyon. The excellent **visitor center** ( ☎ 435-676-2676; Hwy 12; ⊙ 9am-6pm summer, 10am-4pm spring & fall, closed Oct-Apr) provides regional maps, hiking information, historical displays, local crafts and hands-on kids' displays. Red Canyon is in the **Dixie National Forest Powell Ranger District** ( ☎ 435-676-8815; www.fs.fed.us/dxnf; 225 E Center St, Panguitch; ⊙ 8am-4:30 Mon-Fri).

## Activities

Hiking, mountain biking, horseback riding and ATV riding are the primary activities at Red Canyon. Pick up the trail map brochure at the visitor center, which details all the routes.

Several moderately easy **hiking trails** begin near the visitor center: The 0.7-mile/30-minute **Arches Trail** passes 15 arches as it winds through a canyon; the 1-mile/30-minute **Pink Ledges Trail** winds through red-rock formations. For a harder hike, try the 2.8-mile/2-4 hour **Golden Wall Trail**. Check at the visitor center for current trail conditions.

If you like **horseback riding**, you can arrange a guided ride with **Red Canyon Trail Rides** ( ☎ 435-834-5441, 800-892-7923; brycecanyonmotel.com; Hwy 12, 5 miles west of Hwy12/63 junction; 2hrs $30, half day $40, all day $85) through the Bryce Canyon Pines Motel (p137), or with **Ruby's Red Canyon Horseback Rides** ( ☎ 435-834-5341, 800-468-8660; www.rubysinn.com; 1000 S Hwy 63; 1.5hrs $28, half-day $45, all day $79), based at Ruby's Inn (p137).

Unlike much of the region around Bryce, **mountain-biking trails** abound at Red Canyon. The best is the **Thunder Mountain Trail**. Five miles of this loop trail are paved and suitable for families; the other 7.8 are strenuous and involve sand and switchbacks (ride uphill on the pavement and downhill on the dirt). Rent a bike at **Ruby's Inn** (half-day $20, all day $35) from the Chevron Station across the street; you can also rent a bike rack for your car. Red Canyon also includes **ATV trails**; call Ruby's about ATV rentals.

## Sleeping & Eating

It's a 20-minute drive from Red Canyon to Bryce, or 10 minutes to Panguitch.

**Red Canyon Campground** (p135) is scenic and beautifully maintained by the USFS. If you can't secure a site, try **Red Canyon RV Park** ( ☎ 435-676-2690; tent $10, RV hookup $20; closed Oct-Mar), at the Hwy 12/89 junction, which also operates a small store.

On Hwy 12, just east of the Hwy 89 junction, **Harold's Place** ( ☎ 435-676-2350; www.haroldsplace.net; cabin $65; ☒ ☒ ) maintains 20 cozy, modern, pine-paneled log cabins and a good **restaurant** (for around here) that serves breakfast and dinner; the specialty is trout. **Western Town Resort** ( ☎ 435-676-8770, 866-231-2956; www.silveradowildwest.com; Hwy 89 at Hwy 12; r $89-120; ☒ ☒ ☐ ) offers 80 standard motel rooms behind faux–Wild West shop fronts. You'll also find a restaurant and various activities like square dancing.

# Zion & Bryce Canyon

# MAP SECTION

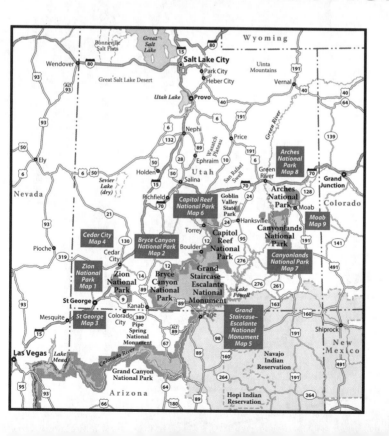

Map 1 **Zion National Park**

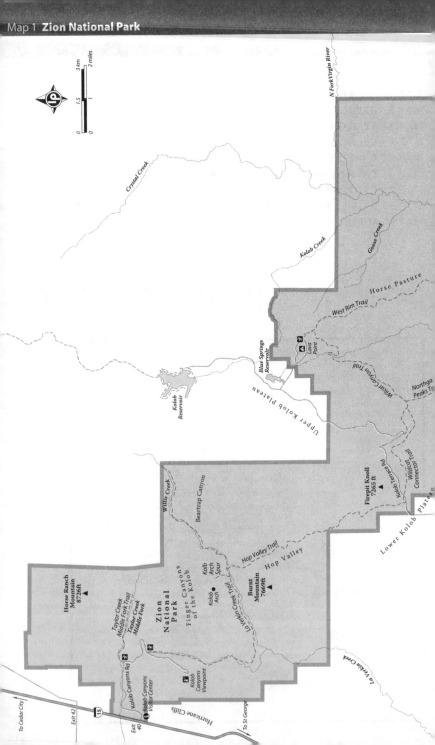

3 km
2 miles
1.5
1
0
0

N Fork Virgin River

Crystal Creek

Goose Creek

Kolob Creek

Horse Pasture

West Rim Trail

Blue Springs Reservoir

Lava Point

Wildcat Canyon Trail

Northga
Peaks Tr

Upper Kolob Plateau

Kolob Reservoir

Willis Creek

Beartrap Canyon

Firepit Knoll
7265 ft

Kolob Terrace Rd

Wildcat
Connector Trail

Lower Kolob Plateau

Hop Valley Trail

Hop Valley

Kolob
Arch
Spur

La Verkin Creek Trail

Burnt
Mountain
7669ft

Horse Ranch
Mountain
8726ft

Taylor Creek Middle Fork Trail

Taylor Creek Middle Fork

Zion
National
Park

Finger Canyons of the Kolob

Kolob
Arch

Kolob Canyons Rd

Kolob Canyons
Visitor Center

Kolob
Canyons
Viewpoint

Hurricane Cliffs

La Verkin Creek

To Cedar City

Exit 42

Exit
40

15

To St George

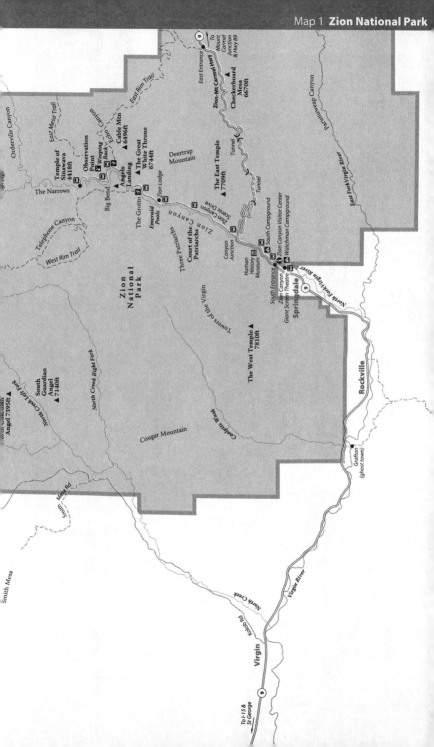

Map 1 **Zion National Park**

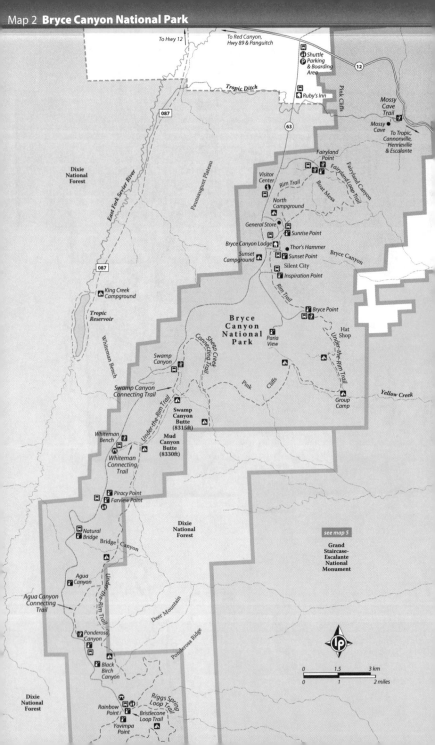

Map 2 **Bryce Canyon National Park**

To Hwy 12

To Red Canyon,
Hwy 89 & Panguitch

Shuttle
Parking
& Boarding
Area

Tropic Ditch

Ruby's Inn

Pink
Cliffs

12

63

Mossy
Cave
Trail

Mossy
Cave

To Tropic,
Cannonville,
Henrieville
& Escalante

Dixie
National
Forest

East Fork Sevier River

Paunsaugunt Plateau

087

Fairyland
Point

Visitor
Center

Rim Trail

Boat Mesa

Fairyland Canyon

Fairyland
Loop Trail

North
Campground

General Store

Sunrise Point

Bryce Canyon Lodge

Thor's Hammer

Bryce Canyon

Sunset
Campground

Sunset Point

Silent City

Inspiration Point

087

Rim Trail

King Creek
Campground

Bryce Point

Hat
Shop

Tropic
Reservoir

Whiteman Bench

Bryce
Canyon
National
Park

Paria
View

Under-the-Rim Trail

Swamp
Canyon

Sheep Creek Connecting Trail

Swamp Canyon
Connecting Trail

Under-the-Rim Trail

Swamp Canyon
Butte
(8315ft)

Pink

Cliffs

Yellow Creek

Whiteman
Bench

Mud
Canyon
Butte
(8330ft)

Group
Camp

Whiteman
Connecting
Trail

Piracy Point

Farview Point

Natural
Bridge

Bridge Canyon

Dixie
National
Forest

see map 5

Grand
Staircase-
Escalante
National
Monument

Agua
Canyon

Agua Canyon
Connecting
Trail

Under-the-Rim Trail

Deer Mountain

Ponderosa
Canyon

Ponderosa Ridge

Black
Birch
Canyon

Dixie
National
Forest

Rainbow
Point

Riggs Spring Loop Trail

Bristlecone
Loop Trail

Yovimpa
Point

0        1.5        3 km
0        1        2 miles

Map 3 **St George**

**INFORMATION**
Chamber of Commerce.................... **1** B3
Dixie Regional Medical Center........ **2** C5
Interagency Information Center....... **3** B6
Library.......................................... **4** B4
Little Professor Books.................... **5** B4
Walgreens..................................... **6** A3
Zions Bank.................................... **7** B3

**SIGHTS & ACTIVITIES**
Bicycles Unlimited......................... **8** B4
Brigham Young Winter Home.......... **9** B3
DUP Museum................................ **10** B3
Mormon Tabernacle....................... **11** B4
Mormon Temple............................ **12** B4
Pioneer Center for the Arts............ **13** B3
Red Rock Bicycle Company............ **14** A4

**SLEEPING**
Ancestor Inn................................. **15** B3
Best Inn & Suites........................... **16** D3
Best Western Abbey Inn.................. **17** B5
Best Western Coral Hills.................. **18** B3
Best Western Travel Inn.................. **19** B3

Budget Inn.................................... **20** B5
Chalet Motel................................. **21** C3
Comfort Inn.................................. **22** C3
Comfort Suites.............................. **23** B3
Coronada Vacation Village............. (see 32)
Days Inn....................................... **24** C3
Dixie Palm Motel........................... **25** B3
Econo Lodge.................................. **26** B3
Greene Gate Village....................... **27** B4
Holiday Inn................................... **28** A5
Howard Johnson's.......................... **29** B5
Motel 6........................................ **30** C3
Quality Inn................................... (see 17)
Ramada Inn................................... **31** D3
Sands Motel.................................. **32** C3
Settlers RV Park............................. **33** D4
Seven Wives Inn............................ **34** B3
Singletree Inn............................... **35** B3
Sullivan's Rococo Inn..................... **36** A4
Sun Time Inn................................. **37** B3
Super 8 Motel................................ **38** B5
Travelodge.................................... **39** C3

**EATING**
Ancestor Square............................ **40** B3
Bean Scene................................... **41** C3
Bear Paw Coffee Company............. **42** B3
Chuck-A-Rama............................... (see 16)
Irmita's........................................ **43** A4
Jazzy Java..................................... **44** A3
Painted Pony................................. (see 40)
Samurai 21.................................... (see 16)
Sullivan's Rococo Steak House...... (see 36)

**ENTERTAINMENT**
Fine Arts Center Theater................ **45** C4
St George Musical Theater.............. **46** B4

**TRANSPORT**
Enterprise..................................... **47** C3
Greyhound Bus Stop...................... **48** B5

**OTHER**
Smith's Supermarket...................... (see 6)

# Map 4 Cedar City

**INFORMATION**
Cedar City & Brian Head Tourism
& Convention Bureau.................... **1** D2
Chamber of Commerce................... (see 1)
Library............................................. **2** D2
Mountain West Books..................... **3** D3
Valley View Medical Center........... **4** D1
Zions Bank...................................... **5** D3

**SIGHTS & ACTIVITIES**
Braithwaite Fine Arts Gallery......... **6** D3
Cedar Cycle..................................... **7** D3
Mormon Tabernacle (Rock Church).. **8** D3
Municipal Pool................................ **9** D3

**SLEEPING**
Abbey Inn........................................ **10** C2
Bard's Inn B&B............................... **11** D3
Best Value Inn................................. **12** D3
Best Western El Rey Inn.................. **13** D3
Best Western Town & Country Inn.. **14** D3
Big Yellow Inn................................. **15** D2
Cedar City KOA............................... **16** D1
Comfort Inn.................................... **17** C2
Crystal Inn...................................... **18** B2
Garden Cottage B&B....................... **19** D3
Motel 6............................................ **20** B2
Ramada Limited.............................. **21** D3
Stratford Court Hotel...................... **22** D3
Super 7 Motel.................................. **23** D3
Super 8 Motel.................................. (see 18)

**EATING**
Blue Kat Cafe.................................. **24** D3
Pastry Pub...................................... **25** D3
Sulli's Steakhouse.......................... **26** D3

**ENTERTAINMENT**
Adams Memorial Theater................ **27** D3
Randall Jones Theater..................... **28** D3
Heritage Center.............................. **29** D3

**OTHER**
Laundromat..................................... (see 16)

**TRANSPORT**
Enterprise....................................... **30** D2
Speedy Rental................................. **31** D2

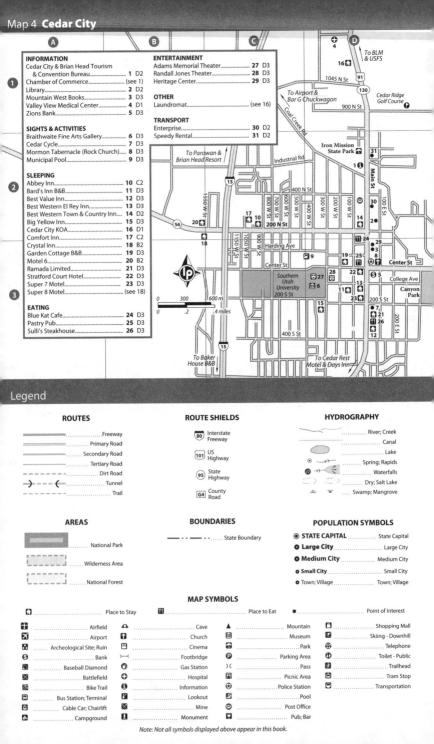

# Legend

**ROUTES**
............. Freeway
.......... Primary Road
.......... Secondary Road
.......... Tertiary Road
.......... Dirt Road
.......... Tunnel
.......... Trail

**ROUTE SHIELDS**
Interstate Freeway
US Highway
State Highway
County Road

**HYDROGRAPHY**
........... River; Creek
........... Canal
........... Lake
........... Spring; Rapids
........... Waterfalls
........... Dry; Salt Lake
........... Swamp; Mangrove

**AREAS**
.......... National Park
.......... Wilderness Area
.......... National Forest

**BOUNDARIES**
.......... State Boundary

**POPULATION SYMBOLS**
STATE CAPITAL ............ State Capital
Large City ............ Large City
Medium City ............ Medium City
Small City ............ Small City
Town; Village ............ Town; Village

**MAP SYMBOLS**
.......... Place to Stay
.......... Place to Eat
.......... Point of Interest

.......... Airfield
.......... Airport
.......... Archeological Site; Ruin
.......... Bank
.......... Baseball Diamond
.......... Battlefield
.......... Bike Trail
.......... Bus Station; Terminal
.......... Cable Car; Chairlift
.......... Campground

.......... Cave
.......... Church
.......... Cinema
.......... Footbridge
.......... Gas Station
.......... Hospital
.......... Information
.......... Lookout
.......... Mine
.......... Monument

.......... Mountain
.......... Museum
.......... Park
.......... Parking Area
.......... Pass
.......... Picnic Area
.......... Police Station
.......... Pool
.......... Post Office
.......... Pub; Bar

.......... Shopping Mall
.......... Skiing - Downhill
.......... Telephone
.......... Toilet - Public
.......... Trailhead
.......... Tram Stop
.......... Transportation

*Note: Not all symbols displayed above appear in this book.*

Map 5 **Grand Staircase–Escalante National Monument**

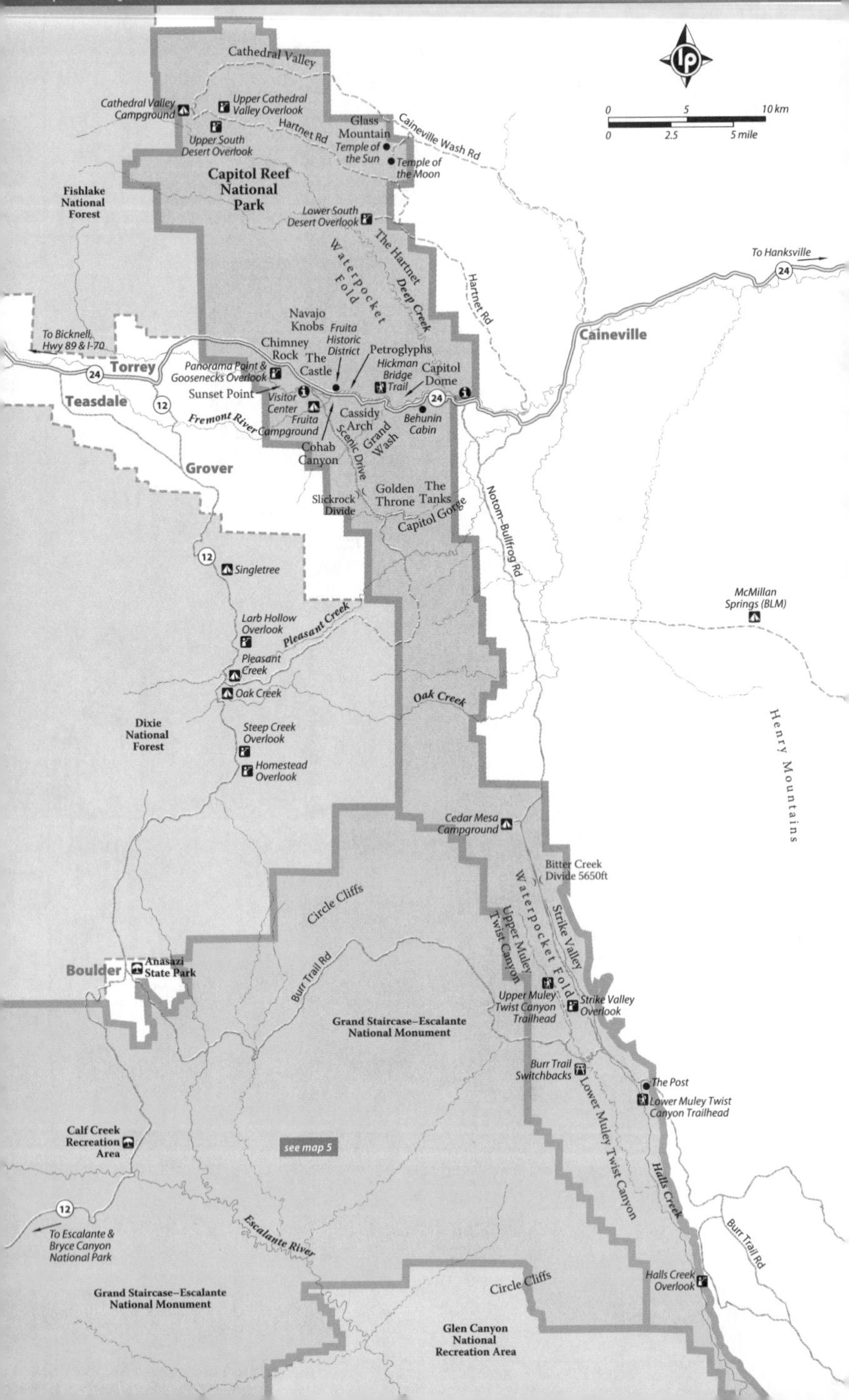

# Map 6 **Capitol Reef National Park**

Cathedral Valley

Cathedral Valley Campground

Upper Cathedral Valley Overlook

Hartnet Rd

Glass Mountain
Temple of the Sun
Temple of the Moon

Caineville Wash Rd

Upper South Desert Overlook

Capitol Reef National Park

Fishlake National Forest

Lower South Desert Overlook

Waterpocket Fold

The Hartnet

Deep Creek

Hartnet Rd

To Hanksville
24

Caineville

To Bicknell, Hwy 89 & I-70

Navajo Knobs
Chimney Rock
Fruita Historic District
Petroglyphs
The Castle
Hickman Bridge Trail
Capitol Dome

Torrey
24

Panorama Point & Goosenecks Overlook

Teasdale
12

Sunset Point

Visitor Center
Fruita Campground

24

Fremont River Rd

Cassidy Arch
Grand Wash

Behunin Cabin

Grover

Cohab Canyon

Slickrock Divide

Golden Throne
The Tanks

Notom-Bullfrog Rd

Capitol Gorge

12
Singletree

McMillan Springs (BLM)

Larb Hollow Overlook

Pleasant Creek

Pleasant Creek
Oak Creek

Dixie National Forest

Steep Creek Overlook

Homestead Overlook

Oak Creek

Henry Mountains

Cedar Mesa Campground

Bitter Creek Divide 5650ft

Circle Cliffs

Waterpocket Fold

Strike Valley

Upper Muley Twist Canyon

Boulder
Anasazi State Park

Burr Trail Rd

Upper Muley Twist Canyon Trailhead

Strike Valley Overlook

Grand Staircase–Escalante National Monument

Burr Trail Switchbacks

The Post
Lower Muley Twist Canyon Trailhead

Calf Creek Recreation Area

Lower Muley Twist Canyon

Halls Creek

see map 5

Burr Trail Rd

12
To Escalante & Bryce Canyon National Park

Escalante River

Grand Staircase–Escalante National Monument

Circle Cliffs

Halls Creek Overlook

Glen Canyon National Recreation Area

0 ——— 5 ——— 10 km
0 ——— 2.5 ——— 5 mile

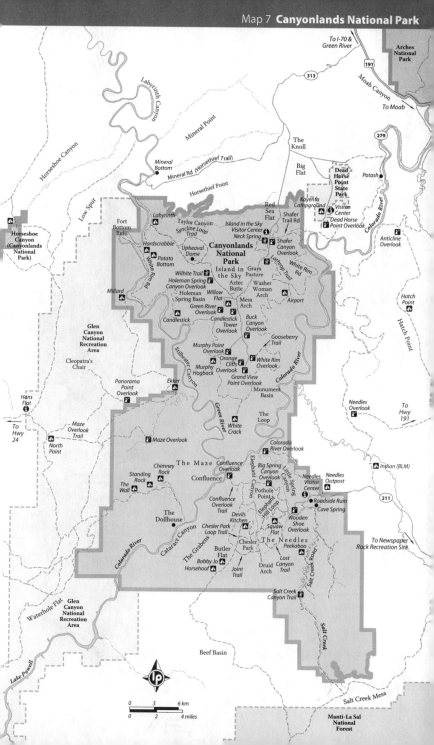

Map 7 **Canyonlands National Park**

To I-70 &
Green River

Arches
National
Park

191

Moab Canyon

To Moab

313

279

The
Knoll

Mineral Point

Labyrinth Canyon

Horseshoe Canyon

Mineral Point

Big
Flat

Dead
Horse
Point State
Park

Potash

Mineral
Bottom

Mineral Rd (Horsethief Trail)

Horsethief Point

Low Spur

Visitor
Center

Dead Horse
Point Overlook

Colorado River

Anticline
Overlook

Horseshoe
Canyon
(Canyonlands
National
Park)

Fort
Bottom
Ruin

Labyrinth

Taylor Canyon

Syncline Loop
Trail

Island in the Sky
Visitor Center
Neck Spring

Red
Sea
Flat

Shafer
Trail Rd

Kayenta
Campground

Hardscrabble

Upheaval
Dome

Canyonlands
National
Park

Shafer
Canyon
Rd

White Rim
Rd

Hatch
Point

White Rim Rd

Wilhite Trail

Island in
the Sky

Grays
Pasture

Lathrop Trail

Potato
Bottom

Holeman Spring
Canyon Overlook

Holeman
Spring Basin

Aztec
Butte

Willow
Flat

Washer
Woman
Arch

Millard

Mesa
Arch

Airport

Green River
Overlook

Candlestick

Candlestick
Tower
Overlook

Buck
Canyon
Overlook

Glen
Canyon
National
Recreation
Area

Cleopatra's
Chair

Gooseberry
Trail

Colorado River

Murphy Point
Overlook

Orange
Cliffs
Overlook

White Rim
Overlook

Stillwater Canyon

Murphy
Hogback

Grand View
Point Overlook

Monument
Basin

Hans
Flat

Panorama
Point
Overlook

Ekker

Needles
Overlook

To
Hwy
191

To Hwy
24

Maze
Overlook
Trail

Green River

The
Loop

North
Point

White
Crack

Maze Overlook

Colorado
River Overlook

Indian (BLM)

The Maze

Confluence
Overlook

Big Spring
Canyon
Overlook

Little Spring Canyon

Needles
Visitor
Center

Needles
Outpost

Chimney
Rock

Confluence

Elephant Canyon

Pothole
Points

211

Standing
Rock

Roadside Ruin

Cave Spring

The
Wall

Confluence
Overlook
Trail

Devils
Kitchen

Squaw
Flat

Wooden
Shoe
Overlook

The
Dollhouse

Elephant Hill Loop

Cataract Canyon

Chesler Park
Loop Trail

Colorado River

The Grabens

Butler
Flat

Chesler
Park

The Needles

Peekaboo

To Newspaper
Rock Recreation Site

Salt Creek Road

Bobby Jo
Horsehoof

Joint
Trail

Druid
Arch

Lost
Canyon
Trail

Waterhole Flat

Glen
Canyon
National
Recreation
Area

Salt Creek
Canyon Trail

Salt Creek

Lake Powell

Beef Basin

Salt Creek Mesa

Manti-La Sal
National
Forest

0      3      6 km
0      2      4 miles

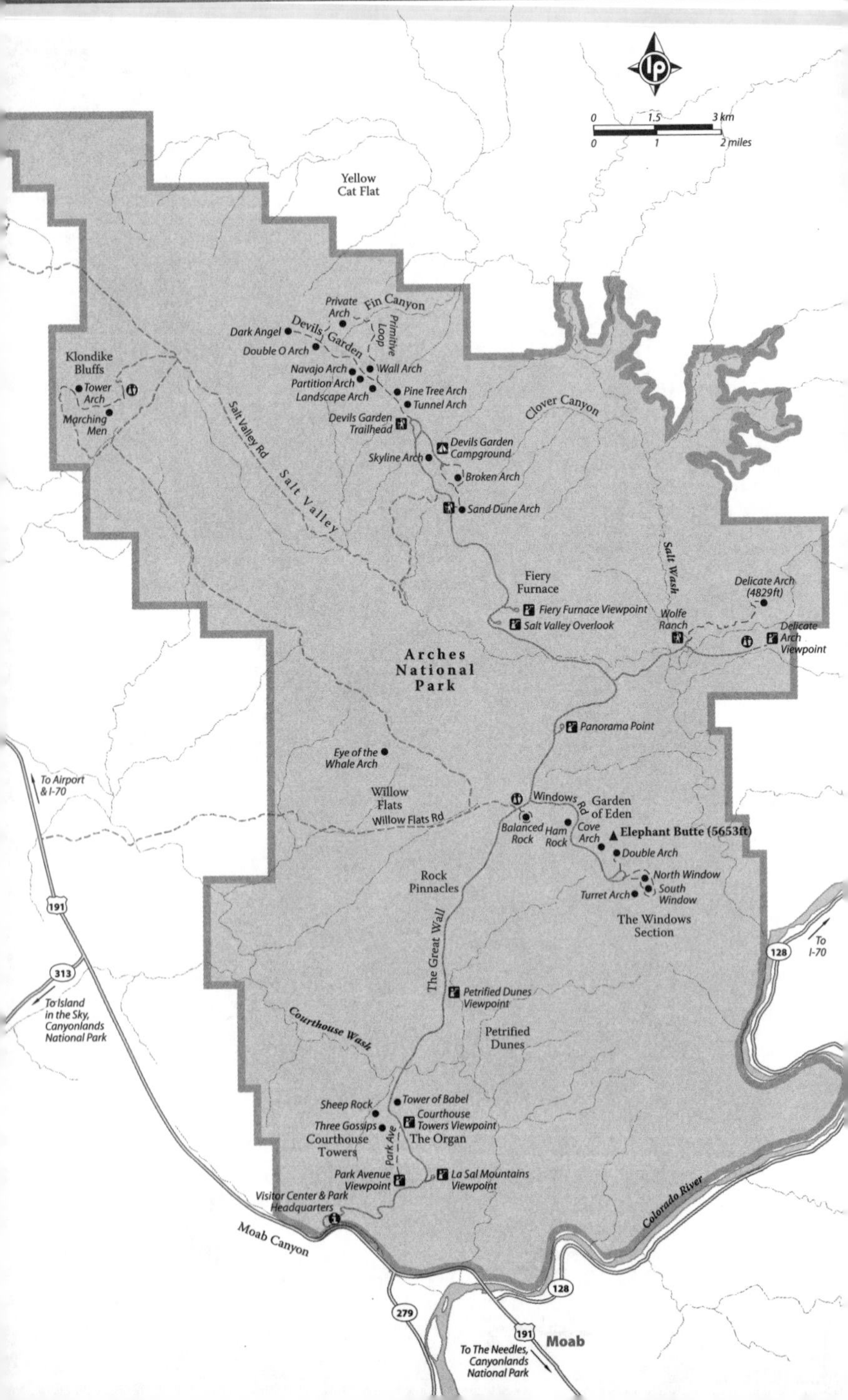

# Map 8 **Arches National Park**

Yellow
Cat Flat

Fin Canyon

Private
Arch

Primitive Loop

Dark Angel

Devils Garden

Double O Arch

Wall Arch

Navajo Arch

Pine Tree Arch

Partition Arch

Tunnel Arch

Landscape Arch

Devils Garden
Trailhead

Clover Canyon

Devils Garden
Campground

Skyline Arch

Broken Arch

Sand Dune Arch

Klondike
Bluffs

Tower
Arch

Marching
Men

Salt Valley Rd

Salt Valley

Salt Wash

Fiery
Furnace

Fiery Furnace Viewpoint

Salt Valley Overlook

Wolfe
Ranch

Delicate Arch
(4829ft)

Delicate
Arch
Viewpoint

**Arches
National
Park**

Panorama Point

Eye of the
Whale Arch

To Airport
& I-70

Willow
Flats

Willow Flats Rd

Windows Rd

Garden
of Eden

Balanced
Rock

Cove
Arch

Ham
Rock

▲ **Elephant Butte** (5653ft)

Double Arch

North Window

Rock
Pinnacles

Turret Arch

South
Window

The Windows
Section

191

313

To Island
in the Sky,
Canyonlands
National Park

The Great Wall

Petrified Dunes
Viewpoint

Petrified
Dunes

To
I-70

128

Courthouse Wash

Sheep Rock

Tower of Babel

Three Gossips

Courthouse
Towers Viewpoint

Courthouse
Towers

Park Ave

The Organ

Park Avenue
Viewpoint

La Sal Mountains
Viewpoint

Visitor Center & Park
Headquarters

Moab Canyon

Colorado River

279

128

191

**Moab**

To The Needles,
Canyonlands
National Park

0   1.5   3 km
0   1   2 miles

Map 9 **Moab**

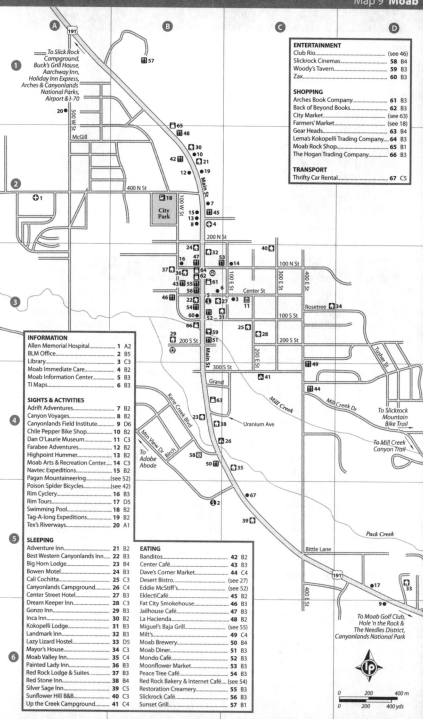

**INFORMATION**

| | | |
|---|---|---|
| Allen Memorial Hospital | **1** | A2 |
| BLM Office | **2** | B5 |
| Library | **3** | C3 |
| Moab Immediate Care | **4** | B2 |
| Moab Information Center | **5** | B3 |
| TI Maps | **6** | B3 |

**SIGHTS & ACTIVITIES**

| | | |
|---|---|---|
| Adrift Adventures | **7** | B2 |
| Canyon Voyages | **8** | B2 |
| Canyonlands Field Institute | **9** | D6 |
| Chile Pepper Bike Shop | **10** | B2 |
| Dan O'Laurie Museum | **11** | C3 |
| Farabee Adventures | **12** | B2 |
| Highpoint Hummer | **13** | B2 |
| Moab Arts & Recreation Center | **14** | C3 |
| Navtec Expeditions | **15** | B2 |
| Pagan Mountaineering | (see 52) | |
| Poison Spider Bicycles | (see 42) | |
| Rim Cyclery | **16** | B3 |
| Rim Tours | **17** | D5 |
| Swimming Pool | **18** | B2 |
| Tag-A-long Expeditions | **19** | B2 |
| Tex's Riverways | **20** | A1 |

**SLEEPING**

| | | |
|---|---|---|
| Adventure Inn | **21** | B2 |
| Best Western Canyonlands Inn | **22** | B3 |
| Big Horn Lodge | **23** | B4 |
| Bowen Motel | **24** | B3 |
| Cali Cochitta | **25** | C3 |
| Canyonlands Campground | **26** | C4 |
| Center Street Hotel | **27** | B3 |
| Dream Keeper Inn | **28** | C3 |
| Gonzo Inn | **29** | B3 |
| Inca Inn | **30** | B2 |
| Kokopelli Lodge | **31** | B3 |
| Landmark Inn | **32** | B3 |
| Lazy Lizard Hostel | **33** | D5 |
| Mayor's House | **34** | C3 |
| Moab Valley Inn | **35** | C4 |
| Painted Lady Inn | **36** | B3 |
| Red Rock Lodge & Suites | **37** | B3 |
| Red Stone Inn | **38** | B4 |
| Silver Sage Inn | **39** | C5 |
| Sunflower Hill B&B | **40** | C3 |
| Up the Creek Campground | **41** | C4 |

**ENTERTAINMENT**

| | | |
|---|---|---|
| Club Rio | (see 46) | |
| Slickrock Cinemas | **58** | B4 |
| Woody's Tavern | **59** | B3 |
| Zax | **60** | B3 |

**SHOPPING**

| | | |
|---|---|---|
| Arches Book Company | **61** | B3 |
| Back of Beyond Books | **62** | B3 |
| City Market | (see 63) | |
| Farmers' Market | (see 18) | |
| Gear Heads | **63** | B4 |
| Lema's Kokopelli Trading Company | **64** | B3 |
| Moab Rock Shop | **65** | B1 |
| The Hogan Trading Company | **66** | B3 |

**TRANSPORT**

| | | |
|---|---|---|
| Thrifty Car Rental | **67** | C5 |

**EATING**

| | | |
|---|---|---|
| Banditos | **42** | B2 |
| Center Café | **43** | B3 |
| Dave's Corner Market | **44** | C4 |
| Desert Bistro | (see 27) | |
| Eddie McStiff's | (see 52) | |
| EklectiCafé | **45** | B2 |
| Fat City Smokehouse | **46** | B3 |
| Jailhouse Café | **47** | B3 |
| La Hacienda | **48** | B2 |
| Miguel's Baja Grill | (see 55) | |
| Milt's | **49** | C4 |
| Moab Brewery | **50** | B4 |
| Moab Diner | **51** | B3 |
| Mondo Café | **52** | B3 |
| Moonflower Market | **53** | B3 |
| Peace Tree Café | **54** | B3 |
| Red Rock Bakery & Internet Café | (see 54) | |
| Restoration Creamery | **55** | B3 |
| Slickrock Café | **56** | B3 |
| Sunset Grill | **57** | B1 |

To Slick Rock
Campground,
Buck's Grill House,
Aarchway Inn,
Holiday Inn Express,
Arches & Canyonlands
National Parks,
Airport & I-70

McGill

City Park

Rosetree

Mill Creek

Mill Creek Dr

To Slickrock
Mountain
Bike Trail

Uranium Ave

To Mill Creek
Canyon Trail

To
Adobe
Abode

Grand

Kane Creek Blvd

Mtn View Dr

Birch

Pack Creek

Bittle Lane

To Moab Golf Club,
Hole 'n the Rock &
The Needles District,
Canyonlands National Park

Trotter St

0    200    400 m
0    200    400 yds

*Nearly twice the size of Rhode Island, 1.9-million-acre Grand Staircase–Escalante National Monument is the largest park in the Southwest.*

## EXPERIENCING
# GRAND STAIRCASE

Its name refers to the 150-mile-long geologic formation that begins on the rim of the Grand Canyon and rises in steps nearly 5500ft to Bryce Canyon and the Escalante River canyons. Together these rock layers represent 270 million years of geologic history in a riot of color. Sections of the monument contain so much red rock that reflected sunlight casts a pink hue on the undersides of passing clouds.

Established in 1996 by President Bill Clinton, Grand Staircase–Escalante links the area from Bryce Canyon National Park east to Capitol Reef National Park and southeast to Glen Canyon National Recreation Area – the last region in the continental United States to be mapped. Managed by the Bureau of Land Management, the monument was created over vehement objections from local residents and legislators who had hoped to develop the area's mining potential, and efforts to revise the management plan and permit greater use of resources continue. Whether or when this might be done remains to be seen. The monument currently welcomes just under a million annual visitors, and many locals are weighing tourism as an alternative to mining.

The monument is unique for a BLM-managed area. While it does allow some uses that would be banned if this were a national park (such as hunting and grazing with proper permits), it allows fewer uses than other BLM lands in order to maintain its 'remote frontier' quality. To this end, development of a tourist infrastructure is minimal and restricted to the park's fringes, leaving a vast desert suitable for scientific research and adventurous exploration.

### WHEN YOU ARRIVE
There are no entrance stations or fees for Grand Staircase–Escalante National Monument (GSENM), which is open 365 days a year. Pick up a map at roadside kiosks outside the monument, or visit the **park website** (www.ut.blm.gov/monument). To talk to a ranger, head to one of the five visitor centers.

### ORIENTATION
The monument encompasses three major areas, divided by geologic significance: The westernmost region contains the **Grand Staircase**, south of Bryce Canyon and west of Cottonwood Canyon Rd. At the center of the park, the

**Kaiparowits Plateau** lies east of Cottonwood Canyon Rd and west of Hole-in-the-Rock Rd. The easternmost section comprises the **Escalante Canyons**, east of Hole-in-the-Rock Rd and southwest of the Burr Trail.

Scenic Hwy 12 skirts the northern boundary of GSENM, from Tropic through Escalante and west of Boulder, while Hwy 89 arcs east of Kanab into the monument's southwest reaches. Four unpaved roads access the park: Three cross the park roughly north to south between Hwys 12 and 89; the fourth leads southeast from Hwy 12 to the Glen Canyon National Recreation Area. The partly paved Burr Trail crosses the monument's northeast corner from Boulder east to Capitol Reef.

Always check with a ranger about weather and road conditions before driving or hiking. In good weather, most roads are passable to cars, but they are dusty, rough and remote. After heavy rain or snow, roads may be impassable, even with 4WD, and should not be attempted if a storm is approaching. After light rains, the clay surface can become dangerously slippery. Always carry extra water and food in case of a breakdown, foul weather or other emergency; help may be hard to find.

See the GSENM map (Map 5) on p149.

## INFORMATION

Obtain information prior to your visit from **Grand Staircase–Escalante National Monument** ( ☎ 435-826-5499; www.ut.blm.gov/monument or http://gsenm.az.blm.gov; PO Box 225, Escalante, UT 84726), or stop by one of five year-round **visitor centers** just outside GSENM.

North of the monument, the **Escalante Interagency Visitor Center** ( ☎ 435-826-5499; www.ut.blm.gov/monument or http://gsenm.az.blm.gov; 755 W Main St, Escalante; ⊗ 7:30am-5:30pm) is jointly run by the BLM, USFS and NPS and provides comprehensive information about southern Utah's federal lands, forests, monuments and national parks.

The **Cannonville Visitor Center** ( ☎ 435-826-5640; 10 Center St, Cannonville; ⊗ 8am-4:30pm) is off Hwy 12, 5 miles southeast of Tropic. Southwest of the monument, the **Kanab Visitor Center** ( ☎ 435-644-4680; 745 E Hwy 89, Kanab; ⊗ 8am-4:30pm) also contains park headquarters. To the south is the **Big Water Visitor Center** ( ☎ 435-675-3200; 100 Upper Revolution Way, Big Water; ⊗ 9am-5:30pm). Just west of Big Water, the **Paria Contact Station** (Hwy 89, 44 miles east of Kanab; ⊗ 8:30am-4:15pm) is open March 15 to November 15.

Rangers at **Anasazi State Park** (p168) in Boulder can also answer questions about GSENM.

### Overnight Permits

You'll need a free permit if you plan to car-camp or backpack in the monu-

> ## HIGHLIGHTS
>
> ✔ Squeezing through narrow slot canyons at **Peekaboo Gulch** (p159) or **Paria Canyon** (p171)
>
> ✔ Tasting the Old West – both its real-life and Hollywood versions – at the **Paria Valley Road & Movie Set** (p171)
>
> ✔ Splashing in the year-round running water of **Calf Creek** (p167)
>
> ✔ Climbing beneath giant yellow **Grosvenor Arch** (p157)
>
> ✔ Finding shapes, faces and figures in the rock formations at **Kodachrome Basin State Park** (p165)

ment. Pick one up at any visitor center, information kiosk or major trailhead. This is dangerous country – always get a permit, let someone know your itinerary and avoid hiking alone.

## Policies & Regulations

Campfires in developed campgrounds are restricted to fire rings; elsewhere in the monument you're allowed to use a fire pan. You may not light fires below the rims of the Escalante and Paria/Hackberry Canyons or on No Man's Mesa. Fires are also prohibited at archaeological sites and in rock shelters or alcoves.

Fishing and hunting is allowed; check seasonal rules and permit requirements at visitor centers. Scavenging is prohibited; leave all plants, rocks, fossils and artifacts where you find them.

Off-road mountain biking and driving are also prohibited in the monument. All vehicles must stay on designated roads, which are open to mountain bikes, cars, 4WD vehicles, ATVs and other off-highway vehicles.

## GETTING AROUND

The only way to get around the monument is on foot or in a private vehicle. High-clearance 4WD vehicles are your best bet, as many roads are unpaved and only occasionally bladed. Note that most off-the-lot SUVs and light trucks are *not* high-clearance vehicles. Heed all warnings about road conditions before entering the monument. If it starts to rain while you're driving, pull over and wait until the road dries again, as you can easily slide off the road or get stuck in the claylike soil.

Buy gasoline whenever you see it. Up north you'll find stations in Tropic, Escalante and Boulder. Down south, gas up in Kanab.

Several companies operate **hiker shuttles**. In Escalante contact **Excursions of Escalante** ( ☎ 435-826-4714, 800-839-7567; www.excursions-escalante.com; PO Box 605, Escalante, UT 84726; ☾ spring-fall). If it's booked, call **Escalante Outback Adventures** ( ☎ 435-826-4967; www.escalante-utah.com; 325 W. Main St, Escalante; ☾ spring-fall). See **Kanab** (p169) for shuttles in the south.

## DRIVING TOURS

Two paved arteries skirt GSENM: To the north, Hwy 12 runs east-west, while to the west, Hwy 89 runs south to Kanab, cuts east into the park's southwest corner, then turns south into Arizona.

Most of the secondary routes listed below are unpaved gravel or dirt roads that quickly become impassible in heavy rain or snow. If it does rain while you're driving, stop and wait for the storm to pass; roads dry quickly, sometimes within 30 minutes. *Never park in a wash.* Contact a visitor center by phone or in person to check road conditions before entering the monument.

While you may be tempted to drive fast on dirt roads, it's impossible to stop quickly. Cross a wash too fast (say, going 15mph to 25mph, depending on steepness) and you could bottom out hard and lose your oil pan. Easy does it.

### SKUTUMPAH & JOHNSON CANYON ROADS

These two roads comprise the monument's westernmost route. A very rough dirt road, Skutumpah (SCOOT-um-pah) runs for 35 miles between Cannonville on Hwy 12 to its junction with paved Johnson Canyon Rd, which continues another 16 miles to Hwy 89, about 9 miles east of Kanab. In dry conditions, Skutumpah takes more than two hours to drive and requires a high-clearance 2WD vehicle, though 4WD is recommended; Johnson Canyon Rd takes less than 30 minutes. Drive south-north to keep the sights in your front windshield.

This very scenic route takes in the **Vermilion**, **White**, **Gray** and **Pink Cliffs**, the latter of which are particularly dramatic. Those who don't have the time or proper vehicle to tackle Skutumpah Rd could drive Johnson Canyon Rd to the 15-mile **Glendale Bench Rd**, which leads east from the Skutumpah junction to emerge on Hwy 89 at **Glendale** (p113). This good dirt road (signed '300 N' in Glendale) is passable to passenger vehicles in dry weather and takes about half an hour, offering peekaboo views of Bryce in the distance. Road signs along the way attest to the skillful aim of local marksmen.

## COTTONWOOD CANYON ROAD

This 46-mile scenic backway heads east, then south, from Kodachrome Basin State Park, emerging at Hwy 89 near **Paria Canyon** (p171). It is the closest entry point into GSENM from Bryce, and it's an easy but sometimes rough drive, passable for 2WD vehicles (RVs and trailers should think twice). About 20 miles south of Hwy 12 you'll reach **Grosvenor Arch**, an unusual yellow-limestone double arch, where you'll find picnic tables and restrooms.

The road continues south along the west side of **The Cockscomb**, a distinctive long, narrow ridge caused by a fold, or monocline, in the Earth's crust. The Cockscomb divides the Grand Staircase from Kaiparowits Plateau to the east; there are superb views in all directions. The most scenic stretch of road lies between Grosvenor Arch and **Lower Hackberry Canyon**, where you'll find good **hiking** (p160). From here the road follows the desolate Paria River valley almost until it reaches Hwy 89.

## SMOKY MOUNTAIN ROAD

Few drivers brave this rough, 78-mile dirt-and-gravel road, passable by ATV or 4WD vehicle only, preferably with high clearance. Even then, expect the route to take more than six hours. From Escalante in the north, it crosses the rugged **Kaiparowits Plateau** and emerges at the **Big Water Visitor Center** on Hwy 89, just west of Glen Canyon National Recreation Area. The prime destination is **Alstrom Point**, 38 miles from Hwy 89, a plateau-top vantage with stunning views that include Lake Powell; ask rangers for directions.

## HOLE-IN-THE-ROCK ROAD

Both the scenery and history are wild along this 57-mile dirt-and-gravel road, which starts five miles east of Escalante and heads southeast, dead-ending at Lake Powell (allow four to five hours one way). It is passable to ordinary passenger cars when dry – except for the last 7 miles, which may require 4WD.

Pioneering Mormons followed this route in 1879–80 on their way to settle new lands in southeast Utah. Little did they know that the precipitous walls of Glen Canyon on the Colorado River would block their path. More than 200 pioneers literally blasted and hammered through the cliff, creating a route wide enough to descend with their 80 wagons – a feat that is honored today by markers along the road. The final part of their route and countless other sights now lie submerged beneath Lake Powell, thanks to the Glen Canyon Dam.

If you don't drive the entire route, at least visit **Devils Garden** (12 miles in), where rock fists, orbs, spires and fingers rise up to 40ft above the sandy desert floor. A short walk from the parking area leads atop giant sandstone slabs – kids love it. You'll also find several hiking trails.

**Dry Fork** (26 miles in) offers the most accessible slot canyon day hikes (p159). While there are no campgrounds or other facilities, dispersed camping is permitted, though you'll need a free backcountry permit. The main road stops short of **Hole-in-the-Rock**, but hikers can descend to **Lake Powell**, a scrambling route that can be done in less than an hour. Sorry, no taxis for the climb back up.

**BURR TRAIL**

The most immediately gratifying, dramatic drive in the area, the Burr Trail heads east from Boulder as a paved road, crosses GSENM's northeast corner and, after 30 miles, reaches **Waterpocket Fold** (p175) in Capitol Reef National Park, where the road becomes loose gravel. Along the way are two trailheads: **Deer Creek** and **The Gulch**; check with rangers for details on these spectacular hikes through riparian zones and red-rock desert.

Just past Deer Creek, the road enters **Long Canyon** beneath towering vertical slabs of red rock. As you leave the canyon, stop at the crest for views beyond of the sheer **Circle Cliffs**, which hang like curtains above the undulating valley floor. Still snowcapped in summer, the **Henry Mountains** rise above 11,000ft on the horizon.

Crossing into Capitol Reef, the road meets the giant, angled buttes of hundred-mile Waterpocket Fold, the 'reef' that blocked 19th-century settlers' passage west. Just ahead, the **Burr Trail Switchbacks** follow an original wagon route through the fold. You can continue to **Notom-Bullfrog Rd** (p178) and north to Hwy 24 or south to Glen Canyon. But if you plan to turn around and return to Boulder, first drive to the base of the switchbacks – the magnificence and scale of the landscape will blow your mind.

## DAY HIKES

Most of the hikes listed below are on marked trails or heavily trodden routes, easily accessible from Hwy 12. A few branch off dirt roads within the monument. Carry at least a gallon of water per person, wear a wide-brimmed hat and sunscreen, and carry food. Purchase USGS 7.5-quadrangle maps at Escalante Outfitters (p166). Whenever possible, avoid walking on cryptobiotic crusts (p275).

These are only a few of the many hikes in the monument. Be sure to ask rangers about others, such as **Sheep Creek**, **Willis Creek** and **The Box**, all easy treks; or **Willow** and **Wolverine**, which are harder.

---

**LOWER CALF CREEK FALLS**
Distance: 6 miles round-trip
Duration 3–4 hours
Challenge: Moderate–Difficult
Elevation Change: Negligible

This trail follows the year-round running creek through a spectacular canyon before arriving at a **126ft waterfall**, a joy on a hot day. Its beauty is no secret; this is probably the most heavily traveled trail in the entire monument. But its easy accessibility – right off Hwy 12 between Escalante and Boulder – makes it a perfect stopover en route to points east or west. You can take dogs with you on this trail too, but they must be leashed.

Park at the **Calf Creek Recreation Area**, between mile markers 75 and 76 on Hwy 12, 15 miles east of Escalante. Though it doesn't climb much, the trail is very sandy and can take a lot out of you. Carry lots of water.

As you work your way toward the falls, you'll pass honeycombed rocks and Navajo sandstone domes, an 800-year-old Native American granary, a box canyon where calves were once herded (hence the name Calf Creek), prehistoric pictographs and lush green wetlands.

Bring lots of water, but don't drink from the creek. The walk out is as strenuous as the walk in, so pace yourself.

## ESCALANTE NATURAL BRIDGE
**Distance: 4 miles round-trip**
**Duration 2–3 hours**
**Challenge: Easy**
**Elevation Change: Negligible**

If you want a short, easy walk with dramatic scenery and you don't mind getting wet, this is a great stopover hike. It's not as demanding as Calf Creek Falls and allows you to play in the water. Kids enjoy skittering upstream along the banks of the Escalante River to **Escalante Natural Bridge**, a giant arch.

Park at the trailhead by the Hwy 12 bridge over the Escalante River, 15 miles east of Escalante and just west of the Calf Creek Recreation Area (p167). On the 2-mile walk upriver, you'll occasionally have to hike through ankle- to knee-deep water, so wear appropriate footwear. The sandy route is well marked and good for families. The big payoff is the 130ft-high sandstone arch with a 100ft span, an awesome sight and well worth the soggy tennis shoes. The arch is on the south side of the river.

## PHIPPS WASH
**Distance: 4+ miles round-trip**
**Duration 2–4 hours**
**Challenge: Moderate**
**Elevation Change: Negligible**

Phipps Wash takes you through a riparian zone, beneath cottonwood trees and alongside a drainage to two formidable arches: **Maverick** and **Phipps.** Expect to get your feet wet, depending on the time of year and drought cycles. Some route-finding skills are necessary for this hike, depending on how far you stray from the drainage.

Start at the trailhead by the **Hwy 12 bridge** over the Escalante River, 15 miles east of Escalante and just west of the Calf Creek Recreation Area (p167). Head downstream along the Escalante River on the well-marked route through private property, then cut southwest into Phipps Wash. Take the first major drainage to the right to reach Maverick Arch, about 1.5 miles from the trailhead. Return to the main wash and continue south toward Phipps Arch, a chunky sweep of rock about 2 miles from the trailhead, which you can reach by scrambling up the east wall of the drainage.

Because this route follows a wash, it's not difficult to find your way – simply stay near the watercourse and crisscross as necessary. But basic orienteering skills are necessary, particularly around the slickrock by Phipps Arch. Carry the USGS Calf Creek 7.5 quadrangle, and seek advice from a ranger.

## SLOT CANYONS OF DRY FORK/COYOTE GULCH
**Distance: 1–4 miles**
**Duration: 1–3 hours**
**Challenge: Easy–Moderate**
**Elevation Change: 200ft, with some climbing & shimmying**

GSENM is famous for its slot canyons, narrow passages and spillways of brightly colored smooth rock. The following are the most accessible. Carry the USGS 7.5-minute quadrangle map for Big Hollow Wash. Use extreme caution, as

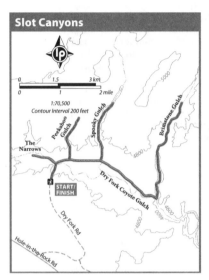

**Slot Canyons**

0    1.5    3 km
0    1    2 mile
1:70,500
Contour Interval 200 feet

The Narrows

Peekaboo Gulch

Spooky Gulch

Brimstone Gulch

START/FINISH

Dry Fork Coyote Gulch

Dry Fork Rd

Hole-in-the-Rock Rd

slot canyons are flash-flood prone. Because they remain in shadow, expect occasionally cool and damp hiking; you'll encounter pools of water in some. Check with rangers for conditions.

From Hwy 12, drive 26 miles down **Hole-in-the-Rock Rd** to Dry Fork Rd (Rte 252), turn left, and drive 1.7 miles to the parking area, bearing left at all junctions. From the parking area, drop below the rim, following cairns into **Dry Fork Wash**. The canyon immediately to the left (west), **The Narrows**, is an easy walk. Double back and head downstream (east), keeping your eyes peeled for the first slot on the left, **Peekaboo Gulch**, which holds a small pond and requires some scrambling. A half mile farther downstream on the left, **Spooky Gulch** is narrower and less challenging, but it's impassable to hefty hikers. Return to the trailhead from here. Don't try to climb up and over Peekaboo to sneak up behind Spooky; you can easily get lost. *Always* hike in and out the same way.

If you want to lengthen your hike, continue to **Brimstone Gulch**, which is less visited and more difficult than the others. Do not climb up and out of slots, then jump down the other side, or you may get trapped below the smooth-walled face you've descended. Check with rangers for more tips on hiking slots.

**LOWER HACKBERRY CANYON**
Distance: 2–6 miles round-trip
Duration: 1–3 hours
Challenge: Easy
Elevation Change: Negligible

This easy, pleasant hike provides welcome relief for drivers tired of sucking dust on **Cottonwood Canyon Rd**; it also makes a good destination for anyone cruising Hwy 89 who wants a taste of the national monument. Hackberry Canyon goes on and on for 26 miles – simply hike for as long as you wish and then return. In all likelihood, you'll have this sculpted, narrow gorge to yourself.

The trailhead is 14 miles from Hwy 89 and takes about half an hour to reach. As you near 14 miles on Cottonwood Canyon Rd, look for a sign for road 430 on the right; from this marker, it's about a quarter mile farther to an unsigned parking area on the left, just before a steep wash. This is the trailhead. Always check with rangers about the road conditions and flash-flood risk before coming.

Just below the parking area is a typically dry wash. Follow it to the right, and in about a quarter mile, you'll reach Lower Hackberry Canyon. Water often flows down the canyon, and many stream crossings are required, but it's not usually deep – normally a few inches. The trail is the beautiful gorge itself.

The first few miles of the canyon are the most narrow and interesting. After a while, the canyon opens up; in early summer, clouds of gnats often choose this point to attack. Hikers can either fight or concede the battle.

# BACKCOUNTRY HIKES

Grand Staircase–Escalante is a mecca for hardcore backcountry adventurers, but entering the monument on foot requires significant route-finding skills – GPS skills don't count. Know how to use a compass and a topographic map, or risk getting lost, even with an electronic route finder. If you get turned around and come to a wash, remember: It's always easier to walk downstream. Talk to rangers before heading out, and don't take unnecessary risks. Be especially aware of the potential for flash floods. For information on hiker shuttles, see p156.

The waterproof Trails Illustrated/National Geographic map ($10) is great, but be sure to carry 7.5-minute USGS maps (available at Escalante Outfitters, p166). For more on safety and what to bring, see the Activities chapter.

Check with rangers about the availability of water; plan to carry and drink *at least a gallon per day. Avoid stepping on cryptobiotic soil crusts.*

## Backcountry Campgrounds

To camp overnight you'll need a free backcountry permit; pick one up at any visitor center (p155), information kiosk or at major trailheads. Talk to rangers about specific regulations regarding dispersed camping. Pack out your trash, and use a camp stove. Fires are allowed only in certain places, and firewood is scarce. Bury human waste in proper catholes (6in deep, at least 200ft from water sources), or consider using human-waste containment bags.

## Backcountry Trails

GSENM offers outstanding treks for serious hikers with advanced abilities. Ask rangers about **Coyote Gulch**, off Hole-in-the-Rock Rd; **Escalante River Canyon**; and **The Gulch**, off the Burr Trail.

---

### BOULDER MAIL TRAIL
**Distance: 16 miles one way**
**Duration 2–3 days**
**Challenge: Difficult**
**Elevation Change: 700ft+ , with multiple elevation changes**

This historic trail was once the supply and mail route between **Boulder** (p167) and **Escalante** (p166). Much of it is unmarked or follows cairns. Most people do the one-way trip in two days, but a third day allows you to do some cross-country wandering and possibly explore **Phipps–Death Hollow Outstanding Natural Area**, a world of gullies, grottoes, spires and other slickrock wonders perched on the east edge of Death Hollow.

The following description is general and is not meant to be your sole route guide; rangers can provide current route conditions and descriptions.

Most hikers begin at the Boulder landing strip and end at the Upper Escalante River trailhead, just outside Escalante. Arrange a shuttle back to your car from the endpoint.

To reach the Boulder landing strip, turn northwest off Hwy 12 (24.8mi northeast of Escalante, 4.2 miles south of Boulder) onto Hells Backbone Rd. Take the first left (McGath Bench Rd; unsigned) and head south for half a mile to the Boulder landing strip; you'll find the trail register a quarter mile past the airstrip.

Trail's end, the well-marked Upper Escalante Canyon trailhead, is north of Hwy 12, three-quarters of a mile east of Escalante.

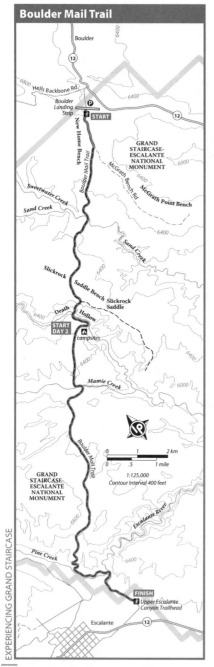

**Boulder Mail Trail**

Boulder

Hells Backbone Rd

Boulder Landing Strip

START

New Home Bench

Boulder Mail Trail

GRAND STAIRCASE-ESCALANTE NATIONAL MONUMENT

McGrath Bench Rd

McGrath Point Bench

Sweetwater Creek

Sand Creek

Sand Creek

Slickrock

Saddle Bench

Slickrock Saddle

Death Hollow

START DAY 2

campsites

Mamie Creek

Boulder Mail Trail

0    1    2 km
0    .5    1 mile
1:125,000
Contour Interval 400 feet

GRAND STAIRCASE-ESCALANTE NATIONAL MONUMENT

Escalante River

Pine Creek

FINISH
Upper Escalante Canyon Trailhead

Escalante

12

### Day 1: Boulder Landing Strip to Phipps–Death Hollow

*(4–5 hours, 5.5 miles)*

The first leg takes you from the flats atop **New Home Bench** down 450ft to the Sand Creek drainage, then 400ft back up to the Slickrock Saddle Bench before making the precipitous 900ft drop into **Death Hollow**. Don't start late: you'll want plenty of light for the final descent.

From the trailhead, stroll south a mile down the Jeep trail and turn right (southwest) at the sign marking the start of the Boulder Mail Trail.

Follow cairns along the west side of New Home Bench, which alternates between red sand and slickrock. After a quarter mile, you'll descend to the confluence of **Sweetwater** and **Sand Creeks**, where cottonwoods offer shade, and there's sometimes water.

Head downstream (left) along the right side of the streambed till you reach a cairn-marked ascent over slickrock. As you round the west side of a capped butte, look for an old telegraph wire overhead.

The line marks the beginning of a climb toward a break in the Slickrock Saddle Bench and could be a good **campsite**. Do *not* follow the telegraph line over the brink of Death Hollow. Instead, follow the cairns just south of the line, down a steep but wide draw into the hollow – a gorgeous, riparian canyon named for mules lost on the steep trip down.

Several **campsites** lie within a quarter mile of where the trail meets the creek; some of the best are 300yd downstream.

### Day 2: Death Hollow to Upper Escalante Canyon Trailhead

*(6–8 hours, 10.5 miles)*

The rest of the hike clambers over several benches. The strenuous 800ft ascent out of Death Hollow is matched only by the final 900ft descent to Pine Creek and the Escalante River.

Head downstream about a half mile from where the trail first entered Death Hollow and look for cairns on the river's west (right) side at a southwest bend. The trail heads directly up the west side of the hollow before leveling out. Look for the telegraph lines on your right.

The trail follows the telegraph line to a slickrock plateau, where it bears right and descends to dry **Mamie Creek**. Turn left (south) at the creek and hike 200ft down the wash to cairns that lead over a rock nose, bearing west (right) over a cracked sandstone formation resembling a giant cerebellum.

Coming into open country, you'll reach **Antone Flat**, a meadow bordered by a spectacular volcanic escarpment. Follow the telegraph line across the meadow.

On the west edge of Antone Flat, a chalky-white slickrock draw may hold water in deep pockets. Head right (northwest) up the draw, following cairns. After a quarter mile, the route bears south (left) along the east side of a broad

## HOW TO HIKE LIKE A GREAT OLD BROAD

Ginger Harmon, now 75 years old, has been hiking all her life. She's been a mountain guide in Nepal and in the Sierra Nevadas, and she's the author of *Walking Europe from Top to Bottom*. For the last 40 years she's been hiking in the Southwest, and for the last 20 her 'home away from home' has been Utah's Escalante region. When asked why she hikes so much, Ginger says, 'I would call it a serious addiction.'

Her addiction now serves a purpose. In 1989, Ginger helped found **Great Old Broads for Wilderness** (www.greatoldbroads.org), a nonprofit advocacy group that seeks to preserve and protect wilderness areas across the US. Sitting around the kitchen table, Ginger and her friends 'felt a bunch of old ladies can make alot of noise about matters that count. I was having such good times in Escalante, I thought I owed it something.'

She helped raise awareness about grazing devastation on the Grand Staircase in the years before it was designated a national monument, and Great Old Broads has since grown to 2500 members nationwide, tackling issues like mining, logging, grazing and OHV (off-highway vehicle) use on public lands. They also organize 'Broad walks' and other trips, but as Ginger says, these are 'outings with a purpose – the purpose to make wilderness warriors.'

Ginger certainly earns her warrior stripes. Every spring and fall she ventures off trail in the southern Utah desert, though she reluctantly admits to slowing down a bit. She used to backpack for 10 days at a time, and now, 'I hate to say it, but I'm down to five days. Every year I have to keep lightening my load. It's amazing what you can take out of your pack to keep doing the thing you love.'

Ginger no longer carries a tent, bivouac sack or Therm-a-Rest pad, and she brings only two outfits: one for day, one for night. She does carry a good sleeping bag, a rain suit and warm fleece clothes: 'To me, to get cold is pure horror.'

Where she doesn't hold back is on her snacks and food ('That's my clothing'). She dehydrates her meals and takes granola bars instead of sports bars, which she calls 'terribly heavy.' Her one grandmotherly constant: 'I like to have a cup of instant soup before dinner. It just seems to make you feel good.'

Ginger says the biggest challenge of desert hiking is 'to get from one water source to the next,' and if there's any single reason why she doesn't hike as long as she used to, it's because she can't carry as much water anymore.

Ginger acknowledges she's never been an average hiker, neither now nor in her youth. She says, 'It's incredible happiness to me, even when you're suffering, and you always suffer on a backpack. But even when I'm suffering, I'm having a good time.

'I have every intention of hiking through my 80s and 90s, until I drop dead,' Ginger maintains, and one is likely to believe her. 'Enthusiasm for life is the bottom line.'
– Jeff Campbell

163

ridge to the final sandy flat. The trail turns west (right), and you'll spot alfalfa fields and Escalante.

After a steep descent (following cairns), the trail swings south (left) toward a rock island atop a hill. Climb over the saddle and down to **Pine Creek**.

The creek's west bank is private, so follow its east bank to the **Escalante River**. Head west (right) a quarter mile until the canyon opens and the trail swings south through the brush, meeting a Jeep road and the **Upper Escalante Canyon trailhead**.

## GUIDED HIKING & WILDERNESS TREKS

For the best multiday trips into GSENM, you can't beat **Escalante Canyon Outfitters** ( ☎ 435-335-7311, 888-326-4453; www.ecohike.com; PO Box 133, Boulder, UT 84716; 4- to 6-day all-inclusive treks $770-1175; ☺ spring-fall). Horses carry gear and packs; superb guides provide excellent interpretation – and do the cooking.

For top-notch, custom-tailored, all-day adventure hikes, **Excursions of Escalante** ( ☎ 435-826-4714, 800-839-7567; www.excursions-escalante.com; PO Box 605, Escalante, UT 84726; $65-100; spring-fall) offers everything from easy photo walks to canyoneering – rappelling into water-filled canyons in wetsuits and swimming in and out of potholes. Stop by the Trailhead Café (p166) in Escalante to learn more.

Looking for fantastic geologic interpretation? Seek out **Earth Tours** ( ☎ 435-691-1241; www.earth-tours.com; PO Box 1426, Boulder, UT 84716; half- to full-day tours $50-75; ☺ spring-fall), run by a PhD in geology who can also speak in lay terms. Stop by the Burr Trail Outpost (p167) in Boulder for more information.

If everyone is booked, **Escalante Outback Adventures** ( ☎ 435-826-4967; www.escalante-utah.com; 325 W. Main St, Escalante; ☺ spring-fall) operates prescriptive hikes.

## OTHER ACTIVITIES

Head up the Aquarius Plateau on **horseback** or drive cattle at **Boulder Mountain Ranch** ( ☎ 435-335-7480; www.boulderutah.com/bmr; call for directions; day rides $35-110), where you can also rent a rustic cabin (p168).

Anglers head up to Boulder Mountain's cool forests and hidden lakes on fly-fishing trips with **Boulder Mountain Fly-fishing** ( ☎ 435-335-7306, 435-231-1823; www.bouldermountainfly-fishing.com; PO Box 1403, Boulder, UT 84716; ☺ Mar-Nov), run by a wonderful storyteller with a great sense of humor.

Learn how to survive in this forbidding wilderness by studying with the **Boulder Outdoor Survival School** ( ☎ 303-444-9779; www.boss-inc.com). Based in Colorado, the school operates a variety of excursions and classes in GSENM.

## SLEEPING & EATING

The best towns for lodging are Escalante (p166), Boulder (p167) and Kanab (p169), as well as Kodachrome Basin State Park. The best places to eat are in Escalante and Boulder.

You'll find two developed **campgrounds** within the monument: Calf Creek and Deer Creek, both in the northern section near Boulder. Down south at the Paria Contact Station (p155), the primitive White House Campground has walk-in tent camping only. For information on developed campgrounds just outside the monument, such as the sites on Boulder Mountain (Hwy 12, between Boulder and Torrey; summer only), contact the visitor centers (p155) or **Dixie National Forest** ( ☎ 435-676-8815; www.fs.fed.us/dxnf). Escalante Petrified Forest (p166) also maintains developed sites.

**Calf Creek Campground** ( ☎ 435-826-5499; www.ut.blm.gov/monument; Hwy 12, 15 miles east of Escalante; $7; ☺ year-round) Surrounded by red-rock canyons (that get hot in summer) beside a year-round creek, this is the most developed campground in GSENM. Its 13 sites include picnic tables, fire pits, toilets and seasonal water but no showers. Leashed pets are allowed, and there are sites for trailers up to 25ft long. Group reservations only. Pack out trash.

**Deer Creek Campground** (www.ut.blm.gov/monument; Burr Trail, 6 miles southeast of Boulder; $4; ⊙ mid-May–mid-Sep) Though it offers just four sites and no water, this pretty camp sits beside a year-round creek beneath tall trees and red-rock formations. Amenities are limited to fire pits, picnic tables and pit toilets. Leashed pets are permitted. Pack out trash.

# AROUND GRAND STAIRCASE

Two main highways border GSENM: Hwys 12 and 89. The sights and services listed below fall along these two routes, from west to east.

## HIGHWAY 12

Recently designated an All-American Road by the Federal Highway Administration, Hwy 12 is one of the most spectacular routes anywhere in the US. Its 125-mile course begins south of Panguitch at Hwy 89, heads east past Bryce Canyon, skirts the northern boundaries of GSENM and ends just west of Capitol Reef, in Torrey.

Stop at the numerous turnouts and scenic viewpoints to see how quickly and dramatically the land changes from wooded plateau to red-rock canyon and from slickrock desert to alpine forest. The most stunning stretch lies between Escalante and Boulder.

Information and visitor centers in Panguitch, Red Canyon, Bryce Canyon and GSENM stock maps and copies of a **route guide** that describes most of the turnouts along Hwy 12. For a new audio tour, due out in 2005, contact the **Garfield County Tourism Office** (☎ 435-676-1160, 800-444-6689; www.brycecanyoncounty.com).

### Kodachrome Basin State Park

Off Cottonwood Canyon Rd, 9 miles south of Cannonville, you'll find this **park** (☎ 435-679-8562; $5 day-use fee), one of the gems of the Utah State Park system. Petrified geysers and dozens of red, pink and white sandstone chimneys – some nearly 170ft tall – stand clustered together and resemble everything from a sphinx to a snowmobile. Visit in the morning or afternoon for the best light, when shadows play on the red rock. Most of the sights lie along hiking and mountain biking trails or dirt roads. The moderately easy 3-mile **Panorama Trail** provides the best overview; the **Eagle View Trail** (0.5 mile, strenuous) and **Sentinel Trail** (1.25 miles, moderate) both feature great views of GSENM from up high. Ride horseback in summer and inquire about stagecoach rides with **Scenic Safaris** (☎ 435-679-8536, 435-679-8787) at Trailhead Station, which also sells groceries, firewood and basic supplies. Say hello to the charming, charismatic proprietors, Bob and Miraloy Ott, who'll help you discern shapes in the rock.

From April through November, Trailhead Station rents six knotty pine **cabins** (☎ 435-679-8536, 435-679-8787; www.brycecanyoninn.com/cabins.htm; $65; ⊙ Apr-Nov; ✗ ✗ ) each with a fridge, microwave and private bath; cabins sleep up to four. The state park operates a **campground** (☎ 801-322-3770, 800-322-3770; www. stateparks. utah.gov; $14, includes park entrance fee; ⊙ year-round) with 26 well-spaced, partially shaded sites, hot showers and flush toilets. Reservations are advised.

### Escalante State Park

Thirty-two miles east of Cannonville and a mile west of Escalante along Hwy

12, this small **state park** ( ☎ 435-826-4466, 800-322-3770; off Hwy 12; campsites $14; ☯ year-round) is most noteworthy for its **petrified forest** of ancient wood, which you can roam along an easy 1.1-mile loop trail. It's not a forest per se – no standing trees of rock – but a hillside of great fossils. There's also a small reservoir where you can rent a **canoe** ($5 for one hour, $10 for four hours, $20 all day). Bring insect repellant. You can stay overnight in a **campground** with 21 tent/RV sites, hot showers, grills, fire pits, picnic tables and a dump station.

## Escalante
### pop 818 / elevation 5600ft
The largest town on Hwy 12, Escalante lies halfway between Bryce Canyon and Capitol Reef National Parks. If you plan to spend a few days in the monument, Escalante makes a good base.

Long populated by radical dropouts and conspiracy theorists, Escalante is undergoing a transformation. Outsiders are moving in, taking over businesses and making the town safe for tourists. And the townspeople seem OK about it.

For regional information, call or visit the **Escalante Interagency Visitor Center** ( ☎ 435-826-5499; www.ut.blm.gov/monument or http://gsenm.az.blm.gov; 755 W Main St; ☯ 7:30am-5:30pm). Near Main and Center Sts is a city information booth (summer only, erratic hours), which provides brochures that detail local historic buildings.

You'll find books, maps, camping and hiking supplies, USGS 7.5-quadrangle maps, high-speed Internet access and liquor at **Escalante Outfitters** ( ☎ 435-826-4266; 310 W Main St).

### SLEEPING & EATING
Pitch a tent or rent a rustic, heated log cabin (shared bath, no air-conditioning) at **Escalante Outfitters Bunkhouse Cabins** ( ☎ 435-826-4266; www.escalanteoutfitters.com; 310 W Main St; tent $14, cabin $40; ☒ ▯ ). Picnic tables and grills are also available.

The single-story, family-owned **Circle D Motel** ( ☎ 435-826-4297; www.utahcanyons.com/circled.htm; 475 W Main St; d $35-55; ☒ ) has low prices and clean – though dated – rooms; some include a fridge and microwave. The modern, ugly, two-story **Prospector Motel** ( ☎ 435-826-4653; www.prospectorinn.com; 380 W Main St; d $57; ☒ ) has standard rooms; skip the restaurant.

The best B&B in town is **Escalante's Grand Staircase B&B Inn** ( ☎ 435-826-4890, 866-826-4890; www.escalantebnb.com; 280 W Main St; d $70-115; ☒ ☒ ▯ ), whose attractive rooms include log-frame beds, country furnishings and richly colored walls.

For a house rental with full kitchen, consider **Wild West Retreat** ( ☎ 435-826-4849, 866-292-3043; www.wildwestretreat.com; 200 E at 300 S; d/q $100/120; ☒ ), a refurbished 1930s barn with a hot tub and large outdoor stone patio; **La Luz Desert Retreat** ( ☎ 435-826-4967, 888-305-4705; www.laluz.net; call for directions; r $125, up to 6 people; ☒ ), a strikingly contemporary adobe home at the desert's edge; or the **Vagabond Inn** ( ☎ 435-826-4266, 866-455-0041; www.vagabondbnb.com; 115 W Main St; $225-275, up to 6 people; ☒ ), a three-bedroom 1890s brick house.

For groceries, **Griffin's** ( ☎ 435-826-4226; 300 W Main St) provides the best produce and some organic items.

There are two happening places to hang out and eat, both with Internet access. For coffee, croissants, sandwiches and burgers, visit the **Trailhead Café** ( ☎ 435-826-4714, 800-839-7567; 125 E Main St; ☯ 8am-8pm, closed Tue & Nov-Apr). For granola and yogurt at breakfast, and homemade pizza and beer at lunch and dinner, visit **Esca-Latte Café** ( ☎ 435-826-4266; 310 W Main St; dishes $5-12; ☯ 8am-10pm daily Mar-Nov, 10am-6pm Tue-Sat winter), at Escalante Outfitters.

## Head of the Rocks
At mile marker 69.8, about 8 miles east of Escalante, pull off the highway for

one of the most arresting roadside views in Utah. The Aquarius Plateau lords over giant mesas, towering domes, deep canyons and undulating slickrock that unfurl in an explosion of color. Farther east, near mile marker 73, stop for coffee and take in canyon views at the must-see **Kiva Koffeehouse** ( ☎ 435-826-4550; www.kivakoffeehouse.com; dishes $2-5; cottage $160-175; ☺ 8am-4:30pm Apr-Nov; ✗ ☺ ). Built to resemble a traditional Native American cliff dwelling, the semicircular building has floor-to-ceiling glass walls and giant raw timber supports. They rent two luxurious **cottages**, also built into the cliff – a perfect hideaway.

## Calf Creek Recreation Area

**Calf Creek** ( ☎ 435-826-5499; www.ut.blm.gov/monument; 15 miles east of Escalante on Hwy 12, between mile markers 75 & 76; $2 day-use fee; ☺ year-round) is the starting point for the only maintained hiking trail (p158) in GSENM. Even if you're not camping here, make it a point to stop when driving between Escalante and Boulder on a hot day. Wade in the cool waters of the year-round creek in the shade of mature cottonwoods, a refreshing treat, especially for kids tired of being cooped up in the car. Watch your footing in the creek, as the mossy rocks can be slippery. You can also picnic here; try for a table by the creek.

## The Hogback

East of Calf Creek, between mile markers 78 and 80, Hwy 12 crosses this narrow ridge with precipitous drop-offs into seemingly bottomless canyons and rolling slickrock desert. There are no guardrails; pull off at designated turnouts to take in the mesmerizing views.

## Boulder

### pop 180 / elevation 6593ft

Until 1940, when Hwy 12 connected it to Escalante, Boulder received its mail by mule. After Salt Lake City, Boulder is the second-largest town in Utah, but it's also the least populated – so remote that the federal government has classified it as a 'frontier community.' Nonetheless, it's home to one of southern Utah's most sophisticated populations. Progressive-minded and more expansive in its worldview than Panguitch or Escalante, Boulder is a diverse collection of down-to-earth people – from artists and farmers to geologists and cowboys – and everybody gets along.

Lorded over by Boulder Mountain (at the southeast end of the Aquarius Plateau) and surrounded by GSENM, Boulder is a great home base for exploring the outdoors, though it offers offers fewer services than does Escalante. To learn more about Boulder online, visit www.boulderutah.com. Many of the town's businesses close in winter; call to verify opening dates.

Stop by the BLM information desk at **Anasazi State Park** (p168), on the east end of town, for information about trips into the surrounding lands, including GSENM and the ruggedly beautiful **Box–Death Hollow Wilderness Area**, up Hell's Backbone Rd (the original mule route to Escalante). The **Burr Trail** (p158) also originates in Boulder.

Equal parts gallery, outfitter, café and local gathering place, the **Burr Trail Outpost** ( ☎ 435-335-7565; Burr Trail & Hwy 12; ☺ 8am-8pm Mar-Oct) is a happening little shop worth a quick visit.

### SLEEPING & EATING

A single-story, 11-room, mom-and-pop motel, **Pole's Place** ( ☎ 435-335-7422, 800-730-7422; www.boulderutah.com/polesplace; 465 N Hwy 12; d $52-66; ✗ ☺ ) was built in the 1990s and is lovingly and immaculately maintained. The **Circle Cliffs Motel** ( ☎ 435-335-7333; www.boulderutah.com/lodging; 225 N Hwy 12; d $50-60; ✗ ☺ ) has three rooms, each with a microwave, fridge and coffeemaker.

## THE THOUSAND LAKES ARE DRY

If you drive from Boulder to Torrey on Hwy 12, you'll pass through lush green forests on Boulder Mountain. But when you arrive in Torrey, glance up at Thousand Lakes Mountain and see how parched and rocky it is, you may wonder, Where are the 'thousand lakes'? Back in the 19th century, a cartographer mixed up the two names on a map he drew. What should have been called Thousand Lakes Mountain is now called Boulder Mountain, and vice versa. The names stuck.

– *John A Vlahides*

With the casual feel of a ranch but the amenities of a luxury hotel, **Boulder Mountain Lodge** ( ☎ 435-335-7460, 800-556-3446; www.boulder-utah.com; Hwy 12 at Burr Trail; d $89-149; ☒ ☒ ☒ ) is the ideal place for day hikers who want high-thread-count sheets and plush terry bathrobes at night. The grounds feature a hot tub, croquet and a bird sanctuary. Some rooms include fridges and microwaves.

On a 160-acre working ranch in a lush green valley with a running creek, **Boulder Mountain Ranch** ( ☎ 435-335-7480; www.boulderutah.com/bmr; Box 1373, Boulder, UT 84716; r $55-60, cabin $60-82; ☒ ) has well-spaced, rustic log cabins that sleep four to six people; all include baths, wood-stoves and outdoor fire rings. You can also rent rooms uphill in the giant log house, whose loft can sleep up to 14 people for a mere $150 per night.

Buy groceries, supplies, beer and gasoline at **Hills & Hollows Country Store** ( ☎ 435-335-7349; Hwy 12, west of town; ☑ 9am-7pm, 24hr gasoline). For good deli sandwiches, draft beer and pizza (after 5pm), stop by **Burr Trail Grill & Deli** ( ☎ 435-335-7503; Hwy 12 at Burr Trail; sandwiches $6-8, pizzas $12-15; ☑ 7am-9pm Mar-Oct). For plain-old diner food such as biscuits and gravy and homemade French fries, head to **Boulder Mesa Restaurant** ( ☎ 435-335-7447; 155 E Burr Trail; dishes $4-8, dinner mains $12-18; ☑ 7:30am-9pm).

**Hell's Backbone Grill** ( ☎ 435-335-7464; Hwy 12 at Burr Trail; breakfast dishes $4-8, dinner mains $12-22; ☑ 7-10am, 5-9pm spring-fall) If you've given up on eating well in southern Utah, take heart: the must-visit Hells' Backbone serves delicious, soulful, earthy preparations of locally raised meats and organically grown produce from its own garden. Save room for lemon-chiffon cake. Make reservations. Breakfasts are excellent.

### Anasazi State Park

On Boulder's north side is **Anasazi State Park** ( ☎ 435-335-7308; www.stateparks.utah.gov; 460 N Hwy 12; $2/person or $6/carload; ☑ 8am-6pm spring-summer, 9am-5pm fall-winter), which includes an outdoor archaeological site of major significance dating back to between the years 1130 and 1175. The museum includes a re-created six-room pueblo, an art gallery and good exhibits about the Anasazi (or Ancestral Puebloan) peoples. The museum also hosts a **BLM information desk** ( ☎ 435-335-7382; ☑ 9am-5pm, closed Nov-Mar) where you can talk to a ranger and get permits and road updates.

### HWY 89

The southern portion of Hwy 89 is not as egregiously scenic as Hwy 12, but it is a highlight. Along it lie Kanab (the region's largest town), dirt access roads to GSENM's southern section and the must-see Paria Canyon–Vermilion Cliffs Wilderness Area.

### Coral Pink Sand Dunes State Park

So strange is this topographical oddity that it could easily have been dubbed 'shocking pink sand dunes,' which the restless winds have gathered and dropped on this 3700-acre spot. For collectors of the bizarre, it's worth the 24-mile, 90-minute round-trip off Hwy 89 to see them, though they have been converted largely into a playpen for off-highway vehicles (OHVs).

A half-mile interpretive dune hike enters a 265-acre conservation area that has been fenced off from the 1200 acres open to OHV riders, whom you'll see coursing over the Sahara-like dunes, their orange flags snapping. Day use is $5, and there's a 22-site campground ($14) with flush toilets and heated showers, paved pull-through sites and fire pits. **Reservations** ( ☎ 800-322-3770) are necessary on weekends. Tent campers should note that the same winds that bring the sands can make camping unpleasant.

A new **visitor center** ( ☎ 435-648-2800; ☽ 9am-9pm, till 4pm in winter) offers displays, toilets, water and soda.

## Kanab
### pop 3500 / elevation 4925ft
Western history – both real and reel – unspools at this remote outpost. Indeed, when an area's main attractions are re-creations of movie sets that were romanticized versions of real Western towns, history becomes a tangled enterprise. But John Wayne really did eat, sleep and film here – as have many other movie stars in 'Utah's Little Hollywood' since the 1930s – and for many that's authentic and Western enough.

Today, tourism is Kanab's economic mainstay, as the town sits at a major crossroads: GSENM is 20 miles away, Zion 40 miles, Bryce 80 miles, the Grand Canyon's North Rim 81 miles and Glen Canyon 74 miles. Those doing the Grand Circle will find this a very convenient stopping point.

### ORIENTATION & INFORMATION
Most businesses lie along Hwy 89, which snakes through town. South of town, the highway continues east along 300 S, leading to the Grand Staircase and eventually Page, Arizona, 73 miles away; Alt Hwy 89 leads south along 100 E to Arizona (3 miles) and onward to the Grand Canyon. All routes are well signed.

The **Kane County Office of Tourism** ( ☎ 435-644-5033, 800-733-5263; www.kaneutah.com; 78 S 100 E; ☽ 8am-8pm Mon-Fri, 9am-5pm Sat, 9am-1pm Sun in summer; 8:30am-5pm Mon-Sat in winter) is the main source for area information.

GSENM's new **Kanab Visitor Center** ( ☎ 435-644-4680; 745 E Hwy 89; ☽ 8am-4:30pm daily, closed weekends in winter) provides road, trail and weather updates for the monument. Top-notch displays focus on archaeology and geology. The **BLM Kanab Field Office** ( ☎ 435-644-4600; 318 N 100 E; ☽ 8am-4:30pm Mon-Fri) offers information on, and issues permits for, the Paria Canyon–Vermilion Cliffs Wilderness Area (p171).

Other services include the **library** ( ☎ 435-644-2394; 374 N Main St; ☽ 9am-5pm Mon & Fri, 9am-7pm Tue-Thu, 10am-2pm Sat), with free Internet access; **post office** ( ☎ 435-644-2760; 39 S Main St); **hospital** ( ☎ 435-644-5811; 355 N Main St); and **police** ( ☎ 435-644-5807; 140 E 100 S). Kanab also offers a large grocery store (open daily) and a bank with a 24-hour ATM.

### SIGHTS
**Frontier Movie Town** ( ☎ 435-644-5337, 800-551-1714; 297 W Center St; ☽ 8am-10pm in summer, 10am-5pm in winter) is a cluster of actual Western movie sets, where gunfights are staged in summer ($16-20 with dinner) and a costume shop can doll you up for $20 a photo. The outdoor grill serves steaks and burgers ($7-14) and cold beer. It's free just to walk through the movie town and gift shop.

Another classic tourist trap is **Moqui Cave** ( ☎ 435-644-8525; www.moquicave.com; adults/teens/children 6-12 $4/2.50/2; ☽ 9am-7pm Mon-Sat summer), 5 miles north of town on Hwy 89. Its oddball collection of fluorescent minerals, dinosaur tracks, cowboy and Indian artifacts, and other flotsam and jetsam – all inside a real cave – add up to actual entertainment.

Also off Hwy 89, a quarter mile from Moqui Cave, is **Best Friends Animal Sanctuary** ( ☎ 435-644-2001, ext 115 for tours; www.bestfriends.org; ☽ 8:30am-5pm), the nation's largest animal sanctuary. Free daily tours last 45 to 90 minutes; longer tours set aside time to meet some of the 1500 animals. This could be the feel-good highlight of your trip. You can also spend the night in any of eight cottages with kitchenettes (members/nonmembers $107/125).

If you want to drink deep the Old West, attend the ever-growing **Western Legends Roundup** ( ☎ 800-733-5263; www.westernlegendsroundup.com), which for five days in late August celebrates all things cowboy, both in life and in film.

### SLEEPING

Kanab hosts a relative surplus of independent budget motels. The town's high season begins when the North Rim of the Grand Canyon opens – around mid-May – and lasts till October, but demand is always the final arbiter.

**Crazy Horse Campark** ( ☎ 435-644-2782; 625 E 300 S; tent $15, RV hookup $20) New owners are sprucing up this large, attractive, 80-site campground, which offers a coin laundry, showers, swimming pool and play areas.

**Hitch'n Post Campground** ( ☎ 435-644-2142, 800-458-3516; 196 E 300 S; tent $18, cabin $22-26) This friendly, 17-site campground is near the center of town.

**Bob-Bon Inn Motel** ( ☎ 435-644-3069, 800-644-5094; www.bobbon.com; 236 N 300 W; r $36-59; ☒ ☒ ☒ ) The 16 rooms here are one of the best deals in Kanab; they are small but newer and very clean, with a modest Western feel.

**Parry Lodge** ( ☎ 435-644-2601, 800-748-4104; 89 E Center St; 1 bed $51-56, 2 beds $57-73; ☒ ☒ ☒ ) Back in the day, all the actors and film crews stayed here, but the rambling, courtyard-style motel has become a faded dowager of the leading lady she once was. Rooms are quite clean, well kept and acceptable, but the only thing special is the aura of days gone by. The restaurant has cut back to only serving breakfast (☽ 7-11am), and the barn quit doing shows years ago.

**Shilo Inn** ( ☎ 435-644-2562, 800-222-2244; 296 W 100 N; r $86-96; ☒ ☒ ☒ ) This is the biggest hotel in town and is a dependable, no-surprise option. The 118 minisuites are very comfortable and include refrigerators, microwaves and coffeemakers.

**Treasure Trail Motel** ( ☎ 435-577-2645, 800-603-2687; www.treasuretrailmotel.net; 150 W Center St; r $44-70; ☒ ☒ ☒ ) For those not counting style points, this motel provides 30 very clean, basic, sizeable rooms.

Other mid-range chain hotels in town include Super 8, Holiday Inn Express and Best Western.

### EATING

**Vermilion Café** ( ☎ 435-644-3886; 4 E Center St; items $4-6; ☽ 7am-2:30pm Mon-Sat, 8:30am-1:30pm Sun) This unexpectedly hip coffeehouse serves breakfast burritos and sandwiches with its array of espresso drinks. It also offers Internet access.

**Rocking V Café** ( ☎ 435-644-8001; 97 W Center St; dinner mains $15-23; ☽ 11:30am-9pm) Both the food and the decor are a stylish mix of rustic and modern Southwest. Burgers and wraps ($6.50-8.50) have flair, and dinners, emphasizing fish and pastas, get even more interesting, particularly with a margarita mixed in. The free Rafters Gallery upstairs is packed with funky, talented local artists.

**Houston's Trail's End Restaurant** ( ☎ 435-644-2488; www.houstons.com; 32 E Center St; mains $10-19; ☽ 6am-9:30pm, breakfast till 11:30am). The waitresses wear six-shooters at this fun Kanab institution, which specializes in down-home Western cooking: order up chicken-fried or rib-eye steak, barbecued ribs or fried chicken. They don't serve beer, but they do have great country breakfasts.

**Nedra's Too** ( ☎ 435-644-2030; 310 S 100 E; items $6-10; ☽ 7am-11pm in summer) Maybe it's the trail talking, but this tastes like perfect Mexican food: steaming plates of cheesy, greasy, unpretentious chimichangas, enchiladas, burritos and Navajo tacos. The salsa is delicious, even if it is only Utah hot.

### SHOPPING
**Denny's Wigwam** ( ☎ 435-644-2452; 78 E Center St; ☽ 8am-9pm Mon-Sat) Denny's is one of the best places in southwest Utah for authentic Western wear, in addition to medicine wheels, moccasins and homemade fudge.

**Willow Canyon Outdoor** ( ☎ 435-644-8884; www.willowcanyon.com; 263 S 100 E; ☽ 7:30am-8pm summer) Half bookstore, half outdoor supply store, this excellent shop can fulfill most of your camping and climbing needs. Books range from outdoor guidebooks to local histories to trade fiction. Plus, they serve espresso.

### GETTING THERE & AROUND
**Green Hound Shuttle** ( ☎ 928-643-6788, 877-765-6840) covers all points from St George to Page, Arizona; and from Bryce to the North Rim of the Grand Canyon. Basic rates are $1 a mile, but vary depending on group size.

**Paria Outpost & Outfitters** ( ☎ 928-691-1047; www.paria.com), at mile marker 21 on Hwy 89, runs trailhead shuttles to the Vermilion Cliffs and Grand Staircase; rates range from $50 to $100 for up to four people. It also offers bike rentals and guided tours.

## Paria Valley Road & Movie Set
Run by the BLM, the Paria (Pie-REE-uh) Movie Set provides a very accessible taste of GSENM. The signed turnoff is 33 miles from Kanab on Hwy 89; from there, a 5-mile dirt road (passable to cars in dry weather) follows an evocative ridge in the Vermilion Cliffs to the movie site.

The original buildings were washed away by floods; today, three rebuilt, plank-walled structures evoke the town-cum-movie set, with creaky swinging doors, raised sidewalks and hitching posts. The real set – the magnificently banded, painted cliffs surrounding you – didn't need any dressing. Informative signs explain the 14-year history of the movie set and the earlier history of the nearby Pahreah ghost town, which the river has just about polished off. A half mile past the movie set is the town cemetery, and a half mile farther is the river and townsite; the road deteriorates, and there's little to see of the stone buildings in the tall brush.

## Paria Canyon–Vermilion Cliffs Wilderness Area
Straddling the Utah–Arizona state line, this wilderness area is one of the region's most popular destinations for day hikers and serious canyoneers – and for photographers. Pick any six postcards from a southern Utah gift shop, and two or three will be from here. With slot canyons that can be hiked for days, and miles of weathered, swirling, fragile slickrock, it's no wonder hiking permits here are as tough to get as Manhattan street parking.

For further information, visit www.az.blm.gov/paria, contact the BLM field office in Kanab (p169) or visit the **Paria Contact Station** ( ☽ 8:30am-4:15pm Mar 15–Nov 15), which is 43 miles from Kanab on Hwy 89, on the Utah side of the wilderness area. The contact station sells topographical maps and guidebooks, offers water and provides updated road and trail conditions. Beside the contact station is the **White House Campground**, with six primitive sites ($5) for walk-in tent camping only.

*continued on p174*

# A GRAND DETOUR

If you're visiting southwest Utah, there's almost no reason not to make a quick detour to one of America's most famous landmarks. The Grand Canyon's North Rim is about 1½ hours south of Kanab and about 2½ hours from Zion National Park, making it a very accessible day trip or overnight destination. On the way back (or there), Hwy 389 in northern Arizona also offers a couple of intriguing, worthwhile stops: Pipe Spring National Monument and Colorado City.

Note: Arizona does not observe daylight saving time, so in summer it's one hour behind Utah time. Remember, you'll gain an hour driving south and lose an hour returning to Utah.

## NORTH RIM OF THE GRAND CANYON

The Grand Canyon is big – almost too big, really – and yet it only takes a couple of hours to get all the picture-postcard photo ops you could ever want. That's what this description is concerned with. For a complete rundown, pick up a copy of Lonely Planet's *Grand Canyon National Park*.

Advantages of the North Rim are that it's higher (at 8200ft) and quieter than the South Rim, sees far fewer visitors, and yet the views are as good or better. Some disadvantages are that it doesn't open until mid-May and offers fewer services.

It's 14 miles from the North Rim Entrance Station to **Bright Angel Point**, where you'll find the visitor center, Grand Canyon Lodge and restaurants. This should be your first destination. The lodge and its open-air deck overlook the classic view, and a paved, wheelchair-accessible 0.3-mile trail leads from here to the point itself. The 3-mile round-trip **Transept Trail** skirts the rim from the lodge to the campground.

Day-trippers' next foray should be the 23-mile drive from the lodge to **Cape Royal** (about 40 minutes one way). This route features a handful of incredible turnouts, including a 6-mile round-trip detour to **Point Imperial**, and it ends at what feels like the edge of the Earth. Along the route is a selection of short, easy trails (0.2 to 4 miles round-trip) that allow you to stretch your legs without making a big commitment; these include the Point Imperial Trail, Roosevelt Point Trail, Cape Final Trail and Cape Royal Trail.

Those with more time and energy should hike a section of the **North Kaibab Trail**, the only North Rim trail that descends into the canyon. The 1.5-mile round-trip to Coconino Overlook is highly rewarding. For an all-day hike you could go as far as Roaring Springs, 9.4 miles round-trip and 3210ft down and back. Day hiking to the canyon floor (more than a mile below the rim) is, shall we say, discouraged.

The **North Rim Visitor Center** ( ☎ 928-638-9875; www.nps.gov/grca; ⏰ 8am-7pm) offers a small bookstore, while the North Rim **switchboard** ( ☎ 928-638-2612) can patch you through to the lodge's front desk, the dining room and other concessions. The dining room serves breakfast, lunch and dinner (when reservations are required). The North Rim also hosts a general store ( ⏰ 8am-8pm), a café ( ⏰ 7am-9pm) and a saloon ( ⏰ 5:30-10:30am, 11:30am-11pm); all are open daily.

If you want to stay overnight, it's easier to find last-minute camping than rooms. The **North Rim Campground** ( ☎ 800-365-2267; http://reservations.nps.gov; 83 sites; $15) is worth checking in person for a cancellation; it also provides public showers. Otherwise, try first-come, first-served **DeMotte Campground** ( ☎ 928-638-2389; 23 sites; $12; ⏰ Jun-Sep), 18 miles

north of the rim. If it's full by the time you arrive, the staff can direct you to free dispersed camping in the adjacent national forest.

You'll need to book far in advance for the **Grand Canyon Lodge** ( ☎ 928-638-2612, 888-297-2757; www.grandcanyonnorthrim.com; d/cabin $91-121). Near De Motte Campground is the low-key, summer-only **Kaibab Lodge** ( ☎ 928-638-2389; www.canyoneers.com; cabin $80-110), which sometimes has last-minute openings. You'll find more lodgings in Jacob Lake, 44 miles from the North Rim, but if you're this far out, there's a better selection of lodgings and restaurants in Kanab (p169).

There's no public transportation to the North Rim, which sits at the end of Hwy 67, 80 miles from Kanab, though Kanab-area shuttles stop here. If you're driving from Las Vegas, allow five to six hours.

## PIPE SPRING NATIONAL MONUMENT

This fascinating **national monument** ( ☎ 928-643-7105; www.nps.gov/pisp; $4, youth 16 & under free, national park passes accepted; ☀ 7am-5pm in summer, 8am-5pm in winter) tends to get overlooked. Most people don't even know what it contains, but it is actually one of the best places to learn about the human history of the Southwest desert.

Pipe Spring was a vital water supply and seasonal home for ancestral Pueblo people and their descendents, the Kaibab Paiute. It later served as an important way station and fortified ranch for Mormon pioneers in the late 19th century.

Today, the national monument sits amid the Kaibab Indian Reservation, and the tribe has worked with the NPS to create an exhibit that tells both their story and the Mormon story side by side. Featuring stunning firsthand accounts, displays tell how each group came to this spot, how they interacted and how they've since fared, and they do so with care, detail and respect for each side's experience. Outside is the spring itself and Winsor Castle, the Mormon's original ranch (little remains of the Native American presence); free tours are offered every half hour.

Pipe Spring is off Hwy 389, 14 miles from Fredonia, Arizona, and 42 miles from Hurricane, Utah.

## COLORADO CITY
### pop 3905 / elevation 5200ft

At first glance, Colorado City looks like any other rural town, until you notice that a number of the houses are so large they're more like compounds, while many have no siding and seem incomplete. These are your first clues to the town's open secret: Colorado City is a polygamist community, one of several along the Utah border. Adherents wear traditional dress, largely based on modesty. Men wear white long-sleeve shirts year-round, while women wear dresses (sometimes over jeans), cover their arms in public and work their hair into long braids. Farming is the economic mainstay, and Colorado City has a reputation for producing very good unpasteurized cheeses (available in the town's one grocery store and in Springdale). Respectful visitors usually receive a very friendly greeting.

And those houses? Their size speaks for itself, and they remain unfinished so residents can avoid paying property taxes.

Colorado City is on Hwy 389, 33 miles from Fredonia, Arizona, and 23 miles from Hurricane, Utah.

*continued from p171*

### HIKING & BACKPACKING

Day hikers have two options: fight like a dog for a day-hike permit for **North Coyote Buttes** – a trailless expanse of slickrock that includes one of the Southwest's most famous formations, The Wave – or day hike the upper portions of three slot canyons (Wire Pass, Buckskin Gulch and Paria Canyon), for which you *don't* need a permit. Either way, these are classic, almost magical, experiences that shouldn't be missed.

**Wire Pass** (3.4 miles round-trip) is doable in about two hours and is the most popular slot canyon day hike. The pass dead-ends where Buckskin Gulch narrows, making it possible to continue along slot canyons for as long as you like. From the **Buckskin Gulch** trailhead, you'll hike about 3 miles to its narrow section. Both trailheads lie along House Rock Valley Rd (4.7 miles west of the contact station), a passable dirt road in dry weather.

It's about 4 miles from the **Paria Canyon** trailhead to its narrow section; the trail starts from the White House Campground.

Due to flash floods, obstacles in these slot canyons change regularly. For example, Wire Pass is mostly level, but one year boulders might mean drops of 4ft, other years 15ft. Always check with rangers before hiking.

Serious canyoneers will want to tackle the five-day trek along 38-mile Paria Canyon to Lees Ferry, Arizona. It involves numerous stretches of ankle- to knee-deep muddy water, some swims and many obstacles, but it's unforgettable. Spring and fall are the best times; permits are required.

See Getting There & Around in Kanab (p171) for trailhead shuttle services.

### PERMITS, FEES & RESERVATIONS

All trails, whether day or overnight, require a $5 fee per person per day. For slot canyon day hikes, you self-pay and register at the trailhead.

For day-hike permits for the North Coyote Buttes, you can **reserve online** (www.az.blm.gov/paria) up to seven months in advance, which is how soon they book up; only 10 are granted per day. Ten walk-in next-day permits are also given out by lottery at the Paria Contact Station at 9am every morning; arrive by 8:30am and hope for the best. Note that the walk-in system may change as a result of hiker complaints.

Overnight permits for the canyons are much easier to get and can also be reserved online up to seven months in advance; only 20 are available per day, and groups are limited to 10 people. No pets, vehicles, horses or campfires are allowed. Voluntary use of human-waste carryout bags is encouraged; the contact station provides them for free.

## Big Water

About 56 miles from Kanab, this small town, whose only traveler service is a convenience store, is notable for two things: It's a well-known polygamist community, and it houses a brand-new, sparkling, national-monument visitor center.

The **Big Water Visitor Center** ( ☎ 435-675-3200; 100 Upper Resolution Way; ☻ 9am-5:30pm, call for winter hours) is worth a visit for its paleontology exhibits, which include a replica of a dig, various bones that have been found in the monument (including the 13ft tail of a duckbill) and a spectacular 9ft-by-45ft mural by expert dinosaur painter Larry Felder.

The south end of **Smoky Mountain Rd** (p157) emerges at Big Water. At this point on Hwy 89, the nearest services are 17 miles east in Page, Arizona.

*Towering slabs of chocolate-red rock, sweeping yellow sandstone arches, giant cream-colored domes and stark gray monoliths jut skyward at Capitol Reef National Park, revealing millions of years of geologic history in a mere 375-sq-mile area.*

# EXPERIENCING
# CAPITOL REEF

Native Fremont Indians called this vast landscape of tilted buttes, jumbled rocks and winding canyons the 'Land of the Sleeping Rainbow.'

The park's centerpiece is Waterpocket Fold, a 100-mile monocline – a buckle in the Earth's crust – that overwhelmed early explorers. They dubbed it a reef, as it blocked their way like a reef blocks a ship's passage. Known also for its enormous Navajo sandstone domes, one of which resembles the US Capitol in Washington, DC, Capitol Reef contains fantastic hiking trails, 800-year-old Fremont Indian petroglyphs and a verdant 19th-century Mormon settlement.

## WHEN YOU ARRIVE

Unlike most national parks, Capitol Reef lacks any entrance stations at the park border. Arriving via Hwy 24, the main paved route through the park, you'll turn south at the signed road to the visitor center, where you can pick up a park brochure and speak with rangers. There is a $5 fee to drive the park's Scenic Drive south of Fruita Campground. Capitol Reef is open year-round.

## ORIENTATION

Hwy 24 cuts through the northern section of this long, thin park, which stretches north-south along **Waterpocket Fold**. The park's Scenic Drive runs 10 miles south from the visitor center.

Capitol Reef's central region is the **Fruita Historic District**. To the far north lies **Cathedral Valley** and its moonscape of towering monoliths, the least-visited section of the park. To the south, the park narrows to hug either side of Waterpocket Fold.

Several unpaved roads access the extreme northern reaches of the park around Cathedral Valley; the easiest route is Caineville Wash Rd, though some stretches require a high-clearance 4WD vehicle. Notom–Bullfrog Rd heads south from Hwy 24, first through private land, then into the park, roughly paralleling Waterpocket Fold. Beyond the Burr Trail Switchbacks, Notom–Bullfrog Rd merges with Burr Trail Rd and continues south to the Glen Canyon National Recreation Area.

See the Capitol Reef map (Map 6) on p150.

## INFORMATION

The **visitor center** ( ☎ 435-425-3791; www.nps.gov/care; Hwy 24 & Scenic Dr; ⏰ 8am-4:30pm, extended summer hours) is also the park headquarters. It's the best and only source for information in the park. Be sure to watch the short film that explains some of Capitol Reef's complex geology. You'll also find a stunning 4ft-by-16ft relief map of the park that took 20,000 hours to create and was crafted using dental instruments. Rangers and interpretive staff offer advice and help plan hikes. Inquire about ranger-led programs.

Despite low annual rainfall amounts and extremely low humidity, occasional summer thunderstorms pose a serious risk of flash floods. Always check the weather with rangers at the visitor center before heading out on a hike.

## POLICIES & REGULATIONS

Capitol Reef's hiking and backcountry use regulations include those listed for all the parks in the Activities chapter. In particular, do not feed the resident deer, as it teaches them not to forage, which can be deadly come winter.

## GETTING AROUND

The park lacks a transportation system. In summer you can drive most dirt roads in a regular passenger car, most notably Notom-Bullfrog and Burr Trail Rds. In more remote regions, such as Cathedral Valley, you'll need a high-clearance 4WD vehicle. Look for gas stations in Torrey and Boulder. Bicycles are allowed on park roads – paved or dirt – but not on trails.

Offering guided hikes in Capitol Reef, **Earth Tours** ( ☎ 435-691-1241; www.earth-tours.com; PO Box 1426, Boulder, UT 84716; half- to full-day tours $50-75; ⏰ spring-fall) is run by a PhD in geology who knows how to translate his knowledge into lay terms. To book biker or hiker shuttle service, contact **Hondoo Rivers & Trails** ( ☎ 435-425-3519, 800-332-2696; www. hondoo.com; 90 E Main St, Torrey) or **Wild Hare Expeditions** ( ☎ 435-425-3999, 800-304-4273; www.color-country.net/~thehare; 116 W Main St, Torrey).

## HIGHLIGHTS

✔ Picking summer fruit right from the trees in **Fruita** (p177)

✔ Hiking The Narrows between sheer, 80-story canyon walls at **Grand Wash** (p180)

✔ **Picnicking** (p177) amid deer herds along the shady banks of the Fremont River, in Fruita

✔ Flirting with vertigo at the **Goosenecks Overlook** (p178)

✔ Hiking beneath sweeping sandstone domes on the **Hickman Bridge Trail** (p181)

## SIGHTS

This chapter's driving tours highlight Capitol Reef's main sights. The park boundaries roughly follow **Waterpocket Fold**, the 100-mile monocline that runs north-south. Hwy 24 crosses the fold, while the park's Scenic Dr parallels it. But the best way to see the fold from within the park is to ascend the **Burr Trail Switchbacks** (p178), then drive north for 3 miles to the **Strike Valley Overlook**. Domes along Hwy 24, such as Navajo and Capitol Domes, are actually part of the fold.

### Fruita Historic District

Offering welcome respite from the menacing red-rock desert, Fruita (FROO-tuh) is a cool green oasis, where mature, shade-giving cottonwoods and fruit-bearing trees line the banks of the Fremont River. The first Mormon homesteaders arrived in 1880, while Fruita's final resident left in 1969.

The park service now maintains the 2700 cherry, apricot, peach, pear and apple trees planted by early settlers, and if you visit between June and October, you can eat ripe fruit straight from the trees for free (there's a nominal fee for any fruit taken from an orchard). To learn what's in season, ask at the visitor center or call the **fruit hotline** ( ☎ 435-425-3791). You're welcome to pick fruit from any unlocked orchard; just follow posted instructions at the gates. Pick only mature fruit and leave the rest to ripen. Near the orchards is a wonderful **picnic area**, where you'll spot roaming deer and hear birdsong in the trees, a rarity in the desert.

> ## WATER, WATER EVERYWHERE
>
> Hidden inside Capitol Reef's towering jumble of rocks and winding canyons are giant natural cisterns that are full of water. These caches are a rare commodity in this arid landscape. John Wesley Powell, the first Western explorer to encounter the reef, found this precious resource and nicknamed the monocline Waterpocket Fold
>
>

You can also visit the old **blacksmith shop**, though it's little more than a shed with period equipment inside (press a button to hear Dewey Gifford, the town's last resident, reminisce about life in Fruita). Across the road is the **Ripple Rock Nature Center**, a family-oriented hands-on learning center. Displays at the **Gifford Homestead** reveal the day-to-day world of a typical pioneer homestead. Fruita also hosts pioneer craft demonstrations and a small store (hours vary seasonally; check at the visitor center), where you can buy handicrafts and reproductions of 19th-century household items.

Just past **Fruita Campground** (p188) the historic district ends, yielding to trails alongside the Fremont River.

## DRIVING TOURS

Two main paved roads access the park: Hwy 24 and the park's Scenic Drive. Both are outlined on the following pages. Many routes through the park follow rough dirt roads that are only bladed four times a year. *Always check road conditions* at the visitor center before heading out. Winter snows may render some routes impassable.

The park sells guides ($1) to two excellent drives: Loop-the-Fold and Cathedral Valley Loop.

The 100-mile **Loop-the-Fold** tour offers the most comprehensive overview of Waterpocket Fold. Part of the route follows Burr Trail Rd, part of it Hwy 12 and part of it Hwy 24 (p178), while about half the trip is on dirt roads generally accessible to 2WD passenger cars with standard or high clearance.

The much rougher, 58-mile **Cathedral Valley Loop** takes in this valley's otherworldly landscapes. Though in places the route requires 4WD and high clearance, you can usually drive a 2WD vehicle the first 15.5 miles of Caineville Wash Rd from Hwy 24 to the striking 400ft monoliths, **Temple of the Sun and Temple of the Moon**, and to **Glass Mountain,** a 20ft mound of fused selenite crystals. This short in-and-out trip offers a taste of Cathedral Valley without the headaches of 4WD. Unless you're driving a high-clearance 4WD vehicle, do *not* attempt the 58-mile loop along Hartnet Rd, which fords the Fremont

River just before rejoining Hwy 24. The turnoff from Hwy 24 to Caineville Wash Rd is at mile marker 98.4.

If you have time for only one backroad trip at Capitol Reef, head up the **Burr Trail Switchbacks**. Better yet, head to Boulder and drive the complete Loop-the-Fold tour. To reach Burr Trail Rd, take **Notom–Bullfrog Rd**, a so-so dirt road – the prettiest stretch lies south of the Bitter Creek Divide.

### HIGHWAY 24
**Route: Torrey to Orientation Pullout**
**Distance: 20 miles one way**
**Speed Limit: 40–55mph**

From Torrey, head east into Capitol Reef on Hwy 24. There is no entrance station; the route is free. Stop at turnouts along the way to read geologic interpretive panels.

The route descends 1300ft in the 11 miles between Torrey and the park visitor center at the Hwy 24/Scenic Dr junction. Make your first stop at **Chimney Rock**, the towering reddish-brown rock formation 8 miles east of Torrey. If you're in great shape, consider hiking the strenuous 3.5-mile loop hike.

Just east of Chimney Rock, turn right at Panorama Point and drive to the **Goosenecks Overlook**. If you make one stop west of the visitor center, make it this one. An easy 0.1-mile walk from the parking area over rock slabs takes you to this dizzying viewpoint 800ft above Sulphur Creek, which twists through the canyon in elegant S curves. The canyon floor represents the oldest rock layer in the park, a whopping 286 million years old. Though the observation platform is fenced in, much of the area around it is open – hold on to little ones! Left of the parking area is the 0.3-mile stroll to **Sunset Point**. Visit the Goosenecks in the afternoon, when the light is best.

Back on Hwy 24, 3 miles farther east, you'll arrive at the Scenic Drive junction, the west end of the Fruita Historic District and home to the park visitor center. For sights along the Scenic Dr south of Fruita, see the **Scenic Drive Driving Tour**.

Rising majestically just north of the junction is **The Castle**; an interpretive panel details its geologic history. East of the visitor center, Hwy 24 skirts the Fremont River and passes through lush green Fruita, the surrounding rock growing paler and more yellow as you approach the park's Navajo sandstone domes. Peer through the windows of the historic Fruita School before stopping at the **Petroglyphs**. Created by Fremont Native Americans, these carvings convinced archaeologists that the Fremont culture was distinct from the Anasazi. The fenced-in boardwalk is wheelchair accessible; bring binoculars or a zoom lens to see detail.

Stop at the turnout just east of the Petroglyphs for views of the park's namesake, **Capitol Dome**, a giant sandstone dome that resembles the US Capitol. This also marks the trailhead for the **Hickman Bridge Trail** (p181). Two miles ahead on the right, peer through the window of the one-room 1882 **Behunin Cabin**, once home to a family of 10.

North of the highway, 2 miles east of the cabin, you'll pass a manmade waterfall. Do *not* swim in it. More accidents (usually compound fractures) occur here than anywhere else in the park. Rocks are slippery, currents strong, and the pool at the bottom shallow.

At **Orientation Pullout**, 9 miles from the visitor center, you'll find restrooms and an information kiosk.

Just past Fruita Campground, where the tree-lined oasis yields to the rocky desert, stop at the self-service fee station and pay $5 to drive the Scenic Dr. Until 1962, when Hwy 24 was rerouted, the drive was part of the main highway and passed through Capitol Gorge, which flooded following rainstorms. Unpaved until the late 1980s, it's a narrow, undulating road with no center stripe. To avoid bottoming out, drive slowly, especially where the road dips into washes. The last stretch of the route into Capitol Gorge remains unpaved.

**Scenic Drive Driving Tour**

Capitol Reef National Park

The following stops in the text correspond to numbered roadside markers. The park used to hand out a brochure detailing the geologic and ecological significance of each stop; at the time of research, these had been discontinued, though the park hopes to distribute an updated version in the near future. The following descriptions are condensed versions of the old material. For more detailed information visit www.nps.gov/care/scenic.htm.

The reddish brown Moenkopi rock escarpment above the first marker **(Stop 1)** is 225 million years old, while the thin, grayish-green layer of shale just above it is part of the Chinle formation, rich in petrified wood. The road soon opens up to a view of the western face of Capitol Reef **(Stop 2)**, which reveals the park's defining geologic features – sedimentary rock, erosion and buckling along Waterpocket Fold.

If it's not raining, turn left and drive a mile up Grand Wash Rd. Where the road ends **(Stop 3)**, you can hike into the wash (see Day Hikes, p180) or take the trail to **Cassidy Arch**, named for outlaw Butch Cassidy, who reportedly hid out here on occasion. In the hills left of the parking area, look for shaft openings at the abandoned Oyler Uranium Mine, which opened in 1904 and mined the radioactive material for use in 'curative' potions. You can walk to the mine, but for obvious reasons it has been sealed.

As you return along the wash, pause **(Stop 4)** for a view of Cassidy Arch amid cliffs on the left. At the base of sheer cliff walls on the right, notice the striated Wingate sandstone, which once was shifting sand dunes on an ancient desert. The next marker **(Stop 5)** offers a glimpse of delicate plant life along the wash, where such highly adaptive species as Apache plume make the most of Capitol Reef's 7in of annual rainfall.

Back on the Scenic Dr, you'll continue through the Moenkopi formation **(Stop 6)**, layers of red shale that formed when this area was a tidal flat – look for telltale ripples in the rock. You'll soon reach **Slickrock Divide (Stop 7)**, a hill between two major drainages. North of here, runoff drains into Grand Wash, while streams to the south channel into Capitol Gorge. As water travels through these washes, it changes the landscape not by carving rock, but by carrying away rubble. Flash floods move a lot of debris all at once. Capping the Moenkopi layer at the next viewpoint **(Stop 8)** is a yellowish gray layer of uranium-rich Shinarump sandstone, deposited along ancient riverbeds and streambeds.

The final 2 miles of the route will knock your socks off as you zigzag through the canyon along the gravel Capitol Gorge Spur. This narrow channel through **Wingate sandstone (Stop 9)** was the original through-road to points east between 1884 and 1962, before Hwy 24 was redirected. The right fork leads to Pleasant Creek.

Soon coming into to view on your left is a massive outcrop of pale **Navajo sandstone (Stop 10)**, a layer more than 1400ft thick in places. It erodes in sweeping contours and comprises the park's most famous domes, including Capitol Dome. The Golden Throne sits 1000ft above this viewpoint, at 6489ft.

The road ends deep within the gorge **(Stop 11)**, one of few passages through Waterpocket Fold. Park here and hike past the Pioneer Register, where early settlers carved their names into the walls, to **The Tanks**, which are natural rock cisterns (see the Capitol Gorge hike, below).

## DAY HIKES

Capitol Reef offers great hiking trails, mostly over loose rock; wear hiking boots with ankle support. There's little shade, and it gets very hot in summer. Drink *at least* one quart of water every two hours of hiking, increase your intake of electrolytes (sodium and potassium) and wear a wide-brimmed hat.

If you're tight on time and want the most variety, stop at the **Goosenecks Overlook** (p178) and hike the Grand Wash and Hickman Bridge Trails. Stop by the visitor center for a thorough list of hikes. Two difficult but worthwhile spurs not described below lead to **Cassidy Arch** (off the Grand Wash Trail) and the **Golden Throne** (off the Capitol Gorge Trail).

### GRAND WASH TRAIL
**Distance: 2.2 miles one way**
**Duration: 45 minutes–1½ hours one way**
**Challenge: Easy**
**Elevation Change: 200ft**

Avoid this hike if rain threatens, as the wash is prone to flash floods. Start from the parking lot at the end of Grand Wash and sign the trail register. This is the park's most dramatic and easily accessible canyon walk. Kids love it, especially The Narrows.

It's an easy stroll up the packed-sand wash from the parking area. The walls inch closer and closer together until, about a mile ahead, you reach **The Narrows**, where the 80-story canyon is just 15ft wide – an awesome sight and a thrill to hike through. The canyon walls shorten as the trail approaches Hwy 24. Return the way you came or arrange for someone to pick you up on the highway.

### CAPITOL GORGE TRAIL
**Distance: 2 miles round-trip**
**Duration: 45 minutes–1½ hours**
**Challenge: Easy**
**Elevation Change: 40ft**

Until recently, this gorge was the primary automobile route through the fold. Pioneers first brought wagons through in the 1880s, and the route remained in use until 1962. The sheer canyon walls are stained with desert varnish (iron oxides), which stand out in dramatic contrast to the rock, especially in black-and-white photographs. Keep your eyes peeled for bighorn sheep, a rare but thrilling sight. Do not take this flood-prone route if rain threatens.

Park at the end of the Scenic Dr. A quarter mile from the trailhead you'll reach a vandalized panel of ancient Fremont petroglyphs. A quarter mile farther is the **Pioneer Register**, a collection of carved names and dates that dates back to the first pioneer passersby in 1871. Despite modern graffiti, you can clearly make out many of the names and dates. Don't be confused by signatures on the right-hand wall. These date to the 1940s, when a USGS survey team lowered its leader over the wall to incise the party's names – vandalism by today's standards.

About three-quarters of a mile from the trailhead, bear left and follow signs to **The Tanks**, which lie atop a fairly steep 0.2-mile spur. These giant cisterns, or water pockets, hold great volumes of water much of the year. They were invaluable to early settlers and remain so for animals. When you're rested and ready, head back the way you came – the onward trail crosses park boundaries into private land.

---

### HICKMAN BRIDGE TRAIL

**Distance: 2 miles round-trip**
**Duration: 1–2 hours**
**Challenge: Easy–Moderate**
**Elevation Change: 200ft**

Capitol Reef's most popular trail, this route is fairly easy for both kids and grandparents. If you're short on time, this hike yields tremendous diversity, including a canyon walk, a stunning natural bridge, long views and spring wildflowers. As the route is largely exposed, it's best to hike it in the early morning. Cairns mark some of the route. This trail connects with the **Rim Overlook–Navajo Knobs Trail** (p182).

From the trailhead on the Fremont River, ascend the red rock cliff via a few easy switchbacks. As you cross an open area of desert vegetation strewn with volcanic black rocks, the highway vanishes behind giant domes of white sandstone. The trail soon drops into a wash, where you can rest in a shady alcove before ascending the slickrock to **Hickman Bridge**. While this chunky yellow arch can be tricky to spot, the trail loops right beneath it for a marvelous appreciation of its mass. Bear left beyond the arch to rejoin the main trail. Be sure to look over the rim and downriver to Fruita, an oasis of green below.

## COHAB CANYON
**Distance: 1.75 miles one way**
**Duration: 1–2 hours**
**Challenge: Moderate–Difficult**
**Elevation Change: 400ft**

If you're with people whose ability or interest in hiking isn't as great as yours, leave them to laze by the river or tour historic sights while you hike this relatively short, initially strenuous hike through Cohab Canyon. This is good workout for energetic teens, whose parents can pick them up an hour later at Hwy 24.

Starting across from the Gifford Homestead north of Fruita Campground, the trail makes a steep quarter-mile ascent atop a rocky cliff. From here the trail levels out though the canyon, then slowly descends to Hwy 24, just east of the Hickman Bridge trailhead. You'll pass striking geologic features on your way through this intimate **hidden canyon**, which protects a small green oasis of piñon and juniper trees (look for lizards). Two short spur trails take you to overlooks of Fruita and the orchards.

About a mile from the trailhead, you'll reach a junction with the **Frying Pan Trail**, another moderate-difficult route that links Cohab Canyon with Grand Wash and Cassidy Arch; it leads atop an escarpment for panoramic views before dropping into Grand Wash. Add 3 miles (one way) if you hike Frying Pan.

## RIM OVERLOOK–NAVAJO KNOBS TRAIL
**Distance: 9 miles round-trip**
**Duration: 4–6 hours**
**Challenge: Difficult**
**Elevation Change: 1494ft**

This hike to Navajo Knobs – twin bumps of Navajo sandstone perched high on the precipitous western edge of Waterpocket Fold – yields unsurpassed views. You'll follow cairns along the slickrock route, which passes Capitol Reef's giant white domes. While this steep climb offers little shade and no water, at least flash floods are not a concern.

Start from the Fremont River along the Hickman Bridge Trail; after 0.3 mile, fork right at the signed junction. Following the draw west (left), the trail skirts the base of magnificent, rounded white peaks. Pause at the well-marked **Hickman Bridge Overlook**, south (left) of the trail. Blending in amid the surrounding rock, the 133ft natural bridge is across a small canyon on the same level as the overlook.

Onward, the trail zigzags through a south-facing side canyon, a pattern that repeats for much of the remaining hike. As you continue climbing, the trail winds past the mouth of three more side canyons before reaching the **Rim Overlook**, 2.25 miles from the trailhead. Gorgeous views encompass a profile of the fold and its north end, the Kaiparowits Plateau (west), Castle Dome (north) and, 1000ft below, the visitor center and Fruita Campground.

After climbing two more sandstone pitches, you'll pass between cliffs (on your right) and a weather tower and find yourself on a broad ledge that faces **The Castle** – a large, eroded, freestanding chunk of Waterpocket Fold. The trail rambles along this ledge to the northwest edge of a west-facing W-shaped canyon. Following cairns, you'll climb the west rim of the W and soon spot the **Navajo Knobs** (6980ft), twins bumps that mark the highpoint on the next promontory. Watch your step as you clamber over loose rock to the double summit. Retrace your steps to the trailhead.

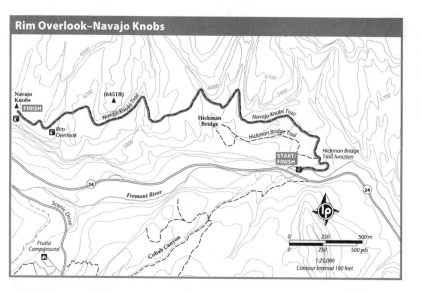

**Rim Overlook–Navajo Knobs**

# BACKCOUNTRY HIKES

For a sense of the vastness of Waterpocket Fold and the ruggedness of the land, there's no better activity than backcountry hiking. Capitol Reef gets extremely hot in summer, however, and dehydration is a serous concern, so plan carefully before backpacking. Be sure to wear a wide-brimmed hat and plan to carry *all* your water – don't count on finding water pockets. Consume *at least* six quarts of water a day and increase your intake of electrolytes (sodium and potassium) to balance the extra fluid consumption. Avoid salt tablets unless directed by a physician.

## Permit Information & Backcountry Camping

Pick up a free backcountry permit and check trail conditions at the visitor center. Ground fires are prohibited in Capitol Reef; bring a camp stove. There are no established campgrounds in the backcountry. *Never* camp in a wash.

## BACKCOUNTRY TRAILS

Talk to rangers before setting out on any of these hikes. In addition to the backcountry trails outlined below, ask rangers about the hike to **Halls Creek Narrows**, a 22-mile round-trip through narrow canyons. Wherever you choose to roam, stay on the trails, don't shortcut switchbacks, and avoid stepping on cryptobiotic soil (see p275).

---

**UPPER MULEY TWIST CANYON**
Distance: 15.7 miles round-trip
Duration: 1–2 days
Challenge: Moderate
Elevation Change: 830ft

---

The upper portion of Muley Twist Canyon is less dramatic than its counterpart (see the next hike), but it offers easier terrain and expansive views from atop the fold. Along the canyon floor you'll pass arches and sculpted sandstone

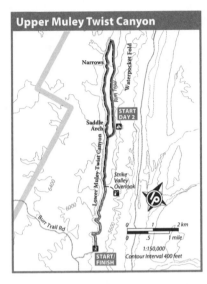

**Upper Muley Twist Canyon**

Narrows
Waterpocket Fold
Rim Trail
START DAY 2
Saddle Arch
Lower Muley Twist Canyon
Strike Valley Overlook
Burr Trail Rd
5600
6000
5000
START/ FINISH

0    1    2 km
0    .5    1 mile
1:150,000
Contour Interval 400 feet

narrows that occasionally hold enough water for a dip.

Though you can approach Upper Muley as a long, difficult day hike, it's better to spend two days and enjoy the scenery. Most people camp near the Rim Trail junction, then hike the Rim Trail Loop without a pack.

To reach the trailhead, drive a mile west of the Burr Trail Switchbacks and turn right on the road leading to the Strike Valley Overlook. With a high-clearance vehicle, you can drive the first 3 miles of the hike to the Strike Valley Overlook trailhead.

### Day 1: Upper Muley Twist Canyon Trailhead to Rim Trail
*(2½–3 hours, 5.3 miles)*
From the trailhead, follow the gravel wash east for a quarter mile, then turn north (left) into Muley Twist Canyon. The canyon is wide and the wash level for the 3-mile hike to the Strike Valley Overlook trailhead, marked by a chain across the wash. The half-mile round-trip jaunt to the **Strike Valley Overlook** is worth the energy, especially if you set down your pack.

Upper Muley Twist Canyon narrows a half mile past the overlook, as steep red sandstone cliffs to the east (right) turn in toward the wash. About 1.2 miles farther you'll arrive at **Saddle Arch**, visible near the rim of the west wall. A sign on the east side of the wash marks the beginning of the Rim Trail Loop. Follow cairns up the canyon's east side.

In about 10 to 15 minutes you'll reach a broad bench capped with juniper trees and camping spots. Avoid treading on the crumbly black cryptobiotic soil. If you want a view, but no shade or potentially high winds, camp at the saddle where the trail crests the fold.

### Day 2: Rim Trail Loop to Upper Muley Twist Canyon Trailhead
*(7½–10 hours, 10.4 miles)*
The Rim Trail Loop is slippery when wet, so use caution. From your campsite, follow cairns up to the east rim for spectacular views. A sign at the top points back down to the Canyon Route, and you'll find several sandy potential campsites.

Follow the ridge north to a highpoint for views north along the fold to the grand white domes near the visitor center (35 miles away). After 1.5 miles of ridge hiking, just before a gap in the fold, the trail plunges toward the west side of the ridge and descends toward Muley Twist Canyon. Several cairned routes lead to the canyon floor, each requiring lots of scrambling.

Turn down-canyon (south) and stay high, close to the east wall. About 300ft past wonderful hat-shaped formations, the trail swings east (left) away from the narrows below. Several deep potholes serve as water-storage tanks.

Beyond the gap in the west wall, the trail returns to the canyon floor. A quarter mile down-canyon, the cairned trail climbs the east wall again, though in dry periods you may be able to continue along the canyon floor. Soon you'll pass **Saddle Arch**, high on the west (right) wall, and a sign for the Rim Route will signal the end of your loop. From here the high red canyon walls wax low and golden, and you'll retrace your route to the trailhead, 5 miles away.

**LOWER MULEY TWIST CANYON**
Distance: 15 miles round-trip
Duration: 1–2 days
Challenge: Moderate–Difficult overnight; Difficult day hike
Elevation Change: 850ft

This loop hike follows the dramatic lower section of Muley Twist Canyon through narrow red walls, then returns through grasslands dotted with colorful hills. The entire region must be relatively dry when you undertake this dangerously flood-prone hike. Check with rangers for current conditions.

Three miles south of the Notom-Bullfrog Rd/Burr Trail junction (29 miles south of Hwy 24), a well-signed road leads right toward **The Post**. The trailhead is at the southwest edge of the parking lot.

The first mile is extremely steep. From the parking lot, follow the well-marked trail west up Waterpocket Fold's red, sloping back. After about an hour of steady climbing, the trail hits sand, and the canyon's red walls come into view to the northeast. You'll level out and cross a sandy area strewn with vegetation, a good potential camping spot.

**Lower Muley Twist Canyon**

*[Map: Lower Muley Twist Canyon showing Circle Cliffs, Headquarters Canyon, The Post, Post Spur Rd, START/FINISH, Norton-Bullfrog Rd, Lower Muley Twist Canyon, Waterpocket Fold, Grand Gulch, campsites. Scale 1:150,000, Contour Interval 400 feet. 0–2 km / 0–1 mile]*

Leaving the wash, the trail bears south to Lower Muley Twist Canyon, staying high on the canyon's east side, then cutting gently to the canyon floor. Sheer red Wingate sandstone walls tower 300ft on both sides.

Continue south through the canyon. After passing two gaps in the west (right) wall, you'll reach a big side canyon to the northeast, home to several good campsites. Back in the main canyon, the trail soon turns from sand to sandstone and continues straight where the main canyon swings west. Mount a sandy plain to more campsites amid sage and junipers.

The hike continues in the same manner – from riverbed to high ground – as the canyon twists south. Each alcove seems bigger, deeper and more graceful than the last. Eventually you'll reach the **canyon narrows**, where the 800ft walls are less than 10ft apart at points – narrow enough to 'twist a mule.'

A quarter mile farther Muley Twist Canyon ends where its riverbed flows into Strike Valley toward Halls Creek. At this point, cairns mark the return trail north to The Post. Strike Valley opens wider the farther north you hike.

## OTHER ACTIVITIES
### Guided Hiking & Wilderness Treks
One of the best guide services in southern Utah, **Hondoo Rivers & Trails** ( ☎ 435-425-3519, 800-332-2696; www.hondoo.com; 90 E Main St, Torrey) operates one-day and multi-day hikes, as well as fantastic horseback and vehicle trips. If it's booked, call **Wild Hare Expeditions** ( ☎ 435-425-3999, 800-304-4273; www.color-country.net/~thehare; 116 W Main St, Torrey).

### Horseback Riding
For half-day or all-day horseback trips, call **Cowboy Homestead Cabins** ( ☎ 435-

425-3414, 888-854-4871; www.cowboyhomesteadcabins.com; half-day $85, all day $150), operated by local cowboys who know the land like the back of their hands. The same goes for **Hondoo Rivers & Trails** (p185).

### Fishing

You'll find surprisingly good fishing in the mountains above Capitol Reef. Stop by **Boulder Mountain Adventures & Alpine Angler's Flyshop** (☎ 435-425-3660, 888-484-3331; www.fly-fishing-utah.net; 310 W Main St, Torrey), where you can find out where to fish or book a daylong or multiday combination horseback/fishing trip.

### Four-Wheel Driving

Plenty of 4WD roads crisscross Capitol Reef. To avoid bottoming out your family sedan, book a guided Jeep trip with **Hondoo Rivers & Trails** or **Wild Hare Expeditions** (p185).

### Kids' Programs

When you arrive at the park, stop by the visitor center to pick up a **Junior Ranger Activity Guide**. Once kids complete certain activities, they return to the visitor center to receive a certificate and badge from a ranger. The visitor center also loans out Family Fun Packs of games and interpretive activities. Be sure to visit the **Ripple Rock Nature Center** (🕑 10am-3pm Memorial Day–Labor Day, closed Sun-Mon), in Fruita, to check out the family-friendly hands-on exhibits.

### Ranger Programs

From May to September, the park offers various programs, including ranger talks, guided walks and evening programs at Fruita Amphitheater. Check at the visitor center for the current schedule.

### Swimming & Wading

Only wade in wide, calm sections of a creek or river – and only if there's no threat of a flash flood; check with rangers. There are three accessible spots. Across the highway from the Chimney Rock parking area, an easy, level trail leads to **Sulphur Creek**. Near the visitor center, hike up Sulphur Creek a mile to a large wading pool shaded by cottonwoods. You can also wade along **Pleasant Creek** at the end of Scenic Dr; get directions from the visitor center.

### Rock Climbing

Technical climbing is allowed, and you don't need a permit. Though you'll find lots of climbable cracks in the Wingate sandstone, be aware that it can flake unpredictably. Follow clean-climbing guidelines, and take all safety precautions. For complete details, check with rangers or visit the park website (www.nps.gov/care).

### Bicycling

The Scenic Drive works well for beginners and intermediates, while experienced mountain bikers love Cathedral Valley, though it becomes a muddy mess when wet. Check road conditions with rangers. You can rent a bike from **Capitol Reef Backcountry Outfitters** (☎ 435-425-2010; www.capitolreefoutfitters.com; 677 E Hwy 24 at Hwy 12; rentals $38-55/day), which also leads rides.

## SLEEPING

There's neither lodging nor food in the park. Eleven miles west of the visitor center, Torrey (p188) is the nearest place to sleep and eat.

*continued on p188*

Most goods and services are available in Torrey.

### GROCERIES & SUPPLIES
**Austin's Chuckwagon General Store & Deli** ( ☎ 435-425-3288; 12 W Main St, Torrey; ☽ 7am-10pm, closed Nov-Mar) sells camp supplies, sundries, groceries, beer and doughnuts. In winter, you'll have to drive 16 miles to **Royal's Food Town** ( ☎ 435-836-2841; 135 S Main St, Loa; ☽ 7:30am-8pm, till 7pm in winter).

### INTERNET ACCESS
Log on at **Castle Rock Coffee & Candy** ( ☎ 435-425-2100; Hwy 12/24 junction, Torrey; ☽ 7:30am-9pm).

### LAUNDRY
Do your wash at **Austin's Chuckwagon Motel** ( ☎ 435-425-3288; 12 W Main St, Torrey).

### LOST & FOUND
Check at the visitor center or call ☎ 435-425-3791.

### MEDICAL SERVICE & EMERGENCIES
In an emergency, dial ☎ 911. For park **police**, dial ☎ 435-425-3791.
   The nearest clinic is the **Wayne Community Health Center** ( ☎ 435-425-3744; 128 S 300 W, Bicknell, 19 miles west of the park on Hwy 24; ☽ 9am-5pm Mon-Fri, 9am-1pm Sat), while the closest hospital is **Sevier Valley Hospital** ( ☎ 435-896-8271; 1000 N Main St, Richfield, 75 miles west of the park on Hwy 24).

### MONEY
There's an ATM at **Austin's Chuckwagon General Store** ( ☎ 435-425-3288; 12 W Main St, Torrey)

### POSTAL SERVICE
For stamps and to mail letters, go to the **post office** ( ☎ 435-425-3716; 75 W Main St, Torrey; ☽ 7:30am-1:30pm Mon-Fri, 7:30am-11:30am Sat) at the Torrey Trading Post.

### SHOWERS
   Pay $4 for a hot shower at **Austin's Chuckwagon General Store** ( ☎ 435-425-3288; 12 W Main St, Torrey) or $3 at **Sandcreek Campground** ( ☎ 435-425-3577, 877-425-3578; 540 Hwy 24).

### TELEPHONES
Pay phones are available at the visitor center and at Fruita Campground.

continued from p186

**Fruita Campground** (☎ 435-425-3791; www.nps.gov/care; Scenic Dr, 1 mile south of visitor center; 71 sites, incl 7 tent-only sites; $10; ☼ open year-round) The park's only developed campground, Fruita provides water, toilets, picnic tables, grills and an RV dump station, but neither showers nor campfire rings. All sites are level, and most are in the shade of mature cottonwood trees. The Fremont River runs right behind the campground. The campground collects gray water from dishwashing; follow instructions in the restrooms. You'll find a pay phone at Loop A. Only group reservations are accepted; otherwise, it's first-come, first-served.

While you won't find water at the first-come, first-served **Cedar Mesa Campground** (☎ 435-425-3791; www.nps.gov/care; Notom-Bullfrog Rd, 23 miles south of Hwy 24; 5 tent sites; free; ☼ open year-round), there are pit toilets, fire grates and picnic tables, not to mention great views east along the fold.

The drive to remote **Cathedral Valley Campground** (☎ 435-425-3791; www.nps.gov/care; Hartnet Jct, Caineville Wash Rd; 5 tent sites; free; ☼ open year-round) requires a high-clearance vehicle and may demand 4WD. The first-come, first-served campground lacks water, but there are pit toilets, fire grates and picnic tables.

# AROUND CAPITOL REEF

## TORREY
**pop 171 / elevation 6843ft**
Eleven miles west of Capitol Reef, Torrey and nearby Teasdale provide the closest lodgings. As Torrey sits 1300ft higher than Capitol Reef, temperatures here are often 10°F cooler. A quiet town built along a Main St (Hwy 24), its primary industry has shifted from logging and ranching to tourism. Torrey shuts down in winter, but in summer there's a whiff of countercultural sophistication in the air. If you're here during the third weekend in July, don't miss the Bicknell International Film Festival (BIFF), just up Hwy 24. This wacky spoof on Sundance includes films, parties and the 'fastest parade in America.'

The town center lies west of the ugly prefab chain motels and gas stations at the Hwy 24/12 junction (aka malfunction junction).

The **Wayne County Travel Council** (☎ 435-425-3365, 800-858-7951; www.capitolreef.org; Hwy 24/12 junction; ☼ noon-7pm Apr-Oct) runs an information booth. For national forest information, head 3 miles west to the **Dixie National Forest Teasdale Ranger Station** (☎ 435-425-3702; www.fs.fed.us/dxnf; 138 E Main St; ☼ 9am-5pm Mon-Fri).

### Sleeping
#### CAMPING
The area's public and private campgrounds are typically open April through October. A mile west of Torrey, **Thousand Lakes RV Park** (☎ 435-425-3500, 800-355-8995; www.thousandlakesrvpark.com; Hwy 24; tent/RV hookup $14/20, cabin $30; ☒ ) provides tent/RV sites, three camping cabins and decent facilities. Nearby, the friendly **Sandcreek RV Park, Campground & Hostel** (☎ 435-425-3577, 877-425-3578; 540 Hwy 24; tent/RV hookup $10/18, cabin $28, hostel r $12) offers tent/RV sites, cabins and beds in its exceptionally nice one-room, eight-bed hostel, as well as showers, a coin laundry, a gift store and an espresso bar.

**Sunglow Campground** (☎ 435-836-2800; www.fs.fed.us/r4/fishlake; $10) sits amid redrock cliffs in Fishlake National Forest, 6 miles west of Torrey, then east on USFS Rd 143. Dixie National Forest runs the small **Oak Creek, Pleasant Creek**

(both $9) and **Singletree Campgrounds** ($10). All three lie above 8000ft on forested Boulder Mountain, between 17 and 22 miles south of Torrey along Hwy 12. Each provides water, but no showers.

### BUDGET–MID-RANGE

**Austin's Chuckwagon Lodge** ( ☎ 435-425-3335, 800-863-3288; www.austinschuckwagon.com; 12 W Main St; r $42-64, 2-/3-bedroom cabins $100-125; ☺ Apr-Oct; ☒ ☒ ☒ ) The best motel in Torrey for service and value, Austin's has spacious motel rooms and cabins with kitchens. Amenities include satellite TV, a hot tub, coin laundry and camper showers ($4).

**Capitol Reef Inn & Café** ( ☎ 435-425-3271; www.capitolreefinn.com; 360 W Main St; r $48; ☺ Apr-Oct; ☒ ) Ten comfortable rooms set back from the road are outfitted with handcrafted wood furniture. Relax in the hot tub or climb the giant kiva to watch the sunset.

**Rim Rock Inn** ( ☎ 435-425-3398; www.therimrock.com; 2523 E Hwy 24; r $59; ☺ Mar-Nov; ☒ ☒ ) On the east side of town, surrounded by red-rock cliffs, the family-owned Rim Rock offers comfortable standard rooms, all with great views.

**Pine Shadows Bungalows** ( ☎ 435-425-3939, 800-708-1223; www.pineshadowcabins.net; 195 W 125 S, Teasdale; cabin $69-75; ☒ ☒ ) Tucked between juniper and piñon pines beneath white cliffs, these five spacious, freestanding cabins with vaulted ceilings and kitchenettes are a good value and make a great hideaway just outside Torrey. Each includes two beds, TV and VCR.

Also worth a look: **Cactus Hill Ranch Motel** ( ☎ 435-425-3578, 800-507-2624; www.cactushillmotel.com; State Rd 112, Teasdale; rooms d/tr/q $48/52/56, cabin d/tr/q $75/85/95; ☺ Mar-Nov; ☒ ☒ ) has motel rooms on a 100-acre ranch and a cozy log cabin on Boulder Mountain. **Cowboy Homestead Cabins** ( ☎ 435-425-3414, 888-854-5871; www.cowboyhomesteadcabins.com; Hwy 12; cabin $64; ☒ ☒ ) features four pine-paneled cabins with kitchenettes 3 miles south of town. **Boulder View Inn** ( ☎ 435-425-3800, 800-444-3980; www.boulderview.com; 385 W Main St; s/d $45/48; ☒ ☒ ) has 11 spotless motel rooms. Skip the Wonderland Motel.

None of the overpriced chain motels – Best Western, Days Inn, Holiday Inn Express and Super 8 – provide a sense of place, except in the views from their prefab windows. However, the **Best Western Capitol Reef** ( ☎ 435-425-3761, 888-610-9600; www.bestwestern.com; 2600 E Hwy 24; r $79-99; ☒ ☒ ) is the best of the lot in terms of amenities.

Nine miles west of Torrey on Hwy 24, Bicknell has several budget motels if Torrey and Teasdale are full.

### TOP END

**Skyridge Inn B&B** ( ☎ 435-425-3222; www.skyridgeinn.com; 950 E Hwy 24; r $115-172; ☒ ☒ ) Every window of this immaculately kept inn opens up to gorgeous views. Decked out in dressed-down country elegance, rooms include local art, down comforters and VCRs; two feature private hot tubs. Guests gather by the fire over sangria and hors d'oeuvres, or soak in the house hot tub.

**Muley Twist B&B** ( ☎ 435-425-3640, 800-530-1038; www.muleytwistinn.com; 249 W 125 S, Teasdale; r $99-109; ☺ Apr-Oct) This big wooden farmhouse with a wraparound veranda looks small against the towering sandstone domes that rise behind it. Rooms at the casual, down-to-earth inn are bright, airy and comfortable.

**The Lodge at Red River Ranch** ( ☎ 435-425-3322, 800-205-6343; www.redriverranch.com; 2900 W Hwy 24, Teasdale; r $125-175; ☒ ) In the grand old tradition of Western lodges, the great room here has a three-story, open-beam cathedral ceiling, a giant fireplace and exposed timber walls decorated with Navajo rugs. Every room is different, and every detail is flawless, from country quilts on the comfy beds to the stone masonry around each room's wood-burning fireplace. Breakfast (not included) is served in the dining room.

## Eating

**Robber's Roost Books & Beverages** ( ☎ 435-425-3265; 185 W Main St; 🕒 9am-9pm Mon-Sat, 10am-3pm Sun May-Nov, weekends only fall & spring, closed Dec-Feb) Linger over coffee on a comfy couch by the fire at Torrey's hip café-bookstore.

**Capitol Reef Café** ( ☎ 435-425-3271; 360 W Main St; breakfast $5-9, lunch-dinner dishes $7-16; 🕒 7am-9pm Apr-Oct; ✖ ) Torrey's best for breakfast and lunch serves a mishmash of vegetable-heavy dishes, salads and sandwiches; it has good dinners too, especially for vegetarians.

**Rim Rock Restaurant** ( ☎ 435-425-3398; 2523 E Hwy 24; entrées $10-25; 🕒 5-9pm daily Mar-Nov, Thu-Sun only Nov-Dec, closed Jan-Feb; ✖ ) Every table features a million-dollar view of towering red-rock cliffs. On the straightforward, meat-heavy menu, choose from great grilled steaks, pastas and fish. There's a full bar. Come before sunset.

**Café Diablo** ( ☎ 435-425-3070; 599 W Main St; appetizers $7-9, entrées $17-28; 🕒 5-10pm Apr-Oct; ✖ ) One of Utah's best, Café Diablo serves outstanding, highly stylized Southwestern food bursting with flavor and towering on the plate. There are delicious vegetarian choices. Save room for dessert. There's also a selection of 23 tequilas (drinkers, request a free ride home). Budget travelers, order appetizers and dessert – you won't leave hungry.

If you're driving east on Hwy 24, stop at **Mesa Market** ( ☎ 435-456-9146; Hwy 24 between mile markers 102 & 103; 🕒 7am-3pm from Easter to the first frost) for straight-from-the-garden organic salads and freshly baked artisan bread from an outdoor stone-hearth oven. That's all the market serves, and it's delicious.

## Entertainment

On Saturdays from 3 to 6pm at **Robber's Roost** (above), there's an open mic and a farmers' market; call about readings. The **Rim Rock Patio** ( ☎ 435-425-3398; 2523 E Hwy 24; 🕒 noon-10pm Mar-Nov), the only place where you can drink beer without ordering food, also serves pizza and ice cream (kids welcome). Play darts or volleyball while you chug-a-lug. The **Wayne Theater** ( ☎ 435-425-3123; www.waynetheater.com; 11 E Main St, Bicknell) shows first-run movies (weekends only) for a pittance and hosts the **Bicknell International Film Festival (BIFF)** in July.

## GOBLIN VALLEY STATE PARK

Melted rock formations from a Salvador Dalí fantasy fill the coliseumlike valley in this small, 3654-acre park in the San Rafael Desert. Visitors are free to roam amid the mushroom-shaped mounds of entrada sandstone. If you stare at them for a while, they do look like little goblins. Kids love the place. A few trails lead out of the valley, and an exposed 21-site **campground** ( ☎ 800-322-3770; www.stateparks.utah.gov; tent $14, $5 day-use fee; 🕒 year-round) provides water and showers; it books up most weekends.

Take Hwy 24 east for 48 miles to Hanksville, then north for 20 miles. A signed, paved road leads 12 miles west to the park entrance.

*Smack amid the Colorado Plateau, Canyonlands is Utah's largest and most rugged national park – indeed, few places encompass such inhospitable terrain. But oh, what majesty!*

NATIONAL PARK SERVICE

## EXPERIENCING
# CANYONLANDS

Vast serpentine canyons tipped with white cliffs loom high over the Colorado and Green Rivers, their waters a stunning thousand feet below the rim rock. Sweeping arches, skyward-jutting needles and spires, deep craters, blue-hued mesas and majestic buttes define the landscape. Canyonlands is a crumbling beauty, a 527-sq-mile vision of ancient Earth.

For anything more than a casual day trip to the main overlooks, you must be self-sufficient. Discounting the inaccessible rivers, most areas are completely waterless, including visitor centers (which do sell bottled water) and campgrounds (only one of which has water in summer). Dirt roads are difficult to navigate, distances are great, many trails are steep and the summer heat can be brutal. It's not hard to understand why, despite its beauty, this is the least visited of all the major Southwestern national parks.

If Zion and Bryce got you excited about canyon country but left you hankering for solitude, Canyonlands is the premier place to indulge your new love.

## WHEN YOU ARRIVE
Canyonlands is open year-round. Admission to the Island in the Sky and The Needles districts, good for seven days, costs $10 per car or $5 per person arriving by motorcycle, bicycle or foot. There is no fee to enter The Maze. Consider purchasing a Local Passport ($25), good for admission to Arches and Canyonlands for a one-year period.

## ORIENTATION
### Main Regions
The Colorado and Green Rivers divide the park into three separate and distinct areas (called 'districts' by the NPS). The river canyons form a Y – the Colorado forms the stem and northeast arm of the Y, while the northwest arm is the Green. Though the districts abut each other, they are inaccessible to one another from within the park – no bridges and few roads mean long drives to see the sights.

Cradled by the two rivers atop the Y is the most developed district, **Island in the Sky**. To reach it from Moab, drive north on Hwy 191 about 40 minutes to Hwy 313; both roads are paved. Southeast of the Colorado, **The Needles** district lies about 75 miles (90 minutes) from Moab via paved Hwys 191 and 211. West of the two rivers, **The Maze** is about 130 miles from Moab, accessible along dirt roads off Hwy 24; take Hwy 191 north to I-70 west to Hwy 24 south. **Horseshoe Canyon**, an unconnected unit northwest of The Maze, also lies off of Hwy 24 via dirt roads.

Island in the Sky and The Needles feature visitor centers, developed campgrounds and paved roads to scenic overlooks, as well as dirt roads and hiking trails. The Maze and Horseshoe Canyon offer only 4WD-accessible dirt roads, hiking trails and primitive campgrounds; few people visit these districts.

See the Canyonlands map (Map 7) on p151.

## HIGHLIGHTS

✔ Losing all perspective on distance at **Grand View Point** (p195)

✔ Bicycling the **White Rim Rd** (p198) at Island in the Sky

✔ Hiking beneath the The Needles' towering spires in **Chesler Park** (p203)

✔ Watching the verdant Green River flow into the clay-red Colorado from the **Confluence Overlook** (p203)

✔ Gazing through **Mesa Arch** (p196) at the rising sun.

✔ Acclimating to silence and solitude in **The Maze** (p205)

✔ Contemplating what it was like to live 11,000 years ago in **Horseshoe Canyon** (p205)

### Major Roads

No roads cross the park. Instead, well-marked secondary spurs from two major highways access Canyonlands' districts.

**Hwy 191** runs north-south through Moab near the eastern park boundary. Take Hwy 191 north to reach Island in the Sky or south to reach The Needles.

West of the park, **Hwy 24** runs north-south through the San Rafael Desert; spur roads connect it to The Maze and Horseshoe Canyon.

Linking these highways to the north is **I-70**, the major east-west freeway through southern Utah. Moab is 30 miles south of I-70 via Hwy 191.

## INFORMATION

Pick up maps, guidebooks and information at the **Moab Information Center** (p219). For information only, call or visit the **Canyonlands NPS Headquarters** ( ☎ 435-259-7164, 435-719-2313; www.nps.gov/cany; 2282 SW Resource Blvd, Moab; ☻ 8am-4:30pm Mon-Fri). The **Canyonlands Natural History Association** ( ☎ 435-259-6003, 800-840-8978; www.cnha.org; 3031 S Hwy 191, Moab) helps the NPS run the visitor centers and Moab Information Center and also serves as a bookseller for the NPS.

The **Island in the Sky Visitor Center** ( ☎ 435-259-4712; www.nps.gov/cany/island; Hwy 313; ☻ 8am-4:30pm, extended hours spring-fall) features exhibits, an excellent introductory video, books, maps, schedules of ranger-led activities and information on permits and campgrounds. **The Needles Visitor Center** ( ☎ 435-259-4711; www.nps. gov/cany/needles; Hwy 211; ☻ 8am-4:30pm, extended hours Mar-Oct) provides books, maps, the same introductory video, excellent exhibits and information on permits and campgrounds; make it a point to see the 25-sq-ft relief map of the park. You'll find a ranger station with books and maps, but no other services, at **Hans Flat**, three to six hours west of **The Maze** ( ☎ 435-259-2652; www.nap.gov/cany/maze; Hans Flat Rd; ☻ 8am-4:30pm).

## POLICIES & REGULATIONS

Canyonlands follows most of the national park hiking and backcountry use regulations outlined in the Activities chapter, with a few exceptions.

On its dirt roads, 4WD vehicles, mountain bikes and street-legal motor-bikes are permitted, but not ATVs. Off-roading is not allowed.

In the backcountry, campfires are allowed only along river corridors; use a fire pan, burn only driftwood or dead, downed tamarisk, and pack out all unburned debris.

Rock climbing is allowed (no permit needed), but only under specific regulations; contact a visitor center for details on restricted areas and permissible climbing hardware.

Pets are not allowed on hiking trails or in the backcountry – even in a vehicle. Make arrangements with a kennel in Moab: **Moab Veterinary Clinic** ( ☎ 435-259-8710), **Spanish Valley Veterinary Clinic** ( ☎ 435-259-5216) or **Karen's Canine Campground** ( ☎ 435-259-7922).

### Backcountry Permits

Permits are required for all backcountry camping, overnight backpacking, mountain biking, 4WD trips and river trips. These are in addition to the park entrance fee. Backpackers pay $15 per group (call for group size limits). Day-use mountain bike or 4WD groups pay $30 for up to three vehicles. River trips cost $30 per group in Cataract Canyon or $20 per group in flatwater areas. Permits are valid for up to 14 consecutive days. Certain backcountry sections of The Needles are open to day use by horses, bikes and 4WD vehicles; permits cost $5 per day per vehicle or per group of up to seven bikes or horses. Horses are allowed on all 4WD trails; contact the park for restrictions on feed and details about day or overnight permits.

You must secure reservations at least two weeks in advance, by fax or mail only, with the **NPS Reservations Office** ( ☎ 435-259-4351, fax 435-259-4285; www.nps.gov/cany/permits.htm; 2282 SW Resource Blvd, Moab, UT 84532). NPS operators answer questions from 8am to 12:30pm (sometimes till 4pm) Monday through Friday (phones are often busy; keep trying). To reserve a backpacking, mountain biking or 4WD trip, contact the NPS no earlier than the second Monday in July for the following calendar year; reservations are particularly recommended for spring and fall. Rafting and day-use reservations are accepted in early January for the same year.

If you don't have a reservation, you can get a permit on a space-available basis the day before or day of your trip from the visitor center in the district in which your trip begins. Though you can call ahead to ask whether permits are available, phone reservations are not accepted.

### GETTING AROUND

The easiest way to tour Canyonlands is by car. Traveling between districts takes two to six hours, so plan to visit no more than one per day. Speed limits vary but are generally between 25 and 40mph. There are no gas stations within the park. Fuel up in Moab, and carry extra gas in the backcountry.

Many **tour operators** guide rafting, hiking, biking and 4WD tours in the park. For a list of outfitters and shuttle services, see Moab.

# ISLAND IN THE SKY

You'll comprehend space in new ways atop the appropriately named **Island in the Sky**, a narrow, 6000ft flat-topped mesa that drops precipitously on all sides, providing some of the longest, most enthralling vistas of any park in southern Utah. The views far into the wilderness are punctuated to the west by the 11,500ft Henry Mountains near Capitol Reef and to the east by the sky-punching 12,700ft La Sal Mountains, which remain snowcapped in early summer. You can stand beneath a sparkling blue sky and watch not one, but multiple thunderstorms many miles from one another, inundating far-off regions with gunmetal-gray sheets of rain while you debate whether to apply more sunscreen.

Offering paved roads and fine views, this is the most easily reached and popular district, welcoming about 260,000 visitors a year. The island is perched atop a sandstone bench called the White Rim, which does form a white border 1200ft below the mesa top. Cliffs below the rim drop another 1500ft into the river canyons.

The small **Island in the Sky Visitor Center** (p192) sits atop the mesa about 2 miles beyond the park boundary and entrance station. From the visitor center, the road heads 12 miles south to Grand View Point. About halfway to the point, a paved spur leads northwest 5 miles to Upheaval Dome. A number of overlooks and trails line each road.

Bring water – Island in the Sky lacks any water sources. And if one of those spectacular thunderstorms heads your way, get in your car or seek shelter immediately.

## DRIVING TOURS

Two main roads cross the mesa top at Island in the Sky, forming a Y. The visitor center and entrance station sit atop the northeast (right) arm of the Y, Grand View Point is at the foot of the Y, and Upheaval Dome caps the northwest (left) arm.

One primary 4WD route, the White Rim Rd (p198), loops around the district about 1000ft below the mesa top.

**GRAND VIEW POINT SCENIC DRIVE**
Route: Visitor center to Grand View Point
Distance: 12 miles
Speed Limit: 25–45mph

Start at the visitor center. About a half mile south, pull off to the left at the **Shafer Canyon Overlook**, where you can peer down a thousand feet. Below is Shafer Trail Rd, the steep access route to the 4WD White Rim Rd.

A quarter mile ahead you'll cross **The Neck** (slow down for great views), where the ridge narrows to 40ft across – eventually this strip will erode away, further isolating the mesa. The road levels out as it crosses **Grays Pasture**, where you might spot a bighorn sheep (if you do, take notes on its size and horns and tell a ranger; the NPS is tracking bighorn numbers as part of a habitat recovery project).

Just past Grays Pasture, take the left turn for **Mesa Arch** (p196). This easy hike is worth every step – especially at sunrise when the arch's underside glows a fiery red. The road to **Upheaval Dome** (p195) bears right here.

A mile past the arch, pull off on the right to take in Candlestick Tower's sheer sandstone walls. Visible to the southwest is The Maze and its many fins and canyons, all capped with white and orange horizontal lines.

Continue 1.5 miles to a turnout for the **Murphy Point Trail** (an easy, two-hour, 3-mile round-trip hike). From the stunning overlook you'll see more of The Maze and snaking Green River. The **Murphy Hogback Trail** (p198) forks left just before the overlook.

Back on the road, half a mile farther on the left, take the paved walkway to the **Buck Canyon Overlook** for spectacular views of the La Sal Mountains. Another

1.8 miles south is the **White Rim Overlook**, a good picnic spot and starting point for the **White Rim Overlook Trail**, an easy, 1.2-mile round-trip hike.

Three-quarters of a mile down the road, just before Grand View Point, the **Orange Cliffs Overlook** offers views west to the Henry Mountains, the last-charted mountain range in the Lower 48. The Orange Cliffs lie southwest, beyond The Maze. Come at sunset when the canyons glow orange in the waning light.

Five hundred feet ahead, the drive ends at **Grand View Point**, where one of the Southwest's most sweeping views unfurls at your feet, rivaled only by the Grand Canyon and nearby **Dead Horse Point** (p206). In the foreground to the southeast, **Monument Basin** contains spires similar to those you'll see in The Needles; to see that district's spires, look south. To spot The Maze, follow the Green River from the northwest to its Confluence with the Colorado. West of the Confluence, **The Doll House** formations mark the edge of The Maze and the head of **Cataract Canyon**, one of North America's most intense stretches of white water.

Stand beside interpretive panel at the overlook and look down at the rock – the south-facing gashes you see occurred when lightning struck a man here in 2003 (he lived). Off to your right is the **Grand View Point Trail** (p197).

## Grand View Point & Upheaval Dome Scenic Drives

Horsethief Point

Taylor Canyon

Island in the Sky Visitor Center
**START - GRAND VIEW POINT**

**Canyonlands National Park**

Shafer Canyon Overlook

Upheaval Dome

Whale Rock Viewpoint

The Neck — White Rim Rd

Dead Horse Point State Park

**FINISH - UPHEAVAL DOME**

Aztec Butte

Grays Pasture

Mesa Arch

Willow Flat

**START - UPHEAVAL DOME**

Green River Overlook

Candlestick Tower Overlook

Buck Canyon Overlook

Holeman Spring Canyon Overlook

0    3    6 km
0    4 miles

Murphy Point

Orange Cliffs Overlook

White Rim Overlook

Monument Basin

Grand View Point Overlook

**FINISH - GRAND VIEW POINT**

Colorado River

Green River

---

### UPHEAVAL DOME SCENIC DRIVE
**Route: Grand View Point Scenic Drive to Upheaval Dome**
**Distance: 5 miles**
**Speed Limit: 35mph**

At the spur junction 6 miles south of the visitor center, turn northwest. A quarter mile from the junction, turn left and drive to the **Green River Overlook** and Willow Flat Campground. Walk to the overlook for views of the silty Green River, the Orange Cliffs and the Henry Mountains. Notice the benches (small mesas) in the foreground, which bear the marks of flash-flood erosion.

Large piñon trees around the parking area are 300 to 400 years old, while most of the blackbrush is more than 100 years old. The hardest thing for such desert plants is simply taking root. Nothing is growing on the parking lot island, nor is anything likely to for another 50 years. Water and cryptobiotic crust (see p275) make all the difference by providing nitrogen and a foothold for plants.

Back on the main road, a half mile farther on the right, pull over at the **Aztec Butte Viewpoint and Trail** (p196). Above the parking area is an ancient granary constructed by ancestral Puebloans.

About 2 miles ahead on the left (past a twisty section of road), you'll reach **Holeman Spring Canyon Overlook,** the only point along this drive that offers long views west across the Green River.

A mile farther, stop at the **Whale Rock Viewpoint and Trail**. Named for its smooth slickrock hump, Whale Rock lies at the end of an easy, mile-long round-trip hike that gains only 100ft. The path is exposed, so use the handrails. Kids love this short scramble.

Three-quarters of a mile ahead, the road ends at the **Upheaval Dome** parking lot and picnic area. To see the dome, stroll the short trail from the parking area.

## HIKING

With the exception of trails that descend to the White Rim, hikes at Island in the Sky are short and moderately easy. For a hike along the mesa top, spend a half day on the **Neck Spring Loop**, near the visitor center, or walk the first mile of the west-trending **Wilhite Trail**, off the road to Upheaval Dome. For a longer trail with views east of the Colorado River and La Sal Mountains, consider a portion of the **Lathrop Trail**, which covers a mile on the mesa before descending to the river.

If you want a longer hike, descend 1000ft to the **White Rim**. The easiest route is the **Murphy Loop**, but it's still a 10-mile, five-hour round-trip. The fastest and most strenuous route, the **Gooseberry Trail** (5.4 miles, four to six hours), is for fit hikers only. Check conditions with rangers before long hikes. Where trails are indistinct, walk on rock or in sandy washes to avoid damaging fragile cryptobiotic crusts.

Dehydration is common and poses a serious risk. Carry and drink *at least* one gallon of water a day. If you're allergic to bug bites, wear long sleeves and pants and/or apply insect repellant in spring and early summer.

**AZTEC BUTTE TRAIL**
Distance: 2 miles round-trip
Duration: 1–1½ hours
Challenge: Moderate
Elevation Change: 225ft

This short hike to the top of a Navajo sandstone dome yields stellar views. Be sure to wear rubber-soled shoes or hiking boots for traction. The first half mile cuts across grassland to the base of the dome. Cairns mark the ascent.

The second half mile is moderately strenuous. The butte levels off at the top, revealing panoramic views and endless sky. Look for the small, ancient **granary**, evidence of an ancestral Puebloan culture, a likely precursor to modern-day Hopis and Zunis. A small spur trail leads to more ruins. This is the only archaeological site at Island in the Sky.

Stay on the trails, as fragile cryptobiotic crust is widespread atop the dome. In summer bring plenty of water and wear a wide-brimmed hat, as the exposed butte offers no shade. In winter the trail may be icy and impassible.

**MESA ARCH TRAIL**
Distance: 0.5 mile round-trip
Duration: 30 minutes
Challenge: Easy
Elevation Change: 100ft

This trail leads to Canyonlands' most photographed arch, one of the best places to watch the sunrise – though don't expect to be alone. As you ascend, notice the trailside cryptobiotic soil, riddled with bubbly minicanyon systems (often likened to browned hamburger meat). This is among the healthiest soil of its kind in the park.

A moderately easy walk up a gentle rise brings you to the arch, an elegant sweep of Navajo sandstone that dramatically frames the **La Sal Mountains**. A thousand feet below, the basin extends in layers of red, brown, green and tan. Look carefully in the near distance to spot a narrow green strip of the **Colorado River**. To your left, through the arch, search atop the red spires for **Washer Woman Arch** (so named for its resemblance to the backside of a crouching laundress).

Resist the temptation to climb on the arch. Climbing is prohibited on most features named on USGS maps. Anyway, one glance over the edge to the sheer drop below and you'll surely get a case of the butterflies. Scamper up the rocks for a look down on the arch.

## GRAND VIEW POINT TRAIL
**Distance: 2 miles round-trip**
**Duration: 1–1½ hours**
**Challenge: Easy**
**Elevation Change: 50ft**

After marveling at hundred-mile views from the roadside observation area, take this easy stroll to the point itself for a better perspective of the massive mesa underfoot. Review the interpretive panels for interesting background. To the right of the panels, the trail descends stone steps to a fairly level, easy walk along the exposed rim – watch the little ones!

You can wander anywhere you want on the rocky promontory, but avoid stepping on cryptobiotic soil; when in doubt, stick to the rocks. To the south, scan the skies over Junction Butte for the peregrine falcons that nest atop it. The trail narrows in places as it passes over slickrock. Follow the cairns.

Scramble atop the rocks at trail's end for spectacular views. The Needles' namesake spires rise to the south, while off to the west

**Grand View Point Trail**

0    250    500 m
0    250    500 yds
1:24,000
Contour Interval 400 feet

Grand View Point Trail

START/FINISH

Grand View Point

White Rim

lie the **Henry Mountains** (on Capitol Reef's eastern flank) and distant **Boulder Mountain** (eastern terminus of the Aquarius Plateau and top step of the Grand Staircase). Glance below to spot the chalky sandstone of White Rim and the placid Green River. If storm clouds start to roll in, particularly from the west, quickly return to your car.

## UPHEAVAL DOME TRAIL
**Distance: 0.4 mile one way to first overlook,**
**0.9 mile one way to second overlook**
**Duration: 1–1½ hours**
**Challenge: Easy–Moderate**
**Elevation Change: 50-200ft**

Another short walk, this trail leads to overlooks of **Upheaval Dome**, one of the park's great geologic mysteries. Scientists disagree over how the feature formed – some suggest it's a collapsed salt dome, while others posit it's the site of a meteorite strike some 60 million years ago. Looking more like

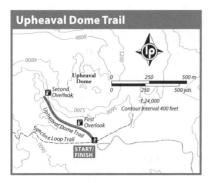

**Upheaval Dome Trail**

a mound of gray sand, the dome rests in a depression – one doesn't look up to it, but down on it, like a bellybutton.

It's an easy stroll to the first overlook. From the parking area, climb to the fork in the trail, bear right and ascend the slickrock to the viewpoint. If your kids yawn every time you start talking geology, wonder aloud whether a UFO might have taken off or landed here. By the look of the place, it's not entirely inconceivable.

To reach the second overlook, return to the fork in the trail and bear left, clambering over slickrock to a final steep descent. The view is similar, but you'll have a broader panorama of the surrounding landscape. If you're pressed for time, skip the second vantage point. Otherwise, the afternoon light here is magnificent.

## BACKCOUNTRY HIKES

After seeing the rugged landscape that surrounds Island in the Sky, you may be champing at the bit to hit the backcountry. Keep in mind, though, that this is unforgiving wilderness – any hike requires proper advance planning.

Aside from White Rim Rd (see Four-Wheel Driving & Mountain Biking, below), there's just one major backpacking route in the district: the **Syncline Loop** (8.3 miles, five to seven hours). If you're fascinated by Upheaval Dome or would like a closer look at the Green River, this is a perfect route with lots of places to camp. However, in summer this largely exposed trail can get blazingly hot. In fact, most park rescues occur along this stretch, primarily because day hikers underestimate the trail, get turned around and/or run out of water. Seek a ranger's advice before attempting this route. You'll need a permit to stay overnight (see Permits, p193).

If you love hiking the mesa top but don't want to stay at Willow Flat Campground, the park issues one permit a day for the **Murphy Hogback** campsite. An easy flat hike across grasslands, through juniper stands and over rocks takes you to this solo site with stunning views. Ask a ranger for details.

## OTHER ACTIVITIES

For details about **river-rafting**, **kayaking** and **canoeing** the Green and Colorado Rivers, see River Running (p228) in the Moab chapter.

### Four-Wheel Driving & Mountain Biking

Blazed by uranium prospectors in the early 1950s, primitive **White Rim Rd** circles Island in the Sky. Accessible from the visitor center via steep Shafer Trail Rd, this 70-mile route is the top choice for 4WD and mountain biking trips. It generally takes two to three days to travel the loop in a 4WD vehicle, or three to four days by bike. As the route lacks any water sources, bicyclists should team up with a 4WD support vehicle or travel with an outfitter (see Mountain Biking in Moab, p225).

The park service limits the number of vehicles. If you arrive without an overnight permit, call the visitor center about possible cancellations or no-shows. Rangers regularly patrol the route to assist motorists whose vehicles break down or who have other problems. They also check permits. Always stay on trails. No ATVs are allowed.

To learn more about the White Rim, pick up *A Naturalist's Guide to the White Rim Trail*, by David Williams and Damian Fagon.

## Kids' Activities

When you arrive at the park, stop by the visitor center to pick up a **Junior Ranger Activity Guide**. Once kids complete certain activities, they can return to the visitor center to receive a special certificate and badge from a ranger.

Kids particularly like the Whale Rock and Mesa Arch Trails, both easy walks with big payoffs. Keep an eye your little ones, especially near overlooks, which are often unfenced.

## Ranger Programs

For information about park attractions and insight on its human and geologic history, attend a ranger-led program. April through October, rangers lead campfire talks and nature walks and speak at key overlooks, notably Grand View Point and Upheaval Dome. Check schedules at the visitor center.

## SLEEPING

You won't find any rooms or restaurants in the park. For a hot meal and a warm bed, drive to Moab. There is one developed campground at Island in the Sky. If it's full, check the campground at Dead Horse Point State Park (p206).

**Willow Flat Campground** ( ☎ 435-719-2313, 435-259-4712; www.nps.gov/cany; 7 miles south of visitor center; 12 sites for tents or RVs under 28ft; $5; ☯ year-round) A quarter mile from the Green River Overlook, down a mile-long dirt spur from the road to Upheaval Dome, this small, first-come, first-served campground provides limited amenities, including vault toilets, picnic tables and fire grates, but no water. Bring your own firewood. Don't expect shade, as most of the vegetation is low and scrubby. Each site accommodates up to 10 people and two vehicles. The campground fills up nearly every night in spring and fall, so arrive early.

# THE NEEDLES

Named for giant spires of orange-and-white sandstone that jut skyward from the desert floor, The Needles offers otherworldly terrain so wholly different from Island in the Sky, it's hard to believe they're part of the same park. Despite paved access roads, however, half as many people visit this district. Why? Perhaps because it's a 90-minute drive from Moab, and once you finally arrive, you have to work harder to appreciate its wonders – in short, you have to get out of the car and walk. But if you expend a little energy, payoffs include peaceful solitude and an opportunity to experience, not just observe, the vast beauty of canyon country.

**The Needles Visitor Center** (p192) lies 2.5 miles inside the park boundary and does provide drinking water. (If you've already visited Island in the Sky, be sure to bring your entrance receipt to avoid having to pay again.) From the visitor center, the paved road continues almost 7 miles to the **Big Spring Canyon Overlook**. Parking areas along the way access several sights, including arches, ancestral Puebloan ruins and petroglyphs. About 3 miles past the visitor center, a side road leads to **Squaw Flat Campground** (p204) and a pump house with year-round water.

Several 4WD and mountain biking trails – formerly uranium mining roads – lead into the backcountry. **Elephant Hill** is the most technically challenging route in the district, with steep grades and tight turns. The route to the **Colorado River Overlook** is easy in a vehicle and moderately easy on a mountain bike; park and walk the final, steep 1.5-mile descent to the overlook. Following the district's main drainage, the **Salt Creek Trail** is moderately easy for vehicles, moderate for bikes.

## DRIVING TOUR

To see the rock spires in the best light, visit in the morning – in the afternoon, the sun drops behind them.

### BIG SPRING CANYON OVERLOOK DRIVE
Route: Visitor center to Big Spring Canyon Overlook
Distance: 6.4 miles
Speed Limit: 35mph

Stop first at the **Roadside Ruin** (a short walk from the visitor center) and stroll the easy 0.3-mile loop trail around this ancient Anasazi granary.

Unless you're bound for the 0.6-mile Cave Spring Trail, bear right at the fork in the road and pull over at the **Wooden Shoe Overlook**, on your left. Scan the cliffs overhead for the namesake rock formation with a tiny arch at its base.

Bypass the turnoff for the campground and continue across the wide, even terrain of **Squaw Flat**. Two miles ahead on the left is a picnic area with shaded tables. The 0.6-mile **Pothole Point Loop** starts from the small parking lot just west of the picnic area. From here the road curls around the point to the moderately easy 2.4-mile **Slickrock Trail**.

Just past this trailhead, the road dead-ends at the **Big Spring Canyon Overlook**. Park along the road and walk out on the rocks for a peek into the shallow canyons. Above the rocks rise hundred-foot formations that look as though they're made of yellowish modeling clay.

## DAY HIKES

The following four trails total 4 miles and are easily doable in a single day. Taken collectively, they offer an overview of the region's human and geologic history. Unfortunately, none of the trails is wheelchair accessible. Cairns often mark sections across slickrock.

If you like long day hikes, The Needles also includes easily accessible backcountry treks you can do in a day (see Backcountry Hikes, p202).

### ROADSIDE RUIN TRAIL
Distance: 0.3-mile loop
Duration: 15–30 minutes
Challenge: Easy
Elevation Change: 20ft

This heavily trodden, well-maintained trail starts out across uneven gravel and finishes over slickrock. The trail's main attraction is a remarkably well-preserved **Anasazi granary** tucked into a gap in the slickrock. If you're here in late spring, keep an eye out for blooming yucca.

At the trailhead, pick up the 50¢ trail brochure – numbers in the pamphlet correspond to numbered trailside posts. You'll learn about the resident plants that manage to survive this harsh climate and how Native Americans used them nearly a thousand years ago in dyes, medicine and meals, among other applications.

## CAVE SPRING TRAIL

**Distance: 0.6-mile loop**
**Duration: 30–45 minutes**
**Challenge: Easy–Moderate**
**Elevation Change: 50ft**

Pungent sagebrush marks this trailhead at the end of a well-maintained mile-long dirt road. Hikers will first reach an abandoned **cowboy camp** whose bunkhouse displays miscellaneous remnants lefts by cowboys in the 19th and 20th centuries. The trail continues beneath a protruding rock lip, then through 6ft sagebrush to **Cave Spring**, one of few perennial water sources in The Needles. Look for the rust-colored pictographs painted on these walls more than a thousand years ago.

From Cave Spring you'll climb two ladders up the slickrock for wraparound views of rock formations, steppes and mesas. Detour from the trail to climb atop the red rock (above the white rock) for awesome views of rock spires and the **La Sal Mountains**.

After crossing the undulating sandstone, the trail drops into a wash and returns to the trailhead. Kids love this hike for the cowboy artifacts, ladders and slickrock scampers.

## POTHOLE POINT TRAIL

**Distance: 0.6-mile loop**
**Duration: 45 minutes**
**Challenge: Easy**
**Elevation Change: 20ft**

This short loop across slickrock features gorgeous views of distant cliffs, mountains and rock formations similar to those along the Slickrock Trail. Acrophobes, take heart: You won't have to stroll beside or peer over any cliffs.

The slickrock itself features naturally occurring dimples that collect water during rainstorms. To the naked eye, these **potholes** appear to be nothing more than mud puddles, but closer inspection reveals tiny organisms that must complete their life cycles before the water evaporates. (For more on potholes, see p263.)

Though this is an excellent walk for contemplative souls and the scientifically inclined, it does lack drama, unless the potholes are teeming with life (which isn't always the case, at least visibly).

## SLICKROCK TRAIL

**Distance: 2.4 miles round-trip**
**Duration: 1½–2 hours**
**Challenge: Easy–Moderate**
**Elevation Change: 70ft**

After ascending a few gentle switchbacks to slickrock, you'll follow cairns along this semiloop trail, which can be tricky to follow in places. Pick up a brochure at the trailhead; it describes four main viewpoints, each marked by a numbered signpost.

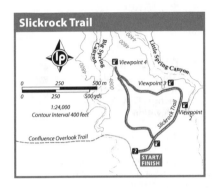

**Slickrock Trail**

0 — 250 — 500m
0 — 250 — 500yds
1:24,000
Contour Interval 400 feet

Big Spring Canyon
Little Spring Canyon
Viewpoint 4
Viewpoint 3
Viewpoint 2
Slickrock Trail
Confluence Overlook Trail
START/FINISH

If you're short on time, at least visit Viewpoint 1 for a panorama you simply can't get from the road. Giant red cliffs hang like curtains below high buttes and mesas, the district's namesake needles touch the sky, and the **La Sal** and **Abajo Mountains** lord over the whole scene.

Bear right at the 'Begin Loop' signpost to reach Viewpoint 2, where hearty vegetation clings to the desert crust and lines the watercourses. Scamper up the rocks for a primo view. At Viewpoint 3 stand atop the giant boulders that ring **Lower Little Spring Canyon**, where purple and gray rock layers offer telltale evidence of an ancient shallow sea.

Viewpoint 4 isn't marked, but you'll know you've arrived at **Big Spring Canyon** once you spot the high promontory that juts over the vast rugged gorge. Watch overhead for birds soaring on thermals. To the north you'll spot **Grand View Point** at Island in the Sky, perched high atop the red Wingate sandstone cliffs.

On the return path you'll face the needles and spires to the south that define this district. The Abajo Mountains lie beyond.

## BACKCOUNTRY HIKES

The Needles is Canyonlands' premier backpacking district, making it hard to get the backcountry permit necessary for an overnight hike. Nothing quite compares to sleeping far from the roar of internal-combustion engines, but if you can't secure a permit, fret not: If you're a strong hiker, many of the best trails are doable in a day.

If you venture off-trail, stay in washes or on slickrock to avoid trampling the fragile cryptobiotic crust.

### Permit Information

Day hikers do not need a permit. For details on overnight permits see Backcountry Permits (p193).

### Backcountry Safety

If you're inadvertently separated from your group, stay put. Wandering expends energy and may make it difficult for rangers to locate you. Carry and drink *at least* one gallon of water per person per day – more if you're backpacking – and balance the increased fluid intake with extra electrolytes (potassium and sodium). Don't take salt tablets unless advised by a physician. Leave your itinerary with someone, especially if you're headed out alone. Cell phones don't always work; to locate a signal, head to the highest peak in safe reach.

### Backcountry Camping

Designated campsites abut most trails; you can request a specific site when applying for your permit. At-large camping is permitted in side canyons that lack designated sites.

Water is scarce in the backcountry. Ask rangers about potential sources and current availability, but plan to pack in all you'll need.

Human waste must be carried out or buried in a 6- to 8in hole at least 300ft from any water sources; consider using human waste containment bags. Carry out used toilet paper.

## Backcountry Trails

In addition to the hike described below, consider the **Confluence Overlook Trail**, a moderate four- to six-hour round-trip hike from the Big Spring Canyon trailhead to watch the silty Green River flow into the muddy red Colorado. Many other hikes connect in a series of loops, some requiring route-finding skills. Among the best are the **Big Spring Canyon** and **Lost Canyon Trails**. For gorgeous scenery, the **Elephant Canyon Trail** to Druid Arch is hard to beat. Archaeology junkies love the rock art along the **Salt Creek Canyon Trail**. Ask rangers for further options and advice.

## CHESLER PARK LOOP & JOINT TRAIL

**Distance: 11-mile loop**
**Duration: 1–2+ Days**
**Challenge: Moderate overnight hike; Moderate–Difficult day hike**
**Elevation Change: 520ft**

Among Canyonlands' most popular backcountry treks, these combined routes cross desert grasslands, pass red-and-white-striped pinnacles and thread between deep, narrow fractures. Though the trails aren't flat, elevation changes are mild and infrequent. You won't find any water.

Park at the Elephant Hill trailhead, 3 miles from Squaw Flat Campground via a gravel 2WD road. From the parking area, the trail climbs to a bench, then undulates over slickrock toward rock spires. At the T-junction, follow signs

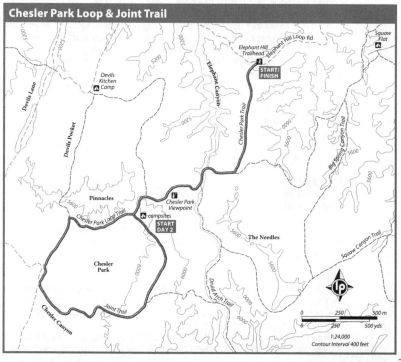

Chesler Park Loop & Joint Trail

to Chesler Park (*not* Druid Arch) and descend 300ft along switchbacks into **Elephant Canyon**. Continue to follow signs along the canyon floor.

The final 0.2 mile to the **Chesler Park Viewpoint** climbs 100 vertical feet, topping out on the rocky pass amid spires 2.9 miles from the trailhead. This marks the beginning of the 5-mile **Chesler Park Loop**. Five campsites lie southeast (left) of the junction.

The next morning, leave your backpack at your campsite and explore the claustrophobia-inducing **Joint Trail**, where the fractured rock narrows to 2ft across in places; the trail junction lies to the south, about midway around the Chesler Park Loop. Pause just east of the Joint Trail for stellar views of the towering **pinnacles** that ring Chesler Park. On the southwest section of the loop, you'll follow a half-mile stretch of a Jeep road. If you stay more than one night, take the side trip to **Druid Arch**.

For most hikers, the *Trails Illustrated* map ($3) should suffice, but if you're inclined to wander, carry a 7.5-minute USGS map.

## OTHER ACTIVITIES

For details about **river-rafting**, **kayaking** and **canoeing** the Green and Colorado Rivers, see River Running (p228) in the Moab chapter.

### Four-Wheel Driving & Mountain Biking

Fifty miles of 4WD and mountain biking roads crisscross The Needles. Stay on designated routes. Motorists and bicyclists must obtain a permit for overnight trips (see Backcountry Permits, p193), but not for day use, with the exception of Lavender and Horse Canyons, which require a $5 day-use permit fee; book in advance or check at the visitor center for cancellations, no-shows or leftovers.

All 4WD roads in The Needles require high-clearance vehicles (many off-the-lot SUVs do *not* have high clearance). Know what you're doing before you set out, or risk damaging your vehicle and/or endangering yourself. Towing fees can run about $1000. If you're renting a 4WD vehicle, check the insurance policy; you might not be covered here. For more information, including 4WD routes and road conditions, check with a ranger when you book your permit. No ATVs are allowed.

### Ranger Programs

From March through October, rangers lead interpretive talks and evening campfire discussions. Check schedules at the visitor center when you arrive in the park.

### Kids' Activities

When you arrive at the park, stop by The Needles Visitor Center to pick up a **Junior Ranger Activity Guide**. Once kids complete certain activities, they can return to the visitor center to receive a special certificate and badge from a ranger. Ask at the visitor center about renting a **Discovery Pack**, which contains binoculars, a magnifying lens and nature guide. Kids especially like the Cave Spring Trail (p201).

## SLEEPING

You won't find any rooms in the park. There is one developed campground in The Needles, and just outside the district is the private Needles Outpost campground, which sells limited supplies. Drive to Moab for lodgings and all other services.

**Squaw Flat Campground** ( ☎ 435-719-2313, 435-259-4711; www.nps.gov/cany; 3 miles west of visitor center; 26 sites for tents or RVs up to 28ft; $10; ☉ year-round) This first-come, first-served campground fills up nearly every day, especially in spring and fall. Unlike the campground at Island in the Sky, this one provides flush toilets and cold running water. Each site includes a picnic table and fire grate, and many lie in the shade of mature juniper trees. If the campground is full, ask at the visitor center about sites on BLM lands, or stay in Moab. Three group sites can be reserved in advance; call the NPS Reservations Office (p193).

**Needles Outpost** ( ☎ 435-979-4007; www.canyonlandsneedlesoutpost.com; Hwy 211; 20 sites; $15; ☾ closed Dec-Mar) If Squaw Flat is full, this privately held campground is an excellent alternative. Campsites sit amid mature juniper trees beside west-facing rock walls that provide morning shade. Hot showers cost $3 for campers, or $5 for the public. Other amenities include flush toilets, fire rings and an RV dump station. The Outpost also accepts reservations. An on-site store sells limited camping supplies, firewood, groceries, beer, ice, gasoline and propane. The **lunch counter and grill** ( ☾ 9am-5pm) serves sandwiches and burgers.

# THE MAZE

A 30-sq-mile jumble of high-walled canyons, The Maze is a rare preserve of true wilderness for hardy backcountry veterans. The colorful canyons are rugged, deep and sometimes inaccessible. Many of them look alike, and it's easy to get turned around – hence the district's name. If you're going to visit The Maze, plan on spending at least three days, though a week may be ideal.

As the district lies west of the Confluence, the only way to reach it from Moab is to drive a 133-mile crescent-shaped route to the **Hans Flat Ranger Station** ( ☎ 435-259-2652; www.nps.gov/cany/maze; ☾ 8am-4:30pm). Take Hwy 191 north from Moab, to I-70 west, to Hwy 24 south. About 25 miles south of I-70, just past the paved turnoff for Goblin Valley State Park (p190), head southeast on the gravel road for 46 miles to Hans Flat. On the way, you'll cross the Glen Canyon National Recreation Area and Orange Cliffs Special Management Unit; if you plan to stop at either one, pick up a permit at Hans Flat.

There is no entrance fee or visitor center, but the ranger station sells books and maps (no food or water). The few roads into the district are very poor and can be closed by rain or snow; bring tire chains if visiting between October and April. You'll need a 4WD vehicle with a short wheelbase and high clearance. If you're inexperienced at four-wheel driving, stay away. You must also be prepared to repair your vehicle and, at times, the road. For more advice and a full list of necessities, contact the ranger station in advance of your trip.

The **Maze Overlook Trail** requires that hikers carry at least a 25ft length of rope to raise and lower packs. Camping is at-large, and you'll find several reliable water sources (ask a ranger for locations). You can drive a 2WD vehicle to the North Point Rd junction, 2.5 miles south of Hans Flat, then hike 15 miles to the Maze Overlook.

# HORSESHOE CANYON

A separate unit of Canyonlands, west of the northern reaches of Island in the Sky, Horseshoe Canyon shelters millennia-old Native American rock art. The centerpiece is the **Great Gallery**, which consists of superb Barrier Canyon–style pictographs that date to between 2000 BC and AD 500. The heroic, life-size figures are magnificent. Artifacts recovered in this district date back as far as 9000 BC.

Damaging the rock art is a criminal offense. Don't touch or disturb it in any way. Even the oils from your skin can harm the paintings.

The Great Gallery lies at the end of a 6.5-mile round-trip trail that descends 750ft from the main dirt road. Budget for six hours. Rangers lead hikes here on Saturdays and Sundays from April through October; to arrange a group walk, contact the **Hans Flat Ranger Station** ( ☎ 435-259-2652; www.nps.gov/cany/horseshoe; ⊙ 8am-4:30pm).

You can camp on BLM land at the trailhead, though it's not a campground per se, but a parking lot. There is a single vault toilet, but no water or services. If you don't like primitive camping, make this a long day trip from Moab, two hours away. Take Hwy 191 north from Moab, to I-70 west, to Hwy 24 south. About 25 miles south of I-70, just past the turnoff for Goblin Valley State Park (p190), turn east (left) and follow the graded gravel road 30 miles to the Horseshoe Canyon Unit.

# AROUND CANYONLANDS

## DEAD HORSE POINT STATE PARK

The views at Dead Horse Point pack a wallop, extending 2000ft below to the serpentine Colorado River, 12,700ft up to the La Sal Mountains and 100 miles across Canyonlands' stair-step landscape. If you thrive on epic landscapes, you won't regret a side trip here.

The turnoff to Dead Horse is on Hwy 313, just 4 miles north of Island in the Sky (Moab is 30 miles away). Toward the end of the drive, the road traverses a narrow ridge just 30yds across. (Ranchers once herded horses across these narrows – some were forgotten and left to die, hence the park name.) A rough footpath skirts the point for views in all directions. To escape the small (but sometimes chatty) crowds, take one of the short hikes that rim the mesa. Visit at dawn or sunset for the best lighting.

The **visitor center** ( ☎ 435-259-2614; www.stateparks.utah.gov; $7 day-use fee; ⊙ 8am-5pm winter, till 6pm summer) features exceptionally good exhibits, shows on-demand videos and sells books and maps. Rangers lead walks and talks in summer.

The 21-site **Kayenta Campground** ( ☎ 801-538-7220, 800-322-3770; www.stateparks. utah.gov; tent/RV hookup $14; ⊙ year-round) provides limited water, 20-amp RV hookups and a dump station, but not showers. Reservations are accepted between March and October, though you can often find a site if you show up early, even in summer. RV drivers should fill up with gas and water before arriving.

## NEWSPAPER ROCK RECREATION AREA

If you're fascinated by petroglyphs, Newspaper Rock features a single large sandstone face covered with images chipped out by various Indian groups and pioneers over a 3000-year stretch. It's beside Indian Creek on Hwy 211, about 12 miles west of Hwy 191. Make a quick stop here on the way to The Needles or stay at the small creekside campground beneath stands of mature cottonwoods. For more details contact the **BLM Monticello Field Office** ( ☎ 435-587-1500; www.blm.gov/utah/monticello).

### GROCERIES & SUPPLIES

Moab  is your best bet. If you're camping in The Needles, visit **Needles Outpost** ( ☎ 435-979-4007; ⊙ 9am-5pm Apr-Oct).

### LOST & FOUND

Contact park headquarters or a visitor center (see Information, p192).

### MEDICAL SERVICES & EMERGENCIES

In an emergency, dial ☎ 911 or contact a park ranger at the nearest visitor center. If you're unable to reach a ranger, contact the **Grand County Emergency Coordinator** ( ☎ 435-259-8115), the agency in charge of dispatching emergency personnel. The nearest hospital is in Moab.

### TELEPHONES

While cell phones work in many spots atop Island in the Sky, they do *not* work in much of The Needles. Pay phones are available at both visitor centers.

NATIONAL PARK SERVICE HISTORIC PHOTOGRAPH COLLECTION

*Giant windows and sweeping sandstone arcs frame snowy peaks and desert landscapes at Arches National Park.*

# EXPERIENCING
# ARCHES

The park boasts the highest density of rock arches anywhere on Earth – more than 2500 in a 116-sq-mile area – and more wait to be discovered. An easy drive (some say *too* easy) makes the most spectacular arches accessible to all.

But there's nothing like seeing them up close. You'll lose perspective on size, especially at the thin and graceful Landscape Arch, which stretches more than 300ft across, making it one of the largest in the world. Other arches are tiny – the smallest are only 3ft across – but once you train your eye, you'll spot them everywhere, like in a game of 'Where's Waldo?' Arches are constantly in a state of flux, and eventually all of them break and disappear. Remember, the same forces of erosion that create them also cause their ultimate demise.

As you stroll beneath these monuments to nature's power, listen carefully, especially in winter, and you may hear spontaneous popping noises in distant rocks – the sound of arches forming. (If ever you hear popping noises *overhead*, run like the dickens!)

## WHEN YOU ARRIVE

Arches is open year-round. The entrance station lies off Hwy 191, 5 miles north of Moab. Admission, good for seven days, is $10 per car or $5 per person arriving by motorcycle, bicycle or on foot. A Local Passport, good for admission to Arches and Canyonlands for a one-year period, costs $25.

## ORIENTATION & INFORMATION

The park includes 22 miles of paved roads, and most sights lie on or alongside the pavement (see Driving Tours). Crowds are often unavoidable, and parking areas overflow at peak times (weekends, spring through fall). Every year the park takes new measures to handle the problem. The NPS may eventually institute a shuttle system if visitation increases. For now, to keep drivers from parking in dangerous or sensitive areas, rangers have stepped up ticketing for illegally parked cars.

The best strategy is to arrive at the park by 9am, when crowds are sparse and the temperatures not so bad; or visit in the evening after 7pm. If you can't find a designated parking spot at one place, continue to the next. Also, drive carefully; accidents occur when drivers focus on the scenery, not the road – an easy trap to fall into at Arches.

Currently the only way to see Arches is by bicycle or private vehicle, on foot or through an organized tour; for information, see the Moab chapter.

There are no places in the park to buy prepared food, groceries or supplies. For all services, drive to Moab.

In 2004 the NPS began construction of a new **visitor center** ( ☎ 435-719-2299; www.nps.gov/arch; ☽ 8am-4:30pm, longer hours spring-fall), slated for completion in 2005. If you arrive after hours, stop at the parking lot and read the informational panels.

For books and maps by mail or online, contact the **Canyonlands Natural History Association** ( ☎ 259-6003, 800-840-8978; www.cnha.org; 3031 S Hwy 191, Moab, UT 84532); the CNHA also staffs the **Moab Information Center** (p219).

Cell phones do work in the park; to find a signal, ascend the nearest hill. In an emergency, dial ☎ 911 or contact a park ranger. If you're unable to reach a ranger, contact the **Grand County Emergency Coordinator** ( ☎ 435-259-8115), the agency in charge of dispatching emergency personnel.

See the Arches map (Map 8) on p152.

## POLICIES & REGULATIONS

Arches' hiking and backcountry use regulations include those listed for all the parks in the Activities chapter. If you need to board your pet, refer to the list of kennels in Canyonlands.

## SIGHTS

Arches' main sights lie along the park's scenic drive. Be sure to stop at the new **visitor center**. The Canyonlands Natural History Association sells maps and books here, and rangers are on hand to answer questions and help you plan your visit; be sure to ask about ranger-led activities. You can also pick up your reserved tickets for the **Fiery Furnace guided walk** (p212). Stock up on water while you're here; the next water source is 19 miles up the road, at Devils Garden.

## DRIVING TOURS

There is one main park road, with two short spurs that lead to more of the park's major sights. The most popular stops lie closest to the visitor center and park entrance. If you're tight on time, visit **The Windows Section**, off the first spur. The more time you have, the farther you can go.

The park also includes three unpaved roads. **Salt Valley Rd** is generally accessible to passenger cars (though not when wet). It leaves the main road a mile before Devils Garden and heads 9 miles west to the scenic **Klondike Bluffs**.

## HIGHLIGHTS

✔ Marveling at the precariously poised 3500-ton **Balanced Rock** (p213)

✔ Gazing down on the Colorado River from beneath the sweep of **North Window** (p213)

✔ Listening for echoes at **Double Arch** (p211)

✔ Climbing the slickrock slope to **Delicate Arch** (p214)

✔ Negotiating a maze of giant sandstone fins in the **Fiery Furnace** (p212)

✔ Spotting figures and faces in formations such as the **Three Gossips** (p210)

You'll get away from the densest crowds, but you won't be alone. A moderately difficult 3-mile round-trip hike leads to **Tower Arch**.

From Klondike Bluffs, an unnamed, 10-mile 4WD dirt road doubles back to the scenic drive at Balanced Rock. This is best done from north to south (the northbound route tackles a steep and sandy climb that may be impassable).

From Balanced Rock, **Willow Flats Rd** leads due west about 8 miles to Hwy 191. Formerly the main route into the park, it requires a high-clearance or 4WD vehicle. The road doesn't offer any important features, just distant views and solitude.

Check with rangers about road conditions.

## ARCHES SCENIC DRIVE
Route: Visitor center to Devils Garden
Distance: 43 miles round-trip, including spurs
Speed Limit: 25–45mph

Arches Scenic Drive

From the visitor center, the steep road ascends Navajo sandstone, once ancient sand dunes. Stop at the **Moab Fault Overlook**. Below, Hwy 191 parallels a fault line through the Moab Canyon. The rock on the opposite side of the highway stands 2600ft higher and is 180 million years older than the side on which you're standing. Interpretive panels explain the geology.

A mile ahead, stop at **Park Avenue**, where you can take the one-way, 1-mile downhill walk past a giant rock fin that calls to mind a row of New York City skyscrapers. While tiny scrub oaks to the right of the trailhead look young, they may be as much as 100 years old. The light here is best in the morning. If you've got antsy kids who want to hike, but you don't want to, this is your chance for 30 minutes of quiet time; pick them up 1.4 miles up the road, at the Courthouse Towers Viewpoint.

Half a mile past Park Avenue, stop at the **La Sal Mountains Viewpoint**. This laccolithic mountain range developed underground during volcanic activity, then rose to the surface, fully formed, some 24 million years ago. (The Henry Mountains, near Capitol Reef, formed the same way.) Atop the mesa in the distance you'll catch your first glimpse of arches.

As you drive down the road, it may look familiar. Many of the driving scenes in the film *Thelma & Louise* were shot in Arches (this stretch is where they locked the cop in the trunk, while the final scene was shot at nearby Dead Horse Point).

As you descend toward the **Courthouse Towers Viewpoint**, look left for the towers nicknamed the **Three Gossips**, which do indeed resemble three figures whispering to one another. From the viewpoint turnout, look up at the monoliths. These walls were likely once connected by arches that have since fallen away, particularly at **Sheep Rock**. Just ahead in **Courthouse Wash**, unlikely stands of bright-green cottonwood trees offer dramatic proof of how water can transform the parched desert into an oasis.

A mile and a half farther on the right, the undulating landscape at **Petrified Dunes** was once indeed a vast sweep of sand dunes. (Technically, the dunes aren't 'petrified,' as they contain no carbon, the determining element in petrification.) As you continue up the road, particularly in spring, notice the increased density of roadside vegetation. The extra bit of runoff from the pavement makes it possible for these plants to survive; a few feet away, they'd shrivel up.

After a 3-mile ascent, you'll arrive at the 3500-ton **Balanced Rock**, which teeters precariously atop a narrow stone pedestal. Pull over and take the 15-minute loop trail (p213), then turn right onto **Windows Rd**, a 5-mile round-trip spur. You'll find pit toilets beside the parking lot at road's end.

Take the easy, short walks to **North** and **South Windows** (p213) and to **Double Arch**. It's hard to grasp the immensity of these gigantic marvels until you're beside them. If you want a long view of the vast surrounding landscape but are short on time, head to North Window and stand right beneath it. Once you've picked your jaw up off the ground, return to your car and continue the drive.

Back on the main road, stop at **Panorama Point**. The 360-degree view includes an overlook of **Salt Valley**, a onetime salt dome that collapsed when water washed away the salt. Interpretive panels explain the geology.

Two and a half miles past The Windows spur, turn right on the signed spur to **Wolfe Ranch** and Delicate Arch. Pull into the first parking lot (which includes pit toilets) and take the short, easy walk to the primitive 1880s cabin, with its juniper-log walls and shale roof. **Salt Wash**, which is wet year-round, runs from the

## ARCHES AND BRIDGES

What's the difference between an arch and a bridge? All are formed by the erosion of sandstone. An arch forms when water freezes and expands in cracks, causing portions of the rock to break away. A bridge forms when a watercourse passes beneath it, eroding the sandstone from below. That said, rivers dry up or change course over time, and it's sometimes difficult to distinguish a bridge from an arch.

cabin to the Colorado. If you're lucky, you may spot a river otter. Cross the footbridge for a surprisingly close look at a small petroglyph panel, incised by Ute or Paiute Indians sometime after the year 1600 (look but don't touch, as oils from fingers deteriorate the rock). If you're up for a moderately strenuous hike, climb the trail to **Delicate Arch** (p214), the park's premier hike. Otherwise, continue driving to the **Delicate Arch Viewpoint**, a mile beyond the Wolfe Ranch turnout.

Two short trails lead to views of the arch, which has also been nicknamed the 'Schoolmarm's Breeches' and the 'Cowboy Chaps.' Follow the crowds to the right for an easy 50yd walk to the lower view, or bear left for a moderately strenuous half-mile hike and 200ft ascent to the better view.

Return to the main road, turn right and drive 3 miles to the **Salt Valley Overlook** for a perspective down to Wolfe Ranch and Salt Valley, then pull off again at the **Fiery Furnace**. A short walk between split-rail fences leads to the overlook, from which you can peer between the giant fins of Entrada sandstone – at sunset they resemble flames in a furnace. Despite appearances, this is the coolest area in the park in summer. Rangers lead daily guided hikes of this rocky maze, but you must purchase advance tickets at the visitor center. For more on the Fiery Furnace, see Hiking, below.

From here the main road skirts past the Fiery Furnace and the **Sand Dune Arch Trailhead** (p213) to road's end at the **Devils Garden Trailhead**. Refill your canteen and picnic before taking the moderately easy mile-long walk to **Landscape Arch** (p215), whose span is longer than a football field. Drive out the way you came, omitting the spur roads.

## HIKING

Arches is geared more to drivers than hikers. Most of the main sights lie within a mile or two of paved roads. There are a few exceptions, but you won't find an extensive system of trails as at other national parks. Still, you can enjoy several hikes that will take you away from the sound of traffic, at least for a few hours.

Backpacking isn't popular at Arches, but if you're bound and determined, you can do so with a backcountry permit, available in person from the visitor center. There are neither designated trails nor campsites. Due to the fragility of cryptobiotic soils (p275), the park discourages backcountry treks. The closest you'll come to an established backcountry route is the **Devils Garden Primitive Loop**.

If you're fit and would like to join a guided hike through the narrow sandstone labyrinth at the **Fiery Furnace**, you must buy tickets (in person only; adult/child $8/4) at the visitor center. You can reserve tickets up to seven days in advance for the two- to three-hour walks, offered twice daily (morning and afternoon) April through October. Hikes usually book up two days in advance.

If you're an accomplished hiker and want to explore the Fiery Furnace alone, you must still pay a fee, watch a video and discuss with rangers how to negotiate this confusing jumble of canyons before they'll grant you a permit.

**PARK AVENUE TRAIL**
**Distance:** 1 mile one way
**Duration:** 30–45 minutes
**Challenge:** Easy–Moderate
**Elevation Change:** 320ft

You'll walk between towering sandstone monoliths on Park Avenue, so named for the vertical walls' resemblance to the sheer faces of Manhattan skyscrapers. It's a straight shot to the end, all downhill from the trailhead; arrange for a shuttle to pick you up at the Courthouse Towers Viewpoint. You could hike up from the bottom, but the views are better on the descent.

From the trailhead, you'll descend to the Dewey Bridge rock layer, also called mudstone for obvious reasons. (A soft rock that erodes faster than layers above it, mudstone forms the pedestal at Balanced Rock.) In places, the primitive trail crosses uneven terrain; follow the cairns. As you near trail's end, glance ahead to spot the **Tower of Babel**, and left to spy on the **Three Gossips**. From the viewpoint, look for **Baby Arch**, which has just begun to form.

If you want to assess the trail before committing, walk to the second interpretive panel at the end of the paved path; from here, almost the entire route unfurls below. The light is best in the morning.

## BALANCED ROCK TRAIL
**Distance: 0.3-mile loop**
**Duration: 15–20 minutes**
**Challenge: Easy**
**Elevation Change: 20ft**

A 3577-ton boulder atop a spindly pedestal that appears to lean, Balanced Rock shoots from the earth like a fist. Its dimensions are deceiving – you'd never guess that the giant rock weighs as much as a naval destroyer. This short loop around the formation affords an intimate view of erosion at work. The pedestal is made of soft Dewey Bridge mudstone, which erodes faster than the rock above. Eventually, this pedestal will snap, and the boulder will come crashing down.

While you can see the formation clearly from the trailhead, the loop allows you to grasp its actual size (55ft to the top of the pedestal, 128ft to the top of the rock). On the outside of the trail look for narrowleaf yucca, an important desert species that can provide food, soap, needles and rope.

## THE WINDOWS TRAIL
**Distance: 0.6 mile round-trip**
**Duration: 30 minutes–1 hour**
**Challenge: Easy**
**Elevation Change: 140ft**

Perhaps the park's most heavily trodden path, The Windows Trail leads directly to North and South Windows and offers a terrific view of Turret Arch. Rangers lead interpretive talks here from spring through fall; if you're interested, check the bulletin board at the parking area. The trail forks about 500ft from the lot. Bear right for a close look at **Turret Arch** along a short loop that rejoins the main trail.

The left fork climbs to the **North Window**. Stand beneath this arch for one of the park's best views, taking in red-rock cliffs along the Colorado and Castle Valley in the distance. Above you rises the giant smooth sweep of the mature arch, supported by a base of lumpy Dewey Bridge mudstone. **South Window** sits higher than North Window. Though tempting, keep off the arch (climbing is prohibited on most named features).

Two trails lead back to the parking lot from here: the wide, graded main trail and the narrow primitive trail. The latter heads east and then north, features great views and offers brief respite from the crowds; follow the cairns.

## SAND DUNE & BROKEN ARCHES
**Distance: 2.4-mile loop (0.4 mile round-trip to Sand Dune Arch;**
**1.2 miles out-and-back or 2 mile loop to Broken Arch)**
**Duration: 15–30 minutes to Sand Dune; 30 minutes–1 hour to Broken;**
**2 hours for complete loop**
**Challenge: Easy–Moderate**
**Elevation Change: 140ft**

From the Sand Dune Arch parking area, follow the trail through deep sand between narrow stone walls, the backmost fins of **Fiery Furnace** – a good teaser if you haven't already hiked the Furnace. (If you have kids with you, let them run ahead and play in the sand – they can't get lost along this trail.) In less

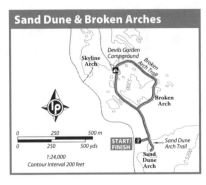

## Sand Dune & Broken Arches

than a quarter mile you'll arrive at **Sand Dune Arch**, which looks something like a poodle kissing a polar bear. Resist the temptation to climb or jump off the 8ft arch.

From here you can bear left to return to your car or bear right across open grassland en route to 60ft **Broken Arch**. At the next fork (the start of the loop trail), grasses give way to piñon pines and junipers along a gentle climb to the arch. The treat here is the walk *through* the arch atop a slickrock ledge. Wear rubber-soled shoes or boots, or you may have trouble climbing to the arch.

When you're ready, return to the parking area or continue north to **Devils Garden Campground**. The route follows cairns over slickrock, passing through stands of desert pines. Watch for new arches forming near the trail. If you're staying at the campground, you can join the loop trail there. From the campground spur it's another half mile back to the start of the loop trail.

This is a good trail for kids, especially the first section, though savvy adult hikers may find it too tame.

---

### DELICATE ARCH TRAIL
**Distance: 3 miles round-trip**
**Duration: 2–3 hours**
**Challenge: Moderate–Difficult**
**Elevation Change: 480ft**

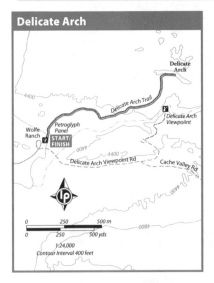

## Delicate Arch

The trail to Delicate Arch may seem interminable on your way up, but the rewards are so great at the top that you'll quickly forget the toil – provided you wear rubber-soled shoes or boots and drink a quart of water along the way. You won't be alone on the trek – this is the most popular long hike at Arches.

Start out behind **Wolfe Ranch**, where a short spur trail leads to a small petroglyph panel. Past the panel, the trail climbs a series of small switchbacks, soon emerging on a long, steady slickrock slope. (This hill is visible from the trailhead, as are the tiny figures trudging up the slickrock like pilgrims.) Take your time on this stretch, especially on hot days. If you keep a steady pace, plan on making it to the top in 45 minutes.

As you approach the arch, the trail skirts a narrow slickrock ledge that may be daunting if you're afraid of heights – if you can push yourself, it's worth every step to round the final corner. To your right, a broad sandstone amphitheater opens up below, and **Delicate Arch** crowns its rim like a proscenium, framing the 12,700ft **La Sal Mountains** in the distance. Circle the rim to the base of the arch, which sits atop a saddle that drops precipitously on either side. (If you bypass the bowl and bear left, it's possible to clamber high atop large flat rocks for a different perspective – and fewer people.)

There is one drawback to this trail. Many people climb up only to take a snapshot before heading back down. Yet one of the great joys of visiting the arch is to linger beside it and soak in the scene. If you do, however, expect someone with a camera to ask or even holler at you to get out of the way. (Edward Abbey predicted this sort of thing; see p216.) To avoid a confrontation (and if you're not scared of heights), head beneath the arch and drop down the other side of it a few yards, where few people venture, least of all the 'industrial tourists.'

---

## LANDSCAPE ARCH TRAIL

**Distance: 2.1 miles round-trip (1.6 miles round-trip to Landscape, half-mile spur to Pine Tree and Tunnel)**
**Duration: 30 minutes–1 hour**
**Challenge: Easy–Moderate**
**Elevation Change: 50ft**

---

Among the world's longest natural stone spans, **Landscape Arch** lies 0.8 mile along the Devils Garden Trail at the north end of the main park road. Along the trail, don't miss the short spurs to Tunnel and Pine Tree Arches. Before setting out, fill up with water at the trailhead parking lot.

From the trailhead, you'll thread through sandstone fins that stand on end like giant wedges. A third of a mile in, bear right at the fork and head downhill to **Tunnel Arch** (on your right) and 45ft **Pine Tree Arch** (on your left). High on a cliff, aptly named Tunnel Arch looks like a subway tube through the Entrada sandstone. In contrast, Pine Tree Arch is meaty, with a bulbous frame around its gaping middle. Look for the gnarled namesake juniper, which juts from the base of the window.

As you approach **Landscape Arch** along the main trail, the terrain opens up,

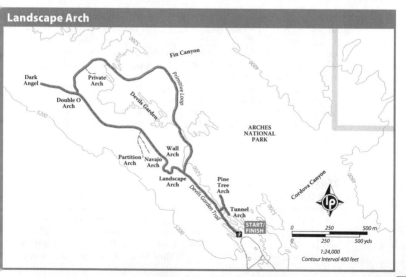

Landscape Arch

## THE BARD OF MOAB

Edward Abbey (1927–89), one of America's great Western prose writers, worked as a seasonal ranger at Arches National Monument in the 1950s, before it became a national park. In his essay collection *Desert Solitaire: A Season in the Wilderness,* Abbey wrote of his time here and described the simple beauty and subtle power of the vast landscape. In one of his essays, perhaps the book's most famous, he bemoaned what he dubbed 'Industrial Tourism' – exploitation of the natural environment by big business acting in cahoots with government, turning the national monument into a 'Natural Money-Mint.'

At the core of the problem: the automobile industry and its paving of the wilderness. Abbey believed passionately in the holiness of the land and felt that tourists who never left their cars ('upholstered mechanized wheelchairs') were robbing themselves of the chance to transcend the mundane, to experience the sanctity of the land and, in so doing, to liberate their consciousness.

But some blame Abbey for contributing to the very thing he decried. Critics argue that by so unerringly evoking in his writing the stark beauty of life in southern Utah's Canyonlands, Abbey inadvertently helped attract thousands of people seeking that very remoteness he described. Nonetheless, his polemic lays out a clear, viable plan for ridding the parks of vehicles, which would free up more room for everyone and leave the parks 'unimpaired for the enjoyment of future generations,' as is the mandate of the National Park Service.

Many of Abbey's predictions have come true – you need only arrive at Arches on a busy weekend and get stuck in a line of SUVs to know that he was, in his way, a prophet. Leave your summer beach reading in your suitcase and instead pick up a copy of *Desert Solitaire*. Not only will you appreciate the desert in new, unexpected ways, you'll also have something to read in the car.

revealing long views to distant ridges (beyond which lie Colorado) and a vast expanse of sky. In the past, visitors could hike right beneath the elegant 306ft sweep of desert-varnished sandstone. But on September 1, 1991, a 60ft slab of rock fell from the arch, nearly killing several hikers. When you notice the cracks on the left side of the arch, it's easy to understand why the NPS closed the trail.

From here you can continue on a moderately difficult out-and-back hike to trail's end at **Dark Angel** spire, adding about 3.4 miles round-trip to your journey. You can also add the difficult **Primitive Loop**, an additional stretch of 4.3 miles. Both lead to **Double O Arch**, where you'll negotiate the narrow edge of a sandstone fin with a 20ft drop on either side. (This rocky route is not suitable for little ones.) Pick up the trail guide at the trailhead or ask a ranger for route details.

### OTHER ACTIVITIES
#### Rock Climbing
Rock climbing is permitted at Arches, but you are prohibited from climbing on any named features. Most routes require advanced techniques. No permits are necessary. Before you set out, ask at the visitor center about current regulations and route closures. Leave dull-colored webbing only when recovery is impossible. Follow established trails or hike in sandy washes or

over slickrock to avoid stepping on fragile macrobiotic crusts. White chalk is prohibited; purchase sandstone chalk at climbing shops in Moab. Remember, it's easier to ascend than descend; always plan your route down, lest you get stuck on a rim.

For a guided canyoneering hike to the Fiery Furnace, contact **Desert Highlights** (p233) in Moab.

## Ranger Programs

Rangers lead several activities from spring through fall, most notably the **Fiery Furnace Guided Hike**. In addition to evening campfire talks at Devils Garden Campground, rangers also hold talks at the The Windows Section. Check current schedules on bulletin boards at the visitor center, the campground and The Windows parking area.

## Kids' Activities

When you arrive at the park, stop by the visitor center and pick up a **Junior Ranger Activity Guide**. Once kids complete certain activities, they can return to the visitor center to receive a special certificate and badge from a ranger.

Arches is very kid-friendly. Distances between sights are short, offering frequent opportunities to hop out of the car and run around (encourage kids to stay on marked trails to avoid crushing the fragile desert soil). Keep an eye out for faces and figures amid the rocks.

# SLEEPING

Arches offers one developed campground, but no rooms or restaurants. Drive the 5 miles to Moab for all services.

**Devils Garden Campground** ( ☎ 877-444-6777, 518-885-3639 for reservations; www.nps.gov/ arch or www.reserveusa.com for reservations; 52 sites for tents, some for RVs up to 30ft; ☻ year-round) The park's only campground sits at the end of the main road, 18 miles from the visitor center. Amenities include water, picnic tables, fire grills, and flush and pit toilets, but no showers. Though tall piñon pines and junipers provide moderate shade, the park gets very hot in summer – this *is* the desert. As you pull into the campground, sites on the right (by the rocks) offer more privacy, while sites on the left boast better views. Two group sites are also available.

From March through October, half the sites are available by reservation only; the remaining sites are first-come, first-served. For same-day availability, do not just drive to the campground. Instead, check at the entrance station or visitor center anytime after 7:30am.

You can reserve sites online or by phone between four and 240 days in advance. Ask about cancellation and no-show fees before you book, particularly if your travel plans are tentative – you could get stuck with the bill.

*If you've been jonesing for civilization, Moab will be a sight for sore eyes.*

# EXPERIENCING MOAB

Shop for groceries till midnight, browse the shelves of indie bookstores, buy a bottle of tequila, make a call from your cell phone, sit down for dinner at 9pm and you'll still find several places to grab a beer afterward. All this culture comes at a price: Corporate chain motels line Main St, T-shirt shops abound, and streetlights and neon signs blot out the night sky. If you're coming from the wilderness, all this activity can be jarring.

Still, there's a distinct sense of fun in the air. Moab bills itself as Utah's recreation capital, and that's why everyone flocks here – to play outdoors. From the hiker to the four-wheeler, recreationists' enthusiasm borders on fetishism.

Now the largest town in southeast Utah, Moab (population 4779) has nearly lost its small-town rural roots, and some residents fear that it's on its way to becoming the next Vail. While the town won't ever become a sprawling suburb (it's surrounded by state and federal lands), it does get overrun with tourists every year, and the impact of all those feet, bikes and 4WD vehicles on the fragile desert is a serious concern. People disagree over how the town should evolve. Talk to anyone and you'll quickly learn that Moab's polarized political debates are yet another high-stakes extreme sport.

One thing is certain: People here love the land, even if they don't always get along or agree on how to protect it. Anyway, if all that neon and traffic and philosophical debating irritate you, remember that you can disappear into the vast desert without a trace in no time flat.

## HISTORY

Tucked beneath high rock walls in a fertile green valley – an important wildlife corridor along the Colorado River – Moab was founded by Mormon ranchers and farmers in the late 1870s after resident Indians' repeated failed attempts to get rid of them. Nothing much changed until the Cold War climate of the 1950s, when the federal government subsidized uranium mining, and Moab's population tripled in three years. In search of 'radioactive gold,' miners bladed a network of primitive roads, laying the groundwork for the region to become a 4WD mecca half a century later. (The miners also left ponds of radioactive tailings, residue from the mineral extraction process.)

Though uranium mining bottomed out in the 1980s when the feds quit paying premiums for the stuff, salt and potash mining continue, as does drilling for natural gas in the surrounding area, a contentious issue.

Hollywood loves Moab and has shot hundreds of Westerns here, mostly from the 1950s to 1970s. But neither the mining boom nor Hollywood has had as much influence on Moab's current character as the humble mountain biker. In the mid-1980s, an influx of fat-tire enthusiasts discovered the challenging and scenic slickrock desert and triggered a massive surge in tourism that continues unabated.

## ORIENTATION

Hwy 191 becomes Main St through Moab. Town follows a fairly typical Mormon grid, in which numbered streets radiate from a central hub – here the intersection of Main and Center Sts. Compass points indicate where you are in relation to that hub: thus, 100 E 300 S is one block east and three blocks south of Main and Center. It's easy once you get used to it.

See the Moab map (Map 9) on p153.

## INFORMATION

Make your first stop the comprehensive, multiagency **Moab Information Center** (Main & Center Sts; 8am-8pm), which serves walk-in visitors only. You'll find extensive information on everything from campground availability and permits to astronomical data and river updates. Choose from an outstanding selection of books and maps on the area, view exhibits and watch a 12-minute video.

The Canyonlands Natural History Association staffs the center in conjunction with the NPS, BLM, Utah State Parks, Grand County and the town.

For information before you arrive, contact the **Moab Area Travel Council** ( 435-259-8825, 800-635-6622; www.discovermoab.com; PO Box 550, Moab, UT 84532; 8am-5pm Mon-Fri). The following are not open to walk-in visitors, but can provide information online and by phone: **Manti–La Sal National Forest Moab Ranger Station** ( 435-259-7155; www.fs.fed. us/r4/mantilasal) and the **BLM** ( 435-259-2100; www.blm.gov/utah/moab).

To learn about Moab's history, visit the **Grand County Public Library** ( 435-259-1111; www.grand.lib.ut.us; 25 S 100 E; 9am-9pm Mon-Wed, 9am-7pm Thu-Fri, 9am-5pm Sat), which also provides T1 Internet service, available by suggested donation ($1/5 minutes).

> ## HIGHLIGHTS
>
> ✔ Rafting the **Colorado River** (p228)
>
> ✔ Biking the **Slickrock Bike Trail** (p226)
>
> ✔ Four-wheel driving **Hells Revenge** (p224)
>
> ✔ Talking politics at **Dave's Corner Market** (p237)
>
> ✔ Hiking beneath **Fisher Towers** (p232) at sunset
>
> ✔ Escaping the heat on the **La Sal Mountain Loop Rd** (p221)
>
> ✔ Strolling and people-watching along **Main St** after dark

Free **newspapers** include *Moab Happenings,* geared to visitors, and the iconoclastic *Canyon Country Zephyr.* Tune to **Moab Community Radio** (89.7 FM and 106.1 FM) for alternative local programming, from folk to funk.

## GETTING AROUND

Rent a car downtown or at Canyonlands Field airport (16 miles north of town via Hwy 191) from **Thrifty Car Rental** ( ☎ 435-259-7317, 800-847-4389; http://moab.thrify. com; 711 S Main St or Canyonlands Field).

You'll find several gas and service stations in town. Obey speed limits, or police will ticket you.

Several companies operate shuttle service to Arches, Canyonlands and environs; some will also shuttle your private vehicle to meet you at a trailhead. Contact **Acme Bike Shuttle** ( ☎ 435-260-2534; www.acmebikeshuttle.com; 702 S Main St), **Atomic Transfer** ( ☎ 435-259-6475; www.moab-canyonlands.com/atomic; 438 N Castle Dr), **Coyote Shuttle** ( ☎ 435-259-8656; 55 W 300 S) or **Roadrunner Shuttle** ( ☎ 435-259-9402; www.roadrunnershuttle. com, 197 W Center St).

For details on getting to Moab, see Planning the Trip (p59).

## SIGHTS

Moab exists primarily as a destination for recreationists and as a base for visitors to Arches and Canyonlands National Parks. Except for government functionaries – Moab is the Grand County seat and home to several federal agency field offices – visitors won't find much to do here by day. That said, several sights are worth a look.

The **Dan O'Laurie Museum** ( ☎ 435-259-7985; www.grandcountyutah.net/museum; 118 E Center St; family/adult/children under 12 $5/2/free; ☺ 1-8pm Mon-Sat, shorter winter hours) preserves and displays regional artifacts and presents exhibits on everything from paleontology and geology to uranium mining and Native American art. If you're interested in learning about the dinosaurs that once roamed Utah, this a great place to start.

Take the self-guided **Moab Area Historic Walking Tour** to see several original buildings and learn some local history. Pick up the pamphlet at the Dan O'Laurie Museum or the Moab Information Center.

An unabashed tourist trap 12 miles south of Moab on Hwy 191, **Hole 'n the Rock** ( ☎ 435-686-2250; www.moab-utah.com/holeintherock; 11037 S Hwy 191; adult/child $4.50/2.50; ☺ 8:30am-7pm, shorter winter hours) is a 5000-sq-ft home-cum-cave carved into sandstone and decorated in knockout 1950s kitsch. Admission covers the 10-minute tour; the petting zoo and gift shop are free.

The nonprofit **Living Rivers** seeks to decommission the Glen Canyon Dam and reestablish a free-flowing Colorado River through the Grand Canyon. Even if you don't agree, catch the fascinating interpretive displays on the walls of **Restoration Creamery** ( ☎ 435-259-1063; www.livingrivers.org/creamery.cfm; 21 N Main St; free admission, ice cream $2-5; ☺ 1-10pm Mar-Oct), which sells delicious ice cream to benefit Living Rivers.

**Moab Museum of Film & Western Heritage** ( ☎ 435-259-2002, 866-812-2002; www.redcliffs-lodge.com; mile marker 14, Hwy 128; free; ☺ 8am-10pm), based at Red Cliffs Lodge 15 miles north of town, is a movie museum that showcases Hollywood memorabilia from films shot in the area; there are also historical displays on local ranches.

### Organized Tours & Outfitters

Moab hosts hundreds of tour and rental companies; the ones listed under each activity are all recommended. For a complete list of tour operators and outfitters, contact the Moab Area Travel Council (p219) or visit the Moab Information Center (p219).

**Canyon Voyages** ( ☎ 435-259-6007, 800-733-6007; www.canyonvoyages.com; 211 N Main St) rents camping and backpacking gear, while **Tag-A-Long Expeditions** ( ☎ 435-259-8946, 800-453-3292; www.tagalong.com; 452 N Main St) rents tents and sleeping bags. Otherwise, many tour outfitters will rent gear only to their trip participants.

# DRIVING & FOUR-WHEEL DRIVE TOURS

People come from around the world to drive in Utah. From paved desert highways for retirees in RVs to vertical slickrock trails for four-wheeling adrenaline junkies, you'll find scenic drives for every taste.

## Scenic Drives

Most of the following drives are paved; exceptions are noted in the individual descriptions.

---

### COLORADO RIVER SCENIC BYWAY (HWY 128)
**Route: Hwy 128 from Moab to Dewey Bridge**
**Distance: 31 miles one way**
**Speed Limit: 35–50mph**

This well-paved route follows the Colorado River northeast of Moab. Add the La Sal Mountain Loop Rd to extend the trip by three to 3½ hours.

Drive north on Main St/Hwy 191 and turn right (east) onto Hwy 128. The road winds through red-rock canyons along the river's serpentine course. Arches National Park lies on the north side of the river for the first 15 miles. Six miles from Hwy 191 you'll reach **Big Bend Recreation Site**, where you can picnic by the river. Seventeen miles from Hwy 191, you'll pass the La Sal Mountain Loop Rd turnoff and **Castle Rock**, a narrow spire that rises above Castle Valley. At mile marker 21, the **Fisher Towers** rise almost as high as the Eiffel Tower (at 900ft, Titan is the tallest). Ten miles ahead, you'll reach the 1916 **Dewey Bridge**, among the first spans across the Colorado. Park and stroll across the suspension bridge to watch rafters running downriver. When ready, return to Moab or double back to the La Sal Mountain Loop Rd. I-70 lies 13 miles north.

---

### LA SAL MOUNTAIN LOOP ROAD
**Route: From Moab to the La Sal Mountains & back**
**Distance: 67-mile loop**
**Speed Limit: 25–45mph**

This route through Manti–La Sal National Forest takes you from the scorching desert into cool green woodlands where you can camp, bicycle, hike or sit by a stream and listen as wind ruffles the quaking aspens. The loop is paved, but it's narrow and lacks any guardrails. Snow closes the road between November and March. Allow three to four hours.

About 15 miles northeast of Moab off Hwy 128, the La Sal Mountain Loop Rd (aka Castle Valley Rd) climbs southeast into the national forest, ascending switchbacks (a problem for large RVs) into the forest. Four miles from the turnoff, look to your left for the spires known as **the Priest and Nuns**, as well as **Castle Rock**. The route winds past junipers and piñon pines, followed by scrub oaks and, finally, alpine slopes of majestic pines, firs and white-barked quaking aspens, whose leaves turn a brilliant yellow-gold in autumn. Here, high above canyon country, you'll gain a fresh perspective on the vastness of the Colorado Plateau.

At the crest, you can turn left on a dirt spur road and climb 5 miles farther to the picnic area and developed campground at **Warner Lake**. For information on hiking and camping, check with national forest rangers (see Information, p219). From the Warner Lake spur junction, the loop road descends to Hwy 191, 8 miles south of Moab.

## POTASH ROAD SCENIC BYWAY
**Route: Hwy 279 south along the Colorado River**
**Distance: 15 miles one way**
**Speed Limit: 30–40mph**

Three miles north of Moab off Hwy 191, the paved Potash Rd (Hwy 279) skirts south along the Colorado. It's named for a potash extraction plant at road's end, where broad sky-blue fields look out of place beneath the red-rock cliffs. Just past the turnoff you'll pass a radioactive tailings pond from Moab's uranium-mining days, while midroute, stunning natural beauty abounds. Such are the region's contradictions.

Highlights along the way include **Wall St** (a favorite of rock climbers), several Indian petroglyph panels (look for signs), dinosaur tracks (bring binoculars for a better look), a 1.5-mile hiking trail to **Corona Arch** (p232) and, near the end, **Jug Handle Arch**, just 3ft wide but 15 times as high. At the Jug Handle parking area, look north to spot more rock art. You'll also find the **Potash Dock** put-in for float trips down the Colorado. Past the potash plant, the road continues as a rough 4WD track into Canyonlands' Island in the Sky district, eventually linking up with Shafer Trail Rd.

## HURRAH PASS ROAD
**Route: Moab to Hurrah Pass**
**Distance: 33 miles round-trip**
**Speed Limit: 5–35mph**

This route starts out west along paved Kane Creek Blvd, off Hwy 191 in Moab, soon passing petroglyph sites and a rock climbing area. The pavement yields to gravel as you enter **Kane Springs Canyon**. About 10 miles in you must ford the creek, which, depending on the weather, may be impassable; 4WD is recommended.

After 15 miles you'll reach 4470ft **Hurrah Pass**. The stupendous scenery includes views *up* to Dead Horse and Grand View Points. South of the pass the road descends toward the Colorado, with views of the potash plant on the opposite bank (look for the fields of blue). At the base of the pass is **Camelot Adventure Lodge** (p236), where – if you've called ahead – you can play a round of disc golf amid the slickrock. When ready, you can double back to Moab or continue south on **Lockhart Basin Road** toward Canyonlands' Needles district.

From here the road is much more difficult (4WD is *mandatory*) and often confusing, eventually emerging about 50 miles south on Hwy 211, just east of **The Needles**. Contact the BLM for maps and information if you want to do the whole route.

## CANYON RIMS RECREATION AREA
**Route: Hwy 191 to Needles & Anticline Overlooks**
**Distance: 22 miles one way to Needles Overlook, 31 miles one way to Anticline Overlook**
**Speed Limit: 45–65mph**

The BLM-administered Canyon Rims Recreation Area lies south of Moab, west of Hwy 191 and east of Canyonlands National Park. Turn west off Hwy 191, 32 miles south of Moab. The paved road leads 22 miles west to the **Needles Overlook**, a great panorama of the national park. About two-thirds of the way

## OHVS & THE BLM

Outside of water rights, no issue is more divisive in southern Utah than who gets to drive on which roads. It's become a litmus test of one's belief: Does all land exist solely for our benefit, or is it in our benefit to protect certain land from all use? In Utah the debate rages over the use of off-highway vehicles (OHVs) on public lands, particularly BLM-managed Wilderness Study Areas.

First, some terminology: An OHV is any motorized vehicle that drives off paved highways, whether it's a knobby-tired ATV, a 4WD vehicle, a pickup truck, a 2WD car or a motorcycle. 'Public lands' refers to BLM (Bureau of Land Management) and USFS (United States Forest Service) areas, which are governed by multiple-use rules that allow logging, mining, grazing, fishing, hunting, skiing, hiking, biking, OHV use and wilderness set-asides, though not all on the same acre. The law charges public-land managers with the 'harmonious balance' of all uses and users.

So far, so good. But no one anticipated the phenomenal growth of OHV use. Over the past two decades, ridership in Utah has increased by 700% to 900%, and the machines have become larger and more powerful, able to reach places once thought inaccessible. OHV use is now considered the second-most damaging activity (after grazing) and poses a threat to the designation of more wilderness in southern Utah.

In Wilderness Study Areas, the BLM is supposed to restrict OHV use until an official wilderness determination can be made. But the BLM is not designating which roads are OK to drive or limiting OHV use in any practical way. OHV users indiscriminately drive existing roads and create new roads at will. This free-for-all effectively tramples the debate, ruining the very wilderness supposedly being studied.

The BLM cites a lack of funds and staff to correct the problem. Furthermore, in 2004 the US Supreme Court ruled the agency couldn't be held accountable for its failure to follow the law and protect proposed wilderness areas.

This is where the public comes in.

If you want to drive dirt roads in southern Utah, respect a 'closed unless posted open' principle, and refrain from driving off road in roadless areas. Until the BLM clarifies road use, this is the most responsible approach for OHV users. Indeed, if everyone did this, the OHV issue would shrink from a war to a vigorous debate.

Also consider helping the BLM do its job. Citizen groups like **Great Old Broads for Wilderness** (www.greatoldbroads.org) and the **Redrock Heritage Coalition** (www.redrock-heritage.org) are gathering hard data on OHV impact and road use to give the BLM the tools it needs. Volunteers are always welcome.

*– Jeff Campbell*

to the overlook, a gravel road stretches 16 miles north to the **Anticline Overlook**, a promontory with awesome views of the Colorado River, Meander Canyon and Hurrah Pass Rd below. The route is passable to both cars and tour buses. Allow four hours for the round-trip from Moab to both overlooks.

If you've already visited the area's other major overlooks (eg Dead Horse and Grand View Points) and have time, this byway makes a good day trip. It's also a good detour on the way to or from The Needles. Don't fret if you miss it, however. The area is especially popular with hikers, campers and ATV enthusiasts. For more information, contact the BLM or stop by the Moab Information Center (see Information, p219).

## Four-Wheel Driving

Four-wheel driving is *huge* in Moab. In the Cold War era, uranium prospectors forged thousands of primitive paths across the vast deserts surrounding town; today most of these are maintained as 4WD routes. If you've never gone four-wheeling, take a guided tour first – it'll blow your mind.

For experienced drivers only, the best-known gulp-and-go 4WD road in Moab is **Hells Revenge**. In the BLM-administered Sand Flats Recreation Area east of town, it follows an 8.2-mile route up and down shockingly steep slickrock. Also for experts, the shared-use **Moab Rim Trail** loops high on the rim rock southwest of town.

Avoid unsigned roads in BLM Wilderness Study Areas, and never drive off road, as you'll likely cause irreparable damage to fragile cryptobiotic soil. The consequences are evident north of town off Hwy 191, where grazing cows have trampled the cryptobiotic soil. Absent this living crust, the desert sands blow free – signs warn motorists of severe dust storms. Without protection, what only *seems* barren now could turn into a veritable wasteland.

For more details about routes, pick up a pamphlet from the Moab Information Center, ask a tour operator or inquire at a 4WD rental agency. Also consider the following recommended books: *4WD Adventures: Utah*, by Peter Massey and Jeanne Wilson, and *Guide to Moab, UT, Backroads & 4-Wheel Drive Trails*, by Charles Wells.

### TOURS & RENTALS

Gearheads and four-wheeling junkies ought not to miss a 50° ascent of slickrock while in Moab. When you're choosing a rental vehicle, remember: Jeeps are the Ferraris of 4WD, and Hummers are the limos. You can also rent an ATV and drive alone on dedicated trails.

For a guided two- to four-hour thrill ride up the slickrock in a Hummer, or to rent your own ATV, call **Highpoint Hummer** (☎ 435-259-2972, 877-486-6833; www.highpointhummer.com; 281 N Main St; adult/child $65-89/39-55). Nobody knows the deep backcountry like good ol' boy **Dan Mick** (☎ 435-259-4567; www.danmick.com). Drive in his 4WD vehicle or yours. He'll also shuttle hikers. Knee-jerk lefties be warned: Dan will push your buttons.

Several excellent companies lead backcountry tours and combination land/river trips; all of the following provide excellent interpretation. **Adrift Adventures** (☎ 435-259-8594, 800-874-4483; www.adrift.net; 378 N Main St) and **Canyon Voyages** (☎ 435-259-6007, 800-733-6007; www.canyonvoyages.com; 211 N Main St) both offer backcountry trips in Chevy Suburbans and lead combination Hummer or Jeep/rafting tours. **O.A.R.S.** (☎ 435-259-5919, 800-342-5938; www.oars.com; 2540 S Hwy 191) and **Navtec Expeditions** (☎ 435-259-7983, 800-833-1278; www.navtec.com; 321 N Main St) hold permits for Canyonlands National Park and guide excellent single- or multiday combination 4WD/hiking/rafting tours. **Tag-A-Long Expeditions** (☎ 435-259-8946, 800-453-3292; www.tagalong.com; 452 N Main St), Moab's biggest outfitter, leads single- or multiday backcountry Jeep/Hummer trips into Canyonlands (including trips to The Maze), as well as land/river combinations.

If you rent a 4WD vehicle, *read the insurance policy* – it may not cover damage from off-road driving and will likely carry a $2500 deductible. Check when you book. Whenever possible, rent a relatively new vehicle. Reputable companies include **Farabee Adventures** (☎ 435-259-7494, 888-806-5337; www.moab-utah.com/farabee; 401 N Main St) and **Cliffhanger Jeep Rental** (☎ 435-259-2599; www.moab-utah.com/cliffhanger; 1551 N Hwy 191, at the Aarchway Inn).

You could also rent a motorcycle from **Elite Motorcycle Tours** (☎ 435-259-7621, 888-778-0358; www.moab.net/elitetours; 1310 Murphy Lane).

## MOUNTAIN BIKING

Moab has been dubbed the mountain biking capital of the world, and it's easy to see why. Challenging trails ascend steep slickrock, wind through woods and travel 4WD roads into the wilds of canyon country.

Mountain biking began in Marin County, California, when a bunch of people started riding beat-up, old-school, fat-tire, single-speed Scwhinns down Mt Tamalpais. As the craze caught on, Moabites realized that the slickrock surrounding town made a perfect 'sticky' surface for mountain bikes' knobby tires.

Two decades later people come from around the world to ride the famous Slickrock Bike Trail and other challenging routes. Considering the high volume of riders, it's important to protect the surrounding desert. Avoid all off-trail riding, and pack out everything you pack in (including cigarette butts).

The busiest seasons are spring and fall. In summer, start riding by 7am at the latest – after that, it's too hot. In winter, snow might cover trails, but you can bike the roads.

Several companies provide **bicycle shuttles** (see Getting Around, p220).

For further reading on mountain biking in Moab, pick up a copy of *Above & Beyond Slickrock*, by Todd Campbell. A fun read by a serious biker is *Rider Mel's Mountain Bike Guide to Moab*, which is small enough to carry on a ride.

> ### DESERT BIKING
>
> Newcomers to desert mountain biking should pay particular heed to safety. Wear a helmet, carry lots of water and bring high-energy foods. Also pack a map and keep track of your route. Don't start out on rough trails – first get your bearings on easier rides. The vibration from riding Moab's rougher trails can loosen headsets, so be sure to check your fittings.
>
> Expect the best, but prepare for the worst. In addition to extra water and food, carry a windbreaker, a wide-brimmed hat, sunscreen, sunglasses, a patch kit, tools and matches. Avoid riding alone, and always tell someone where you're going. Moab may seem like one big theme park, but the desert is unforgiving and should never be underestimated.
>
>

### Tours & Outfitters

When booking a tour or renting a bike, if you don't get good service, turn around and walk out. Lots of fine companies are waiting for your business. Some of the best are listed below. Also ask locals which companies they like most. If you still have a hard time choosing, ask what the outfit serves for lunch. Full-day tours (including bike rental) start at around $100.

**Rim Tours** ( ☎ 435-259-5223, 800-626-7335; www.rimtours.com; 1233 S Hwy 191) leads half-, one- and multiday trips throughout Moab. It also holds permits for Canyonlands National Park, as do **Kaibab Adventure Outfitters** ( ☎ 435-259-7423, 800-451-1133; 91 S Main St; www.moabcyclery.com), **Nichols Expeditions** ( ☎ 435-259-3999, 800-648-8488; www.nicholsexpeditions.com; 497 N Main St) and **Western Spirit Cycling** ( ☎ 435-259-8732, 800-845-6453; www.westernspirit.com; 478 Mill Creek Rd). If you're a diehard, ask about trips to The Maze. All four outfits lead trips to other Southwestern destinations, including Zion, Bryce and Grand Canyon National Parks.

### Bike Rentals

If you want to set out on our own, reserve a rental in advance. Full-suspension bikes start at around $30 per day.

**Rim Cyclery** ( ☎ 435-259-5333; 94 W 100 N; www.rimcyclery.com), Moab's longest-running shop, includes a museum of mountain bike technology. Also consider **Moab Cyclery** ( ☎ 435-259-7423, 800-451-1133; 391 S Main St; www.moabcyclery.com), **Poison Spider** ( ☎ 435-259-7882, 800-635-1792 www.poisonspiderbicycles.com; 497 N Main St; ⏰ 8am-8pm spring & fall, shorter off-season hours) and **Chile Pepper Bike Shop** ( ☎ 435-259-4688, 888-677-4688; www.chilebikes.com; 550½ N Main St). All provide excellent service and helpful websites for planning your trip. Chile Pepper also makes repairs and serves espresso.

**Road biking** is also becoming popular; rent a road bike from Poison Spider.

## Trails

Many mountain biking trails follow 4WD routes; yield to vehicles and horses. Inquire at bike shops about conditions before setting out. Stay on trails, out of water potholes and off fragile cryptobiotic soil crusts. For information about Moab area trails, inquire at bike shops or the Moab Information Center (p219).

**SLICKROCK TRAIL**
**Distance: 12.7 miles round-trip from parking area, main loop trail 9.6 miles**
**Duration: 3–4 hours**
**Challenge: Very Difficult**

The archetypal mountain biking loop, the Slickrock Bike Trail was first forged as a motorcycle trail. It requires top physical fitness and technical savvy. Don't

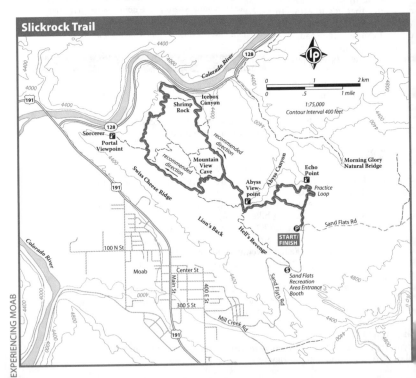

attempt it unless you're an advanced cyclist. Even the initial 2.2-mile round-trip practice loop is difficult and should *not* be your first attempt at mountain biking. If you do find you're in over your head, hike out – don't ride any farther.

From downtown Moab, follow signs from 400 E to the trailhead at the **Sand Flats Recreation Area**. A $2 fee per rider (or $5 per car) is payable at the Sand Flats entrance station. From the parking lot, the trail leads 0.3 mile to the practice loop – turn right here for a good warm-up, or turn left and pedal 0.4 mile to a junction with the main trail.

When you reach the main loop, 2.5 miles from the trailhead, bear left (the gradient is more difficult if you bear right). Painted white dashes on the rock mark the trail route, while yellow markers indicate caution zones or areas of interest. The trail occasionally crosses sand. Highlights include steep drops, vertical climbs and incredible views of the La Sal Mountains and Arches National Park.

Typical riding season for the trail is mid-February through November. At the trailhead you'll find vault toilets but not water.

---

### BAR-M LOOP
**Distance: 7.9 mile loop**
**Duration: 1–2 hours**
**Challenge: Easy–Moderate**

One of a handful of trails in Moab appropriate for families and novice riders, the Bar-M Loop features a gentle gradient and few technical challenges. The loop follows a graded 4WD route and includes slickrock stretches.

To reach the trailhead, drive 7 miles north of town on Hwy 191, and turn right at the Bar-M Chuckwagon, just south of the Hwy 313 turnoff. Park by the kiosk at the south end of the lot.

From the kiosk you'll follow the original highway south. After 1.2 miles, turn left (the second major left from the trailhead). The route gets a bit rougher as it climbs slightly. Follow trailside markers to the start of the loop, 2.3 miles from the trailhead. Turn left and continue to bear left as you make your way around the loop.

The trail skirts the boundary of Arches and boasts great views. If you have a small child, you could even do this trail with the little one on a second seat.

---

### KLONDIKE BLUFFS TRAIL
**Distance: 15.6 miles round-trip**
**Duration: 3–5 hours**
**Challenge: Moderate**

If you're an intermediate biker and have never ridden on slickrock, this trail north of town is a great place to give it a try. Alternating between a 4WD road and slickrock marked with painted stripes, the trail dead-ends at Klondike Bluffs in Arches. Cairns and brown marker posts guide the way.

To reach the trailhead, drive north on Hwy 191 for 16 miles to mile marker 142, and turn right on Klondike Bluffs Rd. (If you reach the airport, you've gone too far.)

From the trailhead, follow the 4WD road 2.7 miles northwest, then bear left (a better-maintained road veers right). At mile 3.8 veer right (away from a road leading north up a wash) and follow trail markers up a small canyon toward the white rocks. Once atop the slickrock, look for **dinosaur tracks** off to the left.

At mile 5.2 the ride tops out. Past a big cairn on the hillside, bear right and leave the road to pedal over slickrock. At trail's end, 1.4 miles ahead, park your bike and walk 0.3 mile to the Klondike Bluffs overlook for a view east to Devils Garden. When ready, return the way you came.

### MOONLIGHT MEADOW TRAIL
**Distance: ±7.5 miles one way, 10 miles round-trip**
**Duration: 2–4 hours**
**Challenge: Moderate**

When it's scorching in Moab, head to the La Sal Mountains for this ride through cool aspen forests and open meadows overlooking the vast desert below. You can make this a one-way downhill ride or a round-trip loop. High-altitude riding can be taxing, so take it easy.

For the one-way downhill, leave a shuttle vehicle at the junction of Geyser Pass Rd and La Sal Mountain Loop Rd (p221). Drive a second vehicle uphill about 8 miles on gravel to Geyser Pass (10,600ft) and park at the trailhead. Follow signs to Moonlight Meadow. The trail eventually emerges downhill at the junction of Geyser Pass Rd and the Trans–La Sal trailhead; descend the road the remaining 2.5 miles to the shuttle car.

For the loop, park at the Trans–La Sal trailhead, about 2.5 miles up Geyser Pass Rd, and bike up to the pass. From there, take the Moonlight Meadow Trail downhill to emerge at your parked car.

## RIVER RUNNING

More than a dozen outfitters run a variety of float trips on the Colorado and Green Rivers. Though permits limit the number of people on the water, favorite takeout beaches can get pretty crowded, and for good reason: This is fun – *really* fun! Whatever your interest, be it bashing through rapids or studying canyon geology, rafting may well prove the highlight of your vacation.

Rafting season runs April to September; jet-boating season lasts longer. Water levels usually crest in May and June. Most day trips cost $35-50, while longer full-day trips start at about $125. Two- to five-day excursions run from about $350 to more than $800 per person. Jet-boat trips cost about $70. Discounts often apply to children accompanying parents. Many companies combine rafting trips with hiking, 4WD or mountain biking trips.

Do-it-yourselfers can rent canoes, inflatable kayaks or rafts. Rates run $30-40 a day for canoes and kayaks, and $65-130 a day for rafts, depending on size (all come with life jackets and paddles). Advance permits are required for trips within the national parks and certain areas outside the parks.

While guided half- and full-day trips are often available on short notice, you should book overnight trips well ahead.

### What Kind of Boat?

Outfitters ply the rivers in a variety of boats. Resembling a rowboat, an **oar rig** is a rubber raft that a guide rows downriver. Also made of rubber, a **paddle boat** is steered by a guide and paddled by passengers. Not technically a raft, a **motor rig** is a large boat driven by a guide (jet boats fall into this category). You can also float in a kayak, inflatable kayak or canoe.

## What Class of Rapids?

Rapids are rated on a scale from one (I) to six (VI), with Class I being still water and Class VI an unnavigable waterfall. Class II rapids are good for novices and families with little kids. Class III are thrilling, while Class IV are borderline scary, depending on your perspective. Class V rapids are technical and dangerous.

## Rafting Tours

Outfitters on guided tours take care of everything, from permits to food to setting up camp and shuttling you back to town.

It's impossible to say who's best, but **Canyon Voyages** ( ☎ 435-259-6007, 800-733-6007; www.canyonvoyages.com; 211 N Main St) and **O.A.R.S.** ( ☎ 435-259-5919, 800-342-5938; www.oars.com; 2540 S Hwy 191) are near the top, as are **Sheri Griffith Expeditions** ( ☎ 435-259-8229, 800-332-2439; www.griffithexp.com; 2231 S Hwy 191) and **Adrift Adventures** ( ☎ 435-259-8594, 800-874-4483; www.adrift.net; 378 N Main St).

Several bigger outfits are geared to large groups and can bash through rapids with the best of 'em. Try **Tag-A-Long Expeditions** ( ☎ 435-259-8946, 800-453-3292; www.tagalong.com; 452 N Main St), **Navtec Expeditions** ( ☎ 435-259-7983, 800-833-1278; www.navtec.com; 321 N Main St) or **Western River Expeditions** ( ☎ 435-259-7019, 888-622-4097; www.westernriver.com; 1371 N Hwy 191).

For educational trips, you can't beat **Canyonlands Field Institute** ( ☎ 435-259-7750, 800-860-5262; www.canyonlandsfieldinst.org; 1320 S Hwy 191). If you're traveling with someone with a physical or mental disability, book with **Splore** ( ☎ 801-484-4128; www.splore.org), based in Salt Lake City.

For guided canoe excursions, call **Red River Canoes** ( ☎ 435-259-7722, 800-753-8216; www.redrivercanoe.com; 1371 N Hwy 191), which provides excellent instruction and interpretation.

For guided jet boat trips, call Adrift Adventures, Navtec or Tag-A-Long.

## Rafting Without a Guide

Good outfitters will provide complete information to help you plan a self-guided trip. Reserve equipment, secure permits and book shuttles far in advance to get what you want. Without a permit, you'll be restricted to several mellow stretches of the Colorado and Green Rivers, but if you want to run Class III and IV rapids in Westwater Canyon or enter Canyonlands on either river, you'll need a permit. Contact the **BLM** ( ☎ 435-259-2100; www.blm.gov/utah/moab) or the **NPS** ( ☎ 435-259-4351; www.nps.gov/cany/permits.htm; 2282 SW Resource Blvd). Strict rules govern sanitation and fires, depending on where you raft; confirm regulations with the appropriate agency.

To rent a raft, canoe or kayak, contact **Canyon Voyages** ( ☎ 435-259-6007, 800-733-6007; www.canyonvoyages.com; 211 N Main St). To rent canoes only, call **Red River Canoes** ( ☎ 435-259-7722, 800-753-8216; www.redrivercanoe.com; 1371 N Hwy 191) or **Tex's Riverways** ( ☎ 435-259-5101; www.texsriverways.com; 691 N 500 W).

For shuttles to or from the rivers, call **Roadrunner Shuttle** ( ☎ 435-259-9402; www.roadrunnershuttle.com; 197 W Center St), **Acme Bike Shuttle** ( ☎ 435-260-2534; www.acmebikeshuttle.com; 702 S Main St), **Coyote Shuttle** ( ☎ 435-259-8656; www.coyoteshuttle.com; 55 W 300 S) or **Black Dogs River Runner Shuttle** ( ☎ 435-259-3512, 800-241-2591; www.rr-ss.com; 3885 Spanish Valley Dr). Roadrunner and River Runner offer the best long-distance service. To get back from the Confluence, you must book a jet boat shuttle *in advance*. Two companies hold permits: **Tex's Riverways** and **Tag-A-Long Expeditions** ( ☎ 435-259-8946, 800-453-3292; www.tagalong.com; 452 N Main St).

## COLORADO RIVER NORTHEAST OF MOAB
Distance: 36 miles
Duration: 2–5 days
Start: Westwater Canyon
End: Takeout Beach

The 36 miles of river northeast of Moab are divided into three distinct stretches. All fall within the jurisdiction of the BLM. Take Hwy 128 from Moab, which roughly parallels the river, making put-in and takeout a breeze.

**Westwater Canyon:** If you're seeking serious white water, this is the place. The first canyon along the Colorado in Utah, Westwater boasts Class III and IV rapids through the oldest exposed layer of rock in the state. Most people make the 17-mile trip in one long day (10 hours) from Moab, though some choose to camp and make it a two-day trip. Most outfitters offer both options. A BLM permit is required.

**Dewey Bridge to Hittle Bottom:** If you like mellow water and simply want to float along, this 7-mile section of flat water is perfect, offering great wildlife watching and scenery. One stretch passes through a bird sanctuary. No permit is required.

**Hittle Bottom to Takeout Beach (Moab Daily):** Also known as Fisher Towers, or simply as The Daily, this is the most popular stretch of river near Moab, perfect for novices who aren't ready for Westwater. Families can safely bring small children without boring their teens. The Daily offers mostly Class I and II rapids, with one short section of Class III. Camp at riverside BLM campgrounds. No permit is required.

## COLORADO RIVER SOUTHWEST MOAB (MEANDER CANYON)
Distance: 63 miles
Duration: 3–5 days
Start: Moab Dock
End: Spanish Bottom, south of the Confluence

The flat-water trip from Moab to the Confluence moves slowly on the wide river. It's a scenic trip, good for mellow souls or novice boaters. You can put in at the **Potash Dock** (see Potash Road Scenic Byway, p222) to shorten the trip by 15 miles.

A mile and a half north of the Confluence, you'll reach **The Slide**, a moderate rapid that you can portage. In the 4-mile stretch from the Confluence to Spanish Bottom, eddies and whirlpools kick in as you approach Cataract Canyon (*do not* miss the takeout). An NPS permit is required to enter Canyonlands. (For a half-day flat-water paddle, put in at Moab and take out at Gold Bar; for a full day, take out at Potash.)

## CATARACT CANYON
Distance: 112 miles
Duration: 3–7 days
Start: Moab
End: Hite

The Class V rapids of Cataract Canyon are legendary. Twenty-six rapids churn and roil over this 14-mile stretch where the Colorado squeezes through narrow canyons. Trips down the Cat are extremely technical and dangerous; there's no room for error.

## THE SCOURGE OF THE COLORADO

As you float down the Colorado, notice the dense stands of wispy-looking trees. These are tamarisk, also called salt cedar, an ornamental tree imported to the US in the 19th century and later planted along the river for erosion control. It has since taken over the banks and is choking the waterway.

A single large tamarisk transpires 300 gallons of water *a day*. Some estimates place the species' combined water consumption as high as one-third of the river's overall flow. If that water were returned to the river, the Colorado might again reach the sea.

The good news? In Death Valley, California, land managers have almost entirely eradicated tamarisk stands, and once-threatened wetlands are rebounding. As you cross the bridge into Moab, and elsewhere along the Colorado, look for charred tree stumps and scorched riverbanks – evidence of the local eradication effort by fire (and herbicides).

Everyone in Moab – indeed, everyone who lives along the Colorado – has something to say about the scourge. If you take a river trip, broach the subject with your guide. To learn more, visit Living Rivers (p220).

The intensity of the rapids fluctuates hugely, depending on snowmelt and drought. Many fail to realize that you have to float on flat water quite a ways to reach the canyon (rafts put in at Potash or Mineral Bottom), and once through the rapids, you'll wind up on flat Lake Powell – though you'll be so high on adrenaline, you probably won't even notice. Peak flow runs mid-May to mid-June. An NPS permit is required; reserve through the NPS.

### GREEN RIVER (LABYRINTH & STILLWATER CANYONS)

Distance: 68–124 miles
Duration: 3–9 days
Start: Green River State Park
End: Mineral Bottom (68 miles) or Spanish Bottom (124 miles)

Discovered by John Wesley Powell during his famed expeditions, this flat-water stretch down the Green is ideal for canoes. You'll pass rock art along the scenic route. Take out at the Confluence or use extreme caution en route to Spanish Bottom, lest you get sucked into Cataract Canyon. An NPS permit is required south of Mineral Bottom.

## HIKING

Carry plenty of water, and wear insect repellant between spring and early summer to repel aggressive gnats.

Contact **Hike! Moab** ( ☎ 435-260-8208; www.hikemoab.com) or **Moki Treks** ( ☎ 435-259-8033, 866-352-6654; www.mokitreks.com) for guided walks with excellent interpretation.

If backpacking and overnight hikes are your speed, check into Canyonlands National Park. Otherwise consider the Canyon Rims Recreation Area (p222), where backpacking trails crisscross the Dark Canyon Primitive Area.

For a moderate-difficult rim hike above Moab, try the **Hidden Valley Trail**, which meanders through this pristine hanging valley in the Behind the Rocks Wilderness Study Area. The trailhead is on BLM land at the end of Angel Rock Rd. Plan on taking four to six hours. Following a series of switchbacks, you'll emerge on the level grassy valley for a mellow 2-mile walk. Carry 3 to 4 quarts of water. Expect shade in late afternoon.

To take in petroglyphs and two spectacular, rarely visited rock arches, hike the moderately easy **Corona Arch Trail**, whose trailhead lies 6 miles up Potash Rd (p222). Follow cairns along the slickrock to **Bowtie** and **Corona Arches**. You may recognize Corona from a well-known photograph in which an airplane is flying through it – this is one *big* arch! The 3-mile walk takes two hours.

The ever-popular, moderately easy **Negro Bill Canyon Trail** is a 2.5-mile walk along a stream whose flow fluctuates based on beaver activity. Scoot down a cool, shaded side canyon to find petroglyphs on the smooth red-rock walls, then continue to the 243ft-wide **Morning Glory Natural Bridge**, which sits at the end of a box canyon. Plan for three to four hours. The trailhead is at a BLM information kiosk 3 miles along Hwy 128, on the right.

The **Fisher Towers Trail** takes you past these towering sandstone monoliths, the tallest of which rises 900ft. The west-facing monoliths get quite hot in the afternoon, so wait for sunset, when rays bathe the rock in color and cast long shadows. (Caution: Many mesmerized hikers linger too long and end up stuck on the trail in the dark. Be sure to bring a flashlight!) The moderate-difficult, 2.2-mile (one-way) trail lies off Hwy 128, 21 miles northeast of Moab; follow signs.

If you're short on time, take the easy 1-mile round-trip hike along **Moon-flower Canyon**, a shaded stroll on mostly level ground that ends at a sandstone bowl beneath hanging gardens. A perennial stream makes this hike a cooler, less dusty alternative. The trailhead lies 1.2 miles from town along Kane Creek Blvd. Look for petroglyphs at the parking area.

To escape the summer heat, head up to the **La Sal Mountains** and hike through stands of white-barked aspens and towering ponderosa pines. You'll find numerous developed campgrounds along La Sal Mountain Loop Rd, including the one at Warner Lake. For more info, contact the Manti–La Sal National Forest Moab Ranger Station (see Information, p219).

## HORSEBACK RIDING

Rates for horseback riding generally range from $30 for a two-hour ride to $60 for a half day and $95 for a full day (including lunch). To combine riding with river-running, contact **Adrift Adventures** ( ☎ 435-259-8594, 800-874-4483; www.adrift.net; 378 N Main St), **Sheri Griffith Expeditions** ( ☎ 435-259-8229, 800-332-2439; www.griffithexp.com; 2231 S Hwy 191) or **Tag-A-Long Expeditions** ( ☎ 435-259-8946, 800-453-3292; www.tagalong.com; 452 N Main St).

**Cowboy Adventures** ( ☎ 435-259-7410; cowboyadventures@hotmail.com) leads trips year-round, including half-, full- or multiday trips in the desert or multiday trips to the La Sal Mountains; it also books combination horseback/rafting expeditions.

**Red Cliffs Adventure Lodge** ( ☎ 435-259-2002, 866-812-2002; www.redcliffslodge.com; mile marker 14, Hwy 128) guides half-day rides (March through November) around Castle Valley, in the red-rock desert north of town.

## ROCK CLIMBING & CANYONEERING

Moab offers solid rock climbing. West of town off Potash Rd, **Wall Street** (Moab's 'El Capitan') gets crowded on weekends and is an excellent spot to meet other climbers. Advanced climbers should check out the BLM-administered **Indian Creek**, off Hwy 211 on the way to Canyonlands' Needles district.

To inquire about good routes and buy gear, check with the rock-climbing specialists at **Pagan Mountaineering** ( ☎ 435-259-1117; www.paganmountaineering.com; 59 S Main St, Ste 2). Another good option is **Gear Heads** ( ☎ 435-259-4327, 888-740-4327; www.survivaltools.net; 471 S Main St; ☯ 8:30am-10pm, shorter winter hours).

Canyoneering expeditions offer chances to rappel into slickrock canyons and hike through cascading water. Arguably the best outfitter, **Desert Highlights** ( ☎ 435-259-4433, 800-747-1342; www.deserthighlights.com; 50 E Center St; guided canyoneering $80-120) leads outstanding trips (with excellent interpretation) to such spots as Arches' Fiery Furnace. For great guided rock-climbing or canyoneering trips, call **Moab Desert Adventures** ( ☎ 435-260-2404, 877-765-6622; 801 Oak St; www.moabdesertadventures.com; guided rock-climbing $110-195). Also check out **Moab Cliffs & Canyons** ( ☎ 435-259-3317, 877-641-5271; www.cliffsandcanyons.com; 63 E Center St; guided rock climbing $90-190).

## OTHER ACTIVITIES

Two companies run one-hour air tours ($99) out of Canyonlands Field: **Slickrock Air Guides** ( ☎ 435-259-6216; www.slickrockairguides.com) and **Redtail Aviation** ( ☎ 435-259-7421; www.moab-utah.com/redtail). Both also operate air shuttles for extended river trips.

Jump out of an airplane or off a cliff with help from **Skydive Moab** ( ☎ 435-259-5867; www.skydivemoab.com; Canyonlands Field; tandem dive $189-229).

Operating the only red-rock disc golf course in Utah, **Camelot Adventure Lodge** ( ☎ 435-260-1783; www.camelotlodge.com; $5 per player) features an 18-hole, par-61 course over canyons, slickrock and cactus-strewn meadows at the base of Hurrah Pass.

The **Moab Golf Club** ( ☎ 435-259-6488; 2750 S E Bench Rd; 9/18 holes $25/37) features an 18-hole, par-72 course.

The Nature Conservancy oversees the 890-acre **Matheson Wetlands Preserve** ( ☎ 435-259-4629; www.nature.org; 934 W Kane Creek Blvd; ☿ dawn-dusk), an important stopover for migrating waterfowl, raptors and shorebirds. Bring binoculars and insect repellant. Guided walks are offered at 8am on Saturdays between March and October.

### Winter Activities

Manti–La Sal National Forest receives tons of light, dry Utah powder, perfect for cross-country skiing. For current information on weather and road conditions and the avalanche risk, call ☎ 435-259-SNOW ( ☎ 435-259-7669) or visit www.avalanche.org.

The La Sals provide a hut-to-hut ski system, which you can access via snowmobile. To reserve a self-guided trip and book the huts, contact **Tag-A-Long Expeditions** ( ☎ 435-259-8946, 800-453-3292; www.tagalong.com; 452 N Main St). **Rim Cyclery** ( ☎ 435-259-5333; 94 W 100 N; www.rimcyclery.com) rents ski equipment, while **Gear Heads** ( ☎ 435-259-4327, 888-740-4327; www.survivaltools.net; 471 S Main St; ☿ 8:30am-10pm, shorter winter hours) rents snowshoes and stocks gear.

## FESTIVALS & EVENTS

Moab loves to celebrate. Event dates vary each year – check with the **Travel Council** ( ☎ 435-259-8825, 800-635-6622; www.discovermoab.com).

Kicking off the season in late March is a **half marathon**. The week before Easter, more than 2000 4WD vehicles overrun town for the **Jeep Safari** (www.rr4w.com), the year's biggest event. Spring also welcomes road cyclists to the **Skinny Tire Festival** ( ☎ 435-259-2698; www.skinnytirefestival.com).

Held in late May, the **Arts Festival** (www.discovermoab.com) keeps growing. In June look for the **Canyonlands Rodeo** ( ☎ 435-259-7089), and in July ride your mountain bike by moonlight during **Moonshadows in Moab** ( ☎ 435-259-2698; www.moonshadowsinmoab.com). The **Grand County Fair** ( ☎ 435-259-5386) arrives in late August or early September.

Motocross racers rev up in September for the **Rumble in the Redrocks Motocross** ( ☎ 435-259-7814; www.racemoab.com). Also in September, mountain bikers come for the post–Labor Day **24 Hours of Moab Mountain Bike Race** ( ☎ 435-259-5533; www.grannygear.com), while road bikers come for the **Moab Century Tour** ( ☎ 435-259-2698; www.skinnytirefestival.com). For a change of pace, attend the **Moab Music Festival** ( ☎ 435-259-7003; www.moabmusicfest.org) to hear chamber music.

October brings the **Moab Gem & Mineral Show** ( ☎ 304-259-2762; www.geocities.com/moabrockclub) and **Fat Tire Bike Festival** ( ☎ 435-260-1182, www.moabfattirefest.com). The latter is one of Utah's biggest biking events and the season's final fling, featuring tours, workshops, lessons, competitions and plenty of musical entertainment. November rings in the **Moab Folk Music Festival** ( ☎ 435-260-2488; www.moabfolkfestival.com).

## SLEEPING

Rates listed below are for double occupancy during high season (March through October). Keep in mind that some places close in winter. Prices range from the least-expensive midweek rate to the most-expensive weekend rate.

Cyclists should ask whether a property provides *secure* bike storage (ie, only one person holds the key – 'bike storage' isn't the same thing). Most lodgings provide coffeemakers, many include refrigerators and some have microwaves; ask when you book. For booking assistance, contact **Moab Central Reservations** ( ☎ 435-259-5125, 800-748-4386; www.moab.net/reservations).

### Camping

Make reservations when possible. For more information and options, visit the **Moab Information Center** (p219) or check the online links at www.moab-utah.com and www.discovermoab.com.

**Up the Creek Campground** ( ☎ 435-259-6995; www.moab-utah.com/upthecreek; 210 E 300 S; $5 per person) Perfect for backpackers, Up the Creek offers 20 tent-only, walk-in sites in a parklike setting within walking distance of downtown. Showers are included ($5 for nonguests).

**Canyonlands Campground** ( ☎ 435-259-6848, 800-522-6848; www.canyonlandsrv.com; 555 S Main St; $18-34) On the main drag, walkable from downtown, Canyonlands is open year-round and provides 140 sites (many are in shade, with RV hookups), eight air-conditioned camping cabins, showers and a swimming pool.

**Sand Flats Recreation Area** ( ☎ 435-259-2444; www.discovermoab.com/sandflats.htm; Sand Flats Rd; $8) If you want to be the first cyclist on the Slickrock Bike Trail in the morning, stay at this campground by the trailhead; it's surrounded by undulating sandstone. You'll find 110 sites with fire rings and pit toilets but no water. There are no reservations.

**Slickrock Campground** ( ☎ 435-259-7660, 800-448-8873; www.moab-utah.com/slickrock/campground.html; 1301½ N Hwy 191; site $18-22, cabin $30) At the north end of Moab, a short drive from downtown, this well-maintained campground offers more than 200 shaded sites, RV hookups and a dump station, air-conditioned camping cabins, a pool, hot tubs and groceries.

**Portal RV Park** ( ☎ 435-259-6108, 800-574-2028; www.portalrvpark.com; site $18-24, cabin $39) Also at the north end of town, Portal provides air-conditioned camping cabins and grassy sites for tents or RVs. There is little shade in summer.

**Archview Resort & Campground** ( ☎ 435-259-7854, 800-813-6622; www.moab-utah.com/archview/archview.html; Hwy 191; site $15-22, cabin $50) Near the Hwy 191/313 junction, Archview includes a pool, gas station and grocery store. Be forewarned: It's completely exposed and bakes in summer.

**Hwy 128/River Rd BLM Campgrounds** ( ☎ 435-259-2100; www.blm.gov/utah/moab; Hwy 128; $10) The best place to stay to beat the heat (other than in the La Sals) is along the Colorado River. Vegetation and the canyon walls provide shade at these 10 BLM campgrounds along a 28-mile stretch of the river. Each includes fire rings and vault toilets but not water. Only group reservations are accepted. Bring insect repellant.

**Canyon Rims Recreation Area** (☎ 435-259-2100; www.blm.gov/utah/moab; Hwy 191; $10) This oft-overlooked recreation area lies 30 miles south of town, just west of Hwy 191 – the middle of nowhere. Its two developed campgrounds feature vegetation and well-spaced sites. The 17-site **Wind Whistle Campground** lies off a paved road 8 miles west of Hwy 191, while the nine-site **Hatch Point Campground** is on the gravel road to the Anticline Overlook, 24 miles from Hwy 191. You'll find drinking water (March through October), fire rings and pit toilets. Only group reservations are accepted.

**La Sal Mountains/Manti–La Sal National Forest** (☎ 435-587-2041, 888-444-6777; www. fs.fed.us/r4/mantilasal, www.reserveusa.com; off La Sal Mtn Loop Rd; $8) When it's 100°F in Moab, the La Sals may be a balmy 75° by day and downright chilly at night. **Warner Lake** sits up high at 9400ft and is one of several developed campgrounds that provides water.

## Budget

**Center Street Hotel** (☎ 435-259-7615, 888-530-3134; linked to www.kokopellilodge.com; 96 E Center St; s/d $35/39; ✗ ✗ ) Part hostel, part hotel, Center Street has private rooms decorated in thrift-store chic, clean shared baths and a shared kitchen. It's great for long stays.

**Kokopelli Lodge** (☎ 435-259-7615, 888-530-3134; www.kokopellilodge.com; 72 S 100 E; d $56-63; ✗ ✗ ) On-site owners carefully tend this clean, old-fashioned eight-room motel. Amenities include a hot tub and secure bike storage.

**Inca Inn** (☎ 435-259-7621; www.moab-utah.com/inca/inn.html; 570 N Main St; d $55; ✗ ✗ ) The service is good and the 23 utilitarian rooms clean at this one-story mom-and-pop motel.

The cheapest beds in town are at the clean, barebones **Silver Sage Inn** (☎ 435-259-4420, 888-774-6622; www.silversageinn.com; 840 S Main St; s/d $45/48; ✗ ) and the rough-around-the-edges **Lazy Lizard Hostel** (☎ 435-259-6057; www.lazylizardhostel.com; 1213 S Hwy 19; s/d/tr/q $22/24/30/36, dormitory $9, cabins $35-47; ✗ ✗ ▯ ).

## Mid-Range

Caveat emptor: some of Moab's chain hotels and motels are substandard and should be skipped. Do yourself a favor and chose from the places listed here. They're all recommended.

### MOTELS

**Adventure Inn** (☎ 435-259-6122, 866-662-2466; www.adventureinnmoab.com; 512 N Main St; d $58-69; ✗ ✗ ) A great indie motel, the Adventure Inn has clean rooms (some with refrigerators) and decent linens, as well as laundry facilities.

**Red Stone Inn** (☎ 435-259-3500, 800-772-1972; www.redstoneinn.com; 535 S Main St; d $55-70; ✗ ▯ ) The small pine-paneled rooms here are decorated with rustic wood furniture, lending a cozy feel to their otherwise utilitarian boxiness. Pets are allowed.

**Landmark Inn** (☎ 435-259-6147, 800-441-6147; www.landmarkmoab.com; 168 N Main St; d $62-78; ✗ ✗ ▯ ) Kids love the 50ft waterslide at this two-story motel within walking distance of downtown. Rooms are spacious, scrupulously maintained and ever so slightly kitschy. Amenities include great bathtubs and a hot tub.

**Big Horn Lodge** (☎ 435-259-6171, 800-325-6171; www.moabbighorn.com; 550 S Main St; d $60-80; ✗ ▯ ) The cozy, old-fashioned knotty-pine paneling is at aesthetic odds with the modern floor-to-ceiling black glass windows at this well-maintained two-story motel on Main St, but service is great. Pets are allowed.

**Best Western Canyonlands Inn** (☎ 435-259-2300, 800-528-1234; www.canyonlandsinn.com; 16 S Main St; d $100-110; ✗ ▯ ) At the crossroads of downtown, this fine chain property offers spacious rooms. Amenities include expanded continental breakfast, a fitness room, a hot tub and laundry. Do not confuse it with the Best Western Greenwell Inn across the street.

**Holiday Inn Express** ( ☎ 435-259-1150, 800-465-4229; www.hiexpress.com/moabut; 1653 Hwy 191 N; d $89-108; ✖ ⚐ ) On the north end of Moab, this boxy prefab motel provides the most comfortable mid- to upper range rooms in town. It's ideal for business travelers and includes expanded continental breakfast and a hot tub.

**Aarchway Inn** ( ☎ 435-259-2599, 800-341-9359; www.aarchwayinn.com; 1551 Hwy 191 N; d $89-95; ✖ ✖ ⚐ ) Another boxy prefab, the Aarchway has the best pool in town. Its spacious rooms are spotless, if ho-hum; several accommodate up to six people. Amenities include kitchenettes and gas grills, a fitness room and hot tub.

If other mid- to upper range motels are full, try the **Moab Valley Inn** ( ☎ 435-259-4419; www.moabvalleyinn.com; 711 S Main St; d $80-85; ✖ ⚐ ). Also consider the standard rooms at **Bowen Motel** ( ☎ 435-259-7132, 435-874-5439; www.bowenmotel.com; 169 N Main St; d $60-80; ✖ ✖ ⚐ ). In a pinch, call **Red Rock Lodge & Suites** ( ☎ 435-259-5431, 877-207-9708; www.redrocklodge.com; 51 N 100 W; d $55-85; ✖ ✖ ).

### B&BS

**Castle Valley Inn** ( ☎ 435-259-6012; www.castlevalleyinn.com; HC64 Box 2602, Moab, UT 84532; rooms/bungalows $95-125/160-175; ✖ ✖ ) Escape the crowds by staying at this top pick off La Sal Mountain Loop Rd, 15 miles northwest of Moab. Book a room in the main house or a freestanding bungalow with full kitchen. The setting is idyllic, the reception warm and the style relaxed and casual. Wind down in the hot tub. Breakfasts include fruit picked fresh from on-site trees.

**Cali Cochita** ( ☎ 435-259-4961, 888-429-8812; www.moabdreaminn.com; 110 S 200 E; r $95-125; ✖ ✖ ) The cozy rooms at this charming brick B&B are decorated with antiques. The innkeepers live off-site, leaving you alone to enjoy the house.

**Dream Keeper Inn** ( ☎ 435-259-5998, 888-230-3247; www.dreamkeeperinn.com; 191 S 200 E; r/cottages $100-125/145) You'll feel like a guest in someone's home at this impeccably kept one-story midcentury ranch house surrounded by lush green lawns. For extra privacy book a cottage. Amenities include a hot tub.

Other B&Bs worth a look include the Southwestern-style **Adobe Abode** ( ☎ 435-259-7716; www.adobeabodemoab.com; 778 W Kane Creek Blvd; r $89-109; ✖ ✖ ) and the modern brick **Mayor's House** ( ☎ 435-259-6015, 888-791-2345; www.mayorshouse.com; 505 Rose Tree Lane; r $80-130; ✖ ✖ ).

## Top End

**Camelot Adventure Lodge** ( ☎ 435-260-1783; www.camelotlodge.com; $125-145 per person per night; ✖ ) On 50 acres by the Colorado River at the base of Hurrah Pass, the five-room Camelot is a bona fide backcountry lodge, unlike anyplace in Moab. The only way here is by 4WD vehicle or jet boat. Ride the camels, play disc golf, hike and mountain bike without driving anywhere. Leave your high heels at home. Rates include three delicious down-home meals (BYOB). This makes an unforgettable retreat for groups of athletically inclined friends. Spend at least two nights here.

**Gonzo Inn** ( ☎ 435-259-2515, 800-791-4044; www.gonzoinn.com; 100 W 200 S; d $129; ✖ ✖ ⚐ ) Smack downtown, Moab's hippest hotel features such stylized custom furnishings as brushed-metal and wood headboards, oversize concrete shower stalls and '50s-retro patio furniture. Amenities include laundry facilities and a hot tub. Pets OK.

**Sunflower Hill Bed & Breakfast** ( ☎ 435-259-2974, 800-662-2786; www.sunflowerhill.com; 185 N 300 E; r $125-175; ✖ ✖ ) The top choice for an in-town B&B, Sunflower Hill offers rooms in two inviting buildings – a cedar-sided early 20th-century home and a 100-year-old farmhouse, both surrounded by manicured gardens and towering cottonwoods. The 12 rooms range in style from dressed-down country to sophisticated elegance. Relax in the hot tub.

**Pack Creek Ranch** ( ☎ 435-259-5505; www.packcreekranch.com; PO Box 1270, Moab UT 84532; cabins $95-225; ✕ ✦ ) This hidden Shangri-la's 11 log cabins are tucked beneath mature cottonwoods and willow trees in the La Sal Mountains, 2000ft above Moab. Most of the individually owned cabins feature wood-burning fireplaces; all have kitchens and gas grills (bring groceries). Ed Abbey is among the artists and writers who have come here for inspiration. Amenities include horseback riding and an indoor hot tub and sauna.

**Red Cliffs Adventure Lodge** ( ☎ 435-259-2002, 866-812-2002; www.redcliffslodge.com; mile marker 14, Hwy 128; r $129-169; ✕ ✦ ✦ ) Part dude ranch, part luxury motel, Red Cliffs has exceptionally comfortable rooms with vaulted knotty-pine ceilings, kitchenettes with dining tables, and private patios, some overlooking the Colorado River. It's perfect for families, as some rooms sleep up to six. Also offers horseback riding and a hot tub.

**Sorrel River Ranch** ( ☎ 435-259-4642, 877-359-2715; www.sorrelriver.com; mile marker 17, Hwy 128; d/ste $209-239/269-329; ✕ ✦ ◻ ✦ ) Southeast Utah's only full-service luxury resort sits on the banks of the Colorado. Every detail is perfect, from handmade log beds (with denim dust ruffles and pillow-top mattresses) to custom-crafted lighting (on dimmers, naturally). Amenities include an on-site spa, fitness facility, salon and hot tub, kitchenettes and horseback riding. Families welcome.

# EATING

Restaurant hours fluctuate seasonally; call before you go. To review menus in advance, pick up the free *Moab Menu Guide* from the Moab Information Center (p219).

## Cafés

Unlike many places in Utah, you *can* get a good cup of coffee in Moab.

**Dave's Corner Market** ( ☎ 435-259-6999; 401 Mill Creek Dr; ✦ 6am-10pm) Get the skinny from locals along with a cup of great shade-grown espresso at this corner store–cum–café owned by the mayor. Stop on your way to or from the nearby Slickrock Bike Trail.

**Mondo Café** ( ☎ 435-259-5551; McStiff's Plaza, 59 S Main St; ✦ 6:30am-7pm) Get jacked on caffeine while you check your email, then play Hacky Sack with the dudes outside.

## Budget

**Jailhouse Café** ( ☎ 435-259-3900; 101 N Main St; dishes $5-7; ✦ 7am-noon) Moab's top breakfast spot serves fluffy omelets and delicious eggs Benedict. Expect a wait.

**Moab Diner** ( ☎ 435-259-4006; 189 S Main St; breakfast $5-7, dinner $7-15; ✦ 6am-9pm) The diner has the fastest service and best value in town, serving classic American greasy-spoon fare, including great breakfasts.

**EklectiCafé** ( ☎ 435-259-6896; 352 N Main St; dishes $5-7; ✦ 7:30am-2:30pm Mon-Fri, 7:30am-1pm Sat & Sun) Sit outside or in at this homey café with a grown-up hippie feel that serves organic coffee, homemade granola, breakfast burritos, quiche and salads. Dinner is served on summer weekends.

**Peace Tree Café** ( ☎ 435-259-8503; 20 S Main St; dishes $4-6; ✦ 8am-6pm) Sit outside and people-watch as you munch on great salads and wraps and sip on freshly squeezed juice.

**Red Rock Bakery & Internet Café** ( ☎ 435-259-5941; sandwiches $4-6; ✦ 7am-6pm) Come here for real bagels and organic coffee, check your email and order a big fat sandwich on homemade bread to take with you on the trail.

**Milt's** ( ☎ 435-259-7424; 300 S at 400 E; 🕙 6am-8pm Mon-Sat) Grab a stool at this tiny 50-year-old diner for scratch pancakes, chili cheeseburgers, fresh-cut fries and milkshakes. It's near the Slickrock Trail.

For the biggest, fattest burritos, head to **Bandito's** ( ☎ 435-259-3894; 467 N Main St; burritos $5-8; 🕙 11am-7pm).

## Mid-Range

All of the following have full bars. Some close in winter.

**Buck's Grill House** ( ☎ 435-259-5201; 1393 N Hwy 191; entrées $9-24; 🕙 5:30-9:30pm) The best in its class, Buck's serves good steaks and such contemporary down-home Southwestern specialties as duck tamales, buffalo meatloaf and elk stew. It also offers a kids' menu and good burgers. Expect big portions. Sit outside on the big patio or inside at an exposed wood table in the attractive, always bustling dining room. There are big portions, kids' menu, good burgers too.

**Eddie McStiff's** ( ☎ 435-259-2337; 59 S Main St; dishes $7-15; 🕙 5:30pm-midnight Mon-Fri, 11:30am-midnight Sat & Sun) Moab's biggest restaurant has something to please everyone, including great pizza, steaks, pastas, salads, burgers, sandwiches and consistently good bar food. McStiff's also brews 13 tasty microbrews.

**Fat City Smokehouse** ( ☎ 435-259-4302; 100 W Center St; dishes $11-18; 🕙 11am-9:30pm) In the back of Club Rio, Fat City serves big plates of Texas-style barbecue ribs and great beef tri-tip. The only drawback: Smoke from the bar wafts into the dining room.

**La Hacienda** ( ☎ 435-259-6319; 574 N Main St; dishes $6-14; 🕙 11am-10pm) For big plates of straightforward Tex-Mex, 'La Ha' is Moab's long-running favorite. Try the sour cream sauce.

**Moab Brewery** ( ☎ 435-259-6333; 686 S Main St; dishes $6-15; 🕙 11:30am-10pm) Serving frosty mugs of house microbrews and plates of everything from tri-tip to tacos and stir-fry to salads, the cavernous brewery is a good bet for families with kids and groups with diverse tastes.

**Miguel's Baja Grill** ( ☎ 435-259-6546; 51 N Main St; dishes $8-12; 🕙 5-10pm) Miguel's makes great fish tacos like you get in Baja and good margaritas too.

**Slickrock Café** ( ☎ 435-259-8004; Center & Main Sts; dishes $6-17; 🕙 8am-10pm) In a historic brick building at the crossroads of town, Slickrock serves three meals a day. Sit near the open windows and people-watch. The vaguely Southwestern menu lists everything from sandwiches to steaks.

**Red Cliffs Lodge** ( ☎ 435-259-2002; mile marker 14, Hwy 128; dinner entrées $12-24; 🕙 6:30-9:30am, 11:30am-2pm, 5-9pm) Every table in the lodge has a stunning view of red-rock buttes and the mighty Colorado. The meat-heavy Western-style dinner menu includes well-prepared prime rib and steaks, while lunch features salads and sandwiches. In nice weather watch the river roll by from the outside deck. Come before sunset.

**Sunset Grill** ( ☎ 435-259-7146; 900 N Hwy 191; dinner entrées $13-21; 🕙 5-9pm Mon-Sat) High on a hill overlooking Moab, the Sunset serves straightforward shrimp cocktail, filet mignon, scampi, chicken and pasta dishes, but the main attraction is the view.

## Top End

Make reservations for the following.

**Center Café** ( ☎ 435-259-4295; 60 N 100 W; dinner entrées $16-28, bistro dishes $6-11; 🕙 5:30pm-close) Hands down southern Utah's best restaurant, the Center Café is what you'd expect of Mendocino, not Moab. The chef-owner cooks with confident style, drawing inspiration from regional American and Mediterranean cuisines: You'll find everything from grilled prawns with white cheddar–garlic grits to pan-roasted lamb loin with balsamic-port reduction. Desserts are superb. Budget travelers, check out the bistro menu.

**Desert Bistro** ( ☎ 435-259-0756; 92 E Center St; dinner entrées $16-29; ⏰ 5:30-9:30pm) Stylized preparations of wild game are the specialty at this down-to-earth, convivial white-tablecloth restaurant, where everything is made in-house, from freshly baked bread to delicious pastries. Service is warm and attentive, and there is a great wine list.

**River Grill at Sorrel River Ranch** ( ☎ 435-259-4642; mile marker 17, Hwy 128; dinner entrées $21-30; ⏰ 7am-9:30am, 11:30am-2pm, 5-9pm) Sit on the wraparound veranda and watch the sun set over the red-rock canyons surrounding Sorrel River Ranch, Moab's only luxury resort. The New American menu changes frequently based on the availability of seasonal ingredients, but expect delicious seared steaks, succulent rack of lamb and fresh seafood flown in from the coast. Come before sunset.

## ENTERTAINMENT

The **Moab Arts & Recreation Center** ( ☎ 435-259-6272; www.moabcity.state.ut.us/marc; 111 E 100 N) holds everything from yoga classes to special events; call for schedules. Kids love the water slides at **Butch Cassidy King World Water Park** ( ☎ 435-259-2837; 1500 N Hwy 191).

Great for kids and grandparents, **Canyonlands by Night & Day** ( ☎ 435-259-2628, 800-394-9978; www.canyonlandsbynight.com; 1861 N Hwy 191, north of the river bridge; adult with/ without dinner $34/44, child with/without dinner $26/32 ⏰ nightly spring-fall) runs a two-hour guided sunset boat trip on the Colorado (including a light show on the canyon walls), with an optional barbecue dinner beforehand.

For unapologetic tourist fun, **Bar-M Chuckwagon** ( ☎ 435-259-2276, 800-214-2085; www.barmchuckwagon.com; Hwy 191, 7mi north of Moab; adult/child $23/12) starts the evening with a gunfight in the faux Western town, followed by a meaty cowboy dinner and Western music show. Reservations are suggested.

See first-run movies at **Slickrock Cinemas 3** ( ☎ 435-259-4441; 580 Kane Creek Blvd).

Moab has a number of bars – or as they're called in Utah, 'private clubs.' Hear live music Friday and Saturday nights or sing karaoke weeknights at the raucous **Club Rio** ( ☎ 435-259-6666; 100 W Center St). Frat boys shoot pool and do shots at **Zax** ( ☎ 435-259-6555; 96 S Main St). Rough-cut drinkers head to **Woody's Tavern** ( ☎ 435-259-9323; 221 S Main St). Chug-a-lug pitchers of microbrews at **Eddie McStiff's** ( ☎ 435-259-2337; 59 S Main St) or the **Moab Brewery** ( ☎ 435-259-6333; 686 S Main St); both serve good bar food.

## SHOPPING

Moab boasts *two* indie bookstores, across the street from one another. **Back of Beyond Books** ( ☎ 435-259-5154; 83 N Main St; ⏰ 9am-10pm) carries a comprehensive selection of regional guides, histories, political nonfiction and magazines. **Arches Book Company** ( ☎ 435-259-0782; 78 N Main St; ⏰ 7:30am-9pm), a general bookstore with good fiction, also carries the *New York Times* and serves locally roasted coffee.

For camping gear, the best place is **Gear Heads** ( ☎ 435-259-4327, 888-740-4327; 471 S Main St; ⏰ 8:30am-10pm, shorter winter hours).

Of the many Native American craft shops and galleries, the two best are **The Hogan Trading Company** ( ☎ 435-259-8118; 100 S Main St; ⏰ 9am-10pm, shorter winter hours) and **Lema's Kokopelli Gallery** ( ☎ 435-259-5055; 70 N Main St; ⏰ 9am-10pm, shorter winter hours).

The **Moab Rock Shop** ( ☎ 435-259-7312; 600 N Main St) is a rock hound's paradise.

For no-frills wine tasting, visit the surprisingly good **Spanish Valley Winery** ( ☎ 435-259-8134; www.moab-utah.com/spanishvalleywinery; call for directions; ⏰ noon-7pm Mon-Sat, shorter winter hours). Also worth a look is the **Castle Creek Winer y** at Red Cliffs Lodge (opposite).

## GROCERIES & SUPPLIES

Moab's main grocery store is **City Market & Pharmacy** (☎ 435-259-5181; 425 S Main St; ☯ 6am-midnight, shorter winter hours). For health food, visit the nonprofit **Moonflower Market** (☎ 435-259-5712; 39 E 100 N; ☯ 9am-8pm Mon-Sat, 10am-3pm Sun). Swanny City Park hosts a **farmers' market** (400 N 100 W; ☯ 8am-11:30am Sat May-Oct).

## INTERNET ACCESS

Log on at **Red Rock Bakery** (p237), **Slickrock Café** (p238), **Mondo Café** (p237) or the **library** (p219).

## LAUNDRY

**Moab Speed Cleaners** (☎ 435-259-7456; 702 S Main St; ☯ 8am-7pm) has limited hours but provides on-site staff and the cleanest facility.

## MEDICAL SERVICES & EMERGENCIES

In an emergency dial ☎ 911 or contact the **Moab Police** (☎ 435-259-8938; 115 W 200 S). For emergency medical care, head to **Allen Memorial Hospital Emergency Room** (☎ 435-259-7191; 719 W 400 N). For nonemergency care, stop by **Moab Immediate Care & X-Ray** (☎ 259-5276; 267 N Main St; ☯ noon-8pm).

Cell phones work in Moab but not in river canyons. When rafting, a satellite phone is essential. For search and rescue, contact the **Grand County Emergency Coordinator** (☎ 435-259-8115).

## POSTAL SERVICE

Moab offers a full-service **post office** (☎ 435-259-7427; 50 E 100 N; ☯ 8am-5pm Mon-Fri, 9am-1pm Sat)

## SHOWERS

Head to **Archview Campground** (p234), **Canyonlands Campground** (p234), **Lazy Lizard Hostel** (p235) or **Poison Spider Bike Shop** (p226).

## TRASH & RECYCLING

Take bottles to the **County Recycling Service** (☎ 435-259-8640; 1000 E Sand Flats Rd; ☯ 8am-4pm Mon-Sat)

## WATER

If you're northbound, take Hwy 191 north to Hwy 128 east and continue 100 yards to **Matrimony Springs**, on the right; southbound drivers should stop at the **Phillips 66 Station** (Main St & 300 S), which provides a spigot on the island out front.

*The history of southern Utah is almost literally written in stone, and it lies jumbled on the desert's skin like a pile of dried bones.*

# HISTORY

From the uplifted, eroded sandstone of the Colorado Plateau to the petrified skeletons of dinosaurs; to the carved etchings of ancestral inhabitants; to the 'stone spectacles' of Mormon prophet Joseph Smith; to the modern-day scars left by mining, grazing and an army of wheels and feet: the desert's story remains sun-baked and exposed under a domed blue sky for anyone to read.

## FIRST PEOPLES

It's not known when humans first arrived in the Southwest. Most likely, nomadic peoples migrated from Asia across a land bridge between Siberia and Alaska, making their way south between 23,000 and 10,000 years ago. We know they arrived by at least 10,000 BC, as archaeologists have dated spearheads found among the remains of woolly mammoths and other Ice Age mammals.

However, Native American creation stories say that the people have always been here, or that they descended from the spirit world. Mormons tell their own unique story (p245).

However they arrived, these early groups were primarily hunters, and apparently very good ones. By 8500 BC, most large prehistoric mammals were extinct – some possibly hunted to that fate, though many were unable to adapt to the drying glacial climate. Southwest inhabitants pursued progressively smaller prey and developed plant-gathering skills. This led to what scholars call the Archaic period, which lasted roughly from 5500 BC to AD 100.

The term 'Archaic' refers as much to the period's hunter–gatherer lifestyle as it does to a block of time. As a survival method, hunting and gathering proved remarkably adaptive and resilient in the Southwest. People lived nomadically in small, unconcentrated groups, following the food supply of seasonal wild plants and such small animals as rabbits. Shelters were temporary, and caves were often used. The people became skilled at basketry, probably the most functional craft for groups on the move.

Eventually, people established semiregular settlement patterns and started to cultivate crops such as primitive corn, beans and squash. By AD 100 several distinct cultures had emerged. Ancestral Puebloans dominated the Colorado Plateau, which encompasses southern Utah, southwest Colorado

# TIMELINE

**60 million years ago** Colorado Plateau uplifts, creating Grand Staircase; rivers pick up speed.

**23,000 BC– 10,000 BC** Nomadic peoples migrate from Asia over Bering Strait land bridge to North America.

**5500 BC–AD 100** Archaic cultures occupy southwest Utah.

**200 BC–AD 1200** Ancestral Puebloans develop vibrant culture and towns on Colorado Plateau.

**1100** Southern Paiutes migrate to region and flourish for 700 years.

**1776** The Domínguez-Escalante expedition traverses the Colorado Plateau, encountering Kaibab Paiutes.

**1847** Brigham Young declares Salt Lake City 'the right place' for Mormon settlement.

**1848** Mexico cedes possession of the region to the US.

**1850** The US establishes the official Territory of Utah.

**1869** John Wesley Powell rafts the Colorado River and begins geologic survey of southern Utah.

**1896** Utah is declared the 45th state.

**1919** Zion National Park is created.

**1928** Bryce Canyon National Park is created.

**1930** Completion of Zion–Mt Carmel Hwy opens southwest Utah to increased tourism.

**1964** Canyonlands National Park is created.

**1971** Arches and Capitol Reef National Parks are created.

**1996** Grand Staircase–Escalante National Monument is created.

**2000** Zion National Park institutes a mandatory shuttle system to relieve car congestion.

and northern portions of Arizona and New Mexico. Ancestral Puebloans were originally called the Anasazi – Navajo for 'ancient enemy' – though this is no longer the preferred term.

The Ancestral Puebloans dominated the region from around 200 BC to AD 1500, though in southern Utah they vanished earlier, around 1200. There's no consensus over why they abandoned the region when they did. It was likely a combination of drought, soil erosion, disease and competition from new groups. But like the cultural distinctions between these original peoples, the edges and extent of influence remain unclear.

The Ancestral Puebloans adopted irrigated agriculture, became highly accomplished basket makers and potters and believed in an involved cosmology. They are best known for their cliff dwellings, pueblo villages and ceremonial underground chambers known as kivas. While southern Utah contains far fewer of these ancient structures than surrounding states, it does boast abundant Ancestral Puebloan rock art.

Another people that lived in southern Utah concurrently with Ancestral

Puebloans were the Fremont, who migrated from the north and continued a seminomadic existence, preferring hunting and gathering to farming and villages. The Fremont disappeared from the region at about the same time as Ancestral Puebloans. Their rock art is also widespread.

## SOUTHERN PAIUTES & SPANIARDS

As Ancestral Puebloans departed, Southern Paiutes moved in, beginning around 1100. Comprising a dozen or so distinct bands, Paiute territory extended from California's deserts east to Colorado, and from Utah's Great Basin south to Arizona's Painted Desert. Kaibab Paiutes lived near what is now Zion National Park, and their modern-day reservation surrounds Pipe Spring National Monument on the Arizona Strip.

In general, Southern Paiutes followed the same survival strategy as Archaic peoples – wandering with the seasons, hunting small animals, gathering wild plants and tending a few modest crops. A staple of their diet was the piñon, or pine nut, and they continued the tradition of fine basketry. By contrast, their shelters and even their clothes weren't made to last more than a season.

They lived largely in peace for more than half a millennium. No one coveted the unyielding land they called home, and yet, according to the Paiutes, they found abundance in it. Deer were plentiful, the winters around present-

## WRITTEN ON THE LAND

Anywhere in southern Utah you may encounter it: the crude outlines of human figures and animals, painted handprints, squiggled lines etched into desert varnish. Rock art is mysterious and awesome and always leaves us wondering: Who did this, and why? What were they trying to say?

Dating from at least 4000 BC to as late as the 19th century AD, rock art in southern Utah has been attributed to every known ancestral and modern people. In fact, one way archaeologists track the spread of ancestral cultures is by studying their distinctive rock art styles, which tend to be either abstract or representational and anthropomorphic. Representational rock art is almost always more recent, while abstract designs appear in all ages.

Petroglyphs of bighorn sheep in southwest Utah.

COURTESY OF ZION NATIONAL PARK CAT#160

We can only speculate about why rock art was created and what it means. This symbolic writing becomes obscure the moment the cultural context for the symbols is lost. Much of the art was likely the work of shamans or elders communicating with the divine. Some of the earliest, abstract designs may have been created in trance states. Certain figures and motifs seem to reflect a heavenly pantheon, while other rock art may tell stories – real or mythical – of successful hunts or battles.

More prosaic explanations also exist. Some rock art may have marked tribal territory, and some may have been nothing more than idle doodling. Even Ancestral Puebloans must have gotten bored waiting for the rain to pass.

day St George were mild, and in summer they fished mountain lakes. The ever-growing number of Europeans on the continent didn't know of them, and gold-hungry 16th-century Spanish explorers like Coronado never reached their territory.

Then, in 1776, the same year the US declared its independence from Britain, the Domínguez-Escalante expedition encountered Kaibab Paiutes while skirting the western edge of the Colorado Plateau. In the first recorded European impressions of them, Father Escalante described 'a large number of people, all of pleasing appearance, very friendly and extremely timid.'

The Spanish expedition had two goals: to open a communication route to California and to spread Christianity among the Indians. But the Spanish never made it farther west, nor did Spain fund the establishment of any Utah missions. Afterward, the Southern Paiutes were left mostly, but not entirely, alone. The Spanish Trail had been cut, and occasional trappers wandered through, as did strange diseases and even Ute and New Mexican slave traders, who stole Paiute children to sell for horses and goods elsewhere.

Rangers reconstruct remains of an Ancestral Puebloan granary.

By the early 19th century the Paiutes could weather the passing wagon trains, which trampled grasses and crops, but smallpox and measles were decimating them. By mid-century, some Paiute tribes, like the Kaibab, had dwindled by two-thirds before they'd ever had to fight or strike a deal with a pioneer.

## ARRIVAL OF THE MORMONS

In 1847, Brigham Young and party arrived atop Utah's Great Salt Lake valley. Seeking to escape Illinois due to persecution for their beliefs, the Mormons were charged by their prophet Joseph Smith to find a new Zion out west, where they could build a heavenly city on earth, what they called the State of Deseret. They were looking, in other words, for what Southern Paiutes had long enjoyed – the solitude and freedom from interference this harsh land provided. As the story goes, a Young sat upright out of his sickbed long enough to say, 'This is the right place.'

The Mormons were not your average pioneers, and Young was not an average leader. The plan was to build an independent nation, a theocracy outside the boundaries of the US. Within a year, however, the rapidly expanding

Brigham Young (center, seated, in white hat) and party enroute to 'Dixie' aka St George, ca 1870.

## REVELATION

At age 18, Joseph Smith received his first heavenly visit, when the angel Moroni revealed to him the location of golden tablets buried in the woods near his home in New York. The angel returned three more times, once a year. After the fourth visit, Smith was allowed to take the golden tablets home and, using 'stone spectacles' provided by the angel, read and transcribe the indecipherable word of God.

Three years later, in 1830, these revelations were published as the *Book of Mormon*, and the Church of Jesus Christ of Latter-Day Saints was established, with Smith as its president.

Smith's revelation is an epic story concerning the arrival in the Americas some 4000 years ago of one of Israel's lost tribes and of Jesus Christ's further teachings to believers here. In the end, the story comes down to a battle between two brothers – the virtuous Nephi and the sinful Laman – with the Lamanites ultimately prevailing.

Dark-skinned, barbaric and turned from God, the Lamanites were, Mormons believe, the ancestors of modern-day Native Americans. Bringing the Lamanites back into the light of God was a task the first Mormons hoped to complete before the expected, imminent gathering up of saints.

There's much more to the story and to the Mormon faith – which is one of the world's fastest-growing religions, with more than 11 million members. If you're curious, open the *Book of Mormon*. There's one in every hotel room in Utah.

country caught up with them. The 1848 Treaty of Guadalupe Hidalgo turned the Mexican territory into a US one, and the concurrent discovery of gold in California attracted streams of passing miners, and with them, Manifest Destiny.

In 1850 the Territory of Utah was established, with Young as territorial governor. If Young despaired over the political fate of his beloved Deseret, he didn't let on. Instead, he aspired to settle an empire larger than Texas as fast as he could. He sent Mormon pioneers in all directions to plow, irrigate and farm the desert into submission, which they did. The Mormons succeeded, because they were zealously dedicated to their faith, tempered by their journey to Utah along the Mormon Trail, and organized. They attacked the land as a cohesive group, fired by visions of God, not gold.

Everywhere they went in southern Utah, Mormons displaced Paiutes, appropriating water sources and the best land. They also 'adopted' the Paiutes and gave them the only practical support they would receive, which they came to depend on. The *Book of Mormon* claims that American Indians are one of Israel's lost tribes, so bringing them back into the fold was, and continues to be, a particularly important Mormon mission. If the end result for the 'timid' Paiutes turned out to be the same as for native tribes elsewhere, it was reached by a largely more respectful road.

## A MASSACRE, A WAR & STATEHOOD

With their modern-day prophets, polygamous practices and theocratic territorial government, Mormons were perceived as a threat by federal authorities and everyday citizens, whom the Mormons called Gentiles. In the 1850s tensions ran high, and minor clashes were common. Then, in 1857, it all came to a head.

In the mountains outside St George, building religious hysteria and fear of a federal invasion led the Mormons – with the help of local Paiutes – to slaughter 120 innocent California-bound pioneers. Details of the Mountain Meadows Massacre are still debated today, but the incident confirmed the government's worst fears, prompting the US Army to surround and subdue Salt Lake City that same year.

No one was killed and hardly a shot fired in the so-called Mormon War, which had two main repercussions: It instituted a secular government in Utah, beneath which the religious hierarchy continued to operate for a decade or more, and it curtailed territorial ambitions, reducing the size of Utah.

Through the Civil War and beyond, the territory petitioned for statehood, but it was continually denied, even as states around it were accepted. Animosity between Mormons and the federal government lingered. For moral reasons, and perhaps because they had nothing else on which to hang their denials, Washington made polygamy the sticking point. Finally, in 1890 the Mormon Church officially repudiated polygamy and asked its followers to do the same. Six years later Utah won statehood.

## JACOB HAMBLIN & JOHN WESLEY POWELL

No history of southern Utah would be complete without mentioning the exploits of two extraordinary explorers: Jacob Hamblin and John Wesley Powell. The first was a Mormon pioneer and the latter a US government employee, but they transcended their job descriptions as few ever do.

GRAND CANYON NATIONAL PARK

Tau-Gu, chief of the Paiute, overlooking the Virgin River with JW Powell, ca 1873.

In their efforts to be self-sufficient, the Mormons established several missions in southern Utah in the 1850s: The Iron Mission, centered around Cedar City, mined ore and smelted iron for construction, while the Cotton Mission, centered around St George, grew cotton for Mormon use and export. Neither mission was ultimately successful. However, the Mormons also sent missionaries south to convert the Southern Paiutes, and its phenomenal success was largely due to Jacob Hamblin, who arrived in 1854.

Dubbed the 'Mormon Leatherstocking,' Hamblin gained the respect and trust of native tribes across the Southwest. He deeply believed that if he always told the truth, listened and never shed Indian blood, he would be safe. Hamblin became a peacemaker who negotiated important treaties and, with native assistance, explored southern Utah as no white man had before him.

One-armed John Wesley Powell is most famous for being the first to descend the length of the Colorado River through the Grand Canyon in 1869. His goal was not adventure, however, but to survey and explore the land and peoples of southern Utah for science. Thanks to his passion and rigor, Powell and his survey teams' geologic and ethnological work largely form the basis of what we know about southern Utah today.

In 1870, Hamblin was instrumental in securing Powell a welcome among

Southern Paiutes. As Hamblin had done, Powell demonstrated fundamental human respect and so earned the Paiutes' assistance.

Powell was also something of a prophet, as his assessment of the right and wrong ways to settle the desert have proven accurate. At the time, the US shook with visions of transforming the Southwest into a garden of Eden. The persistence of this delusion, even in its diluted modern form, may well prove to be a damaging self-inflicted wound for the nation.

## EXPLOITATION & CONSERVATION

The amount of arable land in Utah is less than 5%, and in the south that figure is less than 1%. What farmland there is and towns there are depend entirely on rivers. The rain that falls in the desert is hardly enough to work up a good spit.

Twentieth-century development in the Southwest has been slow to recognize and adapt to this fact. The specifics are too complex for this chapter, but

### THE REDROCK WILDERNESS ACT: A CITIZENS' PROPOSAL

Any attempt to conserve land in the Southwest stirs intense passions, and the Redrock Wilderness Act is a doozy. If passed, it would set aside 9.1 million acres of nearly pristine southern Utah desert as Congressionally designated wilderness areas, the most restrictive type of public lands. These prohibit motorized vehicles, resource extraction, road building and infrastructure development. Indeed, people are only permitted to enter such areas on foot.

Nearly 80% of Utah's land already lies in public hands, 65% of which is owned by the federal government. The Redrock Wilderness Act would change the status of about 15% of these existing federal lands. Opponents of the act frequently say that Utah has already done enough. Putting even more land off-limits to resource extraction and road building is unfair. Why not, they say, focus conservation efforts on Montana or South Dakota – they have plenty of land, right?

Land, yes. Wilderness, no. And there's the rub.

Precious little land in North America remains pristine enough to qualify as wilderness. Southern Utah – the last US region to be settled and mapped – has more than most. Much of Utah is already federally protected to some degree, but proponents say this amount and these protections aren't enough.

In 1985 the BLM itself identified 3.2 million acres for further possible wilderness designation in southern Utah, but a citizens' group did their own inventory and suggested that 5.9 million acres could be added to that total. In 1989 they formalized their plan as a Congressional bill dubbed 'The Citizens' Proposal' – which was eventually renamed America's Redrock Wilderness Act. The bill has since been reintroduced into every new session of Congress, before whom it sits today.

Among those who support the bill are 161 Congresspersons and 15 Senators, perhaps a half to three-quarters of Utah residents, and virtually every known conservation and environmental group. If it passes, it would add nearly 10% to the current 95.3 million acres of official wilderness in the US (two-thirds of which lie in Alaska).

To learn more, contact the **Southern Utah Wilderness Alliance** (SUWA; ☎ 801-486-3161; www.suwa.org).

suffice it to say that projects have repeatedly failed, often spectacularly and expensively, and yet the attempts continue. Politicians have dammed countless rivers across the Southwest to control and divert their flow and create power; the Colorado River has been dammed twice: by Hoover Dam in 1936 and Glen Canyon Dam in 1964, among the world's largest.

And still no Eden.

Mining has experienced various heydays – from the great 19th-century silver mines to coal, oil and even uranium mining around Moab in the 1950s. This extraction has exacted a high toll on the slow-healing desert.

Today, desert cities are well established, and politics demands they be supported, even as the economic and environmental costs keep growing exponentially.

At the same time, Americans have long recognized the rare beauty of these lands and made efforts to preserve them. In fact, the first paintings of such Western landmarks as the Grand Canyon and Zion Canyon, by Albert Bierstadt and Thomas Moran, were instrumental in sparking the 19th-century US conservation movement.

Originally protected as a national monument, Zion became a national park in 1919, the same year as the Grand Canyon. Since then, national parks and monuments have accumulated steadily in southern Utah, culminating in the establishment of Grand Staircase–Escalante National Monument in 1996. Given the region's ever-increasing tourism, it's not likely to be the last.

# ZION NATIONAL PARK

Ancient peoples undoubtedly knew and entered Zion Canyon, for they left written evidence, but to Kaibab Paiutes it was a place to be avoided, particularly after sunset. Mysterious and foreboding, the canyon was for them inhabited by trickster gods who were capricious and even willfully malicious.

COURTESY OF ZION NATIONAL PARK CAT2393.8

Tunnel worker during construction of Zion–Mt Carmel Tunnel 1928-30.

In 1776 the Domínguez-Escalante expedition passed nearby but did not enter Zion, and the same held true for famed mountain man Jedediah Smith in the 1820s. The first white person to enter the canyon was Nephi Johnson, a Mormon pioneer who ventured south with Jacob Hamblin in 1854 on the mission to convert Indians. In 1858, at the behest of Brigham Young, Johnson explored the upper reaches of the Virgin River, looking for good places to settle. One can only imagine what he must have felt as he entered the canyon alone, his Paiute guide waiting safely behind.

Mormons did not settle in the canyon till 1863, when Isaac Behunin built the first cabin. Behunin is credited with bestowing the name Zion, though when Brigham Young first visited in 1870, he disagreed with the assessment. Whether due to the arduous journey or the forbidden tobacco Behunin was growing, Young proclaimed it 'Not Zion,' a name that stuck among Mormons for some years.

John Wesley Powell explored Zion in 1872, but it was Clarence Dutton, a poet–geologist in Powell's employ, who captured its grandeur. Upon seeing the canyon, he wrote: 'In coming time it will, I believe, take rank with a very small number of spectacles, each of which will, in its own way, be regarded as the most exquisite of its kind which the world discloses.'

In a 1908 official report, a government surveyor first suggested preserving the canyon as a monument, and a year later President Taft signed the proclamation creating Mukuntuweap National Monument. In 1919 the name and designation were changed, and Zion National Park was born.

Original Zion lodge, ca 1929, which was destroyed by fire in 1966.

Within a year, park visitation doubled to about 3690 people – hardly crowded, but still a lot considering road conditions and its remote location. To facilitate regional tourism, a railroad spur was extended to Cedar City in 1923, and in 1930 the Zion–Mt Carmel Hwy and its tunnel were completed, offering a paved route into and through Zion. In 1930, 55,000 people are said to have seen this natural wonder, and they've been coming ever since.

# BRYCE CANYON NATIONAL PARK

Bryce Canyon nestles alongside the Paunsaugunt Plateau, a name that is derived from a Paiute Indian term meaning 'home of the beavers.' Fur trappers who roamed the area between 1800 and 1850 made no mention, however, of Bryce's striking scenery. Neither did Spanish traders who traversed southern Utah in the 19th century. During his 1869 survey, John Wesley Powell stuck to the rivers and passed right by. Captain Sutton, a member of the survey, described the distant terrain as seeming 'traversable only by a creature with wings.'

Mormons pioneers struck south in the 1850s, initially settling along the Mormon Corridor (present-day I-15), though they searched the entire Paunsaugunt Plateau for arable land. They found some atop the plateau and along the canyon floor, and in the mid-1870s a small group settled in the adjacent valleys, which seemed well suited for grazing livestock.

Ebenezer Bryce's log cabin, ca 1929.

Among the latter was Ebenezer Bryce, who moved south with his ailing wife, Mary, hoping the climate would restore her health. The Bryces stayed in the area for five years. When Mary's condition did not improve, the couple moved to southeastern Arizona in 1880. But he left behind his name and the now famous epithet, 'It's a hell of a place to lose a cow.'

Like Zion Canyon, Bryce was popular among tourists and conservationists at the turn of the 20th century, though it was even more difficult to reach. It wasn't until 1915, when JW Humphrey became founding supervisor of Utah's Sevier National Forest, that Bryce's fate would be sealed.

Seeing the spectacular canyon, Humphrey sought to establish Bryce among the region's primary tourist attractions. In 1916 he brought in photographers to take the first pictures of the canyon for a promotional article that appeared in a Union Pacific Railroad publication. Word was out. With a small appropriation, Humphrey built a road up the plateau in 1916, opening the way for tourists to stop at the park on their way to the Grand Canyon.

In 1919, the same year Zion became a national park, the Utah State Legislature recommended that Bryce also be protected. Four years later President Harding established Bryce Canyon National Monument, and in 1928 Bryce became Utah's second national park.

# SOUTHERN UTAH'S OTHER PARKLANDS

### ARCHES NATIONAL PARK
The first reliable account of a European visiting Arches dates to June 9, 1844, when Denis Julien carved his name and the date into a rock. However, it wasn't until the 1880s and 1890s that Mormons permanently settled in nearby Moab (Ute Indians had violently thwarted a previous effort in the 1850s).

In the early 20th century, several settlers, including the editor of the first newspaper, touted the region's geologic wonders, attracting the attention of the Rio Grande Western Railroad. Recognizing the potential of Arches as a tourist destination, the railroad lobbied the government for federal protection. In 1929 President Hoover established the national monument, and in 1971 Congress declared it a national park.

### CAPITOL REEF NATIONAL PARK
Capitol Reef's European-American cultural history dates back to 1872, when Mormon settlers first planted fruit trees along the banks of the Fremont River near the town of Junction. Once their trees flourished, the settlers renamed the town Fruita.

In the following decades, Torrey resident Ephraim Porter Pectal sought to promote interest in 'Wayne Wonderland,' a nickname given to the Waterpocket Fold, which lies in Wayne County. Soon after being elected to the state legislature in 1933, Pectal lobbied President Roosevelt to establish Wayne Wonderland National Monument. In 1937 Roosevelt signed a proclamation creating the mercifully renamed Capitol Reef National Monument, and in 1971 President Nixon established it as a national park.

### CANYONLANDS NATIONAL PARK
Following settlement of Moab in the 1880s, ranchers used much of the land in what is now Canyonlands as winter pasture for grazing herds, a practice that continued through 1975. In the 1950s the federal government subsidized uranium exploration, spurring mining operations in southern Utah. Though these efforts unearthed little of the radioactive element, mining roads opened this once remote landscape to tourism.

In the early 1960s, the superintendent of Arches National Monument lobbied for further protection, calling for establishment of 'Grand View National Park.' His concept was modified to include surrounding lands, and in 1964 President Johnson established Canyonlands National Park, which originally protected 257,640 acres. In 1971 Congress expanded the park to its present size of 337,598 acres.

## GRAND STAIRCASE–ESCALANTE NATIONAL MONUMENT

Grand Staircase–Escalante National Monument (GSENM) is southern Utah's most controversial set-aside, established by President Clinton in 1996 under the federal Antiquities Act. Many of Utah's Republican majority believed the president was 'appeasing his Sierra Club constituents' by establishing a monument in a state that had not supported him in either election. (Utah remains the only state never to have carried a Democratic president.) Counties in southern Utah sued the federal government, claiming the executive branch lacked jurisdiction to declare a national monument. In 2004 a federal court ruled that the president had acted within his bounds. Today, the monument is named in the Redrock Wilderness Act, which if passed would further restrict land use in the region.

COURTESY OF ZION NATIONAL PARK CAT:2366

*As home to one of the world's densest concentrations of spectacularly exposed rock formations, this region is a prime destination for travelers and geologists alike.*

# GEOLOGY

In every direction lies dramatic evidence of soft, colorful rocks carved by the awesome power of water.

## PLATEAU COUNTRY

Spanning portions of Utah, Colorado, New Mexico and Arizona, the Colorado Plateau is a geologic anomaly. Surrounded by land that has been tortuously buckled and jumbled over millions of years by the extreme forces of the shifting earth, the plateau floats like a raft on an idyllic cruise. Evidence of its long-term stability is readily apparent in the horizontal layers of sediment that have changed little from the day they were laid down.

The contrasting ruin of the surrounding region is apparent to the west, where thinning and stretching of the Earth's crust has proceeded with such vigor that mountain ranges have collapsed onto their sides and entire valleys have fallen thousands of feet. To the east, forces of collision have crumpled the land to form the mighty Rocky Mountains.

Starting out as a shallow basin collecting sediment from nearby mountains, the entire Colorado Plateau was uplifted some 60 million years ago. This uplift was not a particularly traumatic event – about the only exciting thing that happened was that the plateau split along deep cracks called faults. Over time these cracks have eroded to form stupendous cliffs that subdivide the Colorado Plateau into many smaller plateaus – Kaibab, Markagunt and Paunsaugunt, to name a few.

Along the western edge of the Colorado Plateau looms a line of high, forested plateaus that tower 3000ft above desert lowlands and valleys. Named the **High Plateaus** in 1880 by geologist Clarence Dutton, the term today refers to the flat-topped mesas that characterize Zion and Bryce Canyon National Parks and Cedar Breaks National Monument. Each of the High Plateaus is distinctly bounded by major faults that result in valleys and sheer cliffs.

From an aerial perspective, these plateaus and cliffs form a remarkable staircase that steps down from southern Utah into northern Arizona. Topping the **Grand Staircase** like festive icing are the **Pink Cliffs** of the Claron Formation so extravagantly exposed in Bryce. Below them jut the **Gray Cliffs** of various Cretaceous formations. Next in line are the magnificent **White Cliffs** of Navajo Sandstone that make Zion justly famous. These are followed by the **Vermilion Cliffs** near Lees Ferry, Arizona, and finally the **Chocolate Cliffs**. One of the best views of the Grand Staircase lies along Hwy 89A between Kanab, Utah, and Jacob Lake, Arizona, where the steps rise majestically into the northern highlands.

Another way of understanding the Grand Staircase is to visualize that the top layers of exposed rock at the Grand Canyon form Zion's basement, and that Zion's top layers in turn form the bottom layers of Bryce Canyon National Park. In other words, the parks could be stacked on top of each other. Hypothetically, a river cutting a canyon at Bryce would eventually form another Zion Canyon, and over time create another Grand Canyon.

This is the tableau that characterizes the national parks of the Southwest, from Arches in the northeast corner of the Colorado Plateau to Zion in the southwest corner. In a sense it's a remarkably homogenous region, but at the same time, the forces of erosion have carved an amazingly intricate and diverse landscape that's difficult to comprehend. Each park and national monument reveals an astonishing geologic story that goes far beyond the

## A ROCK PRIMER

Rocks are divided into three large classes – sedimentary, igneous and metamorphic – though only sedimentary rocks are well represented on the Colorado Plateau.

**Sedimentary** rocks originate as vast accumulations of sediments and particles that cement together over time. Transported by streams or by wind, the sediments typically settle in horizontal layers that preserve many features that reveal how they were deposited. Geologists further subdivide sedimentary rocks into three common types. *Mudstone* (or shale) is comprised of tiny flaky particles that settle horizontally and are cemented together with calcium carbonate. These flat particles stack so close together that there's little room for cement, so mudstone is consequently very soft and breakable. *Sandstone* consists of sand particles that stack poorly and leave lots of room for cement, resulting in a very hard, durable rock. *Limestone* lies at the opposite end of the spectrum from mudstone, as it consists of little more than calcium carbonate, a strong cement that erodes easily when wet.

**Igneous** rocks are relative newcomers to the Colorado Plateau, arising from molten magma that has either cooled underground or erupted to the surface as lava or volcanic ash. The Henry Mountains are an example of magma that blistered up under a thin layer of sedimentary rock, then hardened like an old pimple to form what's called a laccolith. While lava flows and other volcanic activity can be found at various sites around the plateau, they're more of an anomaly in this land of carefully layered sediments.

**Metamorphic** rocks are those that start out as either sedimentary or igneous rocks and then transform under intense heat or pressure into other rock types. Such events haven't occurred in the stable layers of the Colorado Plateau, so these rocks are absent from the region. However, metamorphic rocks are exposed along the floor of the Grand Canyon, suggesting that these rocks form a basement layer beneath the entire plateau. One day far in the future, when rivers carve deep enough, metamorphic layers will likely be exposed here as well.

scope of this brief introduction. Interested visitors are encouraged to take advantage of the books and literature available at each visitor center to help fill in the gaps. Offering a basic introduction is *Pages of Stone*, by Halka and Lucy Chronic, while a more technical and colorful overview is provided in *Geology of Utah's Parks & Monuments*, edited by Douglas Sprinkel and a team of specialists.

## A FOUR-ACT PLAY

Perhaps the simplest way to approach the geologic story of the Colorado Plateau is to think of it as a four-act play. The first act would feature sedimentation, followed by lithification, then uplift, and finally erosion. While this is an oversimplification, and there's overlap between the scenes, it offers a framework for understanding the region's geologic history.

More than 250 million years ago, the Plateau Country was a shallow sea off the west coast of the young North American continent (which at the time was merged with other continents into a giant supercontinent known as Pangea). This time period, known as the **Paleozoic Era**, marked the dramatic transition from primitive organisms to an explosion of complex life forms that spread into every available niche – the beginning of life as we know it. Fossils, limestone and other sediments from this era now comprise nearly all exposed rocks in the Grand Canyon, and they form the foundation that underlies all of the Colorado Plateau.

At the close of the Paleozoic, the land rose somewhat and the sea mostly drained away, though it advanced and retreated numerous times during the **Mesozoic Era** (250 million to 65 million years ago). **Sedimentation** continued as

## THE GRAND STAIRCASE

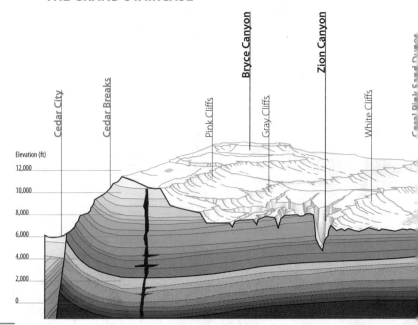

eroding mountains created deltas and floodplains, and as shallow seas and tidal flats left other deposits. Meanwhile, the rise of an island mountain chain off the coast apparently blocked moisture-bearing storms, and a vast Sahara-like desert developed across the region, piling thousands of feet of sand atop older floodplain sediments.

Nearly all of the plateau's exposed layers derive from this ceaseless shifting of sediments during the Mesozoic. Today, both hard and soft layers interweave in dozens of colorful bands with equally colorful names, each layer providing evidence of a period of wind, mud, sand or water. For example, the rusty Chocolate Cliffs of the Moenkopi Formation, as seen along Hwy 24 at Capitol Reef's west entrance, signal a time when tides ebbed over coastal lowlands, leaving behind ripple marks and mud cracks. Zion's monolithic White Cliffs of Navajo Sandstone and Arches' soaring spans of Entrada Sandstone preserve evidence of mighty sand dunes.

Over millions of years the weight of the accumulated layers (roughly 3 miles thick) compacted loosely settled materials into rocks cemented together with mineral deposits – a process called **lithification**. Sandstone, siltstone and mudstone are each cemented together with calcium carbonate. Variations in particle size and quantities of cement account for these layers' differing strengths – weakly bonded rocks crumble easily in water, while more durable rocks form sheer cliffs and angular blocks.

About 60 million years ago North America began a dramatic separation from Europe, sliding west over another part of the earth's crust and leaving behind an ever-widening gulf in the Atlantic Ocean. This movement caused the continent's leading edge to **uplift**, forever transforming the face of the

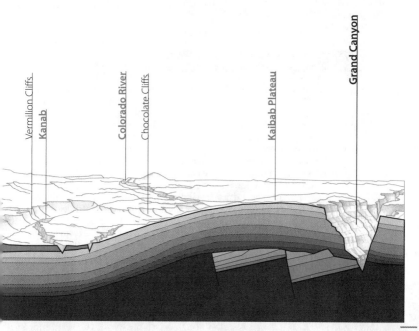

continent by raising the Colorado plateau more than a mile and creating the Rocky Mountains to the east. Though the plateau avoided the geologic turmoil that deformed much of western North America, the forces of uplift did shatter the plateau along fault lines into stair-step subplateaus.

Uplift also set the stage for the final act in this geologic drama. After several hundred million years as a stable, low-lying repository for sediments from surrounding highlands, the plateau finally rose into the limelight, fully exposed to the elements. Furthermore, creation of the Rocky Mountains provided headwaters for great rivers that would chisel the newly risen plateau in their rush to the sea.

Nearly every aspect of the plateau country landscape is shaped by **erosion**, and several factors make these forces particularly dramatic in the Southwest. First are the region's colorful rock layers themselves. As these layers rose, gravity enabled watercourses to gain momentum and carve through stone, while sporadic rainfall and an arid climate ensured the soft layers would otherwise remain intact. These factors have remained consistent over millennia, enabling fragile hoodoos, fins and arches to develop.

Water is perhaps the most dramatic shaping force. Summer flash floods tear through soft rock with immense power, tumbling house-sized boulders down narrow slot canyons and scooping out crumbling sediments like pudding. Zion's Virgin River is often referred to as 'a red ribbon of liquid sandpaper' due to its relentless downward gouging. Those who witness summer thunderstorms will notice how quickly desert waters turn red with dissolving rock.

Seeming at first glance 'solid as a rock,' calcium-carbonate cement actually dissolves easily in rainwater, releasing sand particles and weakening adjacent formations as it sloughs off. The liquefied cement flows down rock faces, then hardens again as it dries, leaving drippings that look like candle wax – a common feature on rock faces in Bryce Canyon. Over time this leaching away of the cement widens cracks and creates isolated fins that further split and dissolve into hoodoos, windows, arches and other fantastic forms.

In winter, storm erosion works in tandem with another equally powerful force. As rainfall seeps into cracks, it freezes and then expands with incredible pressure (20,000 pounds per square inch), forcing open crevices and prying loose blocks of stone. At higher elevations (Bryce Canyon, for example) this freeze-thaw cycle is repeated more than 200 times each year, exacting a tremendous toll on the landscape.

## DESERT VARNISH

Though the dark shiny coating on countless rock surfaces has borne the name *desert varnish* for many years, scientists have only recently determined its origins. They originally thought that this golden to blackish iridescent varnish resulted from minerals leached from cliff faces in rainstorms. Careful analysis has revealed, however, that the likely source is airborne dust sticking to the rock. Bacteria in the dust collect minute amounts of manganese, iron and silica, which over very long periods of time coat the rock in a dark varnish. Petroglyphs etched into such varnish thousands of years ago by Native peoples still look as fresh as the day they were made – vivid proof of how slowly new varnish accumulates.

Similar dark streaks on some cliff faces are not desert varnish, but tannic acid from coniferous trees on overhanging cliffs, which spills down in runoff from cracks and hanging valleys.

# READING THE PARKS
## Zion National Park

Part of the High Plateaus, Zion is located on the southwest corner of the Colorado Plateau and marks the transition from the stable plateau country to the tectonically active Great Basin to the northwest. Separating the regions is a 160-mile line of cliffs along the Hurricane Fault. In the park's **Kolob Canyons** section, sheer 2000ft cliffs jut abruptly from this fault line as if they rose out of the ground just yesterday.

Zion is famous for such massive cliffs, which expose thousands of feet of white to orange Navajo Sandstone. Perhaps nowhere else in the world do these rock formations reach such grand proportions. Bisecting the park, the beautiful **Virgin River** continues its steady march – cutting downward about 1000ft every million years, so rapidly in fact that side tributaries can't keep up and are left as 'hanging valleys' high on cliff faces.

Zion's soaring cliffs were once immense sand dunes – look closely and you'll see fine diagonal lines of 'cross-bedding' that preserve marks of ancient winds that swept these dunes. Calcium carbonate accounts for the white base color, which is often stained reddish by iron oxides. In the freshly exposed rocks of Kolob Canyons, the red is evenly distributed, while most oxides have leached out of **Zion Canyon's** ancient weathered cliffs, leaving the uppermost layers whitish.

The dynamic interplay between Navajo Sandstone and underlying Kayenta Shale largely determines the structure of Zion Canyon. Through the 14-mile **Narrows**, for example, the river flows entirely between sandstone walls, but at the point where it cuts deeply enough, the river readily erodes the softer shale underneath the sandstone cliffs and dramatically widens the canyon.

## Bryce Canyon National Park

Oddly, Bryce is not a canyon at all, but a series of amphitheaters gouged from the gorgeous **Pink Cliffs** like big bites from a loaf of bread. The park's central Claron Formation results from soft siltstone that settled to the bottom of a giant freshwater lake 60 million years ago. Traces of manganese and iron account for this layer's pink and orange hues.

About 15 million years ago, the lakebed lifted 11,000ft, cracking from the stress along countless parallel joints, while farther east the **Aquarius Plateau** rose 2000ft higher. The significant valley between the plateau and Bryce was carved by the Paria River, which over the past million years has begun to nip at the park's cliffs. Looking over the landscape from **Inspiration Point** today, you'll notice the similarities between Bryce's rock layers and those of the distant Aquarius Plateau.

On a smaller scale, runoff along joints on the canyon rim forms parallel gullies with narrow rock walls, or fins, that ultimately erode into the isolated columns known as hoodoos. The layers are so soft that in heavy rains they would quickly dissolve into muddy little mounds, except that siltstone layers alternating with resistant limestone bands give the layers strength as they erode into towering hoodoos. Many hoodoos end up with a cap of harder limestone at the apex, protecting the softer material beneath.

Bryce features dramatic formations at all stages of development, from newly emerging fins to old weathered hoodoos beaten down into colorful mounds. You can easily use your imagination to visualize how these amazing structures are created as the cliffs retreat ever backward.

## Grand Staircase–Escalante National Monument

This vast, complex region contains examples of nearly every rock type and structural feature found in the Plateau Country. Revealed here are more than 200 million years of geologic history and one of the world's most exceptional fossil records of early vertebrate evolution. The entire period that dinosaurs ruled the earth is preserved here in remarkable detail, and scientists have explored only a handful of hundreds of sites so far.

The Monument encompasses not only its namesake feature on the western edge, but it also protects the rarely visited **Kaiparowits Plateau** at the center of the park and the celebrated slot canyon mazes of the **Escalante River** in the east. At least 14 different geologic layers document Mesozoic seas, sand dunes and slow-moving waters that teemed with abundant life. Examples are as varied as the magnificent lavender, rose, burgundy and peach colors of volcanic ash in the Chinle Formation at **Gingham Skirt Butte** or the ancient sand dunes preserved in towering 300ft bluffs of Wingate Sandstone at **Circle Cliffs**.

Few other features characterize this place like the slot canyons of the Escalante, carved by fast-moving waters that become entrenched in resistant sandstone channels and cut downward rather than spreading outward. At their upper ends these canyons begin as modest draws winding through the slickrock like tiny veins before feeding into increasingly larger arteries that eventually empty into the Colorado River. Domes, arches, waterfalls and a wonderland of sculpted sandstone make this a challenging but delightful place to visit.

## Capitol Reef National Park

We've described the Colorado Plateau as floating serenely while all the lands around it are crumpled by the forces of the shifting earth. Capitol Reef is the exception to that rule.

Along a narrow, 100-mile stretch, the earth's surface is bent in a giant wrinkle, exposing more than a dozen rock formations in tilted and upended strata. This type of feature is known as a monocline, and the **Waterpocket Fold** is one of the longest contiguously exposed monoclines in the world. Dubbed a reef by early explorers, who found it a barrier to travel, the fold is capped with bare rounded domes of Navajo Sandstone that reminded them of the US Capitol in Washington, DC – hence the name Capitol Reef.

Another sandstone layer, the **Wingate Formation**, gives this fold a line of distinctive sheer red cliffs on the west side. A third sandstone layer, **Entrada Sandstone**, forms the mysterious freestanding pinnacles and walls of **Cathedral Valley**. Various other formations add so much color and structural diversity that this park is considered without equal in a region chock-full of spectacular parks.

While just four canyons cut across the Waterpocket Fold, a baffling maze of side canyons crisscrosses the park in myriad directions. All formed along clefts and other weak points in the rock, where moisture collects (natural pools of water atop the fold account for its name Waterpocket Fold) and eventually scours out ever-expanding gullies.

## Canyonlands National Park

Like Grand Canyon National Park, Canyonlands is defined by the mighty canyon of the Colorado River. Though the river has carved through 300 millions years of the Earth's history, only the oldest 125 million years' worth of rock layers remain – a staggering testament to the power of erosion. When you gaze into the canyon depths from Grand View Point, you're only looking at the middle slices of a giant geologic cake, with the top layers eaten away and the bottom layers not yet exposed.

Canyonlands is even more diverse than the Grand Canyon, possessing not just two converging river canyons, but intervening high mesas and a complex landscape of slickrock canyons, spires and arches. Cradled between the two rivers, the **Island in the Sky Mesa** is a tableland of Wingate Sandstone topped with scattered buttes and domes of Navajo Sandstone. Below the mesa, slopes plunge 2000ft to the rivers past a shelf of White Rim Sandstone halfway down. The rivers themselves twist and turn along meandering paths inherited from the Miocene (about 10 million years ago), when the land was still a flat plain.

To the west lies **The Maze**, an incomprehensibly convoluted landscape explored mostly by expert adventurers. East of the rivers is **The Needles**, where colorful red and white bands showcase a complicated, 250-million-year-old history of retreating and advancing oceans. The red layers formed in rivers after the ocean's retreat, while white layers represent beaches that fronted ancient oceans.

Any discussion of the region would be incomplete without mentioning the subterranean band of salt deposits left from an evaporating sea 300 million years ago. Around Moab, this band is 3000ft thick, and it stretches under both Canyonlands and Arches National Parks. Water has seeped into the layer in places and washed away the salt crystals, undercutting and fracturing overlying rock formations. In other places, the compressed salt layer has taken on a plastic consistency and domed up, warping and cracking thinner rock layers. Together, these forces shape large sections of the parks, notably Canyonlands' Needles district.

## Arches National Park

Compared to the other parks, Arches' geologic makeup is relatively easy to understand. Ancient rock layers rose atop an expanding salt dome, which later collapsed, fracturing layers along the dome's flanks. These cracks then eroded along roughly parallel lines, leaving fins of freestanding Entrada Sandstone.

Arch formation is more a matter of happenstance than a predictable pattern, as people pay scant attention to the countless 'almost' arches that crumble into oblivion. But in a few lucky cases, rock slabs flake from the sides of fins in just the right way to create small openings that grow into arches as water seeps into cracks, freezes and dislodges more pieces.

At times the rock itself assists the process by releasing tremendous internal pressures stored within its layers, which causes more slabs to pop off. The uniform strength and hard upper surfaces of Entrada Sandstone are the perfect combination for creating such beautiful arches, and today the park is famous as the greatest concentration of natural stone arches in the world.

In the last 10 million years, erosion has removed roughly a vertical mile of rock, carrying away all older materials save for the freestanding fins. This process continues today, so even as brittle arches occasionally collapse, new ones are always in the making. See if you can find examples of arches in all stages of their formation

*The harsh and arid landscape of the Colorado Plateau asks a lot of the plants and animals that make their homes here. Water is always a problem – either it wafts away in the scorching sun or it's frozen solid in winter.*

# ECOSYSTEM

The few times it does come in plenty – delivered by afternoon thunderstorms in the late-summer monsoon season – it comes down so hard and fast and rushes off so quickly that few living things can take advantage of its fleeting presence. Elsewhere, slickrock canyons and sandy flats offer little in the way of usable habitat, and virtually nothing can carve out a living on the countless sheer cliffs that dominate the region. Plants and animals, however, have found remarkable ways to survive on the plateau, and their presence is one of the best reasons for visiting this equally fascinating landscape.

Though the Colorado Plateau is relatively homogenous, each of the parks and monuments offers a unique assemblage of ecosystems, ranging from sere deserts to cold, wet mountain glades. Within a few short miles it's possible to travel from glimpses of roadrunners and scorpions to sightings of marmots and quaking aspens, particularly at **Zion National Park**, where high mesas abut plunging canyons, with few transition habitats in between. Although Zion's southwest corner is a low-desert region, the rest of the park consists mainly of riparian habitats along creeks and rivers beneath mesas capped with high mountain forests.

Focused more narrowly on a high-elevation landscape, **Bryce Canyon National Park** includes boreal species not found at the other parks and excludes many of the water and desert habitats found elsewhere in the Southwest. This park also shelters an important population of the endangered Utah prairie dog. Though mostly desert, **Grand Staircase–Escalante National Monument** encompasses a vast, diverse region with one of the country's richest selections of endemic plants, including 11 plant species found nowhere else in the world.

**Capitol Reef National Park** is a high-desert landscape of piñon-juniper woodlands and desert shrub communities scattered across bare rocky slopes. Elevations ascend at the park's far north end into montane ponderosa pine forests and descend at the southern tip of the park into arid desert habitats. **Canyonlands National Park** is similar, but lower and drier. Although rocks dominate, 80% of the park is still covered by desert shrub, grassland and piñon-juniper woodland. Running through the park are the Green and Colorado Rivers, lined with riparian woodlands. **Arches National Park** is also in the high-desert region, though 40% of the land is covered by piñon-juniper woodland and a rich understory of more than 100 plant species.

To learn more about the plants and animals of the Plateau Country, track down *A Naturalist's Guide to Canyon Country*, by David Williams, which describes many of the region's common flora and fauna.

## LIFE ZONES

With few exceptions, the parks and monuments of the Colorado Plateau protect desert zones with rather uniform habitats. Only a few mesas and slopes rise high enough to support mountain plants and animals, creating 'sky islands' scattered far and wide in a sea of desert. This isolation promotes endemism (the evolution of unique species), because barriers formed by sheer canyons and large rivers separate populations into small units that cannot interbreed.

The rapid rate of erosion on the Colorado Plateau also has a profound effect on the area's ecosystems. Unlike other regions, where eroded materials accumulate and cover vast areas with homogenous soils, erosion on the plateau carries sediments away. Plants have nowhere to live except on freshly exposed bedrock, and because each rock layer has its own distinctive composition and chemistry, this profoundly limits the species that can grow there. Despite these differences, however, it's possible to identify broad bands of vegetation that characterize the Plateau Country.

**Desert scrub** is the habitat that will make most people feel like they're in the desert. It's the hot, dry zone below 4000ft where scraggly shrubs cling to life on sandy flats. Dominating the habitat are low-growing blackbrush, shadscale, Mormon tea and sagebrush. Annual precipitation is likely to average less than 8 in, a number that includes winter snows as well, so it isn't very much rain (actually, most of the rain ends up running over bare rocks and washing away before plants can even use it).

Perhaps the most widespread habitat is the open woodland of piñon pine and Utah juniper that covers huge tracts of Capitol Reef, Canyonlands and Arches National Parks. **Piñon-juniper woodland** ('P-J woodland'

Ponderosa pine

for short) grows mostly between 4000ft and 7000ft. Due to competition for water, trees are spaced widely here, though they still provide shade for many understory plants, as well as food and shelter for numerous animals. In some areas the trees grow in distinct lines, following cracks in the rock where water gathers after a rain.

Growing in a narrow band between 7000ft and 8500ft, **ponderosa pine forest** indicates the presence of increased rainfall at higher elevations. In Zion, however, ponderosa pines grow at lower elevations, because porous Navajo Sandstone is full of water, demonstrating once again how water dictates where plants can grow in this region. Ponderosa pine and boreal forests thrive in Zion and Bryce Canyon (with a few stands in Grand Staircase–Escalante) but are absent in the lower-elevation Capitol Reef, Canyonlands and Arches.

**Boreal forest** above 8500ft has much in common with Rocky Mountain forests, even supporting many of the same plants and animals. This is a zone of cool, moist woodland and rainfall that exceeds 20 inches a year, conditions that favor trees like spruce, Douglas fir and quaking aspen. This forest populates a few high mesas in Zion, but the best examples are found at lookouts in Bryce, particularly at road's end, near Rainbow Point.

Due to intensive grazing, the **grassland** that once covered much of this region has been largely replaced by desert scrub and alien weeds. Early explorers' journals describe a lush grassy landscape, though you'd hardly know it today. In areas of deeper sand and soil, where shrubs don't grow well, it's still possible to find pockets of galleta and Indian ricegrass.

Readily available water supports another set of unique habitats, ranging from **hanging gardens** clustered around cliffside seeps to **riparian woodland** lining perennial creeks and rivers. The presence of precious water attracts many plants and animals to these habitats. Monkeyflowers, columbines and ferns mark spots where springs flow from sandstone cliffs. Riverbanks that were once home to majestic cottonwood and willow stands are more likely today to harbor highly invasive tamarisk.

## LIFE THROUGH THE SEASONS

Seasons on the Colorado Plateau are as complex as the landscape itself. Within a short distance, you may encounter a wide variety of climatic extremes. Even as desert lowlands erupt into full bloom, towering mesa tops may still be buried under many feet of snow. Plant and animal life cycles are likewise highly variable.

April ushers in the first long spells of fair weather, interrupted by lingering wet winter storms. Flowers

Roadrunner

## POTHOLES

A miracle of life unfolds wherever desert rains accumulate in what seem like lifeless, dusty bowls among the rocks. Hiding in the dust are the spores and eggs of creatures uniquely evolved to take advantage of ephemeral water. Within hours of rainfall, beetles, crustaceans, insects, protozoa and countless other organisms hatch and start swimming in this brew of life. Though most are microscopic or very small, there are also oddly shaped, 1- to 2in tadpole shrimp that resemble prehistoric trilobites. Toads and frogs arrive the night after a rain and lay eggs that hatch quickly. Unlike amphibians in other areas, which can take months or years to develop, these tadpoles are champion athletes that emerge from the water in two to three weeks. No matter how productive a pothole may seem, however, its lifespan is limited by evaporation. All too soon, water levels drop, and everything turns to dust again. By then all the organisms have retreated into dormancy to wait for the next drenching rainstorm, which may be years or even decades away.

Because each pool is a fragile ecosystem, hikers should exercise special care when they find a pothole. If necessary, remove only a little water, and don't jump or swim in the water, because body oils, sunscreens and insect repellants can harm resident life. These creatures have nowhere else to go! Even when dry, these pools need our attention because the 'lifeless' dust is actually full of eggs and spores waiting to spring into life again.

begin to emerge, and frog calls reverberate in the night. Filling the air with song and activity, migrant birds arrive in numbers that continue to grow into May. Mammals likewise seem eager to take advantage of the short season between winter cold and searing summer heat. Chipmunks and squirrels lead the charge, bounding energetically amid the rocks and trees.

By June, however, temperatures begin to soar, and animal activity slows to a crawl. Day temperatures of 100°F and higher are the norm through August, though torrential afternoon thunderstorms alleviate the agony for a few hours each day. This June-through-August window is a great time to observe wildflowers.

Clear, cool days make autumn an ideal time to visit the parks, though by then wildflowers have gone to seed and many birds have already made the journey south. Left behind are resident animals – mammals fattening up for hibernation and a handful of birds feasting on plentiful seeds. Some resident species remain active through winter, especially at lower elevations, where temperatures remain moderate and snow rarely falls.

## ANIMALS GREAT & SMALL

Wildlife in the parks ranges from secretive bighorn sheep and prehistoric condors to scampering lizards and nosy ringtail cats, all scattered across a vast and wild region. Only rarely do animals congregate in large or conspicuous numbers. In summer most animal activity takes place in the early evening or at night, when temperatures drop slightly. **Bird-watching** can be a particularly rewarding activity, as more than 300 species inhabit or pass through the area, including California condors, which were newly introduced into the region after nearly reaching extinction. Stop by a visitor center and purchase a few field guides to help identify the many plants and animals you might see.

## Large Mammals

Although bighorn sheep stand guard on inaccessible cliff faces, elk and deer wander through mountain meadows, and mountain lions lurk in forest nooks, your chances of seeing such large mammals are relatively slim. They'll probably show up when you least expect them, so keep your eyes open!

### MOUNTAIN LIONS

Mountain lion

Even veteran wildlife biologists rarely see a **mountain lion**, though a fair number reside in Plateau Country. Like their favorite prey, mule deer, mountain lions mostly hang out in forested areas. Reaching up to 8ft in length and weighing as much as 160lb, this solitary animal is a formidable predator that rarely bothers humans.

### MULE DEER

Forests and meadows are the favored haunts of mule deer, who typically graze in the early evening light. Uncommon when settlers first arrived, and soon hunted out, mule deer nearly vanished around the turn of the 20th century, then quickly rebounded as their predators were eliminated. Today they frequent campgrounds and developed areas, often moving upslope to avoid summer heat and returning downslope as winter approaches. Zion shelters both a distinct high-country population and a canyon-dwelling herd that rarely seem to interact.

### BIGHORN SHEEP

Mule deer

Like solemn statues, **bighorn sheep** often stand motionless on distant cliff faces or ridgelines, distinguished by their distinctive curled horns. During breeding season, males charge each other at 20mph and ram horns so loudly that the sound can be heard for miles. Bighorns are making a slow and tedious recovery after hunting and diseases introduced by domestic sheep drove their populations to record lows. Bring binoculars to spot this animal, as close sightings are rare and typically brief.

## Small Mammals

Small mammals are much more abundant than their larger cousins, and many types of squirrels, chipmunks and small carnivores can be spotted on a given day.

## PRAIRIE DOGS

Although prairie dogs once numbered in the billions across the West, a century of shooting and poisoning at the hands of ranchers drove the Utah prairie dog to near extinction by 1950. This cheeky, dynamic animal was as important as the grassland ecosystem it depended on, but decades passed before anyone realized how critical this loss was and tried to reverse it.

In 1974 scientists established a small prairie dog colony in the meadows at Bryce Canyon National Park and carefully monitored these small rodents (named 'dogs' by the Lewis and Clark expedition because the animals communicate with barks). Each March, as snows begin to melt, about 300 prairie dogs emerge from hibernation and begin a luxurious summer of calling, mating and fattening up on sweet grasses. The meadows around the visitor center and campgrounds are now home to this rare animal, and many park visitors stop by to watch their lively antics. When grasses dry out in July, prairie dogs return underground to begin their eight-month hibernation. The park asks that you stay out of the colonies and avoid the temptation to feed or pester the animals.

Look for them around campsites and picnic grounds and along trails or roadside stops.

### CHIPMUNKS & SQUIRRELS

Several species of small, striped chipmunks and ground squirrels are ubiquitous in the parks. The gold-, black- and white-striped **Uinta chipmunk** is especially common along the canyon rim in Bryce and on Zion's forested plateaus. Though it resembles a chipmunk, the **golden-mantled ground squirrel** lacks stripes on its head. Both species scamper through the forest, eagerly searching for nuts and seeds. They also love to beg for handouts, but resist the urge to feed them.

On open desert flats you're more likely to see the **antelope ground squirrel**, one of the few mammals active during the daytime. Look for its white tail, which it carries over its back like a reflective umbrella, shielding it from the sun as it darts between shady patches.

In comparison, the speckled gray **rock squirrel** is drab. This large, bold squirrel often visits campgrounds, where it inquisitively explores unattended gear or sidles up close to campers. True to its name, the rock squirrel nearly always inhabits rocky areas.

Chipmunk

### WOOD RATS

Although they bear a superficial resemblance to city rats, wood rats are extraordinary, gentle creatures with many interesting attributes. The Colorado Plateau's four species all share a maddening propensity for stealing small shiny objects like watches or rings and leaving bones, seeds or other small objects in exchange – hence the animal's common nickname, the packrat. Wood rats are also famous for building massive stick nests (packrat middens) that are used by countless generations. Upon dismantling these middens and examining their contents, biologists have been able to document more than 50,000 years of environmental prehistory in the region.

### CANYON MICE
No other mammal seems better adapted to the Southwest's slickrock canyons than the tiny canyon mouse. This nimble resident of rocky terrain is the only mammal biologists found living on The Jug, an isolated mesa in Canyonlands surrounded by sheer cliffs. Here they are seven times more abundant than in other areas, showing how well they fare in the absence of competition.

### PORCUPINES
Looking much like an arboreal pincushion, the porcupine spends its days sleeping on the high branches of trees in piñon-juniper woodlands. It's easy to overlook this strange creature, though on occasion you might encounter one waddling slowly through the forest. It's most active at night, when it gnaws on the soft inner wood of trees or waddles around in search of flowers and berries.

Porcupine

### BEAVERS
Strange though it may seem, some of the first explorers to wander across the Colorado Plateau came in search of prized beaver pelts. Limited to the few large rivers, beavers have never been common, but they are frequently sighted, because most park visitors flock to the rivers. In Zion their persistent nocturnal gnawing on large cottonwood trees presents something of a quandary. Wire mesh protects the base of some trees, but the park must still address the bigger question of how to restore the original balance of beavers, spring floods and cottonwoods that existed before humans forced the river into its current channel.

Beaver

### RINGTAIL CATS
One of the area's most intriguing creatures is the nocturnal ringtail cat, which looks like a masked housecat with a raccoon tail. It preys on mice and squirrels, but will eat carrion, birds or fruit in a pinch. Fairly common in rocky areas near water, ringtails may make an appearance around campsites at night, though they are generally secretive.

# Birds

Whether you enjoy the graceful flight of golden eagles atop towering cliffs or the bright songs of warblers amid riverside thickets, there's no question that the Colorado Plateau's 300-plus bird species are among the region's premier highlights.

### SMALL BIRDS

The first birds many people encounter are **white-throated swifts**, which swoop and dive in great numbers along cliff faces and canyon walls. Designed like sleek bullets, these sporty 'tuxedoed' birds seem to delight in riding every wind current and chasing each other in noisy, playful pursuit. Flying alongside the swifts are slightly less agile **violet-green swallows**, a familiar sight around campgrounds and park buildings. Both species catch all their food 'on the wing.'

Golden eagle

Also common around campgrounds, or perched on fences and wires, are gentle **mourning doves**. You may hear either their mournful cooing or the rushing whistle their wings make when they suddenly bolt into flight. Subsisting almost entirely on dry seeds, doves must also find water to drink each day. They can rehydrate enough in one minute to go 24 hours without drinking again.

Whereas most birds perch crosswise on branches and wires, the **common nighthawk** perches lengthwise. But you're more likely to see this dark, narrow-winged bird at sunset, when it darts across the evening sky in search of moths. Its distinctive nasal call is a hallmark sound of the desert evening.

Another bird with a unique call is the **blue grouse**. This resident of mountain forests vocalizes from the ground and has such a deep call that you almost feel it in your bones. Most sightings occur when a startled grouse erupts from your feet into flight. On rare occasions you may spot a male as it puffs up its chest and drums to attract a female.

The stirring song of the **canyon wren** is for many people the most evocative sound on the plateau. So haunting is this song it hardly seems possible that this tiny reddish rock-dweller could produce such music. Starting as a fast run of sweet tinkling notes, the song fades gracefully into a rhythmic cadence that leaves you full of longing.

In contrast, the garrulous call of the **Steller's jay** can grate on your nerves like a loud rusty gate. But this iridescent blue mountain bird makes up for it with wonderfully inquisitive and confiding mannerisms. It seems to have no fear of humans and eagerly gathers around picnic tables and campsites, hoping for leftovers.

Steller's jay

Rafters and riverside hikers will almost certainly meet the brilliant **blue grosbeak**, with its loud, complex songs. This bird scours dense thickets for tasty insects and grubs, and males often ascend to high perches to defend their territory.

### LARGE BIRDS

Of the various owls that reside on the Colorado Plateau, none is as familiar as the common and highly vocal **great horned owl**, which regularly fills the echoing canyons with its booming 'hoo-hoo hooo hooo' calls. This is among the largest and most fearsome of all raptors, and when one moves into the neighborhood, other owls and hawks hurry on to more favorable hunting grounds or run the risk of being hunted down as prey themselves. This bird's glaring face and prominent 'horns' (actually long erect feathers) may startle hikers as it peers down at them from a crevice or dark cavity.

Great horned owl

The threatened **Mexican spotted owl** has garnered considerable media coverage over the years. In California and the Pacific Northwest, this owl nests solely in old-growth forests that are being logged, but the subspecies that lives in the Plateau Country makes its home in rugged canyons. Sightings are rare but thrilling.

Commanding vast hunting territories of some 50 sq miles, powerful **golden eagles** are typically observed in passing as they travel widely in search of jackrabbits and other prey (up to the size of an adult deer). Boasting 7ft wingspans, they are among the area's largest birds, second in size only to recently arrived California condors. Watch for the characteristic golden tint on the eagle's shoulders and neck.

Given their endangered status in recent decades, **peregrine falcons** are surprisingly common throughout the region. Here they find plenty of secluded, cliffside nesting sites, as well as one of their favorite food items, white-throated swifts, which they seize in midair. Look for the falcon's long, slender wings and dark 'moustache.'

Peregrine falcon

Certainly the most ubiquitous large bird is the **common raven**, a bird that seems to delight in making a noisy scene with its raucous calls and ceaseless play. This bird is an especially common sight along roadsides, where roadkill provides it with a steady supply of food.

Visitors may be surprised to see **wild turkey**. Formerly hunted out, this flashy game bird has been making a slow comeback in areas where it's protected, particularly in Zion Canyon. In the mating season each spring, males fan out their impressive tails and strut around to impress females.

## CONDORS

When critically endangered California condors were released at Vermilion Cliffs in 1996, the experience of visiting the Colorado Plateau was profoundly altered. As was the case when wolves were reintroduced to Yellowstone National Park, visitors seem utterly fascinated by the condors. With 9.5ft wingspans and horridly wrinkled featherless heads, these birds are an unforgettable sight.

It's a miracle that condors are around at all, seeing as their world population declined to fewer than two dozen birds in the 1980s. Many assumed these gigantic prehistoric birds were on the brink of extinction. Following a massive captive breeding effort, however, wild condors once again fly in the Southwest. While most reside in the Vermilion Cliffs and Grand Canyon, they wander far and wide in search of large animal carcasses and are observed more frequently to the north. You never know when one will soar overhead.

Condor populations are far from secure, however, despite having enough food and room to roam. The true test will be whether the species can successfully reproduce. Pairs laid one egg in 2001 and two eggs in 2002. These efforts failed, but one nest was successful in 2003, hopefully marking the beginning of this majestic bird's return to the wild.

## Amphibians & Reptiles

Amphibians and reptiles seldom garner the attention they deserve, but a surprising range of beautiful and unique species call the area home. Lizards and snakes are well represented throughout the region, while frogs and toads are usually very common around water.

### AMPHIBIANS

Bleating choruses of common **canyon tree frogs** float up from boulder-strewn canyon streams each night. Gray-brown and speckled like stone, these tiny frogs dwell in damp crevices by day, emerging at night (and sometimes late afternoon) to sing beside rocky pools.

Occupying a similar habitat (since water occurs in limited patches) is the aptly named **red-spotted toad**, a small species with (you guessed it) red-tipped warts covering its body. Its nighttime song around breeding pools is a high musical trill.

More secretive, and thus rarely encountered, is the 10- to 12in **tiger salamander**, the region's only salamander. Spending the majority of its life in a burrow, this creature emerges when abundant water triggers its breeding cycle. In order to fully develop, a larval salamander requires a water source that will last one to three years, although some larvae never change into the adult form and become sexually mature while still in the larval stage.

### LIZARDS

Perhaps the region's most abundant and widespread reptile is the **eastern fence lizard**, a 5- to 6in creature you'll likely see perched atop rocks and logs or scampering across the trail. During breeding season, males bob enthusiastically while conspicuously displaying their shiny blue throats and bellies. Females have dark, wavy crossbars on their backs and only a pale bluish wash underneath.

Bold in comparison is the greenish **collared lizard**, a large-headed species with striking black bands around its neck. This fearsome lizard eats just about every small animal it can overpower. Because it has little to fear, it often perches conspicuously atop large boulders, scanning for movement in all directions.

You may also encounter the curiously flattened **horned lizard**, which looks like a spiny little pancake. This lizard's shape is an adaptation to its exclusive diet of ants. In order to survive on this nutrient-poor diet, horned lizards must eat lots of ants and consequently have extremely large stomachs that lend it its short, round appearance.

Fence lizard

### SNAKES

The Colorado Plateau is excellent habitat for snakes, though visitors seldom encounter more than a few resident species. Most common is the **gopher snake**, which is easily mistaken for a rattlesnake because it vibrates its tail in dry leaves when cornered or upset. Sporting an attractive tan body with dark brown saddles, this 6- to 8ft constrictor preys upon rodents and small birds. In *Desert Solitaire*, author Edward Abbey recounts how he befriended a gopher snake that lived beneath his trailer in Arches National Park. He thought its presence would keep rattlesnakes away, and it seemed to work.

Nothing compares to the jolt of terror and adrenaline prompted by the angry buzz of a **rattlesnake**. Both humans and wild animals react with instinctive fear, even though rattlesnakes rarely strike unless provoked. These mild-mannered creatures would rather crawl away unharmed than provoke a confrontation. At least three very similar species reside in the region, but only rarely does a visitor get close enough to tell them apart.

Another snake that keeps its distance is the **striped whip snake**. This extremely slender 5ft snake moves like lightning when alarmed and can climb into trees and bushes so quickly it seems like it's falling away from you. It uses this speed to capture lizards, snakes and rodents.

Rattlesnake

## Fish

Although the Colorado River and its tributaries are often described as 'too thin to plow and too thick to drink,' these waters were once home to 14 fish species, nearly all of them unique to these waters and highly adapted to extreme conditions. Unfortunately, following the introduction of grazing, dams and other man-made changes to the landscape, some 40 introduced species are now outcompeting these native fish.

One representative native species is the threatened **Colorado pikeminnow**, North America's largest minnow, which weighs up to 100lb and reaches 6ft in length. Once so abundant that they were pitchforked out of irrigation canals, pikeminnows are in drastic decline, as many man-made dams block their 200-mile migration route. Three other endangered fish, the **humpback chub**, **bonytail chub** and **razorback sucker**, suffer similar fates. It's unclear whether they will survive the changes being made to the rivers.

Humpback chub

## Other Creatures

Due to the Colorado Plateau's virtually impassable canyons and rivers, the region's smallest resident species have evolved into myriad colorful local forms. Boasting more than 1300 distinct subspecies, the **darkling beetle** eventually catches the eye of nearly every visitor. These squat-bodied, long-legged beetles trundle across sandy areas in search of edible vegetation. When disturbed, they lower their heads and lift their rear ends high into the air – if would-be intruders probe any closer, the beetle emits a squirt of noxious, though nonpoisonous, chemicals.

Observant hikers will spot the ubiquitous **ant lion**, which in its larval form makes perfectly conical pits in sandy soils. Lurking at the bottom of these pits, the larva waits for hapless insects to slide in, then grabs them with its fierce jaws and sucks them dry. These ugly little grubs metamorphose into gossamer-winged adults that look like large damselflies.

Dangerous in its allure, the fuzzy-bodied **velvet ant** is actually a wasp in disguise. Covered in orange or red hairs, this small insect is a common sight on sandy trails. Children and adults may be tempted to pick up the cuddly looking bug for closer inspection. Beware: It delivers a particularly painful sting.

A good example of a specially adapted species is the famous **Zion snail**, found nowhere else in the world except the hanging gardens of Zion Canyon, where it grazes on algae and plants amid the thin sheets of water that trickle from the Navajo Sandstone. It takes a sharp eye, but you can find these tiny dark snails on the wet walls of The Narrows or Weeping Rock.

## PLANT LIFE

The Colorado Plateau's complex landscape supports an equally diverse mix of plant species. Many are specific to the plateau, while others are drawn from adjacent biological zones such as the Great Basin, Mojave Desert and Rocky Mountains. Each park and monument boasts a list of hundreds of species, and no two places are alike.

Most species are adapted in some way to the Southwest's arid environment, either laying dormant until rains arrive or toughing it out through dry spells. If you arrive in wet season or after a drenching rain, you may be lucky enough to witness the region at its full splendor, when flowers carpet the landscape in all directions.

What you'll witness more often, however, is the plodding life of plants that struggle to conserve every molecule of precious liquid. Many plants sport hairy or waxy leaves to prevent evaporation, while others bear tiny leaves. At least one common plant, Mormon tea, has done away with water-wasting leaves altogether and relies on its greenish, wiry stems for photosynthesis. Most species have long taproots to penetrate the soil in search of water.

This mixed assemblage comprises a fascinating puzzle that interested visitors can patiently piece together. For help identifying common plants, turn to *Wildflowers of Southwestern Utah,* by Hayle Buchanan, or *Wildflowers of Zion National Park,* by Stanley Welsh. Serious enthusiasts can tackle *A Utah Flora,* also by Stanley Welsh.

## Trees

Due to their prominence and longevity, trees serve as excellent indicators of different life zones and local environmental conditions. For example, piñons and junipers do particularly well on desert slopes between 4000ft and 7000ft. **Piñon pines** are well known for their highly nutritious and flavorful seeds, sold as 'pine nuts' in grocery stores. These same seeds have long been a staple for Native Americans, and many animals also feast on the seeds when they ripen in the fall. Piñons bear stout rounded cones and short paired needles. Together with **Utah junipers**, piñon pines form a distinctive plant community that covers millions of acres in the Southwest. Blue, berrylike cones and diminutive scalelike needles distinguish junipers. Sadly, land managers trying to improve the region for cattle have systemically torn up both species over vast areas.

Mingling with piñons and junipers in some canyons is the beautiful little **Gambel oak**, whose dark green leaves turn shades of yellow and red in autumn and add a classy palette of color to an already stunning landscape, particularly in Zion Canyon. Often growing in dense thickets, oaks produce copious quantities of nutritious, tasty acorns long favored by Native Americans and used to make breads, pancakes, soups and ground meal.

The stately **ponderosa pine** defines the forested belt between 6000ft and 8500ft, in many places forming nearly pure stands that cover many acres. To identify this species, look for large spiny cones, needles in clusters of three, and yellowish bark that smells like butterscotch.

At higher elevations, ponderosa pines mingle with other trees that characterize the Rocky Mountain boreal forest. Evidence from packrat middens suggests that between 20,000 and 12,000 years ago, the **Douglas fir** was one of the region's dominant species, though today they are restricted to isolated mountaintops and north-facing ravines. Identified by its single needles and cones with three-pronged bracts on each seed, this relict of an earlier time dramatically demonstrates how the region's vegetation has changed since the Ice Age.

Found amid damp mountain meadows, **Quaking aspen** is imme-

Douglas fir

diately recognizable by its smooth, white bark and circular leaves. Every gust of wind sets these leaves quivering on their flattened stems, an adaptation for shaking off late snowfalls that would otherwise damage fragile leaves. Aspen groves comprise genetically identical trunks sprouting from a common root system that may grow to more than a hundred acres in size. By budding repeatedly from these root systems, aspens have what has been called 'theoretical immortality' – some aspen roots are thought to be more than a million years old.

Rivers and watercourses in this harsh desert landscape are lined with thin ribbons of water-loving plants that can't survive anywhere else. Towering prominently over all others is the showy **Fremont cottonwood**, whose large, vaguely heart-shaped leaves rustle wildly in any wind. Hikers in the canyons' scorching depths find welcome respite in the shade of this tree. In spring, cottonwoods produce vast quantities of cottony seed packets that fill the air and collect in every crack and crevice. **Box elder** is another common streamside plant and a popular ornamental plant in city parks and yards. It issues winged, maplelike seeds and bears trifoliate leaves that resemble those of poison ivy.

Since 1920 the aggressive weedy **tamarisk** has largely replaced native streamside plant communities. Though this delicately leaved plant from Eurasia sports a handsome coat of soft pink flowers through the summer, its charm ends there, for this plant robs water from the soil and completely overwhelms such native species as cottonwood and willow. Producing a billion seeds per plant and spreading quickly, this species now dominates virtually every source of water in the Southwest deserts.

## Shrubs

**Blackbrush** covers large tracts of desert in this region. Presenting a somber face on an already barren habitat, this dark shrub reaches great ages and is only rarely replaced by young seedlings. Vehicle tracks made through blackbrush stands in the 1950s have yet to be erased by new blackbrush. Life is spare for this plant. With wiry stems, shrunken leaves and petalless flowers, it looks more dead than alive.

Scattered amid the blackbrush are a few other shrubs, including **narrowleaf yucca**, a stout succulent related to agave and century plants. Growing in a dense rosette of thick leaves that reaches 2ft high, this plant sends up a 5ft stalk of creamy flowers. A night-flying moth pollinates these flowers; in exchange, the caterpillars eat a few of the plant's seeds. Yuccas favor sandy sites, while blackbrush predominates on thin gravelly soils.

Poison ivy

Triggered by spring rains, the common **cliff rose** paints rocky slopes with its flamboyant white blossoms. You're more likely to 'hear' this plant before you see it, as bees and insects swarm to its fragrant flowers. Though its resinous, fernlike leaves taste bitter, deer still munch on this plant in winter.

Learn to identify **poison ivy** before wandering into plateau country. Particularly in moisture-laden canyons, this toxic plant grows in thickets that hikers must inevitably tackle or else circumvent with great difficulty. Distinguished by round, ivory-colored berries and oaklike leaves that grow in clusters of three, poison ivy may cause a severe itchy rash when touched. From summer into fall, the leaves turn brilliant shades of red, adding their gorgeous hue to the desert landscape.

As might be expected, the juicy black **canyon grape** is a favorite food among many different kinds of mammals and nearly 100 species of birds. Ripening in mid- to late summer, its fruit is rather tart when eaten from the vine, but it makes a delicious jelly, juice or wine. Its vines snake over bushes and rocks in damp canyons, particularly in Zion Canyon, where its maplelike leaves turn yellow, orange and red in the fall.

A distinctive shrub in montane forests is **greenleaf manzanita**, which flourishes along the rim at Bryce Canyon. This shrub bears silky smooth reddish bark and leathery leaves. Countless bees alight on its pale pinkish flowers, while mammals and birds relish its delicious dark-red fruit.

### Wildflowers

A surprisingly large variety of wildflowers thrive in the Colorado Plateau's arid, rocky landscapes. While late-winter precipitation triggers some plants to flower, many others bloom following midsummer thunderstorms.

Seeps, springs and stream banks are fantastic places to search for some of the most dramatic flower displays. The brilliant crimson flash of **Eaton's monkeyflowers** amid lush greenery comes as something of a shock for hikers who've trudged across miles of searing baked rock. These red flowers with widely flared 'lips' are extremely attractive to hummingbirds.

Golden columbine

Columbines are also common at the seeps and springs, though some species range up into forested areas as well. The gorgeous **golden columbine** is most common in wet, shaded canyon recesses. **Rock columbine** grows amid Bryce Canyon's hoodoos, where its vivid blue flowers contrast sharply with the red-rock cliffs. The flowers of both species hold pockets of nectar that attract large numbers of butterflies and hummingbirds.

The showy **prince's-plume** boldly marks selenium-rich desert soils with a 4ft stalk of dainty bright yellow flowers. By using selenium in place of sulfur to manufacture its amino acids, this plant renders itself poisonous to herbivores and grows in soils that other plants can't tolerate. For a time, prospectors thought of this plant as an indicator of places to dig for uranium, but this is more likely a bit of local legend.

Raising eyebrows whenever encountered by hikers, the oddly inflated **desert trumpet** presents its loose arrangement of tiny yellow flowers anytime between March and October. Just below the flowers, the stem balloons out like a long slender lozenge. Old stems

## CRYPTOBIOTIC CRUSTS

One of the desert's most fascinating features is also one of its least visible and most frag-ile. Only in recent years have cryptobiotic crusts begun to attract attention and concern. These living crusts cover and protect desert soils, literally gluing sand particles together so they don't blow away. Cyanobacteria, among Earth's oldest living forms, start the process by extending mucous-covered filaments that wind through the dry soil. Over time these filaments and the sand particles adhering to them form a thin crust that is colonized by microscopic algae, lichens, fungi, and mosses. This crust absorbs tremendous amounts of rainwater, reducing runoff and minimizing erosion.

Unfortunately, this thin crust is instantly fragmented under the heavy impact of footsteps, not to mention bicycle, motorcycle and car tires. Once broken, the crust takes 50 to 250 years to repair itself. In its absence, the wind and rains erode desert soils, and much of the water that would otherwise nourish desert plants is lost. Many of these soils formed during the wet climates of the Pleistocene and may be irreplaceable in today's arid condi-tions. Tragically, as soon as the crust is broken and soil is lost, grasses will be permanently replaced by shrubs, whose roots fare better in the thinner soils.

Visitors to the Southwest bear a special responsibility to protect cryptobiotic crusts by staying on established trails. Look closely before you walk anywhere – intact crusts form a rough glaze atop the soil. At all costs, avoid walking or camping on these ancient soils.

maintain this shape and are just as curious as the liv-ing plant. Sometimes wasps drill into the plant and fill its hollow stems with captured insects as food for developing larvae.

In peak years **evening primroses** are so abundant that it looks like someone scattered white tissues over the sandy desert. Appearing in April, the 3in flowers open at sunset and close by morning, thus avoiding the day's heat and conserving water. At night large, hummingbird-like sphinx moths dart from flower to flower, collecting nectar and laying eggs.

### Other Plants

Although they could be classified with wildflowers, cacti are a group of plants unique unto themselves. Prominent cacti include various members of the prickly pear group, familiar for their paddle-shaped pads that resemble beaver tails. In fact, one of the most common species is called **beavertail cacti**. Both the pads and fruit are commonly eaten after proper prepara-tion. Be aware that the spines (glochidia) detach easily on contact and are highly irritating.

Matching the image of the classic beautiful cacti, stunning **claret cup cacti** shine like iridescent jewels in the dusty desert landscape, where they are the first to bloom in spring. Their deep scarlet flowers burst

Evening primroses

forth from as many as 50 stems per clump, blooming simultaneously for several days.

**Maidenhair fern** deserves special mention because it adds bright green color to countless desert oases. Lacy and delicate, this fern requires a continuous supply of water but otherwise does well in an imposing landscape. You'll recognize it by its leaves, arranged like an open hand from a central wiry black stem.

A close examination of juniper tree branches reveals an extremely abundant but easily overlooked plant – yellow-green **juniper mistletoe**. Parasitic, but apparently not harming its host trees, mistletoe produces tiny fruits that birds such as robins and bluebirds absolutely love. Carried in the birds' digestive tracts, the seeds adhere to new tree branches once excreted.

Formerly widespread across vast tracts of the desert, grasses like **Indian ricegrass** and **galleta** now survive only in relict patches. Along with this loss, an entire food chain of animals that relied on grasslands has also declined, evidenced by local extinctions of bears, wolves, elk, bighorns and pronghorns. Bearing large nutritious seeds, ricegrass was also an important staple for Native Americans in the Southwest. If you happen across a patch of such grasses, take a moment to realize this is now a rare and fragile plant community.

## STRESSES ON THE SYSTEM

With the highest concentration of protected lands in the continental United States, and excellent management by a variety of agencies, it seems that most of the damage to this landscape is a thing of the past. Unfortunately, grazing, mining and military exercises are still creating new scars on lands around the region's parks and monuments. Ironically, the worst damage may now come from the the huge influx of recreationists and visitors who seem to be loving the land to death.

In a region where life hangs by a fragile thread, the heavy trampling of human feet leaves lasting impressions. Desert crusts, wet meadows and riverside campsites are slow to recover from such use, and repeated visits can cause permanent damage. The effects may accumulate so gradually they go unnoticed. Scientists in Bryce Canyon estimate that 3% of the vegetation disappears each year from people wandering off trail among the hoodoos – just tiny little bites that build up over time. Desert crusts are of particular concern, and all the parks have active 'Don't Bust the Crust' programs to educate people about their impact on desert soils.

Desert vegetation grows so slowly that scars left by early prospectors, ranchers and explorers still look

Galleta

fresh. Even protected parkland remains damaged in many areas from long-ago visitors. Cows have had such a devastating impact on the desert that it no longer functions as the same ecosystem. Only on a few inaccessible mesa tops do fragments of ancestral plant communities survive. Today's dry, brushy desert hardly resembles the landscape that existed even half a century ago, and it's not likely to recover for centuries to come.

Plants that adapt best seem to be invasive weeds, which have quickly taken over sites damaged by cows and human activities. Introduced plants like Russian thistle (tumbleweed) and cheatgrass pose a serious problem, as they can force out native plants and animals, creating extensive monocultures. Cheatgrass even alters the chemistry of the soil, possibly rendering it unusable to other plants. Many invasive plants are practically impossible to remove once they gain a foothold.

Harder to quantify is the pall of air pollution that often hovers over the region. Emanating from distant cities, cars and factories, this hazy smog severely compromises the remarkable beauty of this wild landscape and serves as a grim reminder of modern life. Perhaps seeing how our impacts spread outward into wild areas can be a gentle prod to all visitors to reconsider the ways we live their lives.

Despite all these impacts, this crusty old landscape remains a land of serene beauty with the power to move the hearts of every visitor. Memories of colorful cliffs, silent canyons, and sunset shadows will persist long after any visit, and the vast empty spaces of this desert wilderness beckon you to return time after time.

# APPENDIX

## Zion National Park

### GENERAL PARK INFORMATION
**Zion National Park** ☎ 435-772-3256; www.nps.gov/zion
**Kolob Canyons Visitor Center** ☎ 435-586-0895
**Zion Canyon Visitors Bureau** ☎ 888-518-7070; www.zionpark.com
**Cedar City & Brian Head Tourism & Convention Bureau** ☎ 435-586-5124, 800-354-4849; www.scenicsouthernutah.com
**East Zion Tourism Council** ☎ 435-648-2174; www.eastziontravelcouncil.com
**St George Area Convention & Visitors Bureau** ☎ 800-869-6635; www.utahsdixie.com

### ACCOMMODATIONS
**Xanterra Parks & Resorts** ☎ 888-297-2757, 303-297-2757 (outside US); www.xanterra.com
**Zion Lodge** ☎ 435-772-3213, 888-297-2757, 303-297-2757 (reservations); www.zionlodge.com
**Watchman Campground** ☎ 800-365-2267; http://reservations.nps.gov

### ACTIVITIES
**Zion Backcountry Desk** ☎ 435-772-0170
**Canyon Trail Rides** ☎ 435-679-8665, 435-772-3810; www.canyonrides.com
**Springdale Cycle Tours** ☎ 435-772-0575, 800-776-2099; www.springdalecycles.com
**Zion Adventure Company** ☎ 435-772-1001; www.zionadventures.com
**Zion Cycles** ☎ 435-772-0400; www.zioncycles.com
**Zion Rock & Mountain Guides** ☎ 435-772-3303; www.zionrockguides.com

### MAPS
**National Geographic** ☎ 800-437-5521; www.nationalgeographic.com
**USGS** ☎ 888-275-8747; www.usgs.gov

## TOUR OPERATORS
**Southern Utah Scenic Tours** ☎ 435-867-8690, 888-404-8687; www.discover-the-west.com

## TRANSPORTATION
**St George Shuttle** ☎ 435-628-8320, 800-933-8320; www.stgshuttle.com
**Red Rock Shuttle** ☎ 435-635-9104

## USEFUL ORGANIZATIONS
**Zion Canyon Field Institute** ☎ 435-772-3264, 800-635-3959; www.zionpark.org
**Zion Natural History Association** ☎ 435-772-3264, 800-635-3959; www.zionpark.org

# Bryce Canyon National Park

## GENERAL PARK INFORMATION
**Bryce Canyon National Park** ☎ 435-834-5322; www.nps.gov/brca
**Garfield County Tourism Office** ☎ 435-676-1160, 800-444-6689; www.brycecanyoncountry.com

## ACCOMMODATIONS
**Xanterra Parks & Resorts** ☎ 888-297-2757, 303-297-2757 (outside US); www.xanterra.com
**Bryce Canyon Lodge** ☎ 435-834-5361, 435-772-3213 (summer reservations), 888-297-2757 (winter reservations); www.brycecanyonlodge.com
**North Campground** ☎ 877-444-6777; www.reserveusa.com

## ACTIVITIES
**Backroads** ☎ 800-462-2848, 510-527-1555; www.backroads.com
**Canyon Trail Rides** ☎ 435-679-8665; www.canyonrides.com
**Rim Tours** ☎ 435-259-5223, 800-626-7335; www.rimtours.com
**Scenic Rim Trail Rides** ☎ 435-679-8761, 800-679-5859; www.brycecanyonhorseback.com
**Western Spirit Cycling** ☎ 435-259-8732, 800-845-2453; www.westernspirit.com

## MAPS
**National Geographic** ☎ 800-437-5521; www.nationalgeographic.com
**USGS** ☎ 888-275-8747; www.usgs.gov

## TOUR OPERATORS
**Bryce Canyon Area Tours & Adventures** ☎ 435-834-5200, 800-432-5383; www.brycetours.com

## TRANSPORTATION
**Red Rock Shuttle** ☎ 435-635-9104
**St George Shuttle** ☎ 435-628-8320, 800-933-8320; www.stgshuttle.com

## USEFUL ORGANIZATIONS
**Bryce Canyon Natural History Association** ☎ 435-834-4600, 888-362-2642; www.brycecanyon.org

# Grand Staircase–Escalante National Monument

### GENERAL PARK INFORMATION

**Grand Staircase–Escalante National Monument** ☎ 435-826-5499; www.ut.blm.gov/monument or http://gsenm.az.blm.gov
**Big Water Visitor Center** ☎ 435-675-3200
**Cannonville Visitor Center** ☎ 435-826-5640
**Kanab Visitor Center** ☎ 435-644-4680
**Kane County Office of Tourism** ☎ 435-644-5033, 800-733-5263; www.kaneutah.com

### ACCOMMODATIONS

**BLM campgrounds** ☎ 435-826-5499; www.ut.blm.gov/monument

### ACTIVITIES

**Boulder Mountain Fly-Fishing** ☎ 435-335-7306; www.bouldermountainfly-fishing.com
**Boulder Mountain Ranch** ☎ 435-335-7480; www.boulderutah.com/bmr
**Boulder Outdoor Survival School** ☎ 303-444-9779; www.boss-inc.com
**Earth Tours** ☎ 435-691-1241; www.earth-tours.com
**Escalante Canyon Outfitters** ☎ 435-335-7311, 888-326-4453; www.ecohike.com
**Excursions of Escalante** ☎ 435-826-4714, 800-839-7567; www.excursions-escalante.com

# Capitol Reef National Park

### GENERAL PARK INFORMATION

**Capitol Reef National Park** ☎ 435-425-3791; www.nps.gov/care
**Wayne County Travel Council** ☎ 435-425-3365, 800-858-7951; www.capitolreef.org

### ACCOMMODATIONS

**Fruita Campground** ☎ 435-425-3791; www.nps.gov/care/camp.htm

### ACTIVITIES

**Boulder Mountain Adventures & Alpine Angler s Flyshop** ☎ 435-425-3660, 888-484-3331; www.fly-fishing-utah.net
**Cowboy Homestead Cabins** (guided horseback tours) ☎ 435-425-3414, 888-854-4871; www.cowboyhomesteadcabins.com
**Earth Tours** ☎ 435-691-1241; www.earth-tours.com
**Hondoo Rivers & Trails** ☎ 435-425-3519, 800-332-2696; www.hondoo.com
**Wild Hare Expeditions** ☎ 435-425-3999, 800-304-4273; www.color-country.net/~thehare

### MAPS

**National Geographic** ☎ 800-437-5521; www.nationalgeographic.com
**USGS** ☎ 888-275-8747; www.usgs.gov

### USEFUL ORGANIZATIONS

**Capitol Reef Natural History Association** ☎ 435-425-3791; www.nps.gov/care/nha.htm

# Arches & Canyonlands National Parks

## GENERAL PARK INFORMATION

**Arches National Park** ☎ 435-719-2299; www.nps.gov/arch
**Canyonlands National Park** ☎ 435-259-7164, 435-719-2313; www.nps.gov/cany
**Island in the Sky Visitor Center** ☎ 435-259-4712; www.nps.gov/cany/island
**Needles Visitor Center** ☎ 435-259-4711; www.nps.gov/cany/needles
**The Maze** (Hans Flat Ranger Station)%435-259-2652; www.nps.gov/cany/maze
**Moab Area Travel Council** ☎ 435-259-8825, 800-635-6622; www.discovermoab.com

## ACCOMMODATIONS

**Devils Garden Campground** (Arches) ☎ 877-444-6777, 518-885-3639 (reservations); www.nps.gov/arch, www.reserveusa.com (reservations)
**Squaw Flat Campground** (The Needles, Canyonlands) ☎ 435-719-2313, 435-259-4711; www.nps.gov/cany
**Willow Flat Campground** (Island in the Sky, Canyonlands) ☎ 435-719-2313, 435-259-4712; www.nps.gov/cany
**Moab Central Reservations** ☎ 435-259-5125, 800-748-4386; www.moab.net/reservations

## ACTIVITIES

(refer to the Moab chapter)

## MAPS

**National Geographic** ☎ 800-437-5521; www.nationalgeographic.com
**USGS** ☎ 888-275-8747; www.usgs.gov

## TOUR OPERATORS

**Canyonlands by Night & Day** ☎ 435-259-2628, 800-394-9978; www.canyonlandsbynight.com
(also refer to Moab chapter)

## TRANSPORTATION

**Bighorn Express** ☎ 888-655-7433; www.bighornexpress.com
**Roadrunner Shuttle** ☎ 435-259-9402; www.roadrunnershuttle.com

## USEFUL ORGANIZATIONS

**Canyonlands Natural History Association** ☎ 435-259-6003, 800-840-8978; www.cnha.org

# BEHIND THE SCENES

## THIS BOOK

This first edition of Zion & Bryce Canyon National Parks was researched and written by Jeff Campbell, John A Vlahides and David Lukas. Coordinating author Jeff Campbell researched and wrote the Zion National Park chapter, as well as the Introduction and the majority of Highlights, Itineraries, Activities, Planning, History and the Appendix. He also collaborated with John A Vlahides on the Grand Staircase–Escalante National Monument chapter. John A Vlahides researched and wrote the Bryce Canyon, Capitol Reef, Canyonlands and Arches National Parks chapters, as well as the Moab chapter. He also collaborated with Jeff Campbell on the Grand Staircase–Escalante National

## THE LONELY PLANET STORY

The story begins with a classic travel adventure: Tony and Maureen Wheeler's 1972 journey across Europe and Asia to Australia. There was no useful information about the overland trail then, so Tony and Maureen published the first Lonely Planet guidebook to meet a growing need.

From a kitchen table, Lonely Planet has grown to become the largest independent travel publisher in the world, with offices in Melbourne (Australia), Oakland (USA) and London (UK).

Today Lonely Planet guidebooks cover the globe. There is an ever-growing list of books and information in a variety of media. Some things haven't changed. The main aim is still to make it possible for adventurous travelers to get out there – to explore and better understand the world.

At Lonely Planet we believe travelers can make a positive contribution to the countries they visit – if they respect their host communities and spend their money wisely. Since 1986 a percentage of the income from each book has been donated to aid projects and human rights campaigns, and, more recently, to wildlife conservation.

Monument chapter, and contributed to Itineraries, Activities, Planning, History and the Appendix. David Lukas researched and wrote the Geology and Ecosystem chapters.

## CREDITS

Zion & Bryce Canyon National Parks was commissioned, developed and produced in Lonely Planet's Oakland office by Kathleen Munnelly, who also served as project manager. Designer manager Candice Jacobus designed the cover, color pages and template for the series and the title. She also oversaw layout done by Hayley Tsang. Cartographer Bart Wright created the maps, and David Lauterborn was the editor. Wendy Taylor proofed, Jennye Garibaldi helped research illustrations and Ken DellaPenta compiled the index. Regional Publishing Manager David Zingarelli guided the project.

## ACKNOWLEDGEMENTS

Many thanks to Zion National Park for the use of its historic photos, and especially to Leslie Newkirk, who was so helpful in providing them.

Thanks also to the National Park Service and Grand Canyon National Park for additional historic photos.

Humpback chub (p271) and Evening primrose (p275) illustrations courtesy the US Fish & Wildlife Service.

Poison ivy illustration (p273) courtesy the USDA-NRCS PLANTS Database / Britton, NL, and A Brown. 1913. *Illustrated flora of the northern states and Canada. Vol. 2: 484.*

Galleta illustration (p276) courtesy USDA-NRCS PLANTS Database / Hitchcock, AS (rev A Chase). 1950. *Manual of the grasses of the United States.* USDA Misc. Publ. No. 200. Washington, DC.

# INDEX

## A

## B

# CLIMATE CHARTS

### Salt Lake City 4222ft (1286m)

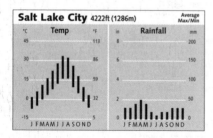

### Cedar City 5800ft (1768m)

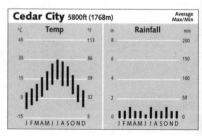

### Kanab 4925ft (1501m)

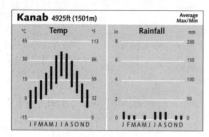

### Moab 4934ft (1503m)

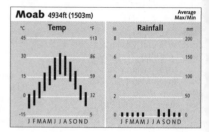

## LONELY PLANET OFFICES

### Australia
Locked Bag 1, Footscray, Victoria 3011
☎ 03 8379 8000  fax 03 8379 8111
talk2us@lonelyplanet.com.au

### USA
150 Linden Street, Oakland, California 94607
☎ 510 893 8555, Toll Free 800 275 8555
fax 510 893 8572
info@lonelyplanet.com

### UK
72–82 Rosebery Ave, Clerkenwell,
London, EC1R 4RW
☎ 020 7841 9000  fax 020 7841 9001
go@lonelyplanet.co.uk

**www.lonelyplanet.com**
**Lonely Planet Images:**
**www.lonelyplanetimages.com**